T0214281

Communications
in Computer and Information Science 1097

Commenced Publication in 2007
Founding and Former Series Editors:
Phoebe Chen, Alfredo Cuzzocrea, Xiaoyong Du, Orhun Kara, Ting Liu,
Krishna M. Sivalingam, Dominik Ślęzak, Takashi Washio, Xiaokang Yang,
and Junsong Yuan

More information about this series at http://www.springer.com/series/7899

Auhood Alfaries · Hanan Mengash ·
Ansar Yasar · Elhadi Shakshuki (Eds.)

Advances in Data Science, Cyber Security and IT Applications

First International Conference on Computing, ICC 2019
Riyadh, Saudi Arabia, December 10–12, 2019
Proceedings, Part I

Springer

Editors
Auhood Alfaries
Princess Nourah Bint Abdul
Rahman University
Riyadh, Saudi Arabia

Ansar Yasar ⓘ
Hasselt University
Hasselt, Belgium

Hanan Mengash
Princess Nourah Bint Abdul
Rahman University
Riyadh, Saudi Arabia

Elhadi Shakshuki
Acadia University
Wolfville, NS, Canada

ISSN 1865-0929   ISSN 1865-0937 (electronic)
Communications in Computer and Information Science
ISBN 978-3-030-36364-2   ISBN 978-3-030-36365-9 (eBook)
https://doi.org/10.1007/978-3-030-36365-9

This Springer imprint is published by the registered company Springer Nature Switzerland AG
The registered company address is: Gewerbestrasse 11, 6330 Cham, Switzerland

Preface

A very warm welcome to the proceedings of ICC 2019. In light of the Saudi Arabia vision 2030, Princess Nourah Bint Abdulrahman University (PNU) held the International Conference on Computing on-campus, during December 10–12, 2019, in Riyadh, Saudi Arabia. At our conference, we brought executives, professionals, educators, researchers, and practitioners from across the world to one hub. In this hub, we spoke of tomorrow's challenges, suggested solutions, shared trading ideas, and analyzed and discussed current developments in information technology within data science, cybersecurity, network and IoT, as well as information technology and its applications.

ICC 2019 had five keynote speakers from all corners of the world and four technical tracks dealing with the aspects of data science, cybersecurity, networks and IoT, information technology and its applications. All submitted papers underwent a rigorous peer-review process by a Technical Program Committee (TPC) consisting of an international group of interdisciplinary scientists and engineers. The accepted papers were then revised according to the referees' comments for camera-ready submission to the conference. These papers covered a broad range of topics within the field of: big data and analytics, bioinformatics, distributed systems, AI, network security, access control, ubiquitous computing, IoT networks, software engineering, and computer-aided design. ICC 2019 received 174 paper submissions. Each paper received a minimum of 3 reviews, and we accepted 53 papers (an acceptance rate of 38%).

One of the goals of ICC 2019 was to foster collaboration among the scientists and the practitioners developing the concepts to solve various real-world problems. It was our wish and hope that the people participating in the conference would find common ground on which they could learn from each other, and that the conference would engender future fruitful scientific activities. Such collaborative endeavours are necessary for the development of the cutting-edge solutions embodied within our society and its fabrics.

We wish to thank the general chairs, the local arrangements chairs, the publicity chairs, the TPC and reviewers, the participants, and, most importantly, the researchers who submitted the articles to make this event a success. Furthermore, we would like to extend our gratitude to PNU who supported the organization of this conference at every stage.

November 2019

Auhood Alfaries
Hanan Mengash
Ansar Yasar
Elhadi Shakshuki

Organization

General Chairs

Auhood Abd. Al Faries   Princess Nourah Bint Abdulrahman University, Saudi Arabia

Hanan Almengash   Princess Nourah Bint Abdulrahman University, Saudi Arabia

Ansar Yasar   Hasselt University, Belgium

Hend Al-Khalifa   King Saud University, Saudi Arabia

Local Arrangements Chairs

Dua Nassar   Princess Nourah Bint Abdulrahman University, Saudi Arabia

Evon Abu-Taieh   Jordan University, Jordan

Ghadah Aldehim   Princess Nourah Bint Abdulrahman University, Saudi Arabia

Hanan Aljuaid   Princess Nourah Bint Abdulrahman University, Saudi Arabia

Hanen Karamti   Princess Nourah Bint Abdulrahman University, Saudi Arabia

Heba A. Kurdi   King Saud University, Saudi Arabia

Hessah Aleisa   Princess Nourah Bint Abdulrahman University, Saudi Arabia

Mada Alaskar   Princess Nourah Bint Abdulrahman University, Saudi Arabia

Manel Ayadi   Princess Nourah Bint Abdulrahman University, Saudi Arabia

Myriam Hadjouni   Princess Nourah Bint Abdulrahman University, Saudi Arabia

Samiah Chelloug   Princess Nourah Bint Abdulrahman University, Saudi Arabi

Steering Committee

Hadil Ahmed Shaiba   Princess Nourah Bint Abdulrahman University, Saudi Arabia

Heba A. Kurdi   King Saud University, Saudi Arabia

Mai Alduailij   Princess Nourah Bint Abdulrahman University, Saudi Arabia

| Maali Alabdulhafith | Princess Nourah Bint Abdulrahman University, Saudi Arabia |
| Shiroq Al-Megren | Massachusetts Institute of Technology (MIT), USA |

Technical Program Committee Members

Safia Abbas	Ain Shames University, Egypt
Nagwan Abdulsamie	Princess Nourah Bint Abdulrahman University, Saudi Arabia
Mohammad Syuhaimi Abrahman	The National University of Malaysia, Malaysia
Maysoon Abulkhair	King Abdulaziz University, Saudi Arabia
Hanan Adlan	Princess Nourah Bint Abdulrahman University, Saudi Arabia
Shaimaa Ahmad	Princess Nourah Bint Abdulrahman University, Saudi Arabia
Muna Ahmed	Princess Nourah Bint Abdulrahman University, Saudi Arabia
Issam Al Hadid	The University of Jordan, Jordan
Hassanin Al-Barhamtoshy	King Abdulaziz University, Saudi Arabia
Fahad Al-Zahrani	UQU, Saudi Arabia
Heyam Albaity	King Saud University, Saudi Arabia
Lamia Albraheem	King Saud University, Saudi Arabia
Hend Alkhalifa	King Saud University, Saudi Arabia
Abdulhadi Alqarni	Jubail University College, Saudi Arabia
Elsayed Alrabie	Menoufia University, Egypt
Nazek Alturki	Princess Nourah Bint Abdulrahman University, Saudi Arabia
Sarra Ali. Ayouni	Princess Nourah Bint Abdulrahman University, Saudi Arabia
Romana Aziz	Princess Nourah Bint Abdulrahman University, Saudi Arabia
Ammar Belatreche	Northumbria University, UK
Jawad Berri	Sonatrach - Algerian Petroleum and Gas Corporation, Saudi Arabia
Dalila Boughaci	INCA/LSIS, LRIA/USTHB, Algeria
Omar Boussaid	ERIC Laboratory, France
Hsing-Lung Chen	National Taiwan University of Science and Technology, Taiwan
Salim Chikhi	MISC laboratory, University of Constantine 2, Algeria
Amer Draa	Mentouri University, Algeria
Ridha Ejbali	National School of Engineers (ENIG), Tunisia
Tamer El-Batt	Nile University, Egypt
Ali El-Zaart	Beirut Arab University, Lebanon
Dalia Elkamchouchi	Princess Nourah Bint Abdulrahman University, Saudi Arabia

Hela Elmannai	SUPCOM, LTSIRS, Tunisia
Rania Ghoniem	Princess Nora bint Abdulrahman University, Saudi Arabia
Said Ghoul	Philadelphia University, Jordan
Myriam Hadjouni	Princess Nourah Bint Abdulrahman University, Saudi Arabia
Monia Hamdi	Princess Nourah Bint Abdulrahman University, Saudi Arabia
Salem Hasnaoui	National Engineering School of Tunis, Tunisia
Sahar Ismail	Shoubra, Benha University, Egypt
Musfira Jilani	Dublin City University, Ireland
Laetitia Jourdan	Inria/LIFL/CNRS, France
Yasser Kadah	Cairo University, Egypt
Okba Kazar	Computer Science Department, Université de Biskra, Algeria
Houssain Kettani	Dakota State University, USA
Rami Khawaldeh	The University of Jordan, Jordan
Kamel Khoualdi	King Abdulaziz University, Saudi Arabia
Sufian Khwaldeh	The University of Jordan, Jordan
Hamid Laga	Murdoch University, Australia
Slimane Larabi	USTHB University, Algeria
Jamel Leila	Princess Nourah Bint Abdulrahman University, Saudi Arabia
Andrew Mccarren	Dublin City University, Ireland
Nouredine Melab	Université Lille 1, France
Kamal E Melkemi	University of Batna 2, Algeria
Haithem Mezni	SMART Lab, Tunisia
Hala Mokhtar	King Saud University, Saudi Arabia
Ahmed Morgan	Umm Al-Qura University, Saudi Arabia
Hala Mostafa	Princess Nourah Bint Abdulrahman University, Saudi Arabia
Achour Mostéfaoui	Université Nantes, France
Abdellatif Moustafa	Umm Alqura University, Saudi Arabia
Dua Abd. Nassar	Princess Nourah Bint Abdulrahman University, Saudi Arabia
Salima Ouadfel	University Mentoury, Algeria
Imed Romdhani	Edinburgh Napier University, UK
Oumemeima Saidani	CRI - Centre de Recherche en Informatique, France
Roselina Sallehuddin	Universiti Teknologi Malaysia, Malaysia
Sahbi Sidhom	Lorraine University, France
Najlaa Soliamn	Princess Nura Bin Abdelrahman, Saudi Arabia
Miguel Solinas	National University of Cordoba, Argentina
Abdulhamit Subasi	Effat University, Saudi Arabia
Elankovan Sundararajan	Faculty of Information Science and Technology, National University of Malaysia, Malaysia

Nazik Turki   Princess Nourah Bint Abdulrahman University,
                             Saudi Arabia
Brent Wilson   George Fox University, USA
Ansar Yasar   Universiteit Hasselt - IMOB, Belgium
Ali Zolait   University of Bahrain, Bahrain

Contents – Part I

Cyber Security

A Comparative Study of Three Blockchain Emerging Technologies:
Bitcoin, Ethereum and Hyperledger 3
Dalila Boughaci and Omar Boughaci

Comparison of Supervised and Unsupervised Fraud Detection 8
Ashay Walke

Cybersecurity: Design and Implementation of an Intrusion Detection
and Prevention System 15
Shaimaa Ahmed Elsaid, Samerah Maeeny, Azhar Alenazi,
Tahani Alenazi, Wafa Alzaid, Ghada Algahtani, and Amjad Aldossari

Detailed Quantum Cryptographic Service and Data Security
in Cloud Computing 43
Omer K. Jasim Mohammad and Safia Abbas

The Effects of the Property of Access Possibilities and Cybersecurity
Awareness on Social Media Application 57
Bedour F. Alrashidi, Aljawharah M. Almuhana,
and Alanoud M. Aljedaie

A Blockchain Review: A Comparative Study Between Public Key
Infrastructure and Identity Based Encryption 69
Lujain Alharbi and Dania Aljeaid

Data Science

ɛrbeng:- Android Live Voice and Text Chat Translator 85
Abanoub Nasser, Ibram Makram,
and Rania Ahmed Abdel Azeem Abul Seoud

Improving Accuracy of Imbalanced Clinical Data Classification Using
Synthetic Minority Over-Sampling Technique 99
Fatihah Mohd, Masita Abdul Jalil, Noor Maizura Mohamad Noora,
Suryani Ismail, Wan Fatin Fatihah Yahya, and Mumtazimah Mohamad

Learning Case-Based Reasoning Solutions by Association
Rules Approach 111
Abdelhak Mansoul, Baghdad Atmani, Mohamed Benamina,
and Sofia Benbelkacem

Stochastic Local Search Based Feature Selection Combined
with K-means for Clients' Segmentation in Credit Scoring   119
  Dalila Boughaci and Abdullah A. K. Alkhawaldeh

Real Time Search Technique for Distributed Massive Data Using
Grid Computing   132
  Mohammed Bakri Bashir, Adil Yousif, and Muhammad Shafie Abd Latiff

Analytical Experiments on the Utilization of Data Visualizations.   148
  *Sara M. Shaheen, Sawsan Alhalawani, Nuha Alnabet,
  and Dana Alhenaki*

A Tweet-Ranking System Using Sentiment Scores
and Popularity Measures   162
  Sumaya Aleidi, Dalia Alsuhaibani, Nora Alrajebah, and Heba Kurdi

Event-Based Driving Style Analysis   170
  Zubaydh Kenkar and Sawsan AlHalawani

Swarm Intelligence and ICA for Blind Source Separation.   183
  Monia Hamdi, Hela ElMannai, and Abeer AlGarni

Shiny Framework Based Visualization and Analytics Tool
for Middle East Respiratory Syndrome   193
  Maya John and Hadil Shaiba

Ensemble Learning Sentiment Classification for Un-labeled Arabic Text   203
  Amal Alkabkabi and Mounira Taileb

Predicting No-show Medical Appointments Using Machine Learning   211
  Sara Alshaya, Andrew McCarren, and Amal Al-Rasheed

Cancer Incidence Prediction Using a Hybrid Model of Wavelet Transform
and LSTM Networks.   224
  Amani Alrobai and Musfira Jilani

Enhanced Support Vector Machine Applied to Land-Use Classification   236
  Hela ElMannai, Monia Hamdi, and Abeer AlGarni

Predicting Students' Academic Performance and Main Behavioral
Features Using Data Mining Techniques   245
  Suad Almutairi, Hadil Shaiba, and Marija Bezbradica

Crime Types Prediction   260
  Hanan AL Mansour and Michele Lundy

Intensive Survey About Road Traffic Signs Preprocessing, Detection
and Recognition   275
  Mrouj Almuhajri and Ching Suen

Machine Learning for Automobile Driver Identification Using
Telematics Data   290
  Hanadi Alhamdan and Musfira Jilani

Employee Turnover Prediction Using Machine Learning   301
  Lama Alaskar, Martin Crane, and Mai Alduailij

Predicting Saudi Stock Market Index by Incorporating GDELT Using
Multivariate Time Series Modelling.   317
  Rawan Alamro, Andrew McCarren, and Amal Al-Rasheed

Author Index   329

Contents – Part II

Information Technology and Applications

EMD for Technical Analysis 3
  Jürgen Abel

Enhancement of the Segmentation Framework for Rotated Iris Images...... 16
  Fati Oiza Salami and Mohd Shafry Mohd Rahim

Domain and Schema Independent Ontology Verbalizing 30
  Kaneeka Vidanagea, Noor Maizura Mohamad Noora,
  Rosmayati Mohemada, and Zuriana Abu Bakara

The Effect of User Experience on the Quality of User Interface Design
in Healthcare 40
  Hanaa Alzahrani and Reem Alnanih

Saudi Arabia Market Basket Analysis 52
  Monerah Alawadh, Israa Al-turaiki, Mohammed Alawadh,
  and Shahad Tallab

Determining the Best Prediction Accuracy of Software Maintainability
Models Using Auto-WEKA 60
  Hadeel Alsolai and Marc Roper

Shark Smell Optimization (SSO) Algorithm for Cloud Jobs Scheduling 71
  Yusra Mohamed Suliman, Adil Yousif, and Mohammed Bakri Bashir

A Visual Decision Making Support System for the Diabetes Prevention..... 81
  Fatima Zohra Benhacine, Baghdad Atmani, Mohamed Benamina,
  and Sofia Benbelkacem

Sensor-Based Business Process Model for Appliance Repair............. 93
  Mayada Elsaid, Ayah Alhamdan, and Sara Altuwaijri

A Multi-labels Text Categorization Framework for Cerebral
Lesion's Identification...................................... 103
  Hichem Benfriha, Baghdad Atmani, Belarbi Khemliche,
  Nabil Tabet Aoul, and Ali Douah

Fuzzy Adaptation of Surveillance Plans of Patients with Diabetes 115
  Mohamed Benamina, Baghdad Atmani, Sofia Benbelkacem,
  and Abdelhak Mansoul

Arabic Real-Time License Plate Recognition System   126
  Shaimaa Ahmed Elsaid, Haifa Alharthi, Reem Alrubaia, Sarah Abutile,
  Rawan Aljres, Amal Alanazi, and Alanoud Albrikan

Exploring Barriers Mobile Payments Adoption: A Case Study
of Majmaah University in Saudi Arabia   144
  Rana Alabdan

A Method for 3D-Metric Reconstruction Using Zoom Cameras   161
  Boubakeur Boufama, Tarik Elamsy, and Mohamed Batouche

Bellman-Ford Algorithm Under Trapezoidal Interval Valued
Neutrosophic Environment   174
  Said Broumi, Deivanayagampillai Nagarajan,
  Malayalan Lathamaheswari, Mohamed Talea, Assia Bakali,
  and Florentin Smarandache

Design and Implementation of Secured E-Business Structure
with LTL Patterns for User Behavior Prediction   185
  Ayman Mohamed Mostafa

Association Rules for Detecting Lost of View in the Expanded
Program on Immunization   201
  Fawzia Zohra Abdelouhab, Baghdad Atmani,
  and Fatima Zohra Benhacine

Hybrid Model Architectures for Enhancing Data Classification
Performance in E-commerce Applications   214
  Ayman Mohamed Mostafa, Mohamed Maher, and M. M. Hassan

Performance Dashboards for Project Management   228
  Samiha Brahimi, Aseel Aljulaud, Anwar Alsaiah, Norah AlGuraibi,
  Mariam Alrubei, and Haneen Aljamaan

Neural Iris Signature Recognition (NISR)   241
  Ali Mehdi, Safaa Ahmad, Rawand Abu Roza, Mohammed Alawairdhi,
  and Mousa Al-Akhras

Healthcare Information System Assessment Case Study
Riyadh's Hospitals-KSA   252
  Muna Elsadig, Dua' A. Nassar, and Leila Jamel Menzli

Network and IoT

OpenCache: Distributed SDN/NFV Based in-Network Caching
as a Service   265
  Shiyam Alalmaei, Matthew Broadbent, Nicholas Race,
  and Samia Chelloug

Comparative Study of the Internet of Things Recommender System   278
    Halima Bouazza, Laallam Fatima Zohra, and Bachir Said

High DC-Gain Two-Stage OTA Using Positive Feedback
and Split-Length Transistor Techniques   286
    Jamel Nebhen, Mohamed Masmoudi, Wenceslas Rahajandraibe,
    and Khalifa Aguir

Automated Detection for Student Cheating During Written Exams:
An Updated Algorithm Supported by Biometric of Intent.   303
    Fatimah A. Alrubaish, Ghadah A. Humaid, Rasha M. Alamri,
    and Mariam A. Elhussain

Integration of Internet of Things and Social Network: Social IoT
General Review   312
    Halima Bouazza, Laallam Fatima Zohra, and Bachir Said

Enhanced Priority-Based Routing Protocol (EPRP)
for Inter-vehicular Communication   325
    Amaliya Princy Mohan and Maher Elshakankiri

Author Index   339

Cyber Security

A Comparative Study of Three Blockchain Emerging Technologies: Bitcoin, Ethereum and Hyperledger

Dalila Boughaci[1]([envelope])[iD] and Omar Boughaci[2]

[1] Computer Science Department, LRIA-FEI- USTHB,
BP 32 El-Alia Bab-Ezzouar, 16111 Algiers, Algeria
dboughaci@usthb.dz, dalila_info@yahoo.fr
[2] El-IDRISSI, Algiers, Algeria
omar.boughaci@gmail.com
http://www.usthb.dz

Abstract. A blockchain is a decentralized peer to peer data sharing mechanism that enables fast and trusted transactions between users on Internet by using cryptographic techniques. This new technology can be used for data control and doing transactions, secure payment and smart contracts, and much more. The aim of this paper is to explain the main concepts of blockchains. Also we give a comparative study of three well-known emerging technologies which are: Bitcoin, Ethereum and Hyperledger.

Keywords: Blockchain · Cryptography · Bitcoin · Ethereum · Hyperledger

1 Introduction

Blockchain is an important innovation for data sharing and trusted transactions on Internet. It is a sequence of hash-chained blocks where a block is a set of secured transactions and each block contains the hash of the previous block and a nonce. Blockchain is an emerging technology pattern that can be used in various domains in particular in transaction networks, finance and banking and much more. It can reduce cost and risk, enhances security level and gives new opportunities for innovation and growth. Also, it can be used to share and process any kind of data in a secure way, through an untrusted network. This can be ensured by using cryptographic techniques and hashing functions.

Blockchain have been used in various domains. Among them we cite: trading finance and financial services such as online payment and digital assets [5]. Also, it can be used in Healthcare service [7], in Manufacturing [1], in Supply chain management [9], in Security services [14], in electronic commerce [11], in Smart contracts [4] and Internet of things-IoT [7,8].

Due to the importance of the blockchain innovation, several frameworks have been done. These technologies can be divided into three main generations which are [13]:

© Springer Nature Switzerland AG 2019
A. Alfaries et al. (Eds.): ICC 2019, CCIS 1097, pp. 3–7, 2019.
https://doi.org/10.1007/978-3-030-36365-9_1

- The first generation (denoted Blockchain 1.0) such as Bitcoin cryptocurrency system: this generation is dedicated to currency, payments, money transfers and remittance services.
- The second generation (denoted Blockchain 2.0) such as Bitbond: this generation adds some sophisticated functionalities of smart-contracts.
- The third generation (denoted Blockchain 3.0) such namecoin: this generation is dedicated to financial markets.

In this paper, first we give the main concepts of the blockchain technology and its benefits. Then we compare three well-known technologies which are: Bitcoin, Ethereum and Hyperledger. Ethereum and Hyperledger are open-source platforms. Bitcoin is a public blockchain.

The rest of this paper is organized as follows: Sect. 2 gives an overview on blockchain. Section 3 compares three main blockchain platforms proposed in the literature. Finally, Sect. 4 concludes and gives some perspectives.

2   Main Concepts of a Blockchain

The blockchain can be defined as a chain of records called linked blocks. The blocks contain transactions chained together, creating a chronological order over blocks and transactions [6]. The blockchain can be viewed as a data structure resistant to modifications from the attackers. When a change takes place in the parent block this leads to change in the child's hash, and change in the grandchild's hash and so on, updating a block requires forcing a recalculation of all blocks following it [2]. As shown in Fig. 1, the blockchain is a sequence of blocks arranged as links in the chain and each block references the previous block by the block's fingerprint (also called Block hash). The Block hash is obtained by computing the content of the block.

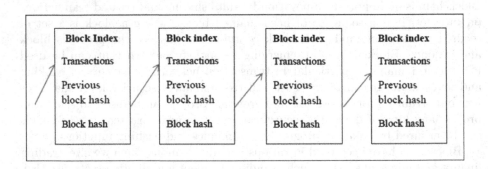

Fig. 1. Example of a blockchain containing four blocks

Each block consists of a sequence of transaction, the hash of the previous block and a nonce. The transactions is the data to be transferred. The nonce: is a random number generated by the computer. It is a key to protect the blockchain.

The block Index is a number generated by the system (Block 1, Block 2, etc). The hash of the previous block is the previous block's fingerprint. The block hash is the hash of the current block which is the current block's fingerprint. The block hash is a combination of the nonce and data of the block. All is hashed according to SHA256 method. A hash is used for identifying attempts to change data in blocks. For instance, in the cryptocurrency blockchain system such as Bitcoin, the transactions are stored in "Ledgers" in every nodes of the currency network. Ledger is the unit or the system of blocks. The transaction is then the asset transfer over the ledger. The ledger is a trusted source of data where participants can endorse transactions and permits to verify the transaction and avoid change in transactions. A new block including the new transaction can be added to the blockchain when it is valid. The validation is done by all the miners' nodes through a consensus algorithm such as the Proof-of-work (POW) and the Proof of stake.

3 Comparative Study

In this section, we compare three well-known blockchain technologies which are: Bitcoin, Ethereum and Hyperledger.

- Bitcoin is the first popular implementation of blockchain. Bitcoin is a cryptocurrency system proposed in 2008 by Nakamoto [10]. It is dedicated to banking and finance sector [10,12]. Bitcoin uses blockchain mechanism to track and verify transactions. Bitcoin provides several benefits such as the law cost of transaction, the direct rapid transaction and the no need to the third party (the bank for example) [3]. More details about the system can be found at this link: https://bitcoin.org/.
- Ethereum: which is sophisticated and an open-source blockchain platform built by the Ethereum Foundation in 2014. Ethereum is a decentralized system dedicated to smart contracts to speed up payments. It facilitates holding crypto-assets as well as creating crypto-currencies and smart contracts. A contract is set of conditions under which transactions occur. It is a set of scripts or codes stored in the blockchain network that acts as a distributed virtual machine. When a specific event happens then an action is done [4]. More details can be find at https://ethereum.org/.
- Hyperledger: which is an open-source blockchain hosted by the Linux Foundation. It is a collaborative business blockchain including leaders in finance, banking, supply chain, manufacturing, Internet of thing and technology. Several implementations have been proposed such as: Fabric Hyperledger, Indy Hyperledger, Sawtooth and roha Hyperledger. More information about the platform can be found at this URL: https://www.hyperledger.org/.

Table 1 summarizes the key points of the four blockchain platforms described below.

Table 1. Comparison between the three popular blockchain platforms

	Bitcoin	Hyperledger	Ethereum
Application	Crypto-currency	General platform	General platform
Ownership	Publicity	Open-source Linux Foundation	Open-source Ethereum Foundation
Energy saving	No	Yes	No
Smart contract	Native	Dockers	Ethereum Virtual Machine
Language	Golang, C++	Golang, java	Solidity, serpent, LLL
Data model	Transaction based	Key-value	Account- based
Currency	BTC	none	Ether
Consensus algorithms	Peer of work (PoW)	Practical Byzantine Fault Tolerance (PBFT)	Peer of work (PoW)

4   Conclusion

Blockchain is a sophisticated technology for doing secure transactions over Internet. The aim of this paper was to give a background on blockchain technology and its benefits. Also, we compared three popular platforms which are: Bitcoin, Ethereum and Hyperledger. It would be nice to study in detail the different consensus algorithms used to validate blockchain transactions. On the other hand, we plan to develop a blockchain based platform for business and finance.

References

1. Angrish, A., Craver, B., Hasan, M., Starly, B.: A case study for blockchain in manufacturing: "FabRec": a prototype for peer-to-peer network of manufacturing nodes. CoRR abs/1804.01083 (2018)
2. Bashir, I.: Mastering blockchain. Packt Publishing, Ltd. ISBN 978-1-78712-544-5. OCLC 967373845 (2017)
3. Böhme, R., Christin, N., Edelman, B., Moore, T.: Bitcoin: economics, technology, and governance. J. Econ. Perspect. **29**, 213–238 (2015)
4. Brent, L., et al.: Vandal: a scalable security analysis framework for smart contracts. CoRR abs/1809.03981 (2018)
5. Crosby, M., Pattanayak, P., Verma, S., Kalyanaraman, V.: BlockChain technology: beyond bitcoin (PDF) (Report). Sutardja Center for Entrepreneurship and Technology Technical Report. University of California, Berkeley (2015)
6. Decker, C., Seidel, J., Wattenhofer, R.: Bitcoin meets strong consistency. In: Proceedings of the 17th International Conference on Distributed Computing (2016)
7. Dwivedi, A.D., Srivastava, G., Dhar, S., Singh, R.: A decentralized privacy-preserving healthcare blockchain for IoT. Sensors **19**(2), 326 (2019)
8. Han, R., Gramoli, V., Xiwei, X.: Evaluating blockchains for IoT. In: NTMS 2018, pp. 1–5 (2018)
9. English, S.M., Nezhadian, E.: Application of bitcoin data-structures and design principles to supply chain management. CoRR abs/1703.04206 (2017)

10. Nakamoto, S.: Bitcoin: a peer-to-peer electronic cash system (2008). https://bitcoin.org/bitcoin.pdf
11. O'Leary, D.E.: Open information enterprise transactions: business intelligence and wash and spoof transactions in blockchain and social commerce. Int. Syst. Acc. Financ. Manag. **25**(3), 148–158 (2018)
12. O'mahony, D., Peirce, M., Tewari, H.: Electronic payment systems. Artech House, Norwood (1997)
13. Swan, M.: Blockchain thinking : the brain as a decentralized autonomous corporation [Commentary]. IEEE Technol. Soc. Mag. **34**(4), 41–52 (2015)
14. Salman, T., Zolanvari, M., Erbad, A., Jain, R., Samaka, M.: Security services using blockchains: a state of the art survey. IEEE Commun. Surv. Tutor. **21**(1), 858–880 (2019)

Comparison of Supervised and Unsupervised Fraud Detection

Ashay Walke[✉]

Indian Institute of Technology, Kharagpur, Kharagpur, West Bengal, India
ashay17awalke@gmail.com

Abstract. Fraud Detection is a challenging problems in Machine Learning. The most commonly used evaluation metric for fraud detection which is a binary classification Machine Learning problem is Area Under the Receiver Operating Characteristic curve (AUROC). In this paper we will show that AUROC is not always the correct metric to evaluate the performance of a classifier with high imbalance. We shall rather show that Area Under the Precision Recall curve (AUPR) is a better evaluation metric for the same. We will compare and contrast various supervised as well as unsupervised approaches to optimize the Area under PR curve for fraud detection problem.

Keywords: Fraud detection · Anomaly detection · Supervised vs unsupervised detection

1 Introduction

A Binary Skewed Data set [1], as the name suggests is a data set containing one of the class in Majority. Training a classifier for Skewed data sets is one of the challenging problems in Machine Learning. A common example for this issue is fraud detection: a very big part of the data set, usually more than 95%, describes normal activities and only a small fraction of the data records should get classified as fraud. In such a case, if the model always predicts "normal", then it is correct 95% of the time. At first, the accuracy and therewith the quality of such a model might seem surprisingly good, but as soon as we perform some analysis and dig a little bit deeper, it becomes obvious that the model is completely useless. As even though it has an accuracy of 95%, It is not able to classify the fraudulent activities.

2 About the Dataset

The datasets contains transactions made by credit cards in September 2013 by european cardholders. This dataset presents transactions that occurred in two

---

Supported by Department of Mathematics, Indian Institute of Technology, Kharagpur.

A. Alfaries et al. (Eds.): ICC 2019, CCIS 1097, pp. 8–14, 2019.
https://doi.org/10.1007/978-3-030-36365-9_2

days, where we have 492 frauds out of 284,807 transactions. The dataset is highly unbalanced, the positive class (frauds) account for 0.172 % of all transactions.

It contains only numerical input variables which are the result of a PCA transformation. Features V1, V2, ... V28 are the principal components obtained with PCA, the only features which have not been transformed with PCA are 'Time' and 'Amount'. Feature 'Time' contains the seconds elapsed between each transaction and the first transaction in the dataset. The feature 'Amount' is the transaction Amount, this feature can be used for example-dependant cost-senstive learning. Feature 'Class' is the response variable and it takes value 1 in case of fraud and 0 otherwise.

3 Supervised Techniques

Given the fact that we have a labelled data set, we try implementing Supervised Machine Learning Techniques. Supervised learning is the Data mining task of inferring a function from labeled training data. The training data consist of a set of training examples. In supervised learning, each example is a pair consisting of an input object (typically a vector) and a desired output value (also called the supervisory signal). A supervised learning algorithm analyzes the training data and produces an inferred function, which can be used for mapping new examples. An optimal scenario will allow for the algorithm to correctly determine the class labels for unseen instances. This requires the learning algorithm to generalize from the training data to unseen situations in a "reasonable" way.

3.1 Gradient Boosting Machine

When we try to predict the target variable using any machine learning technique, the main causes of difference in actual and predicted values are noise, variance, and bias. Ensemble helps to reduce these factors (except noise, which is irreducible error) An ensemble is just a collection of predictors which come together (e.g. mean of all predictions) to give a final prediction. The reason we use ensembles is that many different predictors trying to predict same target variable will perform a better job than any single predictor alone. Ensemble techniques are further classified into Bagging and Boosting. Boosting is an ensemble technique in which the predictors are not made independently, but sequentially. This technique employs the logic in which the subsequent predictors learn from the mistakes of the previous predictors. Therefore, the observations have an unequal probability of appearing in subsequent models and ones with the highest error appear most. (So the observations are not chosen based on the bootstrap process, but based on the error). The predictors can be chosen from a range of models like decision trees, regressors, classifiers etc. Because new predictors are learning from mistakes committed by previous predictors, it takes less time/iterations to reach close to actual predictions. But we have to choose the stopping criteria carefully or it could lead to overfitting on training data. Gradient Boosting is an example of boosting algorithm.

Gradient boosting is a machine learning technique for regression and classification problems, which produces a prediction model in the form of an ensemble of weak prediction models, typically decision trees. The objective of any supervised learning algorithm is to define a loss function and minimize it. Let's see how maths work out for Gradient Boosting algorithm. Say we have mean squared error (MSE) as loss defined as:

$$LOSS = MSE = \sum (Y_i - Y_i^p)^2$$

Y_i is the ith target value and Y_i^p is the ith prediction.

We want our predictions, such that our loss function (MSE) is minimum. By using gradient descent and updating our predictions based on a learning rate, we can find the values where MSE is minimum.

$$Y_i^p = Y_i^p + \alpha * \delta \sum (Y_i - Y_i^p)^2 / \delta Y_i^p$$

which simplifies to $Y_i = Y_i^p - 2 * \alpha * \sum (Y_i - Y_i^p)$

α learning rate and $\sum (Y_i - Y_i^p)$ is the sum of residuals

So, we are basically updating the predictions such that the sum of our residuals is close to 0 (or minimum) and predicted values are sufficiently close to actual values.

3.2   XGBoost

Extreme Gradient Boosting (XGBoost) [5] is similar to gradient boosting framework but more efficient. Specifically, XGBoost used a more regularised model formalization to control overfitting, which gives it better performance, which is why it's also known as 'regularized boosting' technique. It has both linear model solver and tree learning algorithms. Moreover, it has the capacity to do parallel computation on a single machine. This makes XGBoost at least 10 times faster than existing gradient boosting implementations. It supports various objective functions, including regression, classification and ranking. Main difference between GBM and XGBoost is in their objective function. In case of XGBoost Objective Function = Training loss + Regularization. The parameters of the model are

- Booster: We have options like gbtree, gblinear and dart.
- learning_rate: Similar to learning rate in GBM.
- max_depth: Its same as we used in GBM. It controls over fitting.
- gamma: Node splitting will be performed only if loss reduction is more than gamma. So, this makes algorithm conservative.
- lambda and alpha: Lambda is coefficient of L2 regularization and alpha is for L1.

4   Unsupervised Techniques

Given the fact that we are having a labelled data set, using Supervised techniques seems the best opinion. But given the fact that our data set is extremely imbalanced, we can remove the labels from our data set and we can convert the problem into an anomaly detection problem or outlier detection problem which is an unsupervised problem. Hence we try and apply various outlier detection techniques which are Unsupervised.

4.1   TEDA

TEDA-Cloud which is a statistical method based on the concepts of typicality and eccentricity able to group similar data observations. Instead of the traditional concept of clusters, the data is grouped in the form of granular unities called data clouds, which are structures with no pre-defined shape or set boundaries. TEDA-Cloud is a fully autonomous and self-evolving algorithm that can be used for data clustering of online data streams and applications that require real-time response. TEDA is an online clustering algorithm. TEDA algorithm aims to generalize and avoid any restrictive assumptions inherited from traditional statistical methods and probability theory, such as independence of individual data samples from each other, inability to work with very large data sets and prior assumptions of data distribution (e.g. Gaussian). Traditional statistical approaches are often very suitable for random processes, however might violate or ignore the dependence of data in real processes, such as climate, physical, social, economic and so on [7].

4.2   Angle-Based Outlier Detection in High-Dimensional Data

Detecting outliers in a large set of data objects is a major data mining task aiming at finding different mechanisms responsible for different groups of objects in a data set. All existing approaches, however, are based on an assessment of distances (sometimes indirectly by assuming certain distributions) in the full-dimensional Euclidean data space. In high-dimensional data, these approaches are bound to deteriorate due to the notorious "curse of dimensionality". We have a novel approach named ABOD [2] (Angle-Based Outlier Detection) and some variants assessing the variance in the angles between the difference vectors of a point to the other points. This way, the effects of the "curse of dimensionality" are alleviated compared to purely distance-based approaches. A main advantage of our new approach is that our method does not rely on any parameter selection influencing the quality of the achieved ranking. In a thorough experimental evaluation, we compare ABOD to the well-established distance-based method LOF for various artificial and a real world data set and show ABOD to perform especially well on high-dimensional data. Comparing distances becomes more and more meaningless with increasing data dimensionality. Thus, mining high-dimensional data requires different approaches to the quest for patterns. Here, we propose not only to use the distance between points in a vector space but primarily the directions of distance vectors. Comparing the angles between pairs of distance vectors to other points helps to discern between points similar to other points and outliers. This idea is motivated by the following intuition. Consider a simple data set as illustrated in the figure below.

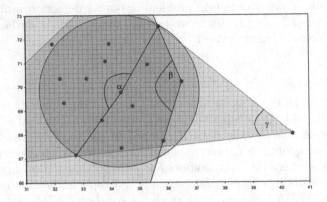

Fig. 1. Intuition of angle-based outlier detection

5   Evaluation Metric

The Evaluation metric generally used in the supervised cases is AUROC. The ROC curve is created by plotting the true positive rate (TPR) against the false positive rate (FPR) at various threshold settings. The true-positive rate is also known as sensitivity, recall or probability of detection in machine learning. The false-positive rate is also known as the fall-out or probability of false alarm and can be calculated as (1 specificity).

$$sensitivity = \frac{TP}{TP + FN}$$

$$specificity = \frac{TN}{TN + FP}$$

If is often said that AUROC is misleaeding when if comes to imbalanced datasets. We propose that AUPR which is the Area Under the Precision Recall is a better metric for imbalanced datasets Precision is a ratio of the number of true positives divided by the sum of the true positives and false positives. It describes how good a model is at predicting the positive class (Q2). Where as Recall is calculated as the ratio of the number of true positives divided by the sum of the true positives and the false negatives. Recall is the same as sensitivity. The precision and recall can be calculated for thresholds using a function that takes the true output values and the probabilities for the positive class as output and returns the precision, recall and threshold values, and hence we plan to use a new metric termed as area under the PR-Curve [4].

$$precision = \frac{TP}{TP + FP}$$

$$recall = sensitivity = \frac{TP}{TP + FN}$$

6   Results

A detailed comparison of the area under PR curve as well as the area under the
ROC curve for various supervised as well as unsupervised algorithms can be seen
in the Table 1. We can see that, even though we removed the labels from our data
set and treated our problem like an outlier detection problem we see compare
able results when it comes to the area under the Precision Recall curve. We see
that the AUPR curve for TEDA is almost compare able with that of XGBoost.
This shows that even if we remove the labels from our data set in an imbalanced
problem both, the supervised as well as unsupervised methods perform nearly
the Supervisd techniques such as MLP and GBM. Hence, even with the huge
loss of information of labels we are seeing comparable results using Supervised
and Unsupervsied techniques.

Table 1. Comparision of AUPR and AUROC for various algorithms for the dataset

Technique	Algorithm	AUROC	AUPR
Supervised	DL MLP	0.85	0.83
Supervised	GBM	0.86	0.8532
Supervised	XGBoost	0.92	0.898
Unsupervised	Isolation forest		0.76
Unsupervised	DBScan		0.72
Unsupervised	TEDA		0.829
Unsupervised	ABOD		0.856

7   Conclusion and Future Work

In the paper, we saw how AUPR is a better metric when it comes to imbalanced
datasets as it focuses more on the minority entries. We see that even after a
very huge loss of information which are the labels i.e when we use unsupervised
techniques the results for AUPR is almost compareable to high performing supervised techniques which shows us that when we plot the points of this dataset in
a space, we will see that the minority will be outliers and when we use unsupervised techniques they are able to detect these outliers with almost comparable
performance as other supervised techniques. In future we could dig deeper upon
using even better unsupervised techniques which will perform better than the
supervised ones.

References

1. Hartl, F.: Thoughts on machine learning - dealing with skewed classes
2. Zimek, A., Kriegel, H.-P., Schubert, M.: Angle-based outlier detection in high-dimensional data. In: KDD (2008)
3. Liu, X.-Y., Wu, J., Zhou, Z.-H.: Exploratory undersampling for class-imbalance learning
4. Davis, J., Goadrich, M.: The relationship between precision-recall and roc curves
5. Chen, T., Guestrin, C.: XGBoost: a scalable tree boosting system
6. Ester, M., Kriegel, H.P., Sander, J., Xu, X.: Density-based spatial clustering of applications with noise
7. Costa, B.S.J., Bezerra, C.G., Guedes, L.A., Angelov, P.P.: Online fault detection based on typicality and eccentricity data analytics

Cybersecurity: Design and Implementation of an Intrusion Detection and Prevention System

Shaimaa Ahmed Elsaid[1,2]([✉]), Samerah Maeeny[1], Azhar Alenazi[1],
Tahani Alenazi[1], Wafa Alzaid[1], Ghada Algahtani[1],
and Amjad Aldossari[1]

[1] College of Computer and Information Sciences,
Princess Nourah Bint Abdulrahman University,
Riyadh, Kingdom of Saudi Arabia
saelsaid@pnu.edu.sa
[2] Electronics and Communications Department, Faculty of Engineering,
Zagazig University, Zagazig, Egypt

Abstract. Cyber security [1, 2] addresses several important issues in network security and performance including intrusion detection, cipher design, security overhead analysis, and tracing. In this article, an intrusion detection and prevention system (IDPS) is proposed and implemented using SNORT and Security Onion tools to detect and prevent anomaly intrusion; misuse of protocol and service ports, DoS based on crafted payloads, DoS based on volume (DDoS), buffer overflow or other cyber-attacks. The proposed system monitors the network or system activities, finds if any malicious operations occur and then prevents it. To show the efficiency of the proposed system, experiments have been done on numerous anomaly intrusion attacks using KDD database. The experimental results yield 96% detection accuracy. The detection and prevention processes take less than 3 s. The results show the feasibility of the methodology followed in this paper under different attack conditions and show the high robustness of the proposed system.

Keywords: Cyber security · Intrusion Detection System (IDS) · Intrusion Prevention System (IPS) · Anomaly detection · SNORT · Security onion

1 Introduction

Nowadays, attackers use various attacks to obtain important information. Many intrusion detection techniques, methods and algorithms help to detect these attacks [3]. The network infrastructure, routers, and DNS servers and keys that bind these systems must not fail together; otherwise, computers will not be able to communicate accurately or reliably [4]. Given the enormity of Cyber security ensuring proper cybersecurity is critical for the company to maintain the integrity of its external and internal financial reports, as well as protecting strategic property information.

© Springer Nature Switzerland AG 2019
A. Alfaries et al. (Eds.): ICC 2019, CCIS 1097, pp. 15–42, 2019.
https://doi.org/10.1007/978-3-030-36365-9_3

1.1   Problem Statement

Computer Networks are exposed to many types of attacks that may lead to data loss, degrade network performance, uncontrolled traffic, viruses etc. [5, 6]. So it is critical to implement a network intrusion detection and prevention systems (NIDPS) in computer networks that have high traffic and high- speed connectivity to detect and prevent all the growing threats to high-speed environments, such as flood attacks (UDP, TCP, ICMP and HTTP) or Denial and Distributed Denial of Service Attacks (DoS/DDoS) [7].

1.2   Our Contribution

With the increasing malicious attacks on computer networks and wireless systems, Intrusion detection and prevention systems (IDPSs) are one of the most reliable technologies to monitor incoming and outgoing network traffic to identify unauthorized usage. In this paper, an IDPS is proposed and implemented using SNORT [8–10] tool where we can design a suitable real network and use real traffic dataset to test the designed IDPS. To demonstrate the weaknesses of our proposed SNORT IDPS, Security Onion [11] is utilized along with SNORT to analyze and correct its alert log file. The proposed system offers:

- No packet filter drops.
- Real-time notification.
- Broad detection coverage
- Resilience to stress.
- Mechanism separate from policy.

2   Related Work

This section surveys the most known existent IDS/IPS systems, analyzes its performance, and provides a comparison among them. Virtual honeypots [12], which simulate a computer on the network and simulate the IPs stack for various OSs and services. Specter is a smart honeypot system, which simulates a Machine of any type, with a set of services for the attackers to use. Specter generates. Specter simply provides a complete simulated machine to be installed on the network. It is considered as an attempt to overcome the shortcomings of intrusion detection systems. Honeypots are simple and easy to configure and do not have complex algorithms. As honeypots captures the malicious traffic, they also capture the new tools used by the black hats. Honeypot detects few false positive and false negative data also [13]. Misuse detection [14, 15] represents knowledge about unacceptable behavior and attempts to detect its occurrence. It proposes a variation of one approach to misuse detection, state transition analysis, by using pattern matching to detect system attacks. Burglar Alarms; a technique proposed by Markus Granum [16] to reduce the risk of false positives and allow identification of novel attacks, focusing on identifying events that should never occur. Applying dedicated monitors to search for instances of such policy violations effectively Places traps for would- be attackers. Table 1 provides a comparison among existent systems.

3 The Proposed IDPS System

In this paper, an anomaly intrusion detection and prevention system is proposed. It is useful for finding attacks like misuse of protocol and service ports, DoS based on crafted payloads, DoS based on volume (DDoS), buffer overflow and other application. The proposed system is a dynamic anomaly detector where the definition of the system behavior is included; audit records produced by the operating system are used by IDS to define the events of interest. If uncertain behavior is considered as anomalous, then the system administrators may be alerted by false alarms.

Table 1. Comparison among existent systems

Techniques	Principle of work	Requirements	Advantages	Disadvantages
Honey pots	A computer system that is set up to act as a decoy to lure cyber-attacks, and to detect, deflect or study attempts to gain unauthorized access to information systems	PC LINUX 7.X	Easy to implement Reliable Easy to understand acceptable performance Low Cost	Narrow vision of honeypots Alarms only when attacked Fingerprinting Can be used when detected by attacker Risk Introduce risks to the environment
Misuse detection	Typical misuse detection approaches: "Network grip" - look for strings in network connections which might indicate an attack in progress Pattern matching - encode series of states that are passed through during the course of an attack It detects a pattern that matches closely activity that is typical of a network intrusion	Snort software	Easy to implement Easy to deploy Easy to update Easy to understand Low false positives Fast	Cannot detect something previously unknown Constantly needs to be updated with new rules Easier to fool
Burglar alarms	Based on site policy alert administrator to policy violations	Sensor nodes	Reliable	Policy-directed Requires knowledge

The proposed system applies cognition based detection model that works on the audit data. The set of predefined rules for the classes and attributes are identified from the KDD training dataset. It uses Decision tree based SVM which merges the Decision tree and SVM techniques to decrease the training and testing time in an efficient way. It detects any anomaly intrusion in three steps:

– Data collection:

This module passes the data as input to the IDS. The data is recorded into a file and then it is analyzed. Network based IDS collects and alters the data packets and in host-based IDS collects details like usage of the disk and processes of the system.

– Feature Selections:

To select the particular feature large data is available in the network and they are usually evaluated for intrusion. For example, the Internet Protocol (IP) address of the source and target system, protocol type, header length and size could be taken as a key for intrusion.

– Analyses

The proposed IDPS analyzes the data where the incoming traffic is checked where the system behavior is studied, and mathematical models are employed to it. The proposed system informs the network administrator with all the required data through email/alarm icons and plays an active part in the system by dropping packets so that it does not enter the system or close the ports. As shown in Fig. 1, the flowchart of the proposed system can be described as follows:

First step: Download snort and security onion on the Ubuntu.
Second step: Configure snort and security onion tools.
Third step: Download normal and intrusion packets real traffic dataset.
Fourth step: Create a network with the same number of devices and IPs as those in the dataset
Fifth step: Simulate the network from which the dataset is driven then enforce network devices to send the dataset packets.
Sixth step: Check if there is an intrusion packet.
Seventh step: If yes, the snort will produce alert contain details about detected intrusion, and use sguil to analyze the alert file and determine the intrusion, then will drop the packet.
Eighth step: If it is not intrusion, the system will allow the packet to cross.

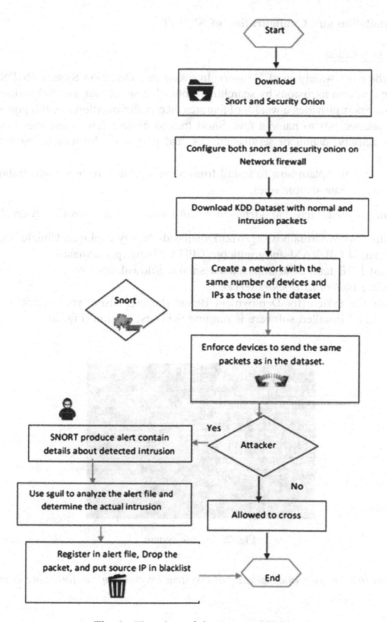

Fig. 1. Flowchart of the proposed IDPS

3.1 Installation and Configuration of SNORT

a. Snort Installation

Snort is the most widely used Network Intrusion and Detection System (NIDS) that detects and prevent intrusions by searching protocol, content analysis, and various pre-processors. Snort provides a wealth of features, like buffer overflow, stealth port scans, and CGI attacks, just to name a few. Snort tries to name a few. Snort tries to detect malicious activity, denial of service attacks, and port scans by monitoring network traffic.

Here, we will explain how to install from Snort website, create a configuration file for snort, and create sample rules.

1. *Download the Oracle VM VirtualBox with Linux Ubuntu operating system16.04.*

   - https://www.virtualbox.org/wiki/Downloads Newly deployed Ubuntu 16.04 Minimum 4 GB RAM and multicore CPU for better performance.
   At least 1 TB hard disk. https://www.snort.org/downloads
2. *Installing ubuntu as a snort server.*
   Prepare the System for Deployment Before starting, ensure your system is up to date and all installed software is running the latest version (Fig. 2).

Fig. 2. Update system

3. *Log in to root user and update your system by running the following command* (Fig. 3):

```
apt-get update -y                          cd daq-2.0.6
```

Fig. 3. Install required updates

4. *Before installing snort, you will need to install required dependencies on your system* (Fig. 4)

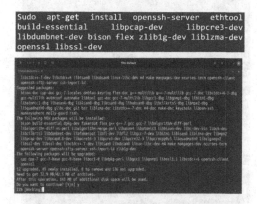

Fig. 4. Install required dependents

5. *Install DAQ*

download the latest version of DAQ with The following command (Fig. 5):

Fig. 5. Install DAQ

6. *Chang the directorory to daq-2.0.6* (Fig. 6):

Fig. 6. Chang directory

7. *Now run the following command to compile and install DAQ* (Fig. 7):

Fig. 7. Run command

8. *Network Interface checking* (Fig. 8)

Fig. 8. Interface checking

9. *Configuring snort Interface(s) which Snort should listen on* (Fig. 9):

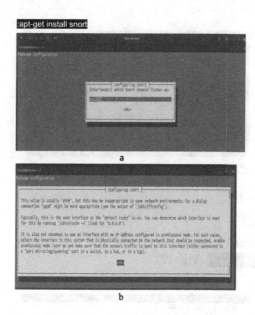

Fig. 9. Configuring snort interface

10. *Update the shared libraries otherwise you will get an error when you try to run Snort* `ldconfig` *(Fig. 10):*

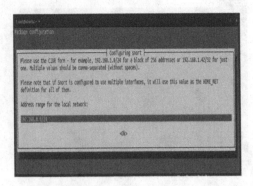

Fig. 10. Address range for the local network

11. *Verify the installation and configuration with the following command* (Fig. 11)

Fig. 11. Update the shared libraries

b. <u>Configure Snort</u>

      Step1:   open/etc./snort/snort.conf   file   in   your   favorite   editor: `gedit/snort/snort.conf` (Fig. 12)

Fig. 12. Open file to sonrt config

Step2: Change the file as shown below (Fig. 13):

```
# Setup the network addresses you are protecting
ipvar HOME_NET 192.168.15.0/24
# Set up the external network addresses. Leave as
"any" in most situations
ipvar EXTERNAL_NET any
var RULE_PATH /etc/snort/rules
var SO_RULE_PATH /etc/snort/so_rules
var PREPROC_RULE_PATH /etc/snort/preproc_rules
var WHITE_LIST_PATH /etc/snort/rules
var BLACK_LIST_PATH /etc/snort/rules
include $RULE_PATH/local.rules
```

Fig. 13. Chang the configuration

Step3: Save and close the file when you are done

Step4: validate the configuration file with the following command (Fig. 14):

Fig. 14. Validate

c. *Testing Snort*

Snort is now ready for testing but before starting, you will need to create a rule set. Let's create a rule to test Snort

Step5: Edit the local.rules file: Add the following lines (Fig. 15):

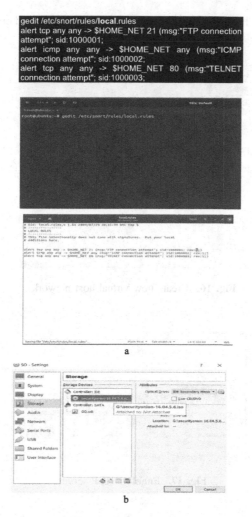

Fig. 15. Edit the rules

Step6: Save and close the file.

The above rules will generate an alert when someone tries to Ping, FTP, or Telnet to the server.

3.2   Installation and Configuration Security Onion

Security Onion https://securityonion.net/ is a free and open source Linux distribution for intrusion detection, enterprise security monitoring, and log management. It includes Elasticsearch, Logstash, Kibana, Snort, Suricata, Bro, Wazuh, Sguil, Squert, CyberChef, NetworkMiner, and many other security tools. The easy-to-use Setup wizard allows you to build an army of distributed sensors for your enterprise in minutes.

1. Create new virtual host only for network of security onion, and enable DHCP server (Figs. 16 and 17).

Fig. 16. Create new virtual host network

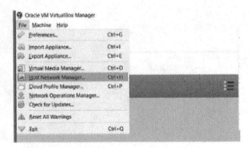

Fig. 17. Enable DHCP server

2. Create VM name, type and version.
3. Determine the size of the memory on which the security onion can be loaded and the size of the virtual hard desk to download security onion (Figs. 18 and 19)

Fig. 18. Specify memory size

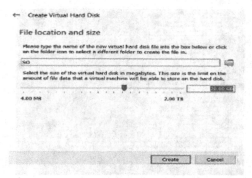

Fig. 19. Specify file location and size

4. Upload the security onion file from your computer to Virtual Box (Figs. 20, 21 and 22).

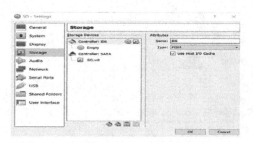

Fig. 20. Upload the security onion

Fig. 21. Edit setting

Fig. 22. Uploading Security onion is done

5. Chose the language and write the password (Figs. 23 and 24).

Fig. 23. Language used

Fig. 24. Password

6. Choose which services to install on security onion, and chose the setup of security onion is DHCP (Figs. 25 and 26).

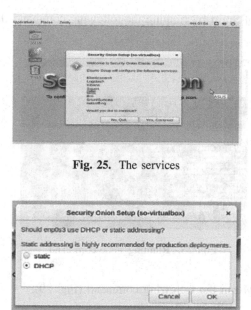

Fig. 25. The services

Fig. 26. Setup of security onion

4 Implementation of the Proposed IDPS System

4.1 Implementation of Intrusion Detection System (IDS)

1. Start Snort in Network IDS mode from terminal and tell it to output any alert to the console (Fig. 27):

Fig. 27. Checking for the statuses

2. Check the status of Snort by running the following command (Fig. 28):

Fig. 28. Running some command

3. On the remote VM run the following command (Fig. 29):

Fig. 29. Start snort in intrusion detection mode

4. Start Snort in Network IDS mode from the terminal and tell it to output any alert to the console (Fig. 30):

Fig. 30. Result of IDS

5. Finally, alert file produced by the proposed IDS.

4.2 Implementation of Intrusion Prevention System (IPS)

Step1: sudo nano etc/network/interfacs
   - Adding networking interface
   - Configure a snort network here (This means you can bridge eth0 with eth1 (pass traffic between them)).
   - All traffic will go through the snort to the website.
   - SNORT will decide which traffic should go and which are not (Fig. 31).

Fig. 31. Add network interface

Step2: network forwarding
sudo nano /etc/sysctl

sudo nano /etc/sysctl.conf

Ipv4 Network forwarding is the final stage of network forwarding (Fig. 32)

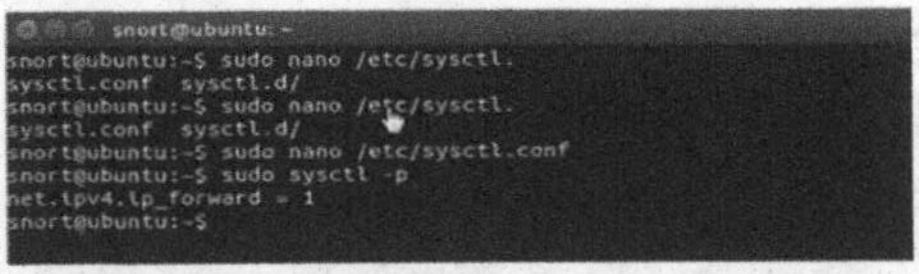

Fig. 32. Network forwarding

Step3: Network checking (Figs. 33 and 34)

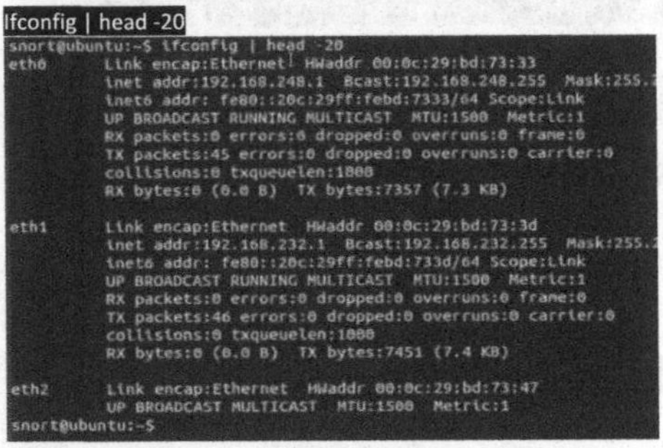

Fig. 33. Network checking

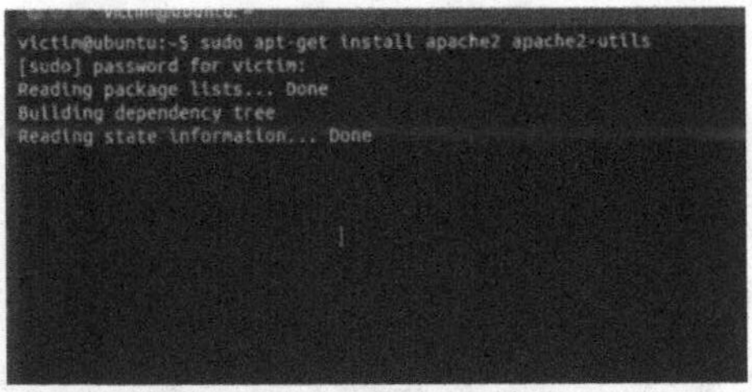

Fig. 34. Installing web server and web victim

Step4: Installing a web server and a victim server.

```
sudo apt-get install apache2 apache2-utils
sudo su
cd /var/www/html/
echo "This is the victim webserver" > index.htm
```

Step5: Editing: for making password protected website (Fig. 35)

Fig. 35. Editing the website

Step6: http pass setting (Fig. 36)

Fig. 36. Setting the http

Step7: Snort setting for the web server (Figs. 37 and 38)

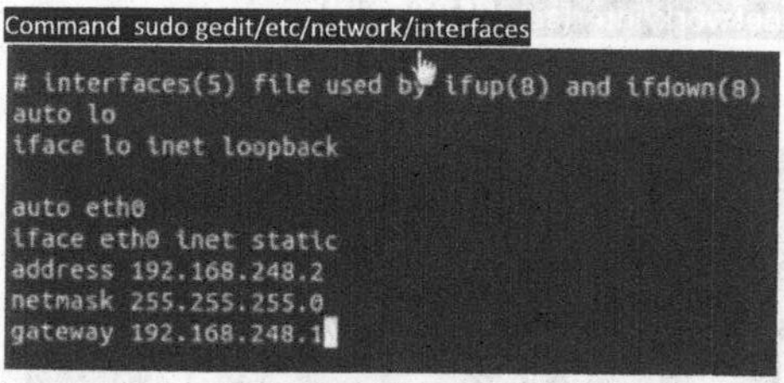

Fig. 37. Link the website with the network

Fig. 38. Final result of the website

Step8: Display the website we set up.
The settings of the KALI network were loaded on Ubuntu, like the website and snort (Fig. 39)

Fig. 39. Setting the intrusion

Step9: sudo nano/etc/network/interfaces (Fig. 40)

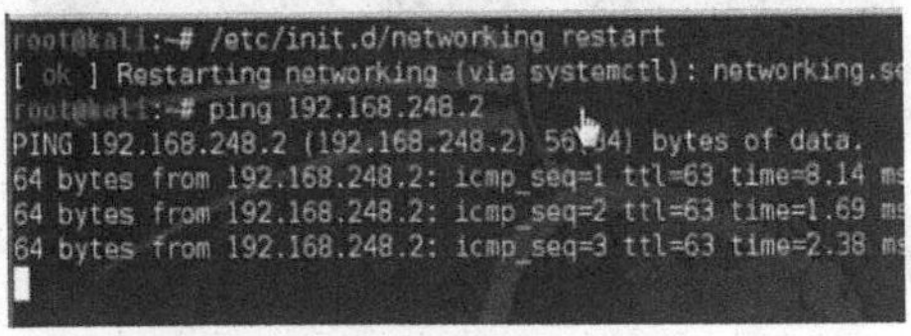

Fig. 40. The snort is working

Step10: Ping website address to make sure the snort is working (Fig. 41)

(a)

(b)

(c)

Fig. 41. Creating IPS rules

Step11: Create rules for the IPS

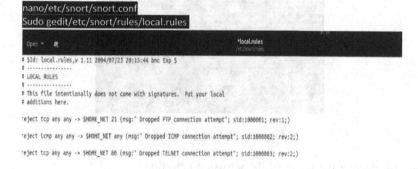

Step12: Running snort in IPS mode (Fig. 42).

Fig. 42. Snort running in IPS mode

Step13: Attacking sites from kali uploaded to Ubuntu (Fig. 43)

Fig. 43. Attacking the website

Step14: display the result of the intrusion detection

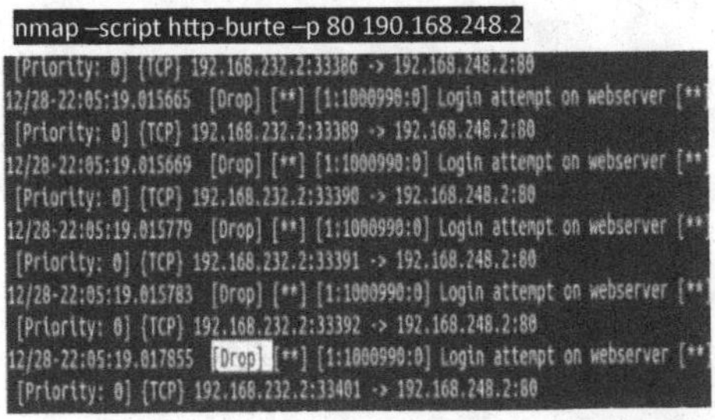

Fig. 44. Final result of dropping the intrusion packet

As shown in Fig. 44 the proposed system was able to detect the intrusion packets and dropped it.

5   Testing the Proposed IDPS System

5.1   Testing the IDS System

1. Open the interface of the sguil tool and write the username and password of Security onion (Fig. 45).

Fig. 45. Sguil interface

2. Test the IDS system by using KDD dataset (Fig. 46).

Fig. 46. Steps of Testing the IDS

3. Real-time alerts appear after you execute this command locate KDD, after executing this command, alerts appear for the intrusion attempts. We will show colors for alerts such as red, yellow, orange. This indicates the infiltration status if red is very bad and if yellow is bad (Fig. 47).

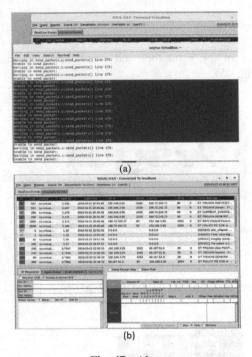

(a)

(b)

Fig. 47. Alerts

Step 4: Figure 48 shows the details, what the hacker try to do with our network, this is details indicate the method of analysis of the sguil to snort accurately and in Fig. 49, the green color means that the IDPS system is running.

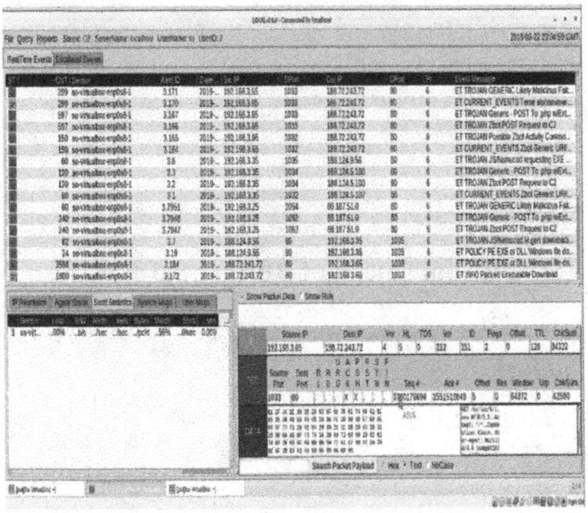

Fig. 48. Details of each alert

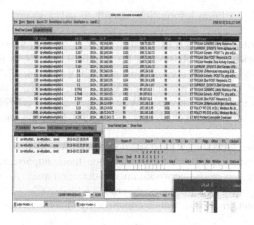

Fig. 49. The green color means that the IDPS system is running. (Color figure online)

6 Conclusion and Future Work

Cybersecurity aims to enhance the protection of networks, IT systems, operational technology systems and their components of hardware and software, their services and their data. In this article, an anomaly intrusion detection and prevention technique is proposed. Anomaly detection is useful for finding attacks like misuse of protocol and service ports, DoS based on crafted payloads, DoS based on volume (DDoS), buffer overflow and other application. The proposed system is a dynamic anomaly detector where the definition of the system behavior is included. The system behavior is defined as an order of different events. For example, audit records produced by the operating system are used by IDS to define the events of interest. In this case, the behavior can be observed only when audit records are created by OS and the events are occurred in strict sequences. If uncertain behavior is considered as anomalous, then the system administrators is alerted by false alarms. The system detects the intrusion packets and prevent it by dropping all its packets.

In the future, we wish to:

– Modify the proposed system to protect the computer network from other types of attack instead of anomalies such as signatures, hybrids and system application in the real world.

References

1. Abu-taieh, E.: Cyber security body of knowledge. In: The 7th IEEE International Symposium on Cloud and Service Computing (2017)
2. Abomhara, M., Køien, G.M.: Cyber security and the internet of things: vulnerabilities, threats, intruders and attacks. J. Cyber Secur. **4**, 65–88 (2015). https://www.researchgate.net/publication/277718176_Cyber_Security_and_the_Internet_of_Things_Vulnerabilities_Threats_Intruders_and_Attacks. Accessed 19 May 2019

3. Solms, R., Niekerk, J.: From information security to cyber security. Comput. Secur. **38**, 97–103 (2013)
4. Bishop, M.: Computer Security. IEEE Secur. Priv. **9**(1), 67–69 (2003)
5. Riordan, J., Duponchel, Y., Rissmann, R., Zamboni, D.: Network attack detection. International business machines corporations, pct/IB2006/050554, 29 June 2008
6. Kumar, S., Spafford, E.: Pattern matching model for misuse intrusion detection. Department of Computer Sciences Purdue University West Lafayette, October1994
7. Ranum, M.J.: Intrusion detection challenges and myths. CEO, Network Flight Recorder, Inc. (1998)
8. Snort documentation. https://www.snort.org/documents. Accessed 20 Mar 2019
9. Top five free enterprise network intrusion-detection tools. http://searchsecurity.techtarget. com/tip/Top-five-free-enterprise-network-intrusion-detection-tools. Accessed 23 Apr 2019
10. Gaur, N: Snort: planning IDS for your enterprise, 13 June 2007
11. Security Onion Solutions. https://github.com/Security-Onion-Solutions. Accessed 25 Dec 2018
12. Kuwatly, I., Sraj, M., Al Masri, Z.: Dynamic honeypot design for intrusion detection. In: IEEE/ACS International Conference (2004)
13. Chaudhary, S., Chaudhary, K.: Distributed honeypots system. Int. J. Adv. Res. Innov. **1**, 29–35 (2013). Department of Computer Science and Engineering
14. Porras, P.A., Kemmerer, R.A.: Penetration state transition analysis-a rule-based intrusion detection approach. In: Eighth Annual Computer Security Applications Conference, pp. 220–229. IEEE Computer Society Press, 30 November-December 1992
15. Llgun, K.: Real-time intrusion detection system for unix. Master's thesis, Computer Science Department, University of California, Santa Barbara, July 1992
16. Advantages and Disadvantages of Burglar Alarms. http://gps-securitygroup.com/advantages-and-disadvantages-of-installing-alarm-security-systems/. Accessed 21 Dec 2018

Detailed Quantum Cryptographic Service and Data Security in Cloud Computing

Omer K. Jasim Mohammad[1]([⊠]) and Safia Abbas[2]

[1] Director of Computer Center, University of Fallujah, Anbar, Iraq
Omerk.jasim@uofallujah.edu.iq
[2] Department of Computer Science, Faculty of Computer
and Information Sciences, Ain Shams University, Cairo, Egypt
safia_abbas@cis.asu.edu.iq

Abstract. This paper presents a holistic security solution for cloud computing environment by proposed a new secured cloud framework, which known as cryptographic cloud computing environment (CCCE) [14, 15]. CCCE entails both a trusted cloud-user and an innovative quantum cryptographic service (QCaaS). QCaaS is a new security service that responsible to solve the key generation, key distribution and key management problems, which emerged through the negotiation between the communications parties (cloud-user and cloud provider). Such service includes a proposed symmetric quantum encryption algorithm that is explained in previous work, usually called quantum advanced encryption standard (QAES). QAES build by the integration between a quantum key distribution (QKD) and an enhanced version of AES using two different modes, On-line and Off-line mode. Additionally, CCCE implemented using the system center manager 2012-SPI, which in turn, installed and configured based bare-metal Hyper-V, it poses more secured data transmission channels by provisioning secret key among cloud's instances. Finally, CCCE reveals a higher secure data transmission comparing to other cloud security systems especially in key generation, key management, defeating almost type of attacks, and the impact rate of the proposed solution on the performance of cloud resources.

Keywords: Cloud computing · Quantum cryptography · Hyper-V · Secure service · Cloud computing security · Key management

1 Introduction

A lot of companies have outsourced parts of their information systems to external suppliers under the phenomenon of information technology outsourcing (ITO) [1]. This development has been reinforced by a cloud computing technology trend [2]. Cloud computing helps companies and cloud users to utilize the hardware, storage, and software components of a third party organization usually called cloud system provider (CSP) instead of managing their own computing infrastructure [2, 3].

In addition, cloud computing offers users the illusion of having infinite hardware computing resources which they can use as they need, without having to concern themselves with precisely how those resources are provided or maintained [4].

© Springer Nature Switzerland AG 2019
A. Alfaries et al. (Eds.): ICC 2019, CCIS 1097, pp. 43–56, 2019.
https://doi.org/10.1007/978-3-030-36365-9_4

Accordingly, cloud computing encompasses three main service's levels, Infrastructure as a service (IaaS), Platform as a service (PaaS) and Software as a service (SaaS), that vary according to the degree of relation with the details of the underlying hardware and software [5–7].

In spite of revenues, which mentioned above, have dramatically changed the information technology scene, the data moving through an open environment and the lack of controlling from cloud-users on their data led to many obstructions. Accordingly, the CSP must preserve users' data confidentiality, integrity, and it is responsible for defeating an insider or an external attack. CSP must adopt various security solutions to guarantee a trust environment for the consumers [8, 9]. One kind of these solutions is cryptographic cloud environment that can provide the confidentiality, integrity, and authentication problems. Classical and quantum cryptosystems provide a method that is efficiently and unconditionally secure to transmit data between different parties in cloud environment. Current context exploits quantum encryption criteria to find an efficient and invulnerable quantum algorithm based on the principles of quantum computations to secure cloud data [10–12].

This paper introduces a secured cloud computing cryptographic environment that entails both trusted user cloud and innovative cloud cryptographic service. This service involves the QAES algorithm that explained in details in [13, 14]. The main contribution of this paper is to build a secure cloud environment and describes the experimental cloud network system. This environment has been built depending on Microsoft System Center Manager 2012-SP1 (MSCM-SP1) and Hyper-V hypervisor. Since our reference implementation is based on the Hyper-V, the Hyper-V terminologies are applied when describing the QCaaS design like creating a template, deploying service, and domain connection.

The rest of the paper is organized as follows: Sect. 2 illustrates the core components of the proposed secure cloud computing cryptosystem. The developed quantum-crypto service (QCaaS) has been given in Sect. 3. Section 4 shows the experimental results and analysis. Finally, Sect. 5 presents the conclusion and future works.

2 Proposed Secure Cloud Computing Cryptosystem

Proposed framework has been structured to provide a secure data transmission to/from cloud data center. Thus, multiple secure mechanisms and a lot of precautions are applied to shield the critical information from unauthorized parties. The proposed framework completely depends on innovative service, quantum cryptography as a service (QCaaS) that involves a proposed encryption algorithm (QAES). QAES is a symmetric encryption algorithm that entails both a new developed version of traditional AES and QKD system (it explained in details in [15]). Figure 1 illustrates the core-contents of proposed secure cloud cryptosystem.

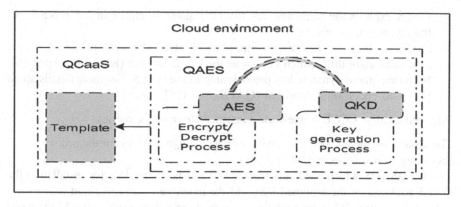

Fig. 1. Proposed cloud computing environment

As shown in Fig. 1, QCaaS responsible on the key generation, key management, and encryption/decryption process. In briefly, QCaaS includes the QAES algorithm that constituted by the integration between the following aspects:

i. **QKD:** is a new technology come up with an idea of how to securely distribute a random key with help of quantum physics. Also, it enables the cloud communication parties (cloud-user, cloud service provider (CSP)) to "growth" a shared secret key without placing any limits on an adversary's computational power and can detect the influence of any third-party eavesdropping on the key exchange. Additionally, QKD provides a potential solution to the key distribution problem by enabling two communication parties connected by a quantum transmission path (optical fiber or quantum network) [11, 12] to continuously produce an unconditionally secure shared secret key or decide not to use a key if detecting an eavesdropper. In order to use such keys with the different security applications in the cloud computing environment, those keys must be deployed between communication parties after then integrated it with any type of modern cryptographic algorithm. Practically, the simulation of QKD designed and developed to work in the distributed computing environment using windows communication foundation (WCF) technique. To generate a secret key based QKD simulator, the basic computation processes such as bases, states, channel, and QKD phases are simulated [13]. For more detailed about the simulation environment, see [15];

ii. **Developed AES algorithm:** is a private key block cipher that processes data blocks of 128 bits with the key length of 128, 192, or 256 bits like the traditional AES [8], but. It is completely depended on QKD in the key generation process. Substantially, the length of key (Kl) determines the number of rounds (Nr) for each cryptographic process. For example, QAES-128 applies the round function 10 times, QAES-192 applies 12 times and QAES-256 applies 14 times [13]. In addition, mathematical criteria of QAES don't contract with the corresponding one in the AES. However, the differences between the QAES and the traditional AES have been given as follows:

 – QAES utilizes the dynamic quantum s-box (DQS-box) that is generated depending on key generation from the quantum cipher. While, AES utilizes astatic S-box and completely based on the mathematical model.

- QAES exploits the generated key from the quantum cipher in order to achieve the cryptographic process.
- QAES replace the key expansion phase in the AES and proposed a new scheduler algorithm, which known as the key controller (KC). KC responsible for arrangement dynamic key provisioning in the QAES. For more details about proposed encryption algorithm (QAES), see [15];

Algorithmically, CCCE framework consists of four major parties:

- The cloud Provider (*CSP*), who provides data storage services for the ordinary VM, according to resources availability (R_a).
- The QCaaS (*Q*), which holds the master key and is responsible for installation the QAES package on the assigned VM and the machine of trusted cloud-user.
- A trust cloud-user (*U*), who probably uses or share a data block at a VM managed by CSP but does not hold the full administrative right of deriving the decryption keys on such VM.
- A trust active directory domain (ADD), usually named as domain controller (*DC*), which responsible for adding *U* to the trusted active users group (*G*). Furthermore, *DC* responsible for managing the credential verification, validation, and the originality for the cloud-user (real user or spammer).

Accordingly, Figs. 2 summarizes the steps of registration process that established between *U* and *CSP*.

- CCCE Algorithm: Login process for U
Initialize CSP, G, U, and Q are ready
While (the registration is available in the cloud data center)
U →Do: send request to CSP
DO ↔ CSP : mutual authentication based Kerberos function
CSP → U : register a MAC for user
DC → U to G : domain controller administrator add user to trust group
End while

Fig. 2. CCCE algorithm: login process

As mentioned above, all CCCE parties connected through the central domain controller (DC) and worked as concurrently. Initially, in order to register a new cloud-user, he/she (U) requests a secure connection form the CSP, then, CSP checks the validity of user (original or spammer attack) based on the Kerberos authentication function [10, 11].Then, CSP adds authenticated user to the user group (G) of domain controller (DC). While, Fig. 3 shows the pseudo code for deploying a cryptographic service (Q).

-   CCCE Algorithm: Renting VM and cryptographic service

Initialize CSP, G, U, Q, Login successfully(Fig2), and Ra are guarantee

      U→ CSP : user request an ordinary VM

      CSP→ R : provider check the resources availability Ra

While (*User Requested Resources* < Ra)

    Initialize DC, G

      For every U in G

        U→ DO: user received assigned VM from CSP

        DC → U: domain administrator registers a VM-info and approved to U.

        U→ CSP: user request a cryptographic service

        CSP→ Q : provider assigns query to service

        Q→ U : negotiation between user and secured service

        Q → qk_1 : secret key build by service

        U → qk_1: secret key build by user

      End for

  Else While

      CSP→ U: unavailable resources.

      U → *CSP*: log out

  Update the G for the next attempt.

End while

Return the Final state

Fig. 3. CCCE algorithm: renting and deploy the proposed service

When a cloud-user wants to achieve a secure transmission for their files, CSP deploys a cryptographic service (Q) to the cloud-user (U) rented machine, then, CSP informs to QCaaS (Q) to start negotiation with cloud-user (U) and build an identical secret key. Accordingly, QCaaS (Q) creates an isolated connection with cloud-user (U).

All mentioned operations will be implemented, if the requested resources by a cloud-user less than the available resources at cloud data center (CSP). Therefore, the CCCE overcomes the key management problem by deploying a new distribution model depending on the four mentioned parties to the specific trusted user.

3   Developed Quantum Crypto-Service

This section describes a proposed quantum cryptographic service in the CCCE. This layer responsible on the key provisioning to cryptographic VMs' and separating both clients' cryptographic primitive and credential accounts based ADD (qcloud.net)-forest. QCaaS optionally applied to the multiple trusted clients, who are renting the VMs. Following sub-sections illustrated the requirements design and the deploying process for the proposed service.

3.1 Requirements Design

In this sub-section, the main requirements of cryptographic service are explained and discussed.

Isolation

The isolation aspect means a separation between traditional VM (instance) and cryptographic VM. As shown in Fig. 4, the traditional VM is a VM that assigned to the authenticated user for renting, then, used for storing files after the administration of Quantum Cloud checking the resource's availability, see Fig. 4.

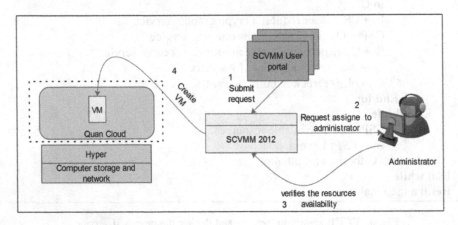

Fig. 4. Traditional VM creating mechanism

Whereas, a cryptographic VM is a VM responsible for key provisioning and management using QAES package (will be explain in sub-section C). However, two types of VMs are connected through central ADD or through a sub-domain in order to defeat an insider attack. Therefore, such separation helps to isolate between the data file and cryptographic privilege, which in turn, create a new VM involves a cryptographic key, see Fig. 5. This cryptographic service optionally associated with each traditional VM depends upon the user selection.

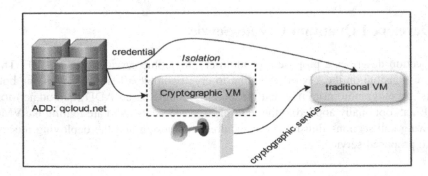

Fig. 5. Deploying cryptographic service to traditional VM

Finally, the key deployment between the trusted client and the secured VM has done through CA and trusted domain connection in order to guarantee the confidentiality of cloud-users.

VM-Service-Template

Virtual-machine-service template (VM-S-T) is used to create a new service and providing a repeatable way of deploying standardized hardware and software settings. VM-S-T classified as VM template (VMT) and service template (ST), VMT defines standard requirements (operating system, CPU, HDD, and so on) for QAES package that published as a service based on library resources. So, the basic function of VMT is to describe the information about a cryptographic virtual machine that is deployed as part of the service.

ST follows the VMT information profile's configuration in order to setup a new cryptographic-VM. In general, the building of cryptographic-ST completely based upon the VMT resource's specifications which are initialized based on VHD files (resident in SCVMM library). Furthermore, in order to create a cryptographic VM-S-T, following steps must be performed:

- Create VMT on the ST designer,
- Select the VHD that contains an operating system (ISO file).
- Configure the virtual hardware (network adapter, capability profiles).
- Configure the operating system (full qualified domain name (FQDN), Internet Information Services (IIS) features, and join domain).
- Configure the cryptographic application package (install web deploy application package).

Accordingly, the template managing is performed through the web console or self-service portal, while all profiles (hardware, operating system, network, and domain controller) resources are stemmed from SCVMM instances. For more details about the creation of the VMT and the ST, see [15].

3.2 Cryptographic Package

This package has been obtained based on the QAES in order to achieve a cryptographic process through the running of the cryptographic-VM. QAES package was established using the installed shield software [14, 15] that provides a subset of the world-class in the package creation functionality, it includes significant functionality which is not available in the current simulator environments. QAES package installed on the cryptographic-VM after configuring the network connection according to ADD (qcloud.net), and Microsoft load balancing mechanism.

Since all transformations and exchanging operations in the Quantum Cloud are performed via web applications. QAES package utilizes the Web Deploy 3.5 [15] to synchronize an IIS server and enables the cloud providers to deploy a cryptographic-VM as a service and available as on-demand. Finally, according to mentioned prerequisite's service design. Many features have been associated with QCaaS like:

- Mini-OS is directly connected with the cloud platform and isolated from the cloud instances.

– Isolation resources for each cryptographic service (Special hardware resources (CPU, HDD, and memory).
– Private network configuration and trusted IP for each trusted client.
– Domain connection for each new cryptographic service.

Consequently, QCaaS assures both the appropriate load for cloud performance optimization and the client controlling activities (client prevents the cloud administrator from gained or preserve his data). Therefore, a secured environment for each client's VM, with no possibility for insiders or external attackers, is guaranteed.

CCCE utilizes an ST to deploy the cryptographic service to Quantum Cloud instances and trust cloud-user. The deploying of QCaaS performed optionally regarding to cloud user selection. Following steps must be followed to deploy a cryptographic service:

• Cloud-user enters the conferred credential over AC service portal.
• Select the Quantum Cloud.
• Choose a cryptographic ST (QCaaS layer1).
• Deploy.

When a trusted cloud-user enters via the portal of AC, a list of predetermined resources being available for cryptographic-ST. Here, AC-service requests additional information depending upon the ST requirements such as QAES package, kind of integration mode, and credential authority. After data verification, AC coordinates with SCVMM and passes the job for processing. Then, SCVMM accepts the job from AC, and verifies that the request matches the capabilities of the user role and the quota that is created in a VM-ST-template. Finally, SCVMM administrator deploys the cryptographic-VM in the CCCE (Quantum Cloud and trusted cloud-user) and installs the QAES package on the selected host. Figure 6 shows the basic steps of deploying QCaaS in the CCCE.

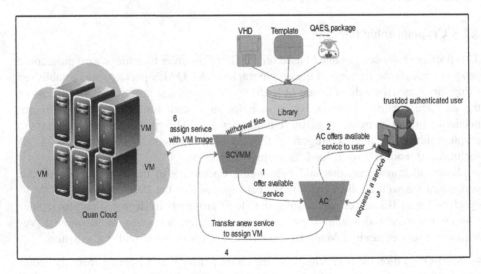

Fig. 6. QCaaS: deploying mechanism

Consequently, many advantages are gained when deploying such cryptographic service like:

- A cryptographic service dynamically worked with one or more of user application's which assign with one or more VMs
- QCaaS can specify a load balancer to spread requests across the assigned VMs.

As a result, QCaaS offers a lot of benefits to the CSP and cloud-user, because it repeatedly runs with each downloading/uploading operation.

4 Experimental Results and Analysis

This section evaluates the CCCE components by discussing and analyzing the observational results. Such results are categorized into three groups, QKD, QAES, and CCCE characteristics. The first and second groups (QKD, QAES) have been discussed in details in [13–15]. However, the obtained results from the last group such as privacy and security of CCCE and the performance of Quantum Cloud environment are discussed in the following sub-sections.

4.1 CCCE Characteristics

This section discusses the main features are gained by the proposed secured cloud computing environment, such as security management, QCaaS roles, encryption/decryption mechanism, and defeating attack.

Security Management
Confidentiality is one of the security management complications that can be assured by encrypting data. Also, other primary barrier of the encryption techniques is still the key management issue. Accordingly, the CCCE has overcome these two barriers by (confidentiality and key management) deploying the QCaaS for each trusted cloud-user. QCaaS supports scalability in dynamic key distribution via two implemented modes and provides independent and trusted communication for each cloud-user. Likewise, it protects the cloud-user cryptographic key through the communication with Quantum Cloud environment. Due to the isolation criteria for the resources, QCaaS prevents an attacker or malicious from extraction information from the cloud. Finally, QCaaS guarantees the following roles:

- Securing the cloud-user: QCaaS provides the encryption/decryption process by cooperating both user's machine and cloud servers, this corporation defeats two types of attacks (man-in – the middle attack and authentication attack).
- User encryption permissions: QCaaS helps the user for encrypting the flying data, which in turn, provides a higher level of security.
- Key Protection: key generation and key distribution processes are critical in any cloud environment, therefore, the keys must be carefully generated and protected.

QCaaS achieves these processes by dynamic key generation based QKD. After then, the keys are expired as soon as the sending or receiving files process completed.

User Controlling Side

Generally, in cloud environment, the encrypted data and the decryption key has to be stored in a storage on cloud servers that is naturally unreliable due to the possibility of being abused by malicious insiders. CCCE addressed this problem by isolating the cryptographic-VM and the ordinary VM depending on the trusted ADD, this feature helps cloud-users to store their data in a plain from. Substantially, QCaaS separates the cryptographic process from storage function. This service has a more controlling feature in the trusted cloud-user to prevent an insider attack from presence the stored data. The domain connection mechanism, reliable hardware, and scalability of QCaaS are helped to provide a client-controlling side. In addition, the cloud-user runs a logging program for user verification, then, when CSP distinguishes him as an authorized user, this request along with the cloud-user ID is sent to the assigned cloud-VM. After finding corresponding data, data and user ID are transmitted to QCaaS to encrypt or decrypt. Such Data through a secure channel with CRM will be accessible for cloud-users. Then, QCaaS removes the whole data related to the process.

4.2   Performance of Quantum Cloud

Performance is a critical part of most cloud computing environment. Many research companies continually show that good performance is essential for a CSP and cloud-user. In this sub-section, the performance of Quantum Cloud is evaluated based on the SCOM server, this evaluation focuses on processor utilization, memory consumption, network bandwidth, and idle of the logical disk. The processor utilization refers to the amount of work handled by a processor and it varies depending on the amount and type of managed computing tasks under cloud datacenter. The memory consumption refers to the memory size that is lost through the executing applications or running VMs on the cloud datacenter. A network bandwidth refers to the capacity of a network connection for supporting transfer an amount of data from one point to another in a given time (usually a second) and it is usually expressed in bits per second (bps). Higher network bandwidth often translates to better performance, although overall performance also depends on other factors. Finally, the idle logical disk refers to the time required for the read/write from the virtual hard disk (VHD) through the period of time.

The evaluation computations are calculated when 6-client machines are connected (Windows 8 as an operating system installed) to the Quantum Cloud at the same time. Two of them implemented a download process, whereas, others implemented an uploading process using different file sizes (10–150 MB). Figures 7 and 8 illustrate the performance of Quantum Cloud regarding to above criteria process efficiency and memory consumption.

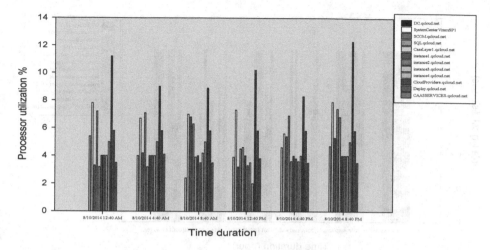

Fig. 7. Processor utilization through the 24 h

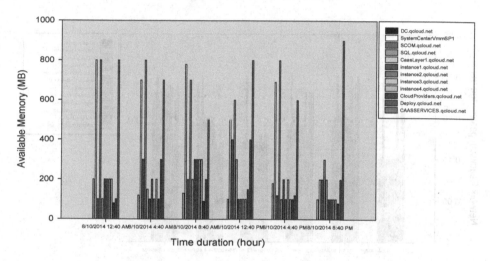

Fig. 8. Memory consumption through 24 h

Accordingly, we conclude that the contributed cryptographic service doesn't effect on the processor utilization or memory consumption. The resources isolation mechanism (quota creation) helps to guarantee a suitable load balancing for cloud environment. On the other hand, Figs. 9 and 10 depict the efficiency of HDD based on the delaying time for read/write operation and the efficiency of network through 24 h of working.

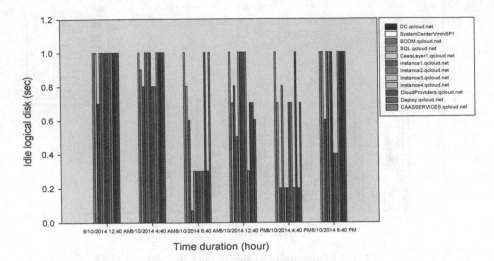

Fig. 9. Idle logical disk through 24 h

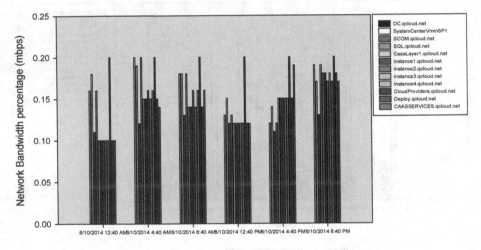

Fig. 10. Network bandwidth through 24 h

According to above analytical Figures, QCaaS does not affect the performance of Quantum Cloud and a normal state of the processor and memory registered. The isolation resources of cryptographic service and central controlling by the domain controller (qcloud.net) helped to guarantee the efficiency of the cloud. Finally, comparing to other cloud computing environments [10, 11, 13], regarding to the cost of resources, our proposed cloud computing environment presents the convincing solutions for the performance, security, and independence for the cloud-users.

5 Conclusions and Future Works

Cloud computing is an emerging trend of distributed computing technology that is very useful in present day to day life, it uses the internet and the central remote servers to provide and maintain data as well as applications. Such applications in turn can be used by the end users via the cloud communications without any installation. Despite the flexibility of data and application accessing and usage that cloud computing environments provide, there are many questions still coming up on how to gain a trusted environment that protects data and applications in the clouds from hackers and intruders. Consequently, a set of critical security issues, such as privacy, confidentiality, integrity, availability, traceability, and reliability must be provided. Since the currently Quantum Cloud environment depends on the QAES algorithm and the cryptographic service, it protects users' data from hacking as much as possible. QAES algorithm accomplished by the combination between the enhanced version of AES and the QKD system. This proposed algorithm prepared as an installer package that is installed and configured on the innovative cryptographic service (QCaaS). The QCaaS is a core contribution to enhance the cloud computing security and gives more controlling ability to a cloud user to manage their VM. The QCaaS solves the key generation, key distribution and key management problems that emerged through the two implemented negotiation modes. Since QCaaS assigned to the two communication parties (cloud user and CSP), it enjoys many advantages like serving the cloud-user secure communication and protecting their sensitive data, verifying and monitoring the identity of the original user depending on qcloud.net and Kerberos authentication function, deploying an encryption service with each VM, and achieving the encryption/decryption processes using QAES.

Moreover, CCCE enjoys certain advantages when compared with the others cloud computing environment [10, 11, 13], especially with respect of secret key generation used in the encryption/decryption process. It can be considered as the first cloud environment that integrates both the CSP principles and the quantum cryptography criteria. CCCE shows that the availability and the reliability of the secret key generation can be easily achieved based on two modes, On-line and off-line. In addition, CCCE poses more secure data transmission by provisioning secret keys among cloud's instances based on innovative cryptographic service QCaaS. CCCE manipulates heavy computing processes that cannot be executed using personal computer only. Finally, cloud data encryption based quantum technology platform dispels all security fears through the cloud data transmission. This technology offers, a simple, low-cost for the data protection, security tools for service's integration, and an efficient disaster recovery.

At the future, deploying the CCCE system to work on the public cloud environment such as Google cloud platform and Amazon EC2 and generalize the CCCE idea to a broader than the field of personal data transfer. In addition, deploying the CCCE system to work on the grid computing environment in order to generalize the system in the most computing paradigms.

References

1. Hill, R., Hirsch, L., Lake, P., Moshiri, S.: Guide to Cloud Computing: Principles and Practice, 1st edn. Springer, Heidelberg (2013). ISBN 1617-7975
2. Ackerman, T.: IT Security Risk Management: Perceived IT Security Risks in the Context of Cloud Computing, 1st edn. Springer, Heidelberg (2013). ISBN 978-3-658-01114-7
3. Chen, C., Lin, J., Wu, X., Wu, J.: Parallel and distributed spatial outlier mining in grid: algorithm, design and application. J. Grid Comput. **13**(2), 139–157 (2015)
4. Wu, K., Liu, L., Liu, J.: Researches on grid security authentication algorithm in cloud computing. J. Netw. **6**(11), 1639–1646 (2011)
5. Liu, H., Ning, H., Xiong, Q., Yang, L.T.: Shared authority based privacy-preserving authentication protocol in cloud computing. IEEE Trans. Parallel Distrib. Syst. **26**(1), 241–251 (2014)
6. Itani, W., Kayassi, A., Chehab, A.: Energy-efficient incremental integrity for securing storage in mobile cloud computing. In: Proceedings of the International Conference on Energy Aware Computing (ICEAC10), Cairo, Egypt, pp. 1–2 (2010)
7. Yau, S.S., An, H.G.: Confidentiality protection in cloud computing systems. Int. J. Softw. Inform. **4**(4), 351–361 (2010)
8. Rahmani, H., Sundararajan, E., Ali, Z.M., Zin, A.M.: Encryption as a service (EaaS) as a solution for cryptography in cloud. In: Proceedings of the 4th International Conference on Electrical Engineering and Informatics (ICEEI 2013), vol. 11, pp. 1202–1210 (2013). Procedia Technology
9. Narayan, E., Malik, M., Singh, A.P., Narain, P.: To enhance the data security of cloud in cloud computing using rsa algorithm. Bookman Int. J. Softw. Eng. **1**(1), 8–11 (2012)
10. Wu, J., Liu, Q., Liao, X.: A secure and efficient outsourceable group key transfer protocol in cloud computing. In: Proceedings of the 2nd International workshop on security in cloud computing, USA, pp. 43–50 (2014)
11. Günther, F., Manulis, M., Strufe, T.: Key management in distributed online social networks. In: IEEE International Symposium on a World of Wireless, Mobile and Multimedia Networks (WoWMM), Lucca, pp. 1–7 (2011)
12. Zhou, M., Mu, Y., Susilo, W., Yan, J., Dong, L.: Privacy enhanced data outsourcing in the cloud. J. Netw. Comput. Appl. **35**(4), 1367–1373 (2012)
13. Jasim, O.K., Abbas, S., El-Horbaty, E.-S.M., Salem, A.-B.M.: A comparative study between modern encryption algorithms based on cloud computing environment. In: Proceedings of the 8th International conference for Internet Technology and Secured Transactions, UK, pp. 536–541 (2013)
14. Jasim, O.K., Abbas, S., El-Horbaty, E.-S.M., Salem, A.-B.M.: Cryptographic cloud computing environment as a more trusted communication environment. Int. J. Grid High. Perform. Comput. (IJGHPC) **6**(2), 38–51 (2014)
15. Mohammad, O.K.J., Abbas, S., El-Horbaty, E.-S.M., Salem, A.-B.M.: Securing cloud computing environment using a new trend of cryptography. In: 2015 International Conference on Cloud Computing (ICCC), KSA (2015)

The Effects of the Property of Access Possibilities and Cybersecurity Awareness on Social Media Application

Bedour F. Alrashidi[1]([⊠]), Aljawharah M. Almuhana[2]([⊠]),
and Alanoud M. Aljedaie[2]([⊠])

[1] Faculty of Computing and Information Technology, King Abdulaziz University,
Jeddah, Kingdom of Saudi Arabia
bedourf2016@gmail.com
[2] College of Computer Science and Software Engineering, University of Hail,
Hail, Kingdom of Saudi Arabia
aljawharahalmuhana@gmail.com, a.aljedaie@uoh.edu.sa

Abstract. Cybersecurity became the third war in the world as it affects the privacy, security, availability, and access possibilities of user's data. Lately, the statistics shows that the users prefer social media application to share their data and updates. Many users believe that only their followers can see their updates while the permissions of access possibilities terms and conditions provided some authority to access the data. To highlight this issue we did a survey in users awareness of accepting access possibility to their data and analyse the risks of allowing/accepting the access possibility of users' data in social media applications. In this paper we propose a Reconnaissance Penetration Testing Methodology (RPTM) that aims to study the process of reconnaissance and information gathering of specific target to show the user's data. In result and discussion we have did a statistical study to find out the level of users awareness in cybersecurity and access possibilities.

Keywords: Cybersecurity · Social media · Penetration test · Social engineering

1 Introduction

The idea of social media sharing has become a critical necessity in one's daily activity. Day after another, new social media applications become trending and the privacy has almost lapsed. People are sharing their life events as text, images and/or videos at social media applications without realizing the consequences of privacy loss [12]. The ignorance of the privacy issues can lead into a difficult and a serious consequences. The lack of awareness about cyber security requirements in majority is a huge factor that could create a lot of critical cases towards one's privacy.

© Springer Nature Switzerland AG 2019
A. Alfaries et al. (Eds.): ICC 2019, CCIS 1097, pp. 57–68, 2019.
https://doi.org/10.1007/978-3-030-36365-9_5

Recently, as the social media technologies increased the security techniques should be also increasing to keep up the high priority of consumers privacy protection. The authorization of access possibilities could leak the users data to a third party. As a result, these data may be used on an unauthorized way. The problem is that not only the authorized data would be accessed but all the consumer's data as well [12]. Even if the consumer's data were protected to a certain point, the pentester can use social engineering to access the required data. Social engineering is a collection of information that are shared publicly such as names, date of birth, locations, photos and other detailed information. Pentesters are capable of using these data to reach sensitive information such as email account, medical records and credit cards. The importance of the awareness of web security should not be underestimated to avoid data leakage. The adequacy and accuracy of social media apps security could be obtained through several testing tools [12].

These tools are used to test how accurate and adequate the app security is and how much information are accessible by a third party. There are many types of social media attacks has been reviewed in [10] and the important one is spamming which mean the use of electronic transmission systems to send messages that the user does not want to receive, the types of spam messages vary, but most are sent to promote the advertising of something such as: goods, services and ideas. The popular Spam Tool known as Mass Mailer.

A threat in online social media apps have been introduced in [11]. It is divided into classical and modern threats. Phishing attack is classified as classical which is actually the most popular way for social engineering and this way aims to steal the data. Location Leakage Attack classified as a modern which aims to get the location informations for different users.

In this paper, a survey was taken to measure the level of the awareness of cybersecurity on access possibility authorization. Based on the survey the RPTM was tested in different social media apps that had been chosen by respondents of the survey.

2   Literature Review

Due to the effects of cybersecurity crimes in the data for governments and companies, the researchers are very interesting and activating in cybersecurity fields which become a trend topic in the world. Many studies have been done related to cybersecurity, penetration testing, access possibility and social engineering.

2.1   Cybersecurity

Many practices and studies have been done in analysing and system detecting to detect the attacks and provide new models of cybersecurity detections and solutions. Rathod et al. [1] provide a novel model for cybersecurity economics and analysis, this study aims to develop a model that reducing fragmented practices of cybersecurity solutions and also helping to reach EU Digital Single Market goal. In [2] a comprehensive cybersecurity audit model have been done to improve cybersecurity assurance by providing a proposal to be used for leading cybersecurity audits in organizations and Nation States.

As shown in [3] the goals for this research is concentrating on the potential to propel inquire about motivation in cybersecurity and train the future generation with cybersecurity abilities and answer basic research addresses that still exist in the mixed learning techniques for cybersecurity instruction and appraisal. Administration and business enterprise aptitudes are too added to the blend to get ready understudies for certifiable issues [3]. Conveyance strategies, timing, organization, pacing and results arrangement will all be surveyed to give a benchmark to future inquire about and extra cooperative energy and coordination with existing cybersecurity projects to extend or use for new cybersecurity and STEM instructive research. This is another model for cybersecurity training, authority, and business enterprise and there is a plausibility of a huge jump towards a further developed cybersecurity instructive strategy utilizing this model [3].

Parekh et al. [4] exhibits and investigates results of two Delphi forms that surveyed cybersecurity specialists to rate cybersecurity points dependent on significance, trouble, and immortality. These evaluations can be utilized to distinguish center ideas cross-cutting thoughts that interface learning in the order. The primary Delphi process distinguished center ideas that ought to be learned in any first seminar on cybersecurity. The second recognized center ideas that any cybersecurity expert should know after graduating from school [4]. In spite of the quickly developing interest for cybersecurity experts, it isn't clear what characterizes essential cybersecurity learning. Starting information from the Delphi forms establish a framework for characterizing the center ideas of the field and, subsequently, give a typical beginning stage to quicken the advancement of thorough cybersecurity training rehearses [4]. These results give an establishment to creating proof based instructive cybersecurity appraisal apparatuses that will recognize and measure compelling strategies for educating cybersecurity. The Delphi results can likewise be utilized to educate the advancement regarding educational module, learning works out, and other instructive materials and strategies [4].

2.2   Penetration Testing and Access Possibility

Currently, penetration testing tools and wayes have been increased dramatically due to the curiosity of hackers and pentester. There are many studies have been done in penetration testing, Tetskyi et al. [5] they study a neural network in view of choosing best penetration testing for web. To take a decision for selecting best tools in penetration test by providing a service to recommend the best. However, Necessities might be nonfunctional (working framework, the nearness of a graphical interface, cost, and so on.) and useful (which assaults can be performed). This administration is an aggregator with the capacity to seek as indicated by determined necessities. Utilizing this administration, the pentester will discover apparatuses that fulfill his necessities as most ideal as, that is, he will get an answer about which apparatus to decide for the particular undertaking of entrance testing. Another very interesting research [6] in penetration testing and tools have been done to debate about the job of the Information Security Management System (ISMS), proficient Moral and specialized Competency required for playing out the penetration n test. Moreover they propose a logical model in penetration test which illustrates the process of includes a thorough way to deal with securing frameworks. A special study was done in [7] penetration testing based on mobile internet and this paper aims to advances a sort of entrance test strategy dependent on mobile Internet. This technique manufactures a test stage with the real system, and after that plan an execution plan of infiltration test program through the vulnerabilities of versatile Internet. The outcomes demonstrate that, the mobile correspondence terminal is influenced most clearly by the web weight test, and the vitality utilization is the greatest.

2.3   Social Engineering

Social engineering is widely used by hackers and it is the most successful way to collect a sensitive data from users. Social engineering in social media life is a considerable endeavor worry because the proclivity of social engineers focusing on workers through these mediums to assault data resources living inside the association. This examination was roused by an apparent hole in scholastic writing of authoritative controls and direction for workers concerning social engineers dangers through social media appropriation. The motivation behind this paper [8] is to propose a social media approach structure concentrating on the viable decrease of social engineers danger through IeT security arrangement control. The structure's advancement included an examination of the essential social engineers through online life challenges close by current data security standard suggestions. The coming about proposition for the SESM (Social Engineering through Web-based social networking) system tends to these difficulties by conceptualizing undertaking execution through the interconnection of applicable existing IT security benchmarks in juxtaposition with their own online networking approach improvement structure. Benchmarking a mobile implementation of the social engineering prevention training tool have been done by Mouton et al. [9] the Social engineers Assault Detection Model form 2 (SEADMv2) has been proposed to assist people identify pernicious social engineers assaults. Earlier to this study, the SEADMv2 had not been actualized as a client friendly application or tried with genuine subjects. This paper illustrate and discuss how the SEADMv2 was executed as an Android application. This Android application was tried on 20 subjects, to determine whether it decreases the likelihood of a subject falling casualty to a social designing assault or not. The comes about demonstrated that the Android execution of the SEADMv2 altogether reduced the number of subjects that fell casualty to social engineering attacks. The Android application moreover essentially diminished the number of subjects that fell casualty to malevolent social engineering attacks, bidirectional communication social engineering attacks and roundabout communication social engineering assaults. The Android application did not have a measurably critical effect on safe.

3 Methodology and Experiment

The methodology of this work can be categorised into two main parts:

3.1 A Survey in Users Awareness of Cybersecurity and Access Possibilities in Social Media Apps

In the this part, we designed a survey to investigate the level of user's awareness and knowledge in access possibilities and cybersecurity risks that might be affect their data privacy in social media apps.

Fig. 1. A survey in users awareness of cybersecurity and access possibilities in social media apps.

Our survey method is an online questionnaire by using google forms and for analysing we used pivot chart in EXCEL. It is a set of prepared questions which are distributed online. The participants are randomly chosen by using the purpose of social media. Figure 1 demonstrates the design of our survey in Users Awareness of Cybersecurity and access Possibilities in Social Media Apps. We planned to do the survey among different users of social media and then we randomly received 260 samples. Table 1 shows the distribution and details of the collected samples.

The Survey questions are designed based on awareness of the risks that gained from allowing the property of access possibility of social media application's terms. We have designed the questions based on difference key points such as:

1. The frequently use of social media applications.
2. The awareness of reading the terms and conditions of social media applications.
3. The user idea about allowing the property of access possibility to user' devices.
4. The user idea about sharing the personal data via social media applications.
5. The user idea about the data privacy when shared at social media applications.

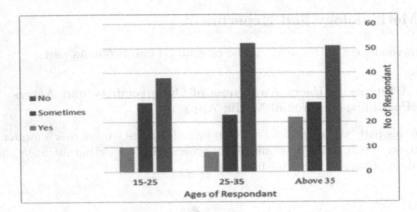

Fig. 2. Reading and accepting terms and conditions for social media application.

Figure 2 shows the number of respondents with different ages in reading and accepting terms and conditions once installing any social media apps. It shows that 54.2% of respondents answer that they accept the terms and condition without reading it. It is clear from the chart that ages greater than 35 are more aware to read the terms and conditions before accepting any applications. The chart in Fig. 3 describes the variety of respondents in accepting and allowing the apps to access their devices in the step of installation. It shows that age above 35 has the highest responded (46%) about not to allow the applications to access to their privacy data. While, the age between 15 to 25 has the highest percentage in allowing the applications to access to their data with (38%). Overall, among the 260 samples we have 113 responses (about 43.5%) that answered YES to a direct question (Are you allow the social media applications to access to your data while

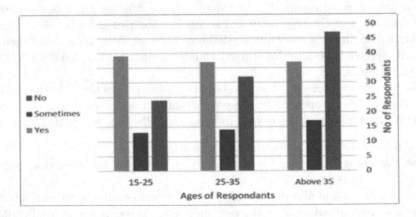

Fig. 3. Accepting the access possibility on installation process of social media application.

installation?) and 103 answered NO which making a percentage 39.6%. However, 16.9% of responders have no idea about what this question means.

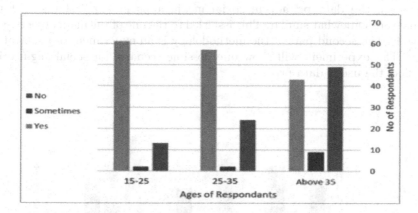

Fig. 4. Allow social media application to access the users data like (Gallery, Camera, Microphone.)

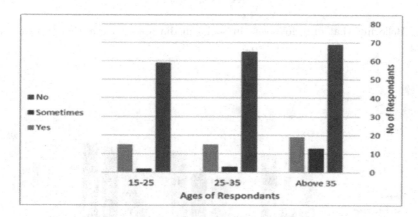

Fig. 5. Share the current location with a new (photo, video, message) in social media apps.

As we planned to exactly check the user awareness and understand of this questions we have directed another question says (Are you allow the social media applications to access to your own data like: Gallery, Microphone, and the Camera) as shown in Fig. 4 and we got 61.9% answered yes among different ages. Figure 5 illustrates that the majority of users among different ages are not share their current locations on their posts at social media apps. Moreover, 50% of the respondents stated in Fig. 6 that no one access their private data (images-files) through social networking applications and programs. While, 25.8% thought that only their allowing-followers can access their address and location through social media applications.

Trust on the data privacy in social media apps in Fig. 7 shows that the responses are somewhat similar. This issue led to the one of the main objective for this study. The second part of the methodology is an experiment of penetration testing. This experiment will show one possible scenario for social engineering that affect the user's data privacy.

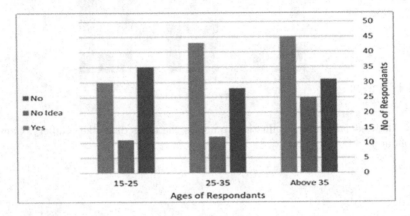

Fig. 6. Believing that only followers in social media apps have authority to see the posts.

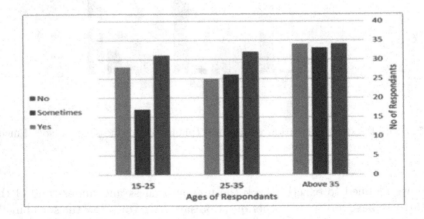

Fig. 7. Trust on the data privacy that have been shared in social media apps.

3.2   A Reconnaissance Penetration Testing Methodology (RPTM)

Reconnaissance Penetration Testing Methodology (RPTM) is a methodology that used to collect information about target users. Figure 8 shows one possible scenario of (RPTM) and how the user's data can be accessed and attacked by all access possibilities of different social media application. This could be happened when the user accepts the terms and conditions of application's licence while downloading the application. When the user agreed to applications' terms and conditions, it means that he/she is agreed to share and use his/her data for any researches studies or advertisements purposes. The user can be the victims of vulnerable access of the IP, Gallery, Contact details and location by pentester.

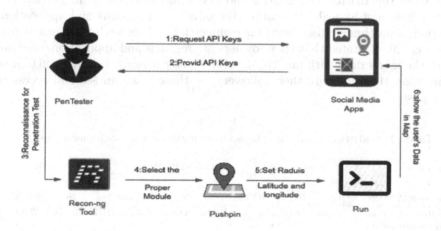

Fig. 8. A reconnaissance penetration testing methodology.

This scenario have been tested by using KALI linux operating system which is designed for a penetration testing purposes. RPTM scenario started once the pentester get application programming interface (API) keys from any social media application. The API keys act between the user and the applications to get access for services. The pentester will reconnaissance for gathering information and this can be done by using a special tool called Recon-ng which is coded in python programming language. Recon-ng provide many modules to access and reach the data, we selected pushpin module in our test. Last step is setting the longitude and latitude for any target place in the maps. Finally, run command will show the saved data on maps and there are many ways to see the information either in text reporting or maps reporting.

4   Result and Discussion

Based on the survey, the RPTM methodology was tested on three most common apps that were chosen by the respondents. The RPTM proved that the pentester is capable to reconnaissance data of social media apps' users based on sharing current locations, and used the information to collect and chance to reach any important data for social engineering purposes. The Table 1 of statistical result in cybersecurity awareness for social media users shows the major five questions that given in the survey and the percentages of answers received based on different range of ages. It is clearly discovered that users between 15–25 are the most users who trust their privacy on the social media applications with percentage of 36.84%. They thought that their data that posted on different applications are protected all the time. Also, 23.68% of the users between 15–25 are stated that the owners of social media applications are never used their data for commercial and research purposes. While, the people between 25–35 have the highest awareness about this matter with 28.92% and in conclusion 57.7% of the participants do not have any idea about weather the owners of programs and applications use their data (images-files-sites) for commercial and research purposes or not. However, 20.8% stated that they (owners of programs and applications) are not share the user's data with any third party for any reasons. However, 46.05% of them know that not only their followers are those who can see and access to their posts.

Table 1. Statistical result in cybersecurity awareness for social media users.

Age range	Between (15–25)			Between (25–35)			Greater than (35)		
No of responders	76			83			101		
Question/Answer	Yes	No	NO idea	Yes	No	NO idea	Yes	No	NO idea
Q1-Read the terms and conditions of Apps when installed in your device?	13.16%	50.00%	36.84%	9.64%	62.65%	27.71%	21.78%	50.50%	27.72%
Q2-Agree to the property of access possibility to your device while installing Apps?	51.32%	31.58%	17.11%	44.58%	38.55%	16.87%	36.63%	46.53%	16.83%
Q3-Only people in your account are viewing your posts	39.47%	46.05%	14.47%	51.81%	33.73%	14.46%	44.55%	30.69%	24.75%
Q4-Trust in the privacy and security of your data that sent in various apps?	36.84%	40.79%	22.37%	30.12%	38.55%	31.33%	33.66%	33.66%	32.67%
Q5-Owners of Apps are using your data for commercial and research purposes	19.74%	23.68%	56.58%	28.92%	21.69%	49.40%	16.83%	17.82%	65.35%

5   Conclusion and Future Work

This paper aims to investigate the level of users awareness in cybersecurity especially access possibilities and privacy to their data in social media application. Firstly, we introduce the concepts of cybersecurity and social engineering in social media apps and different tools of penetration testing that might be used for this purposes. Secondly, we did a literature review in cybersecurity, penetration testing and social engineering, it is noticed that these issues become the most trends topics in recent years. In terms of studying the level of user's awareness a survey has been distributed among different users male and female with different ages. Furthermore, a RPTM methodology has been designed and tested to prove a penetration testing scenario in recon-ng tool. In result and discussion we introduce a statistical study of the level in users awareness in cybersecurity and access possibilities to their data. To sum up, users must have more awareness in cybersecurity, social engineering and access possibility. We recommend in the future studies providing a project to increase users awareness in cybersecurity.

References

1. Rathod, P., Hämäläinen, T.: A novel model for cybersecurity economics and analysis. In: 2017 IEEE International Conference on Computer and Information Technology (CIT), Helsinki, pp. 274–279 (2017)
2. Sabillon, R., Serra-Ruiz, J., Cavaller, V., Cano, J.: A comprehensive cybersecurity audit model to improve cybersecurity assurance: the cybersecurity audit model (CSAM). In: 2017 International Conference on Information Systems and Computer Science (INCISCOS), Quito, pp. 253–259 (2017)
3. Javidi, G., Sheybani, E.: K-12 cybersecurity education, research, and outreach. In: 2018 IEEE Frontiers in Education Conference (FIE), San Jose, CA, USA, pp. 1–5 (2018)
4. Parekh, G., et al.: Identifying core concepts of cybersecurity: results of two Delphi processes. IEEE Trans. Educ. **61**(1), 11–20 (2018)
5. Tetskyi, A., Kharchenko, V., Uzun, D.: Neural networks based choice of tools for penetration testing of web applications. In: 2018 IEEE 9th International Conference on Dependable Systems, Services and Technologies (DESSERT), Kiev, pp. 402–405 (2018)
6. Al Shebli, H.M.Z., Beheshti, B.D.: A study on penetration testing process and tools. In: 2018 IEEE Long Island Systems, Applications and Technology Conference (LISAT), Farmingdale, NY, pp. 1–7 (2018)
7. Jiajia, W.: Research of penetration test based on mobile internet. In: 2016 2nd IEEE International Conference on Computer and Communications (ICCC), Chengdu, pp. 2542–2545 (2016)
8. Wilcox, H., Bhattacharya, M.: A framework to mitigate social engineering through social media within the enterprise. In: 2016 IEEE 11th Conference on Industrial Electronics and Applications (ICIEA), Hefei, pp. 1039–1044 (2016)
9. Mouton, F., Leenen, L., Venter, H.S.: Social engineering attack detection model: SEADMv2. In: 2015 International Conference on Cyberworlds (CW), Visby, pp. 216–223 (2015)

10. Kunwar, R.S., Sharma, P.: Social media: a new vector for cyber attack. In: 2016 International Conference on Advances in Computing, Communication, & Automation (ICACCA) (Spring), Dehradun, pp. 1–5 (2016)
11. Soumya, T.R., Revathy, S.: Survey on threats in online social media. In: 2018 International Conference on Communication and Signal Processing (ICCSP), Chennai, pp. 0077–0081 (2018)
12. Greitzer, F., Strozer, J., Cohen, Sh., Moore, A., Mundie, D., Cowley, J.: Analysis of unintentional insider threats deriving from social engineering exploits. In: IEEE Security and Privacy Workshops (2017). https://doi.org/10.1109/SPW.2014.39

A Blockchain Review: A Comparative Study Between Public Key Infrastructure and Identity Based Encryption

Lujain Alharbi[✉] and Dania Aljeaid

King Abdulaziz University, Jeddah, Saudi Arabia
Lalharbi0064@stu.kau.edu.sa, daljeaid@kau.edu.sa

Abstract. Blockchain is inventive technology that allows passing information without the need for third party or transaction cost. It offers solid properties such as decentralization, transparency, and immutability which make it desirable to adopt in sense of sharing data and maintain its security. However, with the emergence of blockchain technology, new issues have arisen with regards to security in the blockchain authentication and infrastructure. This paper focusing on understanding blockchain and what limitation and challenges adhered with it. Moreover, it reviews and analyzes the different authentication methods and discuss the integration of Identity-based encryption (IBE) and how does it differ than public key infrastructure (PKI) to determine the best method.

Keywords: Authentication · Identity based encryption · Public key infrastructure · Blockchain

1 Introduction

Blockchain is a remarkable evolution of technology that allow anomalously through decentralized lodgers and data mining. It has high expectation to change society and redefine economic and financial transactions, organizations, governments, legal practice and supply chain. By involving the development of many aspects, such as Internet of Things (IoT), cloud computing, Big Data, and robotics due to its unique architecture, the data protection services it provides and its indisputable record that is performed without the need of intermediaries. According to Google Trends [1], The Google Trends of "Blockchain" [1] showed a high interest in this evolved technology since 2015 and the records indicated that blockchain has increased its popularity on in 2017 on a global scale.

Previously, Blockchain was mostly associated with cryptocurrencies but the development of smart contracts has contributed effectively to the growth of blockchain practices and encouraged researchers to adopt it in other fields [2]. Blockchain was first introduced by Satoshi Nakamoto as a product of bitcoin, a solution for the issue of double spending in digital cash. Blockchain is a decentralized distributed ledger that shares and stores the transaction to all participants in a peer-to-peer network. The transactions are verified and stored, and it is hard to be erased arbitrarily [3]. As a distributed ledger and an intermediary eliminator, blockchain can change the internet to

© Springer Nature Switzerland AG 2019
A. Alfaries et al. (Eds.): ICC 2019, CCIS 1097, pp. 69–81, 2019.
https://doi.org/10.1007/978-3-030-36365-9_6

become more reliable peer-to-peer communication and trustworthy for application. Meanwhile, eliminating an intermediary will cut the costs of transaction fees, which are used by the intermediaries to ensure the transactions' completion and verification.

Since blockchain does not depend on transaction cost, this gives blockchain the capability to be trustworthy technology and protect data from tampering. One of the reasons that makes blockchain reliable is because blockchain ensures data integrity and immutability by using cryptographic hash function. Hashing the data stored in blocks and comparing the hash values in each new block attain immutability. Any slight modification made in any block will be known and verified through the blockchain miners [4]. Blockchain can be used as the underlying technology and work in cross-border transactions for many sectors, such as financial sectors, governmental sectors, health sectors, educational sectors, internet of things, etc. [5]. Like any new technology, blockchain faces some challenges and security threats that are under investigating. One of these challenges is the limited size for storing the data [6] due to the fundamental nature of the blockchain in that all data are simultaneously stored in all devices in the blockchain network. Another limitation is that, with the current movement to give the data owners the right to remove and erase all their data from any digital form of storage, the blockchain gives quite the opposite, by ensuring no data are erased, tampered with or modified [6]. Another vulnerability in blockchain is the Public and Private key management and security [7]. Public and Private Key Security is one of the main concerns that has had limited studied in the blockchain. The integrity of the data in the blockchain is reliable in the fact that no one can encrypt or decrypt or sign any transaction except the owner of the private and public key. If the owner of these keys loses access to them, that means all the transactions that have been made using these keys are no longer accessible to the user. The user can view these data, but has no claim over them and can no longer process them or use them in any future transaction [7].

The main contribution of this paper will focus on reviewing blockchain technology and analyze its unique features, applications, and types. Moreover, we will Identify and analyze the different methods on authentication using two infrastructures. As well as the current challenges of blockchain and potential weaknesses will be discussed.

2 Blockchain

2.1 Blockchain Definition

Blockchain is a distributed ledger that is maintained by a group of nodes through consensus protocols [8]. Blockchain was first introduced by Nakamoto in 2008 as a peer-to-peer decentralized network using proof of work to transfer money to avoid any central authority interfering with the transactions [9]. Blockchain consist of a chain of blocks (data packages) that starts with a genesis block, which is considered the first block in the blockchain. The blockchain grows by adding new blocks to the chain. Each block contains a nonce value, timestamp, computed hash value of the block, the hash value of the previous block and a list of multiple transactions. This mechanism ensures tampering resistance and acts as an indicator of any change in blocks. Each transaction contains a set of data, such as the receiver's public key, the sender's public key, the message and the signature of this data, which are encrypted by the sender's private key. A consensus mechanism is used to ensure that the majority of the nodes will agree using a set of rules and procedures on each new block and its transactions' validity before adding it to the chain [4]. This will ensure no tampering is done to any block in the chain because, if one hash value of a block changes its value, then all hashes and validation processes of the block ahead must be recalculated. The process is carried out by incrementing a number called nonce to ensure every block hash is started by a zero [9]. Due to this consensus mechanism, any new transaction will not be added automatically, but will be held on the block for a certain time until its validity is checked, then it will be stored permanently on the ledger [4].

2.2 Blockchain Types

There are three types in blockchain: public, consortium and private. Public means everyone can read, verify and participate in the consensus process. Consortium means that participants in the consensus process need to be authorized, but reading can be either public or private. Private means neither reading or participation in the consensus process is allowed until authorization is granted [2].

2.3 Blockchain Features

The main features of the blockchain is to decentralize systems. The decentralization in the blockchain aims to enhance transparency by eliminating any third-party meddling in the transaction process, which enhances the availability and decreases the risk of single point of failure. Moreover, it allows all anonymous participants in the blockchain to view all blocks' content. The participants' anonymous feature allows an honest transaction confirmation [7]. Blockchain also prevents information tampering and minimizes third-party certification bodies' participation [5]. It helps to avoid single point of failure because data are replicated in every node, and transparency in the blockchain ensures that, in a public blockchain, anyone can access and view the data. As for the trust, this is based on cryptography and the consensus mechanism, unlike the usual method in which the trust is based on the validation of a third party and data are stored permanently and cannot be altered after being added to the blockchain, which saves the data integrity [10].

2.4 Blockchain Applications

Researchers are expanding blockchain use to identity authentication, data protection, network security, identification and certification, defending against DDos attacks, ensuring data integrity, credibility and more. Blockchain can be used in many areas, such as E-governance, IoT, supply chain, voting, medical records, finance, storage, protection of intellectual property, identity certification, insurance and more [5]. The following list will illustrate some of the blockchain applications [5]:

1. Finance, Services: Blockchain can be used as a new method of payment in the service field
2. Intellectual property: Users can retain intellectual creation, such as copyright and trademarks, by saving the hashes of their creations on the blockchain with a timestamp to ensure that their rights are preserved. Smart contracts can help them receive cash when their creations are used
3. Software and the Internet: Blockchain can be used for many purposes in software, but two examples are storing the hashes of system logs and storing the hashes of the databases to ensure no altering is done to the logs and no duplicates of database backups are been made
4. Government: Blockchain is a great tool for governance because it can help in the voting process and eliminate any vote tampering issues by allowing voters to vote using the blockchain and everyone can view the voting progress
5. Supply chain: Tracing supply from the origin until the retailing strokes
6. Internet of Things IoT: Blockchain can be used to authenticate that a message sent to an IoT device is sent by a trusted IOT. For example, it can be used for car renting or room renting based on smart lockers where a key given by the renting agent which will only work will the lock associated to it using smart contracts.

2.5 Blockchain Issues

1. 51% attack. The blockchain consensus mechanism is based on the assumption that all nodes are honest and no group of nodes has the computing power to perform a DDoS attack; this assumption is invalid if a group of nodes have a computing power of over 51% of the system, then it can tamper with system content and perform a DDoS attack [7]. Attackers can use this vulnerability to (1) double spend the coins (double spending), (2) tamper with the transaction information and (3) stop the transaction validation process [8].
2. Private key management issues [7]. User's public and private keys are generated and managed by the user. The blockchain has a vulnerability in which, while generating the signature, there is insufficient randomness, so that the attacker can discover the private key, meaning all the user's information and transactions associated to this private key will be lost [8].
3. The anonymity mechanism may trigger an attack backtrack problem [7]. Due to the anonymity nature of the blockchain it is difficult to track back the attackers. Examples of attacker's criminal activities are [8]: 1. Ransomware: CTB-Locker (2014) and WannaCry (2017) are examples of ransomware used to encrypt users' files and only the attacker can decrypt them if they receive payment in bitcoin. 2. Underground market: bitcoin is used to buy drugs and illegal items in the underground market, such as Silk Road. 3. Money laundering: using cryptocurrency in comparison with other currencies is less vulnerable to money laundering.
4. Fork issue. When a new consensus rule or blockchain version is launched, blockchain will have many scenarios, such as new nodes agreeing or disagreeing with transactions done by the old node. The old node agrees or disagrees with transactions done by the new node and this will result in forking the blockchain

into a soft fork and a hard fork. Hard fork means that blockchain will fork into two completely different chains whereby old nodes and new nodes won't communicate anymore. Soft fork means both old and new nodes will still work in the same blockchain, but the new nodes will ignore and disapprove any transactions done by the old node [2].

5. Performance issues, such as signature verification time delay where the transaction ownership and validation are only proved with a computationally expensive signature done using a private key unlike any normal centralized database whereby authentication is done on connection time. Consensus mechanisms time delay is used to ensure enough consensus and extensive communication needs to be done between the node, which results in a time delay. Another issue is data redundancy because, unlike a centralized database where data are stored in one location with a certain number of backups, the blockchain requires that a replica of the data is stored in every node and an update is required with any new block [4].

6. Blockchain cryptocurrencies face difficulties in adoption by governments because it still doesn't have clear regulations and laws [4].

7. Not only blockchain cryptocurrencies face an issue, also blockchain applications face adoption and integration issues due to the complexity it requires to adapt it from new platforms to new rules and regulations[4].

8. Blockchain technology requires a lot of computation power redundancy in nodes, which consumes a lot of energy [4].

9. Wide application of a cryptographic algorithm may introduce unknown backdoors or vulnerabilities [11].

10. Frequent data cross borders will improve the difficulty of supervision [11].

11. Data cannot be altered or deleted, which eliminates the right-to-be-forgotten [6].

12. Storage is relatively small in size [6]. Because of the nature of a blockchain, where every node needs to have a complete copy of the complete blockchain, this creates an issue due the rapid increase in the transactions. There is a solution introduced which, if applied, the nodes will only have to store the header of the block, called Simplified Payment Verification (SPV) [2].

13. Sensitive data exposure [11].

2.6 Blockchain Authentication

Authentication in blockchain is done using the private key. There are several researches on authentication models that can be used instead of the PKI, which was the first method of authentication in the first blockchain application (bitcoin). These researches gained interest after many attacks were conducted on the blockchain. One of the attacks that was on bitcoin is the Mt.Gox attack where users lost their private keys due to an attack on their wallets [7]. The research on blockchain authentication was trying to find a more secure method of protecting the blockchain users from losing their private keys and, thus, losing the access to their transactions. The security of the blockchain relies on the fact no one can encrypt, decrypt or sign a message except for the owners of the private and public keys.

3 Public Key Infrastructure (PKI)

In the following section, we are going to discuss PKI, PKI usage in blockchain, and applications.

3.1 Public Key Infrastructure (PKI)

A system manages the public and private key and associates it with an identity. PKI should enable users to register, update, revoke and backup their public key. Public key infrastructure includes certification authorities, registration authorities, repositories, and archives. PKI can be done in either of these methods: certificate-based PKI (CA PKI) or Web of Trust PKI [12].

3.2 Certifying Authority (CA)

CA PKI is a centralized method that uses a trusted third party to issue a public key for a user and links it to his/her identity. This CA should be trusted by all parties that use this public key issued by this CA. It is an entity that issues certificate that contains the user's identity and the corresponding public and private key. The CA assures that the identity owner of this certificate is the owner of the public key [12]. The certificate will be issued in the format of X.509 standard that has specification about the certificate content referenced to ISO standards. The certificate contains public key, identity, expiration date and the CA's digital signature. Then, these certificates will be stored in the PKI Repositories [12]. When a certificate is revoked, it will be added to the certificate revocation lists [12]. The issue that CA PKI presents is the single point of failure. If the certifying authority system fails, then all public keys issued by this CA will no longer be trusted and, thus, any information associated with it will be lost. Another issue is if the owner of the public wants to revoke it, then it must be done using the time-consuming process of certificate revocation lists.

3.2.1 Certificate Authority: Breaches and Attacks

There have been several attacks on CA [13].

- CA DigiNotar is one of the security breaches of CA that issued over 500 fake certificates for big companies such as Google.com
- DigiCert Sdn. lost the trust of many browsers after issuing SSL certificates that were weak and enabled attackers to impersonate websites
- TrustWave certificate authority has proven that a CA can use their authority to conduct bad decisions by issuing for a customer a subordinate root certificate, which enables this customer to create SSL certificates for any domain and which can be used for any malicious activities if intended by this customer. TrustWave later revoked this subordinate root certificate.

4 PKI and Blockchain

4.1 PKI Usage in Blockchain

The public key infrastructure (PKI) in the blockchain is used for users' authentication, encrypting data and digital signatures. Public and private key can be viewed at as the user bank account and it associated pin, other users can use the receiver public key to send him/her a message (transaction) and the user can use his/her private key to open the message (transaction). Users in a blockchain can generate public and private keys locally then obtain a certificate associating these keys to his/her identity from the centralized trusted third party, called the certifying authority (CA).Then users can use the PKI as following: first, a message is signed (digital signature) using the private key (Fig. 1 step1). Second, the signed message is encrypted using the receiver public key (Fig. 1 step2). Finally the encrypted message is sent to the receiver and verified by decrypting the message and find the message and sender signature (Fig. 1 step3) [5]. Any encrypted message using a public key can only be decrypted using the associated private key [7]. The message, public key and signature will verify that this message was signed by the owner of the private key that created the published public key. Sending a transaction needs three variables 1. (the message), 2. (public key of message owner-sender) and 3. (public key of receiver) Then we use the private key to sign these three variables; this transaction can then be validated by using the three variables and their signature and comparing the signature to the sender's public key [5]. One flaw of PKI is that the CA is subject to single point of failure of its certifying authority, which can be caused by a hardware failure of a malicious attack [14].

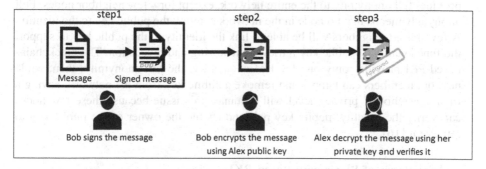

Fig. 1. Sending a message using Public Key Infrastructure (PKI)

4.2 Application of PKI in Blockchain

- *Cecoin:* Cecoin is a distributed certificate scheme based on blockchain and inspired by bitcoin. Cecoin is a replacement of the traditional PKI scheme where users public and private keys are paired to their identities using a certifying authority. Unlike certifying authority where certificates are stored in a centralized manner, Cecoin stores the certificates in a blockchain. Cecoin allows each identity to register multiple certificates; it also allows revocation and validation of these certificates. This distribution feature of Cecoin solves the single point of failure issue raised by CA and guarantees consistent certificates. Cecoin treats the certificates as currencies and validates them using miners with an acceptable cost, then certificates are stored in a certificate library with a large storage overhead [15]

- *Certcoin:* certcoin is a blockchain-based PKI built in Namecoin blockchain that provides identity retention and was introduced by Fromknecht. Users post their identities and public keys in the blockchain linked together as a pair. Certcoin enables a public view to the ledger containing all the public keys and identity pairs. The certcoin mining process enables users to register, update and revoke their public keys. Certcoin keys expire after a certain time, defined after the timestamp of creation. Certcoin does not preserve the privacy of users' activities because the identity is publicly paired to the public key [16–18]

- *Privacy aware blockchain:* privacy aware blockchain PKI should enable users to assign a public key to an identity because, even though this method is looking for anonymity, a public key will always be assigned to an identity, updates to this identity will be assigned public keys, enable searching for valid public keys, verifying public key validity, and enable a public key to be revoked. These requirements are different than the requirement of normal PKI where users can search, verify and revoke knowing the identity of the public key; in this method, users can search, verify and revoke with no disclosure of its owner's identity [16]

- *Axon:* blockchain by its nature provides transparency by using public ledgers and, thus, no privacy. Axon proposes a privacy aware blockchain-based PKI. In the proposal, the identity of the public key owner is not visibly paired. Users have the ability to hide or disclose their identity paired to the public keys. Axon's proposal provides full anonymity to the entire network, except for a few neighbor nodes. Full anonymity means that no node in the network can link the public key to the identity. A few trusted neighbors will be able to link the identity to the public key to support the functionality of public key retrievals, renewing and revocation. The blockchain-based PKI provides only one level of anonymity, the full anonymity; then, while network members can tamper and remove a public key from the network, having a trusted neighbors' privacy level will eliminate this issue because these few nodes can verify the identity, public key pair and enable the owner of the public key to retrieve it [16].

4.3   Advantages of Blockchain-Based PKI

- The nature of blockchain transparency eases and fastens the validation of a certificate [13].
- CA is based on a chain of certifying authorities that all trust each other to issue certificates. The traditional PKI revocation process requires informing all these CA through the use a revocation lists(CRLs). Blockchain-based PKI makes it easy to revoke a certificate because all nodes are connected and communication between them is easy [13].

- Blockchain-based PKI eliminates the man-in-the-middle attack because the certificate information can be validated instantly [13].

4.4   Limitation of Blockchain-Based PKI

- The rapid growth in the blockchain size and its reflection in every node creates an issue for the continuity of the blockchain-based PKI, especially the ones that uses smart contracts, as the size increases. For example, ethereum's size in April 2017 was 20.46 GB and in December 2017 it became 38.89 GB [13].
- Costs of operating blockchain-based PKI are uncertain and rapidly changing [13].
- A certifying authority issues rights based on their ability to access their account. If CA account access information is lost, then this CA won't be able to issue any more certificates [13].

5   Identity-Based Encryption (IBE)

In the following section, we are going to discuss IBE, IBE usage in blockchain, and applications.

Blockchain's nature provide anonymity, which was acceptable in cryptocurrencies but, as the uses of blockchain shift to real world application, the need of knowing user identity has grown for accountability and access control.

Identity-based encryption (IBE) is used to replace the complexity of distributing the public key in public key infrastructure. The IBE scheme works by using the receiver's identity as a public key and uses it to decrypt the message without obtaining a verifier from a certifying authority. The receiver will generate his private key after receiving the message by requesting the private key from a private key generator. PKG generates a master public and a master private key. The PKG will publish the master public key and keeps the master private key. As shown in the figure below (Fig. 2), the master public key combined with the identity will allow any entity to send messages to the ID owner, but only the ID owner can contact the PKG and generate the private key. IBE uses key escrow. The user uses his/her identity as his/her public key and then uses a master key only known to the PKG to generate the private key using a secret master key [19].

This will mean that: (1) PKG has the ability to decrypt or sign any message on behalf of the receiver, (2) make the receiver's private key public, (3) and that the failure of the PKG means the failure of the system depending on it (single point of failure) [13].

A solution to the PKG private key misuse was proposed by Boneh and Franklin to use a distributing private key generator, DPKG. DPKG means the usage of K number of PKG and each one of the K PKG generators is a part of the private key. The receiver will combine these K parts of the private key and then use them as his private key [8].

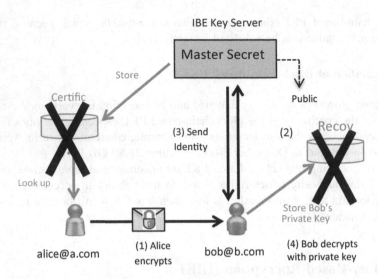

Fig. 2. Identity based encryption

6   IBE in Blockchain

There are several applications as to the use of IBE in blockchain:

- The Medical System [20] was proposed to ensure the medical records are decentralized and not controlled by a central agency to avoid tampering or altering with and patients' records. The system combines the usage of cloud computing to store the data while blockchain is used to store the hashes of these data. The usage of both technologies ensures integrity if any records were manipulated in the cloud, it can be easily discovered by the validation process of its hash in the blockchain. Due to the nature of the healthcare field, users' identities need to be disclosed in every medical service provided for the patients. If patients wants to give a medical institute the permission to view their medical records in the cloud, they should sign a smart contract first in the blockchain using a sign algorithm to give them the permission. IBEs were used for authentication by allowing every patient and medical entity to use their identity to create a public key that can be used to sign any medical disclosure smart contract, add to it or change it. The IBE implementation in this medical system has reduced the overhead of previously contacting any CA to create a pair of public and private keys. Users can simply use their identity as public key while private key is generated securely via a key generating center.
- Another blockchain based application that uses IBE is Verify-Your-Vote (VYV). This application ensures voter eligibility and voting process transparency to guarantee that there is no manipulation with votes. IBE is used in the system to ensure the user's identity is integrant and visible due to the fact that IBE uses the user identity (such as social security number) as a mean to identify the user; users will vote only once, so no prior communication with any entity is required. Elimination of third-party participants removes the possibility of certificate tampering and, thus, vote tampering and cheating [21].

7 Comparison Between PKI and IBE

The working mechanism of PKI and IBE is similar in the concept. Two keys are created, one of the keys is made public key and the other is kept private. The difference is in the method of generating the key pairs [22].

7.1 Generating the Key Pair

- PKI: key generation in either done locally by the client and then certify the key by the CA or generate the key by the CA itself. uses random information to generate the key pairs [22].
- IBE: public key is generated using an identifier of the receiver then the receiver generates his/her private key from a private key generator PKG. IBE uses an identifying information to generate the key pairs [22].

7.2 Centralization and Trusted Third Party

- Certifying authority CA: CA is used in the PKI and is responsible for certifying the public key by associating it to a user and assuring the validity of the information in it. Private key is either generated by the individual or the CA [22].
- private key generator PKG: PKG is responsible for creating and delivering a new private key for the identity holder each time requested by the identity holder using key escrow. Private key is solidly generated by the PKG [22].

7.3 Concepts of PKI vs IBE

- PKI is a certificate management tool. It manages both the technical factors, ethical and regulatory factors and human factors to issue a certificate that binds the public key to the identity [23].
- IBE is an encryption mode where it takes identity information (name, social ID or email, etc.) and uses it as a public key and then operationally extracts a private key from that public key [23].

7.4 Benefits for IBE over PKI

- PKI manages the certificates and registers, issues, stores, and revokes these certificates. This increases the traffic on the network, increases the storage for the certificates and expensive computation power [21]
- IBE is encryption-based with no need for certifications or a third party for the public key creation process, which reduces the overhead of management and trust issues in any third parties, reduces the demand on the bandwidth and storage, and allows holders of private keys to decrypt offline after gaining the private key from PKG [23].

7.5   Limitation in IBE Compared to PKI

- In PKI, the users do not require any entity to deliver the private key to them. However, in IBE, the communication route must be secure to deliver the private key from PKG to users [23].
- The key escrow issue only exists in IBE; PKG can encrypt and sign any messages on behalf of the users. This issue can be eliminated using distributed PKG [23].

8   Conclusion

IBE has been used to solve the certifying authority single point of failure issue. however, it was not widely applied in the blockchain domain. This shortage of application were due to the movement to apply a blockchain-based PKI. blockchain-based PKI is believed to solve the single point of failure represented in traditional PKI by using the decentralized nature of a blockchain. The communication complexity represented in PKI, with the need for previous communication to distribute the public key, is still not solved in PKI at blockchain level and is still not solved by using IBE in blockchain. As a future work we would recommend a new authentication method for blockchain instead of PKI, which is IBE. This recommended solution suggests using IBE for creating public keys from users' identities solves the issue of single point of failure and communication complexity. Nevertheless, replacing PKI with IBE brings out other issue such as PKG key exposure issue. Therefore, the future work will be conducted to guarantee a blockchain-based DPKG that is free of key exposure issues and provide anonymity.

References

1. Google Trends. https://trends.google.com/trends/explore?date=all&q=blockchain. Accessed 31 Mar 2019
2. Lin, I.-C., Liao, T.-C.: A survey of blockchain security issues and challenges. Int. J. Netw. Secur. **19**(5), 653–659 (2017)
3. Nakamoto, S.: Bitcoin: a peer-to-peer electronic cash system, p. 9
4. Niranjanamurthy, M., Nithya, B.N., Jagannatha, S.: Analysis of blockchain technology: pros, cons and SWOT. Clust. Comput. (2018)
5. Liu, L., Xu, B.: Research on information security technology based on blockchain. In: 2018 IEEE 3rd International Conference on Cloud Computing and Big Data Analysis (ICCCBDA), pp. 380–384 (2018)
6. Esposito, C., Santis, A.D., Tortora, G., Chang, H., Choo, K.R.: Blockchain: a panacea for healthcare cloud-based data security and privacy? IEEE Cloud Comput. **5**(1), 31–37 (2018)
7. Yli-Huumo, J., Ko, D., Choi, S., Park, S., Smolander, K.: Where is current research on blockchain technology?—a systematic review. PLoS ONE **11**, e0163477 (2016)
8. Li, X., Jiang, P., Chen, T., Luo, X., Wen, Q.: A survey on the security of blockchain systems. Future Gener. Comput. Syst. (2017)
9. Böhme, R., Christin, N., Edelman, B., Moore, T.: Bitcoin: economics, technology, and governance. J. Econ. Perspect. **29**(2), 213–238 (2015)

10. Gatteschi, V., Lamberti, F., Demartini, C., Pranteda, C., Santamaría, V.: To blockchain or not to blockchain: that is the question. IT Prof. **20**(2), 62–74 (2018)
11. Dai, F., Shi, Y., Meng, N., Wei, L., Ye, Z.: From bitcoin to cybersecurity: a comparative study of blockchain application and security issues. In: 2017 4th International Conference on Systems and Informatics (ICSAI), pp. 975–979 (2017)
12. Kuhn, D.R., Hu, V., Polk, W.T., Chang, S.H.: SP 800-32 introduction to public key technology and the federal PKI infrastructure. National Institute of Standards & Technology, Gaithersburg, MD, United States (2001)
13. Yakubov, A., Shbair, W.M., Wallbom, A., Sanda, D., State, R.: A blockchain-based PKI management framework. In: NOMS 2018 - 2018 IEEE/IFIP Network Operations and Management Symposium, Taipei, Taiwan, pp. 1–6 (2018)
14. Zheng, Z., Xie, S., Wang, H.: Blockchain challenges and opportunities : a survey (2018)
15. Qin, B., Huang, J., Wang, Q., Luo, X., Liang, B., Shi, W.: Cecoin: a decentralized PKI mitigating MitM attacks. Future Gener. Comput., Syst (2017)
16. Axon, L.: Privacy-awareness in blockchain-based PKI, p. 18
17. Fromknecht, C., Yakoubov, S.: CertCoin: a namecoin based decentralized authentication system 6.857 class project, p. 19
18. Fromknecht, C., Velicanu, D., Yakoubov, S.: A decentralized public key infrastructure with identity retention. IACR Cryptol. ePrint Arch. **2014**, 803 (2014)
19. Boneh, D., Franklin, M.: Identity-based encryption from the weil pairing. In: Kilian, J. (ed.) CRYPTO 2001. LNCS, vol. 2139, pp. 213–229. Springer, Heidelberg (2001). https://doi.org/10.1007/3-540-44647-8_13
20. Wang, H., Song, Y.: Secure cloud-based EHR system using attribute-based cryptosystem and blockchain. J. Med. Syst. **42**(8), 152 (2018)
21. Chaieb, M., Yousfi, S., Lafourcade, P., Robbana, R.: Verify-Your-Vote: a verifiable blockchain-based online voting protocol. In: Themistocleous, M., Rupino da Cunha, P. (eds.) EMCIS 2018. LNBIP, vol 341, pp. 16–30. Springer, Cham (2019). https://doi.org/10.1007/978-3-030-11395-7_2
22. Paterson, K.G., Price, G.: A comparison between traditional public key infrastructures and identity-based cryptography. Inf. Secur. Tech. Rep. **8**(3), 57–72 (2003)
23. Bai, Q.: Comparative research on two kinds of certification systems of the public key infrastructure (PKI) and the identity based encryption (IBE). In: CSQRWC 2012, pp. 147–150 (2012)

Data Science

Ɛrbeng:- Android Live Voice and Text Chat Translator

Abanoub Nasser[1(✉)], Ibram Makram[1(✉)],
and Rania Ahmed Abdel Azeem Abul Seoud[2(✉)]

[1] Faculty of Computers and Information, Fayoum University, Fayoum, Egypt
myfirstaccisec@gmail.com, abanoub.nasser77@gmail.com
[2] Department of Electrical Engineering,
Communication and Electronics Section, Faculty of Engineering,
Fayoum University, Fayoum, Egypt
raa00@fayoum.edu.eg

Abstract. Mobile applications become the basics of human's daily life. People worldwide face difficulties in communication due to different languages and culture barriers. So it is important to enable people to communicate faster by bringing people together from across the globe. Ɛrbeng is an Arabic/English Android instant messaging translator application to communicate worldwide that makes the world just got a lot smaller. With the feature of live translation capabilities, Ɛrbeng allows exchanging text messages, voice and video chat as well as online and offline file transmission with anyone regardless of language barriers. Ɛrbeng is an Interlingual based machine translation system. With Interlingua Ɛrbeng becomes an unambiguous and international translation application that based on a client/server Socket programming. Ɛrbeng uses an integrated language platforms that offers comprehensive online communication functions. Ɛrbeng performs live translation with high translation performance, less time consuming and with more enhanced quality of translation.

Keywords: Live translation · Mobile application · Interlingual machine translation · Text generation · Natural language processing

1 Introduction

Due to the differences in cultures and language expansion, the communication process between people is difficult. It is needed to overcome the difference in the culture and the lack of time to learn the foreign language to enhance the communication process. Also, it is needed to help users overcome language barriers. Machine translation could quickly and affordably increase the efficiency of the international operations, expand the market reach, and improve global communications. Machine translation is a powerful tool that has many purposes and can be used in some different ways. Machine translation has evolved to become an essential part of the business and individual consumer life. There is a great business value in enabling new and existing content to be translated with greater efficiency and productivity, lowering costs and increasing Return on Investment (ROI).

© Springer Nature Switzerland AG 2019
A. Alfaries et al. (Eds.): ICC 2019, CCIS 1097, pp. 85–98, 2019.
https://doi.org/10.1007/978-3-030-36365-9_7

Generally, Machine translation methodologies are commonly categorized as three classic approaches; direct, transfer, and Interlingua. The approaches vary in the depth of analysis and rang they try to reach in an independent representation of language meaning or intent. The Direct methodology is considered as a lexicon-based approach. It is based on a word-for-word substitution (with some local adjustment) by using a large bilingual dictionary [1].

The transfer methodology is implemented with three phases: analysis, transfer plus generation. The translation occurs on representations of the source sentence structure and meaning respectively. The first phase includes parsing the input into a source-language-specific intermediate syntactic structure. Then, apply linguistic rules to transform this representation into an equivalent representation in the target-language. Finally, the final target-language text is generated [2]. Interlingual methodology, on the other hand, goes beyond purely linguistic information (syntax and semantics). It involves the deepest analysis of the source language (SL) and the content of texts [1]. The Interlingua-based translation is based on two monolingual stages: analyzing the SL text into an abstract single universal language-independent underlying representation of meaning (the Interlingua), and generating this meaning using the lexical units and the syntactic constructions of the target-language.

Although, the Interlingual-based machine translation has many advantages; it is possibly the least used between the other three approaches. However, there are many promising projects that have generated good prototypes. However, there is a lack of an Arabic/English Live Translation Chat Application. The following section reviews some of those live machine translation projects. SDL is a desktop chat translator application to online chatting between an English speaker and a French speaker. It unifies the translation and provides integration and controls the process flow. BANTER is led by chatting and gaming. It worked on the Mosaic browser, founded Challenge Games with a customer interaction platform. Who'sOn is a real-time chat translation that translates over 40 languages. JusChat is an easy-to-use Android Apps on Google Play for powerful MSN chatting applications. The JustChat window can pretend to be word, excel or any custom application layout. QQ International is a live chat translator available on Windows, Android, and iPhone/iOS. Currently QQ International is available in a 6-language interface, English, French, Japanese, Spanish, German and Korean, and is fully compatible with all other Chinese versions of QQ. iChat transformed online chatting and became an integral part of Apple's OS offering. iChat was an instant messaging software application developed by Apple Inc. for use on its Mac OS X operating system. It supports instant text messaging, audio and video calling.

This paper proposed Ɛrbeng application; it is an Arabic/English Android live voice, video, text and chat translator application. Ɛrbeng is an Interlingual rule-based Machine translation system that connects people all over the world for free. Live translation makes Ɛrbeng the premiere app for global communication. Ɛrbeng connects people with millions of users across the globe for simply meeting new people regardless of regions and languages. With Ɛrbeng, the world is in your hands. Ɛrbeng enables exchange of files, photos and videos with a simple drag and drop. This is done by converting the voice into text then the text is converted to Interlingua. Interlingua is an unambiguous international intermediate language to enhance translation techniques.

Interlingua enables ℰrbeng to support the generation of multiple languages. It currently handles only Arabic\English translation. Also, Interlingua as a language-independent helps to provide grammars and lexicons the required to process each language. ℰrbeng supports the production of high-quality translation by isolating parser and generators so the development of SL and TL component cannot be overlapped that lead to reduce development time.

2 Methodology

ℰrbeng is a high-performance java-based socket-programming client/server communication model. The user requests a query to translate the text. The server manipulates the database to get the required translated text then sends it to the user. MySQL is used for building the structured lexicon that contains the most used words and expressions with the ability to update. ℰrbeng uses an android code for building a user-friendly chat application interface. ℰrbeng builds a user-friendly database for securely saving user information which is easily updated and modified.

ℰrbeng uses the Parse Cloud platform that gives the system the ease of access nature with the ability to create a user account and register with a specific ID with privacy of storing and retrieving data. Also, ℰrbeng links account across networks, resets passwords and keeps data safe and secure. ℰrbeng system enjoys the dynamic powerful web presence without the hassle of maintaining servers; sharing data between web and mobile app or displaying it on a landing page. JavaScript adds custom validations and endpoints to make ℰrbeng more powerful. ℰrbeng with the easy to use, completes with a smart keyboard with auto-correction. The message is delivered fast and accurately. ℰrbeng as a dynamic messaging system sends high-quality written messages, audio messages and video or voice chat fast. Also, it could schedule messages ahead of time. With the group chat features, it makes catching up with multiple friends or messaging your entire family a breeze.

Using ℰrbeng's group chats one could communicate exchanges documents and audio messages with a group of people. ℰrbeng live chat translation application is an Interlingual-based Machine translation system with distinguished quality of translation. Interlingua provides an economical way to make multilingual translation systems. ℰrbeng automates and accelerates global translation tasks and greatly reduces the cost of supporting local language content. ℰrbeng centralizes translation efforts, merging manual, disparate processes into a single, streamlined program. ℰrbeng application has many translation features that could perform a live translation with high translation performance with less time-consuming. Those features are Account privacy, Chat history, Translation Quality, Friendly User Interface. ℰrbeng application also has features of ease of access and ease of use, availability, Instant Messengers. Also, ℰrbeng is a multifunctional communication tool; one could make an Audio/Video call. ℰrbeng could be integrated with existing authoring tools and improves translation efficiency with advanced translation technologies like a videoconference with up to 4 contacts. ℰrbeng system is implemented in three phases. The first phase is the Machine translation phase. The second phase is the chat application (android) phase. The third phase is the Voice recognition phase.

2.1 Machine Translation Phase

The core module of the ɛrbeng system is the Knowledge-based Interlingual machine translation systems phase. It is considered as the most productive of the semantically accurate translations. To enhance the translation, technique Interlingua is used as an intermediate unambiguous international language between two languages. There are two phases to generate the target-language:-

- Analysis Phase: to convert the input text from Source Language into Interlingua as an intermediate stage.
- Generation Phase: to translate the generated Interlingua to the target-language; extract the semantic meaning to obtain the same meaning in the target language.

(1) Analysis Phase: The analysis is performed by analyzing the input text that is resulted from the speech recognizer, into Interlingua. This phase includes many steps and is validated through some rules as shown in Fig. 1. ɛrbeng's vocabulary (non-domain specific) is limited to a vocabulary of about 31,000 distinct word and a domain-specific technical terms with a pre-defined vocabulary, approximately 10,000 words, and phrases.

    (a) *Preprocessor:* applying general transformations like; lemmatization; compound splitting; reordering of phrases to make the two-word orders closer; adding pseudo-tokens for syntactic functions such as subject, predicate, object. English preprocessing includes the removal/adding functional words that systematically lack matches in other languages (articles, personal pronouns, etc. Arabic preprocessing [3, 4] includes:

- Arabic retokenization, splitting off punctuations and numbers from words and removing any diacritics that appears in the input.
- The separation of conjunctions, prepositions, and articles that are normally written jointly with the noun
- Decliticizations. Splits off the class of conjunction particles, articles and all pronominal.

    (b) *Morphological Analysis:* The morphology-based preprocessing of Arabic/English in ɛrbeng system includes breaking up words into a stem and affixive morpheme; splitting Arabic/English compound words, joining separable verb prefixes with verbs and augment words with morphological information. This is done using segmentation that splits up the Arabic letters into segments that correspond to clusters of a stem plus one or more affixation morphemes. An Arabic word is viewed as a concatenation of three regions, a prefix region, a stem region, and a suffix region. The prefix and suffix regions can be null. Prefix and suffix lexicon entries cover all possible concatenations of Arabic prefixes and suffixes.

    (c) *Lexicon:* ɛrbeng uses the Buckwalter lexicon [5] which includes the morphological compatibility category, part-of-speech (POS) and orthographic rules. The lexicon is composed of compatibility tables and an analysis engine. Stem lexicon entries are clustered around their specific lexeme,

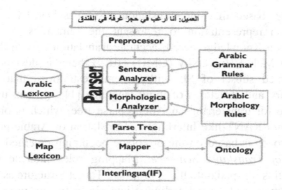

Fig. 1. Ɛrbeng analysis phase (Source Language to Interlingua)

(d) *Parser:* the parser transfers the input sentences to a parsing tree. It would be painful to encode Arabic/English sentences direct into Interlingua without the aid of a parser. Ɛrbeng system uses the SOUP robust parser [6]. SOUP builds a semantic dependency tree that provides the linguistic relationship between sentence units. SOUP provides a spoken language real-time analysis by using context-free semantic grammars. The parser's output represents the meaning of the source text. There is no a single parse tree to cover an entire utterance of speech because such utterances frequently contain multiple segments of meaning. This is why the SOUP parser is used, one of its features is to produce a sequence of parse trees for each utterance, effectively segmenting the input text at parse time. Then a deterministic mapper using regular expressions is applied to convert parses into IF representation. This is done to match the format of the parser's output in the format of the IF representation.

(e) *Mapper:* The mapping rules are used to map lexical items onto semantic concepts, and syntactic arguments onto semantic roles, forming the inter-mediate representations [7]. The first intermediate representation is a frame-based representation which is the Source Feature grammatical structure (F-Structure). The Arabic/English parsing trees are processed using the SL grammar and lexicon to produce a Source F-Structure for each sentence. Ɛrbeng uses an explicit and very restricted domain model-based semantic restrictions to resolve ambiguity (e.g. Phrase attachments) [8]. The Mapper also applies a set of transformation rules to transfer the F-Structure into Interlingua. The mapper refers to the lexicon to build a frame of verbs, nouns, and number combinations for every grammar non-terminal. The mapper represents the parsing trees and maps the syntactic structure by applying a set of mapping rules that are developed by [9].

(f) *Interlingua:* Interlinguas is used as pivot representations that allow the con-tent of a source text to be generated in many different target-languages. An Interlingua [8] is a system for representing the meanings and intentions of language. It explains the formal structure of the language and describes the various different types of concepts that are represented [9]. Ɛrbeng as a knowledge-based machine translation system is based on The KANT-like Interlingua representation to represent the semantics of the expressions. KANT is a Knowledge-based, accurate translation system that developed at Carnegie Melon University (CMU) [10]. Ɛrbeng is designed to translate a well-defined subset of SL with general restrictions that are put on the vocabulary and structures of input language [11]. Ɛrbeng used a developed prototype for transferring an Arabic parse tree, which is obtained from the parser, into KANT-like Interlingua. Translation of Arabic using the Interlingua approach is based on the prototype beginning emerged in [9]

(2) *Generation of Translated Sentence:* Mapping rules indicate how Interlingua representation is mapped onto the appropriate Target Structure as shown in Fig. 2. The mapper maps and splits Interlingua into pieces to start use lexicon to extract feature structure through map rules. The generator is one of the most important components which contain sentence generator and morphological analyzer [12].

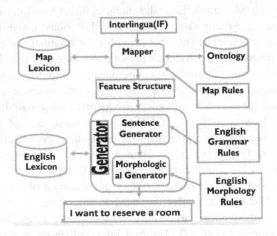

Fig. 2. Ɛrbeng generation phase (from interlingua to target-language)

(a) *Mapper:* The Arabic/English mapper module converts Interlingua representation into an Arabic/English sentence feature-structure representation (FS). This is done by selecting lexical items for each Interlingua concept by using a set of mapping rules and a mapping lexicon [13]. The mapper maps the semantic roles for each Interlingua concept (slots in Interlingua frame) to grammatical functions (slots in FS) [13]. There are different Mapping Rules for Sentence Type. The mapper specifies the type of the sentence then determines the mapping rules that would be applied in each sentence type. The handled Arabic sentence types are:-

- *Verbal Sentence:* Verbal sentence has different patterns. The pattern is defined then the mapping rules are applied to represent verbal sentence into Interlingua.

- *Nominal Sentence:* The representation of the nominal sentence into Interlingua representation is different. The nominal sentence composed of Inchoative and enunciatively, there are some transformation rule must be applied before applied mapping rules.

(b) *Target F-Structure.:* The FS generator generates a target sentence for each Arabic FS Target-language. FS contents reflect the contents of the Interlingua, expressed in terms of the syntactic and lexical properties of the target-language using a monolingual lexicon, morphological generator [14] and syntactic generator [15]. Lexicon stores lexical knowledge, with each entry represented as an FS of feature-value pairs.

(c) *Sentence Generator:* the mapper takes FS as input produces the Arabic \English sentences using a set of mapping rules, a mapping lexicon, morphological generator and syntactic generator [16]. The Syntactic generation rules using rules to construct the grammatically correct Arabic\English sentences. They can be classified into rules that are responsible for:

- Ensuring the agreements between constituents like verb-subject, demonstrated noun-substitute, noun-adjective and number counted noun,
- Handling the end case of dual and plural forms according to the case markings, and Inserting missing fragments for producing the target Arabic \English surface structure in its right form such as prepositions.

2.2   Chat Android Application

Ɛrbeng Mobile application is responsible for sending the translated message between two users as shown in Fig. 3. The first user sends a message with its SL; the server will receive the message for processing. The server translates the message and re-sends the translated message to the second user. The server manipulates the database to get the required translated text then sends it to the client. The client/server Socket programming enables flexibility and high performance. When the client sends a request for a translation, the client initializes a channel between the server and the client. There is a socket that is opened between the live chat application and the server when the user sends a message to another. When the server receives the message, it calls the function [trans (string sentence)] to translate this sentence. The server will check if it is a common expression for pattern match translation or it is a sentence which is needed to be analyzed by generating Interlingua then generate the translated message. The server will divide this message into words and expressions; determine the type of words (adjective, common expressions, decimal number, flags, grand, noun, pronoun, plural, prepositions, question Name, verb) to translate the message. After translating the sentence sends the translated message to the server then the socket is closed.

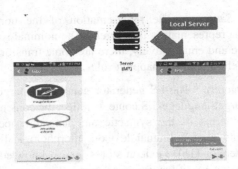

Fig. 3. Application overview

2.3 Voice Recognition

This phase is the most attractive part. It translates the voice of each user in its native language. It consists of three parts (SPEECH-TO-TEXT, TRANSLATION, and TEXT-TO-SPEECH).

- SPEECH-TO-TEXT: - ʕrbeng Android application uses the speech to text conversion feature. The App calls the voice API which is distinguished with its grateful function such as the attribute which determines if the speaker is a man, woman, girl, or boy. The App uses the technique to determine the spoken language and the function which returns the value of the spoken words as text.
- TRANSLATION STAGE: - The translation operation is done so the spoken text pass-through this stage to be translated.
- TEXT-TO-SPEECH:- The next stage is that the translated spoken text will send to the receiver then received as a voice message through the same API but the opposite sequence. When the user determines the spoken voice such as Language. UK the function of speaks will return a voice.

3 Discussion

ʕrbeng enables communication with no fees as it is truly free using your already existing network of Wi-Fi. It means you can message and video call without the need for extra subscriptions. ʕrbeng enables data protection by connecting one across the globe with guaranteed the peace of mind of end-to-end encryption to ensure your privacy. ʕrbeng prides in protecting users and their data by using the latest data protection practices to ensure the identity and information stays safe. The screen shots of the main page that contains Login and Register buttons are shown in Fig. 4. The user types the text then he/she chooses the translation options. The system translates the text into a grammatically corrected one between Arabic and English languages. The Register Page enables the user to create a new account is shown also in Fig. 4. User must insert the following information fields which will be automatically sent to the cloud server:

- *E-mail*: for each user same e-mail for security, privacy.
- *Username:* for the same user insert one username.
- *Password:* contain a combination of alphabet, number.
- *Determine native language*: (ex. AR) or (ex. EN).

Fig. 4. Main Page and Register Page of ɛrbeng live chat translation.

For Login, the app checks the username and password then compare them with the stored information. If the information is matched, the user will successfully login. ɛrbeng has different pages. The User List page contains a list of all users that the sender could contact with online users are marked as shown in Fig. 5.

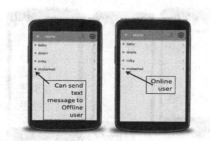

Fig. 5. User list page

Each user has a Profile page that contains much information that includes his/him Profile Picture, Username, E-mail, and registered Language as shown in Fig. 6. Also, the user could update and change his/her username or password by using the Privacy Settings page as shown in Fig. 6. The App will update the database with the new username and password. Finally, there is a Log out page that allows the user to log out from his/her account as shown in Fig. 6.

Fig. 6. Profile page and Change Privacy Settings page

To start the live translation, the user firstly chooses his native language (AR). Then the user composes the message and sends it to the server. The server translates the message into the second user's language (EN). The server sends the translated message to the second user as shown in Fig. 7. The user could send his/her message by the voice. The server also will process the received voice message for translation. The server will send Translated voice message then send it to the receiver with its date and time as shown in Fig. 7. The user also will be able to obtain his/her chat history. The toolbar helps users to interact easily with other contacts by sharing position, contacts or sharing media etc.

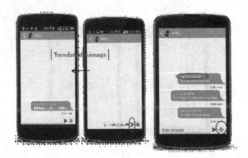

Fig. 7. Sending Text and Voice message

4   System Database

Ɛrbeng stores user personal information as username, email, password, profile picture, so on in a cloud environment. The cloud platform provides a complete backend solution for Ɛrbeng system mobile application. Ɛ rbeng uses the online database which is easily updated and modified for each query or single data record. This allows Ɛrbeng to store data, manage users, and send push notifications, track analytics. The cloud allows file storage of 20 GB and a Database Storage of 20 GB. All Ɛrbeng system users' basic data is stored securely and efficiently in the cloud. The Ɛrbeng system application is a safe and secure social one that connects users via traditional logins or third party social networks accounts. Ɛrbeng system have the feature of locally stores data in the case that the user will not have a network connection. The App could use all the querying and security features that are available for Android. Ɛrbeng system enjoys a dynamic web presence without all the hassle of maintaining a specific server. The user could share data between the web and mobile app with display it on a beautiful landing page.

The database of the system contains two main files: the core file and the analytics file. The core file contains three tables; Users, Chat, Image uploading tables. The Users Table contains columns with user information as; Object ID: private key, single unique User name, encrypted Password, authenticate Author log in Data, Email and Email Verified, native user Language, Online, Created At, Updated At, Acknowledgment read, Phone Number as shown in Fig. 8. The Chat Table contains columns that including the message between users, Object ID, Message, Receiver name, Sender name, Created At, Updated At. The Image Uploading Table contains columns that including more information of users: - Object ID, Image Name, Created At, Updated At, ACL.

ObjectId String	username String	password String	authData undked	emailVerified Boolean	Language String	email String	Online Boolean	createdAt Date
IBJySM8LZj	ibrhm	(hidden)	(undefined)	(undefined)	Arabic	ayfirstaccitac..	true	May 21, 2015, 10:48
a0YYYWe1SE	michaeli	(hidden)	(undefined)	(undefined)	Arabic	mm.tci@yahoo...	true	May 20, 2015, 05:55
P18cBk5XWo	abanoub	(hidden)	(undefined)	(undefined)	Arabic	abanoub.nasser...	true	May 01, 2015, 10:23
d0A08XWcn4	michael	(hidden)	(undefined)	(undefined)	English	michael_8A5811...	true	Apr 28, 2015, 13:10
DhMAXihyqk	mario	(hidden)	(undefined)	(undefined)	Arabic	marionahil1903...	true	Apr 28, 2015, 13:17

Fig. 8. Users table

Ɛrbeng uses the Analytics database to view the App usage, custom analytics in the user-friendly and Parse dashboard, overlay graphs, filtered by date to gain insight into the effectiveness of your usage. The Analytics database contains two tables the Audience Table and the Events Table. The Audience Table shows the daily active installations and the Events Table shows the number of requests on particular day as shown in Figs. 9 and 10.

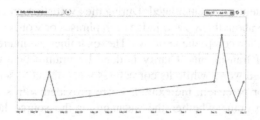

Fig. 9. Audience daily active installations

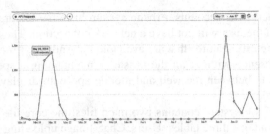

Fig. 10. Events API requests

5 Results

ɛrbeng live translator is developed with a little bit small corpus that could be extendable. After the design of ɛrbeng, the test process is performed with a few phrases and words and the survey was done by both Arabic and English speakers. The ratings of the speakers were based on three different criteria namely clarity, significance and precision, based on the evaluation, the following steps are performed:

1. The election of a set of phrases as a tested data.
2. Perform three kinds of particular tests were namely clarity, significance and precision.
3. Calculate errors based on the analysis of, Word Error rate and Sentence Error rates.
4. Designed of the scoring algorithm for particular tests.
5. Done experimentation using the above tests on the translated data.
6. Analysis of the results.

The clarity, significance, and precision of this translator were tested with randomly selected SL sentences from selected news (sports, world, regional, entertainment, travel, etc.), articles, literature (by both Arabic and English authors) and language officially used on the files, etc.). Compound and complex, as well as simple phrases, are used to evaluate the Arabic Translator. Then the average rating scores for the phrases of the individual translations were then calculated (separately according to clarity, significance, and precision). Percentage of precise sentences, correctly translated sentences and smart sentences are calculated. During the evaluation process, the examiners do not have any clue about the SL and judge each phrases or words as well as in target-language based on its comprehensibility. The examiner is interested only in the comprehensibility of translations. Clarity is done by grammatical errors, mistranslations and un-translated words while its correctness was subject to semantic rules of the Arabic language. For precision, the examiners are provided with source text with the translated text to examine whether the meaning of the source language phrase is protected in the translation.

6 Evaluations

Various methods have been implemented to evaluate the performance of ɛrbeng live chat translation application. Speed of the translation for ɛrbeng depends on many factors like; the size of the agent, the name of language pair, the format of the input text being translated, and Type of Machine translation and how can it learn. With ɛrbeng, the speed could be configured to ranges 3,000 words per minute upwards. This rate is considered a reasonable speed regarding the other applications in the market which has average speed of 2,500 words per day. ɛrbeng customers could translate about 1 billion words per day. The Precision and Recall of ɛrbeng are 88% and 85%. These standard measures a have higher correlation and an intuitive interpretation, which can facilitate insights into how ɛrbeng might be improved. The ɛrbeng software is publicly available. ɛrbeng as a rule-based Interlingual approach leads to a small Word error rate (WER) than statistical-based machine translation systems. This metric is calculated by calculating the number of words that differ between a piece of machine-translated text and a reference translation.

7 Conclusions

ɛrbeng is fairly important in helping people communicated without a human translator or spending months learning a language. ɛrbeng also works for most translation needs. ɛrbeng as an android based application is available to solve problems of practice, application of new technology. With the ease of use of ɛrbeng, it solves envisaged problems of low educated people by strengthening their productivity, enhance their social status and bring about economic transformation. ɛrbeng helps people to learn English with more vocabulary fast. Any learner or tourist that may wish to converse in Arabic are assisted with this Smart Arabic Language Translator. ɛrbeng live chat translation application aims to reduce the distance between different cultures and languages people. With ɛrbeng Language is no longer a problem. Anyone can communicate textually, vocally or in the video without worrying about the language of the contact.

Acknowledgments. Thanks to Michael Maged, Mario Nabil and Maria Osama the Fayoum University, Faculty of Computers and Information for efforts and helpful discussions and feedback. This work was supported by the infrastructure and the High-Tech Platforms of Fayoum University.

References

1. Hutchins, W.J., Somers, H.L.: An Introduction to Machine Translation (Chaps. 1, 4, 17) (Chap. 1, p. 8). Academic Press Limited, London (1992)
2. Nirenburg, S., Wilks, Y.: Machine translation. In: Advances in Computer, vol. 52, pp. 160–189 (2000)

3. Habash, N., Sadat, F.: Arabic preprocessing schemes for statistical machine translation. In: Proceedings of the Human Language Technology Conference of the North American Chapter of the ACL, pp. 49–52. ACL, New York (2006)
4. El Isbihani, A., Khadivi, S., Bender, O., Ney, H.: Morpho-syntactic Arabic Preprocessing for Arabic-to-English statistical machine translation. In: Proceedings of the Workshop on Statistical Machine Translation, pp. 15–22. ACL, New York (2006)
5. Buckwalter, T.: Buckwalter Arabic Morphological Analyzer Version 1.0. Linguistic Data Consortium, University of Pennsylvania, LDC Catalog No.: LDC2002L49 (2002)
6. Gavaldà, M.: SOUP: a parser for real-world spontaneous speech. In: New Developments in Parsing Technology, vol. 23, pp 339—350. Kluwer Academic Publishers, Norwell (2004). Also Published in the Proceedings of the 6th International Workshop on Parsing Technologies (IWPT-2000), Trento, Italy
7. Mitamura, T., Nyberg III, E.H., Carbonell, J.G.: An efficient interlingua translation system for multi-lingual document production. In: Proceedings of Machine Translation Summit III, Washington D.C., The United States, 2–4 July 1991
8. Lonsdale, D.W., Franz, A.M., Leavitt, J.R.R.: Large scale machine translation: an interlingua approach. In: Proceedings of the 7th International Conference on Industrial and Engineering Applications of Artificial Intelligence and Expert Systems, Austin, Texas, The United States (1994)
9. Abul Seoud, R.L.: Generating interlingua from Arabic parsing tree, M.Sc., Faculty of Engineering, Cairo University, Egypt (2005)
10. AlAnsary, S.: Interlingua-based machine translation systems: UNL versus other interlinguas. In: The 11th International Conference on Language Engineering, Cairo, Egypt (2011)
11. Nyberg, E.H., Mitamura, T., Carbonell, J.: The KANT machine translation system: from R&D to initial deployment. In: Proceedings of LISA (The Library and Information Services in Astronomy) Workshop on Integrating Advanced Translation Technology, 3–4 June 1997. Hyatt Regency Crystal City, Washington D.C. (1997)
12. Soudi, A., Cavalli-Sforza, V., Jamari, A.: A prototype English-to-Arabic interlingua-based MT system. In: The Proceedings of the Workshop on Arabic Language Resources and Evaluation - Status and Prospects, The 3rd International Conference on Language Resources and Evaluation (LREC 2002), Las Palmas de Gran Canaria, Spain (2002)
13. Shaalan, K., Abdel Monem, A., Rafea, A., Baraka, H.: Mapping interlingua representations to feature structures of Arabic sentences. In: The Challenge of Arabic for NLP/MT, International Conference, the British Computer Society, London, pp. 149–159 (2006)
14. Shaalan, K., Monem, A.A., Rafea, A.: Arabic morphological generation from interlingua. In: Shi, Z., Shimohara, K., Feng, D. (eds.) IIP 2006. IIFIP, vol. 228, pp. 441–451. Springer, Boston, MA (2006). https://doi.org/10.1007/978-0-387-44641-7_46
15. Shaalan, K., Monem, A.A., Rafea, A., Baraka, H.: Generating Arabic text from interlingua. In: Proceedings of the 2nd Workshop on Computational Approaches to Arabic Script-Based Languages (CAASL-2), pp. 137–144. Linguistic Institute, Stanford (2007)
16. Shaalan, K., Monem, A.A., Rafea, A.: Arabic morphological generation from interlingua. In: Shi, Z., Shimohara, K., Feng, D. (eds.) IIP 2006. IIFIP, vol. 228, pp. 441–451. Springer, Boston, MA (2006). https://doi.org/10.1007/978-0-387-44641-7_46

Improving Accuracy of Imbalanced Clinical Data Classification Using Synthetic Minority Over-Sampling Technique

Fatihah Mohd[1(✉)], Masita Abdul Jalil[1],
Noor Maizura Mohamad Noora[1], Suryani Ismail[1],
Wan Fatin Fatihah Yahya[1], and Mumtazimah Mohamad[2]

[1] Faculty of Ocean Engineering Technology and Informatics,
Universiti Malaysia Terengganu, 21030 Kuala Nerus,
Terengganu, Malaysia
mpfatihah@gmail.com
[2] Faculty of Informatics and Computing, Universiti Sultan Zainal Abidin,
21030 Kuala Nerus, Terengganu, Malaysia

Abstract. Imbalanced datasets typically occur in many real applications. Resampling is one of the effective solutions due to producing a balanced class distribution. Synthetic Minority Over-sampling technique (SMOTE), an over-sampling technique is used in this study for dealing the imbalanced dataset by add the number of instances of a minority class. This technique is used to decrease the imbalance percentage of the dataset by generating new synthetic samples. Thus, a balanced training dataset is produced to replace the class imbalanced. The balanced datasets were obtained and trained with machine learning algorithms to diagnose the disease's class. Through the experiment findings on the real-world datasets, oral cancer dataset and erythemato-squamous diseases dataset from the UCI machine learning datasets, an over-sampling method showed better results in clinical disease classification.

Keywords: Erythemato-Squamous diseases dataset · Imbalanced dataset · Oral cancer · Resampling · SMOTE

1 Introduction

The basic data preparation steps carried out on a computer system is to convert real-world data to a computer readable format. This is a main phase of system development in order to ensure the data quality. Many issues are to be solved in data quality such as the accuracy, completeness, consistency, timeliness, believability, and interpretability [1]. In real application, datasets are imbalanced when at least one class is denoted by only a small number of training set (minority class), whereas other classes are the majority. In this state, classification with a majority class may well accurate, however, the minority class may have a highly error classified due to the effect on traditional training criteria of the larger majority class. Almost classification algorithms (CA) aim to minimize the error rate and the percentage of incorrect prediction of class, where the

© Springer Nature Switzerland AG 2019
A. Alfaries et al. (Eds.): ICC 2019, CCIS 1097, pp. 99–110, 2019.
https://doi.org/10.1007/978-3-030-36365-9_8

difference between types of incorrectly classified are ignored. In specific, this assume that all incorrectly classified have the same cost [2].

To fix the drawback, a resampling on imbalanced dataset before the classification stage using oversampling and under sampling approach is proposed. Oversampling, the Synthetic Minority Over-sampling technique (SMOTE) algorithm is applied in this study to resolve the problem of the class imbalance of oral cancer dataset and erythemato-squamous diseases dataset (ESD) from the UCI machine learning dataset. The remaining of the paper is structured as follows: The next section, presents the related works in oversampling technique. The following section provides a brief description about the Materials and methods used in this study. Next, the findings of the study, are elaborated in experimental and analysis section and lastly the conclusion section address further research issues in this area.

2 Related Works

Class imbalance occurs when one of the classes is less represented. In the training data, this incident will affect the performance of the algorithm for selecting cases. This often occurs when data collection is not enough [3]. Most CA aim to reduce the error rate and the percentage of incorrect classified of class labels [2, 4]. To handle the class imbalance, the resampling methods can be applied in order to provide a balanced dataset [5, 6]. Resampling methods are divided into over-sampling and under-sampling the classes that can be used to balance the dataset [7, 8]. Over-sampling method balances the original class or dataset by increasing the number of minority class data, whereas under-sampling method removes the number of majority class data from the original dataset [2]. Some of the resampling methods are widely used are random over-sampling or under-sampling [9], Synthetic Minority Oversampling Technique (SMOTE) [2], and Adaptive Synthetic Sampling (ADASYN) [10].

Random over-sampling and under-sampling simply increases randomly the number of existing minority or majority class members in the training. This method is known to increase the likelihood of occurring overfitting. Since random over-sampling only duplicates remaining data, it has been identified that random over-sampling does not increase real data to the training dataset and abandon valuable data [9, 11]. To avoid the over-fitting problem, [2] propose the Synthetic Minority Over-Sampling Technique (SMOTE). SMOTE not only increases the size of the training data set, it also increases the variability and creates artificial training dataset based on the original training dataset. Empirically, SMOTE has presented to perform well in many applications. A study proposed by [12], applied synthetic minority over-sampling technique (SMOTE), which created synthetic examples using the minority instances in the current training large piece, which in turn are used to stabilize the training large piece.

Chawla demonstrated the minority class was over-sampled at 50%, 100%, 200%, 300%, 400%, and 500%. The majority class was under-sampled at 10%, 15%, 25%, 50%, 75%, 100%, 125%, 150%, 175%, 200%, 300%, 400%, 500%, 600%, 700%, 800%, 1000%, and 2000%. The amount of majority class under-sampling and minority class over-sampling depended on the dataset size and class proportions. For instance, for the mammography dataset, for the/minority class over-sampled at 50%, 100%,

200%, 300%, and 400% [2]. Farquad and Bose, employed the coil dataset to forecast the clients with a car policy based on his sociodemographic and history of product ownership data, would buy insurance policy or not. The Coil dataset, which is highly class imbalanced and has a 94:6 ratios for class distribution. This dataset contained only 6% of the training data denoted clients who purchased the insurance policy. The remaining 94% records denoted clients who did not desire to purchase an insurance. They employed different standard resampling techniques such as under sampling, over-sampling and SMOTE. The class distribution ratio after hiring the SMOTE is 50:50 [13].

Another study used SMOTE to create one more dataset, where the minority samples were oversampled by 485%, making the ratio of 6:1 to 1:1 [14]. Then, the over-sampling method is also applied to handle highly imbalanced time series classification from seven datasets in the UCR time series repository: Adiac, FaceAll, Words, Swedish Leaf, Two Patterns, Wafer, and Yoga. They applied over-sampling method to oversample the set of 50 positive samples nine times to have a total of 500 positive samples (same size of negative examples). Then, using SMOTE, the most synthetic class distributions is created, since every remaining positive sample has been chosen for producing roughly the same number of new samples. For example, wafer dataset, was oversampled on minority class from 50 samples to 712–6532, majority class was over-sampled from 380–3000 to 382–3402 [15].

Wang also applied resampling technique to overcome the class imbalance problem. The proposed hybrid sampling support vector machine (SVM) approach, combines under-sampling and over-sampling techniques successfully, generates a balanced dataset with less a loss of information and without the addition of a great number of synthetic samples. The finding of the study shows that, the proposed approach out-performs existing over-sampling and under-sampling techniques [4]. Additionally, the SMOTE is used to solve the class imbalanced in the dialectical Arabic dataset. The experiments done using single and ensemble classifiers with and without utilizing SMOTE indicated that, using the word embedding with ensemble and SMOTE can reach 54.54% performance, which is 15% higher improvement on average in F1 score over the base-line (38.87%) [16]. Since, SMOTE has revealed to achieve better than random oversampling and applied in many applications [17], this study utilized SMOTE to overcome the class imbalanced in clinical dataset.

3 Material and Method

Most classification algorithms best perform when the amount of instances in each class is about equal. Thus, to deliberate the maximize accuracy and reduce error in classification, the research methodology of the study covers four phases: data preparation, resampling to imbalanced dataset, and evaluate classifier algorithm. This section first describes the materials used in the experiment: oral cancer dataset (OCDS) and erythemato-squamous diseases dataset (ESD), and then elaborates the resampling technique used in this study.

3.1   Oral Cancer Dataset

OCDS contains 25 attributes or features and 82 instances. The 25 attributes of oral cancer are elaborated into four kinds: demographic, clinical signs and symptoms, histopathological and feature of oral cancer stage is labelled as a class label or target of disease diagnosis (stage one, two, three, and four) [18, 19].

3.2   Erythemato-Squamous Diseases Dataset

The experimental work in this study used ESD dataset from UCI Machine learning depository. ESD dataset has 34 attributes, 33 are linear valued and one is nominal. Patients who diagnosed with disease, were first assessed clinically with 12 attributes. Then samples of skin were evaluated for 22 histopathological features under a microscope analysis. The numbers of instances were 366, while the numbers of attributes were 34 [20–22].

3.3   Resampling Technique

In this method, the minority class is re-sample by generating synthetic data by over-sampling with replacement. This method is raised by a technique that verified successful in handwritten character recognition [23]. Chawla et al. produced synthetic examples in a less application-specific manner, by working in feature space rather than data space [2]. In this study, SMOTE, an over-sampling technique is used for the class imbalanced by expand the number of samples for minority class. This technique will support to decrease the imbalance percentage of the dataset. Figure 1 shows the procedure of SMOTE [2]. The amount of over-sampling is assigned as a parameter of the system. The class with minority number is over-sampled by pleasing each minority class data and presenting synthetic examples along the line segments linking any/all of the k minority class nearest neighbors. Taking upon the number of over-sampling needed, neighbors from the k nearest neighbors are randomly selected.

Figure 2 shows an example of calculation of random synthetic samples. Synthetic samples are produced in the few steps. Begin by taking the difference among the feature vector (sample) under consideration and its nearest neighbor. Then, multiply this difference by a random number between 0 and 1, and expand it to the feature vector under consideration. The collection of a random point along the line segment between two specific features is occurred. This method successfully drives the decision region of the minority class to be more extensive [2].

4   Experiment and Analysis

In this section, Waikato Environment for Knowledge Analysis (WEKA) software is applied to resolve imbalanced OCDS by using SMOTE under the supervised filter function. WEKA is a machine learning tool written in Java, established at the University of Waikato, New Zealand [24, 25]. This data mining software is widely used to resolve the imbalanced data classification [6, 26–28]. In the experiment works, firstly the original OCDS must fit entirely in WEKA memory. Then, the amount of SMOTE and number of nearest neighbours is specified as Fig. 3.

The imbalanced OCDS has instances for stage four, 28 instances for stage three, ten instances for stage two and four instances for stage one. For the training set, 10-fold cross validation is applied. The minority class is oversampled at 35%, 45%, 50%, and 100% of its raw size. Table 1 denotes the outcome of resampling on imbalanced OCDS by SMOTE. The number of resampling instances is 160 instead of 82 instances. All the classes are resampled with a same distribution (25%) with new total instances 160. Balanced OCDS using SMOTE in WEKA software is shown as Fig. 4.

In this study, the ESD data were categorized into six classes. There were 112 instances of the majority class (psoriasis), 72 for lichen planus, 61 for seborrheic dermatitis and the other three classes (pityriasis rosea, chronic dermatitis, and pityriasis rubra pilaris) falls under the category of minority class with the number of instances less than 60. For the training set, 10-fold cross-validations were used. The minority class was oversampled at 100%, 200%, 300%, and 400% of its raw size. Table 2 notes the finding of resampling an imbalance ESD using SMOTE. After the process of over sampling, the number of instances became 660 instead of the original 366 instances. Over sampling has resulted in an almost balanced class distribution among the minority and the majority classes as follows: minority class- pityriasis rosea (14.85%), chronic dermatitis (15.76%) and pityriasis rubra pilaris (12.12%) and majority class- psoriasis (16.97%), seborrheic dermatitis (18.48) and lichen planus (21.82%).

Table 1. Balance class distribution for OCDS by using SMOTE.

Class	Class label	Before resampling	After resampling
1	One	4 (4.87%)	40 (25%)
2	Two	10 (12.19%)	40 (25%)
3	Three	28 (34.15%)	40 (25%)
4	Four	40 (48.78%)	40 (25%)
	Total number of instances	82	160

Table 2. Balanced class distribution for ESD by using SMOTE.

Class	Class label	Before resampling	After resampling
1	Psoriasis	112 (30.6%)	112 (16.97%)
2	Seborrheic dermatitis	61 (16.67%)	122 (18.48%)
3	Lichen planus	72 (19.67%)	144 (21.82%)
4	Pityriasis rosea	49 (13.39%)	98 (14.85%)
5	Chronic dermatitis	52 (14.21%)	104 (15.76%)
6	Pityriasis rubra pilaris	20 (5.46%)	80 (12.12%)
	Total number of instances	366	660

Algorithm SMOTE (M, N, k)
Input: M, N, k
Initialize Number of minority class samples as M; Amount of SMOTE as N; Number of nearest
neighbors as k.

(* If N is less than 100%, randomize the minority class samples as only a random
percent of them will be SMOTEd*)

1. If N < 100
2.   then Randomize the M minority class samples
3.   M = (N/100) * M
4.   N = 100
5. End If

(* The amount of SMOTE is assumed to be in integral multiples of 100*)

6. N = (int) (N/100)
7. k = Number of nearest neighbors
8. numofvar = Number of variables
9. Sample { } { }: array for original minority class samples
10. newindex: keeps a count of number of synthetic samples generated, initialized to 0
11. Synthetic { } { }: array for synthetic samples

(* Compute k nearest neighbors for each minority class sample only. *)

12. For i ← 1 to M
13.   Compute k nearest neighbors for i, and save the indices in the narray
14.   Populate (N, i, narray)
15. End For

(* Function to generate the synthetic samples *)

16. Populate (N, i, narray) n
17. While N ≠ 0
18.   Choose a random number between 1 and k, call it nn
19.   This step chooses one of the k nearest neighbors of i.
20.   For varb ← 1 to numofvar
21.   Compute: dif = Sample [narray[nn]] [varb] – Sample [i] [varb]
22.   Compute: gap = random number between 0 and 1
23.   Synthetic [newindex] [varb] = Sample [i] [varb] + gap * dif
24.   End for
25.   newindex++
26.   N = N – 1
27. End While
28. return (* End of Populate. *)
29. End of Pseudo-Code.
Output (N/100) * M synthetic minority class samples

Fig. 1. SMOTE algorithm.

Algorithm Generate Sample of Synthetic by SMOTE

1. Consider a sample (6,4) and let (4,3) be its nearest neighbor
2. (6,4) is the sample for which k-nearest neighbors are being identified
3. (4,3) is one of its k-nearest neighbors
4. Let:
5. s1_1 = 6 s2_1 = 4 s2_1 - s1_1 = -2
6. s1_2 = 4 s2_2 = 3 s2_2 - s1_2 = -1

   The new samples will be generated as
7. (s1'',s2') = (6,4) + rand(0-1) * (-2,-1)
8. rand(0-1) generates a random number between 0 and 1

Output (N/100) * M synthetic minority class samples

Fig. 2. Algorithm to generate sample of synthetic by SMOTE.

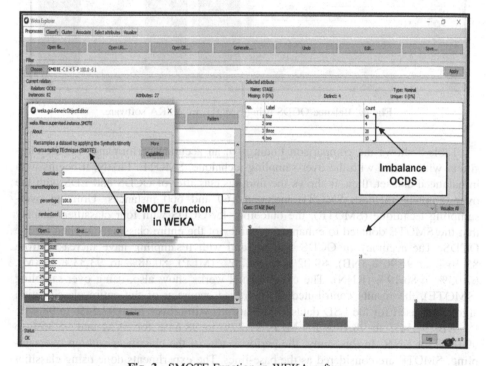

Fig. 3. SMOTE Function in WEKA software.

The effectiveness of the used SMOTE was evaluated by imbalanced and balanced dataset. The performance of accuracy is verified with classification accuracy metric (ACC), with four metrics are defined as true positive (TP), false positive (FP), true negative (TN) and false negative (FN), ACC = (TP + TN)/(TP + FP + FN +TN) [29, 30]. Four machine learning algorithms are trained and tested to classify the OCDS and EDS: Naïve Bayes (NB), Multilayer Perceptron (MLP), Support Vector Machine (SVM), and K-Nearest Neighbor (KNN).

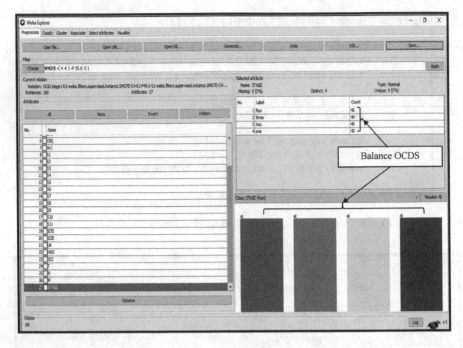

Fig. 4. Balance OCDS using SMOTE in WEKA software.

Table 3 shows the comparison findings of an accurate performance for the classifiers without and with the over-sampling technique, SMOTE. Firstly, it begins with imbalanced dataset, then, it shows the findings classifier of OCDS and EDS with the over-sampling method, SMOTE included 160 and 660 instances. Utilizing over-sampling technique (SMOTE), the outcomes for OCDS with four classifiers display that the SMOTE donated to enhanced accuracy of the entire classifiers applied for the OCDS. The accuracy of OCDS without and with resampling have increased from 85.36% to 91.90% (NB), 89.02% to 94.26% (MLP), 80.48% to 93.33% (SVM), 67.03% to 86.19% (KNN). The experimental works show also, using over-sampling (SMOTE), the results contributed to improved accuracy of the entire classification algorithms used for the ESD dataset. The accuracy improves from 97.54% to 98.48% for NB, 97.54% to 98.18% for MLP, 97.27% to 98.64% for SVM and 95.36% to 99.09% for KNN. In this study, the performances of the classifiers without oversampling, SMOTE are considered as the base-lines. The experiments done using classifier algorithms with and without applying SMOTE shows that, applying SMOTE on OCDS can achieve 91.43% performance and 98.6% on ESD which are more than 10% and 1% enhancement on average in accuracy over the base-line (80.56% and 96.93%).

Table 3. Performance Comparison of Classifiers on OCDS and ESD Dataset with and Without SMOTE in terms of accuracy.

No	CA		OCDS		ESD	
			Base	SMOTE	Base	SMOTE
4	KNN	Accurate	67.07	86.19	95.36	99.09
		Error	32.93	13.81	4.64	0.91
3	SVM	Accurate	80.49	93.33	97.27	98.64
		Error	19.51	6.67	2.73	1.36
1	NB	Accurate	85.37	91.90	97.54	98.49
		Error	14.63	8.10	2.46	1.51
4	KNN	Accurate	67.07	86.19	95.36	99.09
		Error	32.93	13.81	4.64	0.91
Mean accuracy		Accurate	80.56	91.43	96.93	98.60

Figures 5 and 6 plot accuracy performance of the entire classification algorithms applying over-sampling for two imbalanced datasets i.e. oral cancer dataset, erythemato-squamous diseases dataset respectively. The findings obviously present that in almost all classification of two datasets that use over-sampling technique (SMOTE) produces in the improvement of accuracy. Although the accuracy improvement value is quite small, it is valuable for skewed dataset where accuracy of minority class is particularly significant.

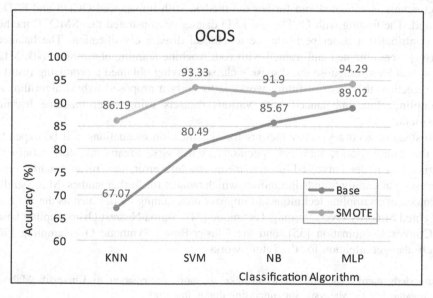

Fig. 5. Accuracy Performance on the OCDS at different percentages of over-sampling.

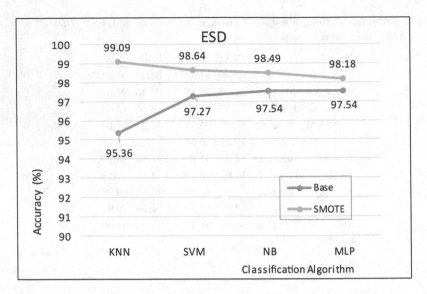

Fig. 6. Accuracy Performance on the ESD at different percentages of over-sampling.

5   Conclusion

Since introduced in 2002 [2], SMOTE has continued to attract attention in big data and many clinical applications for handling class imbalanced [31–33]. Thus, in this study, an oversampling by adopting SMOTE algorithm, typically used to solve the imbalanced class of the dataset was applied. Through classification experiments, SMOTE effectiveness is validated and further the method with imbalanced OCDS and ESD is verified. The finding with OCDS and ESD dataset demonstrated that SMOTE method has contributed a better performance to clinical disease classification. The balanced datasets were obtained and trained with four machine learning algorithms; NB, MLP, KNN, and SVM diagnose the disease's classes. Having obtained a promising result in this direction, the focus of future works is to study a proposed hybrid algorithm for resampling class imbalanced with various datasets using other machine learning classifiers.

Instead of accuracy, other metrics for classification evaluations will be expended for the future works, includes specificity, sensitivity, logarithmic loss, confusion matrix, area under curve, F1 scores, mean absolute error, and mean squared error. Moreover, this study founds limitations which request for further studies. Many studies enhanced oversampling techniques to improve data mining model such as the Majority Weighted Minority Oversampling Technique [34], Sigma Nearest Oversampling based on Convex Combination [35], and the Cluster-Based Synthetic Oversampling [36], which also get attention for the future works.

Acknowledgement. The authors would like to show appreciation to Universiti Malaysia Terengganu (UMT), Malaysia, for supporting during this study.

References

1. Blake, R., Mangiameli, P.: The effects and interactions of data quality and problem complexity on classification. J. Data Inf. Qual. (JDIQ) **2**(2), 8 (2011)
2. Chawla, N.V., Bowyer, K.W., Hall, L.O., Kegelmeyer, W.P.: SMOTE: synthetic minority over-sampling technique. J. Artif. Intell. Res. **16**(2002), 321–357 (2002)
3. Malof, J.M., Mazurowski, M.A., Tourassi, G.D.: The effect of class imbalance on case selection for case-based classifiers: an empirical study in the context of medical decision support. Neural Netw. **25**(1), 141–145 (2012)
4. Wang, Q.: A hybrid sampling SVM approach to imbalanced data classification. Abstr. Appl. Anal. **2014**, 1–7 (2014)
5. Borowska, K., Topczewska, M.: Data preprocessing in the classification of the imbalanced data. Adv. Comput. Sci. Res. **11**, 31–46 (2014)
6. Salunkhe, U.R., Mali, S.N.: Classifier ensemble design for imbalanced data classification: a hybrid approach. Procedia Comput. Sci. **85**, 725–732 (2016)
7. Ali, A., Shamsuddin, S.M., Ralescu, A.L.: Classification with class imbalance problem: a review. Int. J. Adv. Soft Comput. Appl. **7**(3), 176–204 (2015)
8. Haixiang, G., Yijing, L., Shang, J., Mingyun, G., Yuanyue, H., Bing, G.: Learning from class-imbalanced data: review of methods and applications. Expert. Syst. Appl. **73**(2017), 220–239 (2017)
9. Japkowicz, N., Stephen, S.: The class imbalance problem: a systematic study. Intell. Data Anal. **6**(5), 429–449 (2002)
10. He, H., Bai, Y., Garcia, E.A., Li, S.: ADASYN: adaptive synthetic sampling approach for imbalanced learning. In: 2008 IEEE International Joint Conference on Neural Networks (IEEE World Congress on Computational Intelligence), pp. 1322–1328. IEEE (2008)
11. Prati, R.C., Batista, G.E.A.P.A., Monard, M.C.: A study with class imbalance and random sampling for a decision tree learning system. In: Bramer, M. (ed.) IFIP AI 2008. ITIFIP, vol. 276, pp. 131–140. Springer, Boston, MA (2008). https://doi.org/10.1007/978-0-387-09695-7_13
12. Chawla, N.V.: Data mining for imbalanced datasets: an overview. In: Maimon, O., Rokach, L. (eds.) Data Mining and Knowledge Discovery Handbook, pp. 875–886. Springer, New York (2010). https://doi.org/10.1007/978-0-387-09823-4_45
13. Farquad, M.A.H., Bose, I.: Preprocessing unbalanced data using support vector machine. Decis. Support Syst. **53**(1), 226–233 (2012)
14. Rahman, M.M., Davis, D.: Addressing the class imbalance problem in medical datasets. Int. J. Mach. Learn. Comput. **3**(2), 224 (2013)
15. Cao, P., Zhao, D., Zaiane, O.: An optimized cost-sensitive SVM for imbalanced data learning. In: Pei, J., Tseng, V.S., Cao, L., Motoda, H., Xu, G. (eds.) PAKDD 2013. LNCS (LNAI), vol. 7819, pp. 280–292. Springer, Heidelberg (2013). https://doi.org/10.1007/978-3-642-37456-2_24
16. Al-Azani, S., El-Alfy, E.-S.M.: Using word embedding and ensemble learning for highly imbalanced data sentiment analysis in short arabic text. Procedia Comput. Sci. **109**, 359–366 (2017)
17. Santoso, B., Wijayanto, H., Notodiputro, K., Sartono, B.: Synthetic over sampling methods for handling class imbalanced problems: a review. In: IOP Conference Series: Earth and Environmental Science, pp. 012031. IOP Publishing (2017)
18. Mohd, F., Jalil, M.A., Noor, N.M.M., Bakar, Z.A., Abdullah, Z.: Enhancement of Bayesian model with relevance feedback for improving diagnostic model. Malays. J. Comput. Sci., 1–14 (2018). Special Issue December 2018 (Information Retrieval and Knowledge Management Special Issue Publication)

19. Yusof, M.M., Mohamed, R., Wahid, N.: Benchmark of feature selection techniques with machine learning algorithms for cancer datasets. In: Proceedings of the International Conference on Artificial Intelligence and Robotics and the International Conference on Automation, Control and Robotics Engineering, pp. 1–5, Kitakyushu, Japan. ACM (2016)
20. Badrinath, N., Gopinath, G., Ravichandran, K., Soundhar, R.G.: Estimation of automatic detection of erythemato-squamous diseases through adaboost and its hybrid classifiers. Artif. Intell. Rev. **45**(4), 471–488 (2016)
21. Tuba, E., Ribic, I., Capor-Hrosik, R., Tuba, M.: Support vector machine optimized by elephant herding algorithm for erythemato-squamous diseases detection. Procedia Comput. Sci. **122**(2017), 916–923 (2017)
22. Jain, D., Singh, V.: Feature selection and classification systems for chronic disease prediction: a review. Egypt. Inform. J. **19**(3), 179–189 (2018)
23. Ha, T.M., Bunke, H.: Off-line, handwritten numeral recognition by perturbation method. IEEE Trans. Pattern Anal. Mach. Intell. **19**(5), 535–539 (1997)
24. Hall, M., Frank, E., Holmes, G., Pfahringer, B., Reutemann, P., Witten, I.H.: The WEKA data mining software: an update. ACM SIGKDD Explor. Newsl. **11**(1), 10–18 (2009)
25. Smith, T.C., Frank, E.: Introducing machine learning concepts with WEKA. In: Mathé, E., Davis, S. (eds.) Statistical Genomics. MMB, vol. 1418, pp. 353–378. Springer, New York (2016). https://doi.org/10.1007/978-1-4939-3578-9_17
26. Al Najada, H., Zhu, X.: iSRD: spam review detection with imbalanced data distributions. In: Proceedings of the 2014 IEEE 15th International Conference on Information Reuse and Integration (IEEE IRI 2014), pp. 553–560. IEEE (2014)
27. Sabanci, K., Koklu, M.: The classification of eye state by using KNN and MLP classification models according to the EEG signals. Int. J. Intell. Syst. Appl. Eng. **3**(4), 127–130 (2015)
28. Huang, Z., Chan, T.-M., Dong, W.: MACE prediction of acute coronary syndrome via boosted resampling classification using electronic medical records. J. Biomed. Inform. **66**, 161–170 (2017)
29. Mohd, F., Bakar, Z.A., Noor, N.M.M., Rajion, Z.A., Saddki, N.: A hybrid selection method based on HCELFS and SVM for the diagnosis of oral cancer staging. In: Sulaiman, H.A., Othman, M.A., Othman, M.F.I., Rahim, Y.A., Pee, N.C. (eds.) Advanced Computer and Communication Engineering Technology. LNEE, vol. 315, pp. 821–831. Springer, Cham (2015). https://doi.org/10.1007/978-3-319-07674-4_77
30. Mustafa, N., Memon, R.A., Li, J.-P., Omer, M.Z.: A classification model for imbalanced medical data based on PCA and farther distance based synthetic minority oversampling technique. Int. J. Adv. Comput. Sci. Appl. (IJACSA) **8**(1), 61–67 (2017)
31. Geetha, R., Sivasubramanian, S., Kaliappan, M., Vimal, S., Annamalai, S.: Cervical cancer identification with synthetic minority oversampling technique and PCA analysis using random forest classifier. J. Med. Syst. **43**(9), 286 (2019)
32. Basgall, M.J., Hasperué, W., Naiouf, M., Fernández, A., Herrera, F.: An analysis of local and global solutions to address big data imbalanced classification: a case study with SMOTE preprocessing. In: Naiouf, M., Chichizola, F., Rucci, E. (eds.) Cloud Computing and Big Data, vol. 1050, pp. 75–85. Springer, Cham (2019). https://doi.org/10.1007/978-3-030-27713-0_7
33. Elreedy, D., Atiya, A.F.: A comprehensive analysis of synthetic minority oversampling technique (SMOTE) for handling class imbalance. Inf. Sci. **505**, 32–64 (2019)
34. Barua, S., Islam, M.M., Yao, X., Murase, K.: MWMOTE–majority weighted minority oversampling technique for imbalanced data set learning. IEEE Trans. Knowl. Data Eng. **26**(2), 405–425 (2012)
35. Zheng, Z., Cai, Y., Li, Y.: Oversampling method for imbalanced classification. Comput. Inform. **34**(5), 1017–1037 (2015)
36. Lim, P., Goh, C.K., Tan, K.C.: Evolutionary cluster-based synthetic oversampling ensemble (eco-ensemble) for imbalance learning. IEEE Trans. Cybern. **47**(9), 2850–2861 (2016)

Learning Case-Based Reasoning Solutions by Association Rules Approach

Abdelhak Mansoul[1]([✉]), Baghdad Atmani[2], Mohamed Benamina[2], and Sofia Benbelkacem[2]

[1] Department of Computer Science, University 20 August 1955, Skikda, Algeria
mansoul2l@gmail.com
[2] Laboratoire d'Informatique d'Oran (LIO),
University of Oran 1 Ahmed BenBella, Oran, Algeria
Baghdad.atmani@gmail.com, mohamed.benamina@gmail.com,
sofia.benbelkacem@gmail.com

Abstract. Case-Based Reasoning (CBR) is amply used as a method to solve problems in many domains. It involves retrieval and use of past cases to solve a new one. However, using past cases to solve a new one by this methodology is weighing a great deal. In this paper, we present our approach for reducing the search space solution through association rules and focus only interesting cases that meet only these rules. The reduced search space is then used by CBR to compute a solution for the new problem. Through this work, we aim to propose an approach that combines Association Rules and CBR to improve searching solution for similar cases. Thereafter, we test our approach by using real-life datasets.

Keywords: Decision support · Case-Based reasoning · Association rules · Data mining · CBR

1 Introduction

The Case-based reasoning is an artificial intelligence technique based on the reuse of past experiences [1]. It can be considered as adapting old solutions to meet new problems. It has been amply applied to support decision and was widely applied to solve problems and support decision in health care [2, 3]. However, it presents some weaknesses in its two main tasks: the retrieval and the adaptation tasks [3, 4].

Thus, a serious difficulty emerge when finding various similar cases and therefore several solutions, however a choice between solutions must be done. Several works have been conducted on the retrieval task using different strategies and have proposed many solutions. These solutions are from sequential calculation, non-sequential indexing, classification algorithms such as ID3 and Nearest Neighbor Matching [5], Fuzzy Logic [6] and Data mining methods [7]. In this work, we address an approach by investigating the collaboration between CBR and Association Rules.

© Springer Nature Switzerland AG 2019
A. Alfaries et al. (Eds.): ICC 2019, CCIS 1097, pp. 111–118, 2019.
https://doi.org/10.1007/978-3-030-36365-9_9

Motivation and Contribution. As mentioned above, the major retrieval shortcoming is the several closer cases. This fact induces a very hard adaptation to deduce an appropriate solution.

So, the central part of our approach is based on this deficiency, by using a data mining operation: Association Rules. Thus, by using this operation we do better the retrieval of cases and the choice of the solution from a small case base instead of a huge one.

The rest of this paper is structured as follows: In Sect. 2 we give a survey on some related works showing particularly the use of CBR with other technics in medical decision aid. Section 3, deals with our approach. Section 4, presents experimentation and interpretation of results, and finally in Sect. 5 we give the conclusion which summarizes the paper and point out some possible trends.

2 Related Works

CBR is fundamentally related to research in analogical reasoning, and is an active area of research. It has been widely experimented jointly with different methods for computing and reasoning [3, 4, 8]. The combination of CBR with other techniques has been used to avoid the adaptation problem, mainly by using the retrieval task with other reasoning strategies. This is an issue of current concern in CBR research in different fields [3, 9–12].

Schmidt et al. suggested clustering cases into prototypes and remove redundant ones to avoid an infinite growth of case base, the retrieval searches only among these prototypes [13].

Mansoul and Atmani used clustering to enhance CBR retrieval task for diagnosis of orthopaedic diseases [14].

Marling et al. suggested a solution at retrieval task using a three matching algorithms and combined three different measures and fuzzy similarity and they also proposed another solution using a reutilisability measure to select and retrieve a case in addition to check of constraints and a scoring. This method gives the easiest case to adaptation task. This solution was used to propose a menu planer system based on CBR and RBR [8].

Xu used an indexing/matching module based on retrieving only cases that match the important indices of the new case, calculate an aggregate match score for the comparable cases and retrieve only those comparable cases with higher aggregate match scores [15].

Kumar et al. used two distances (Weighted Euclidean, Mahalanobis) to perform retrieval task and eliminate bad cases with an eliminating score [16].

Saraiva et al. used also a CBR-RBR combination for the retrieval task of CBR for to identify gastrointestinal cancer [17].

Balakrishnan et al. proposed a solution for retinopathy prediction based on the combination CBR-Association Rules [11].

3   The Proposed Approach

The problem (case) we handle is characterized by: a set of n attributes and a solution S. Thus, the case or new problem will be defined as follows:

[Case] Attribute$_1$, ..., Attribute$_n$, S[End_Case]

Association Rule and It's Analogy with Case

The analogy of an association rule with the case is well established as shown in Fig. 1.

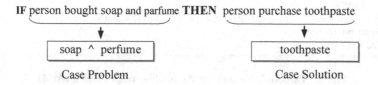

Fig. 1. Association rule example and it's analogy with case.

The Objective. Our aim is to find the closest cases for the new case and from there the relevant solution. We must proceed with this strategy: *reduce* the Searching Case Base, then retrieve the solution. So, to achieve this objective, we must perform the following treatments:

- *Preprocessing.* It's the data preparation for *Association Rules Mining (ArM)*.
- *Initiate ArM.* It generates the relevant cases to be considered for finding the solution of the new case.
- *Initiate CBR.* CBR accomplishes the retrieve, the reuse, the revise and the retain tasks with the relevant cases to search for the solution.

3.1   ArM Processing

Association rules Mining is a procedure (Fig. 2) which finds features occurring toge-ther. Apriori, is one of algorithms with do this task correctly and derives from the works of Agrawal et al. [18]. The reducing space of similar cases can clearly make retrieval of the solution computationally better regarding to only relevant cases (in-teresting solutions) for the new case being processed and more meaningful since only cases validated are retrieved.

As result we will have a set of relevant cases stored as rules in an Association Rules Repository. This processing is done by the following pseudo-algorithm:

```
Input : Case_Base , Output : Relevant_cases
1:Transform(Case_Base, Table_of_Cases); Initialize Support and Confidence
2:Apriori(Table_of_Cases, Ass_Rules)
3:For each Current_Rule in Ass_Rules
        If all attributes of S exists in Current_Rule Then Accepted_Rules(Current_Rule)
          Else  drop (Current_Rule)  End if
        For each Current_case in Case_Base
                For each Accepted_Rule
                    If Current_Case verify Current_Rule Then Accepted_case:= "Yes"
                          Else  Accepted_case:= "No"   Endif
                Next Eccepted_Rule
                Endfor
        Next Current_Case
        Endfor
    If accepted_case:= "Yes" Then  Relevant_cases:= Current_Case(S,D)  Endif
    Next Current_Rule
4:End for
```

Fig. 2. Pseudo-Algorithm for Association rules Mining (ArM).

3.2   CBR Processing

CBR is a methodology that uses a simple principle: Reasoning by reusing past experiences. It is a powerful and frequently applied approach to solve problems. It is conventionally based on four tasks: retrieve, reuse, revise and retain according to Aamodt and Plaza [1]. So, in our study it is used to search for the n closest cases to a new case. We used the k-nn method for the simplicity of its implementation. The process (Fig. 3) will select similar cases, and will extract the preliminary solutions that have been considered for the n similar cases, then those preliminary cases are considered to determine the solution (New_Case_Solution).

This process will be handled by the following pseudo-algorithm.

```
Input : New_Case_Solution ← Ø, Cases_to_Reuse ← Ø,  New_Case(S, Ø)
Output : New_Case_Solution
1:  ArM ()
2:  Initialize k for k-nn
3:  Cases_to_Reuse ← Retrieve(New_Case, Relevant_Cases,k-nn)
4:  Reuse(Cases_to_Reuse, Adapted_Solution)
5:  Revise(Adapted_Solution, Confirmed_Solution)
6:  If Confirmed_Solution accepted Then New_Case_Solution:=Confirmed_Solution;
        Retain_New_Case(S, New_Case_Solution)
    Endif
7:  End
```

Fig. 3. Pseudo-Algorithm for Case-Based Reasoning.

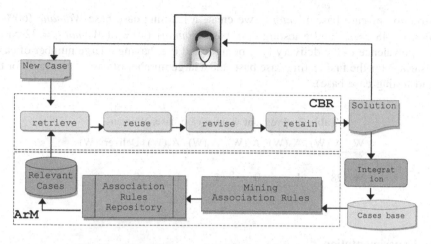

Fig. 4. ArM-CBR reasoning for managing a new case.

4   Experimental Setup

The architecture of the proposed approach (Fig. 4) is based on JColibri [19] and Weka [20]. The JColibri platform is used to build the case base and all the relative operations for CBR and Weka platform is used for *ArM* process. The transferral process between the two platforms is essentially insured by a module written as an application in Java.

4.1   Data Set Description

We use a dataset (Table 1) containing information about caesarian section results of 80 pregnant women with the most important characteristics of delivery problems in the medical field. Each pregnant women is represented by: age, delivery number, delivery time [Premature, Timely, Latercomer], blood pressure [Low, Normal, High] and heart status [Apt, Inept] and Delivery {0, 1} corresponding to delivery "Normal" and "Caesarian" [21].

Table 1. Overview of pregnant women database sample [21].

Data set sample
22, 1, 0, 2, 0, 0
....
32, 3, 0, 1, 0, 1

4.2   Pretreatment

An initial transformation of the data set (Table 1) into a case base named $Woman_N$ (Table 2) is done. It contains a number of cases W_i (pregnant woman) where each case is described by attributes A_1, A_2, A_3, A_4, A_5, and Delivery as a target attribute. After construction of case base $Woman_N$, we create a learning case base $Woman_L$ (60% of $Woman_N$ = 48 cases) and a testing case base $Woman_T$ (40% of $Woman_N$ = 32 cases) with a prevalence of the delivery type being tested (i.e. having a large number of cases "Caesarian" for the first testing case base and a large number of cases "Normal" for the second testing case base).

Table 2. Pregnant women case base: $Woman_N$.

W	$A_1(W)$	$A_2(W)$	$A_3(W)$	$A_4(W)$	$A_5(W)$	Delivery(W)
...						
W_i	28	1	0	2	0	0
...						

4.3   Experimentation

We consider 20 cases for each delivery type randomly taken from the testing case base $Woman_T$ without any initial hypothesis. A comparison of each case under $Woman_T$ is done with the learning case base $Woman_L$ with the following heuristic:

$$\left. \begin{array}{c} \forall\, W_i \in Woman_T \\ and \\ \forall\, W_j \in Woman_L \end{array} \right\{ \begin{array}{c} \text{if Delivery}(A(W_i)) = \text{Delivery}(A(W_j)) \text{ then Concordance} \\ \text{Else Discordance} \end{array} \quad (1)$$

Then, we calculate the error rate of each type of delivery with the formula (2). This rate represents the number of cases differently identified (in term of delivery) in $Woman_L$ compared to the existing delivery in $Woman_T$. The test results are presented in Table 3.

$$\text{Error Rate (ER)} = (\text{misclassified cases} * 100)/\text{Total cases} \quad (2)$$

4.4   Results and Analysis

As mentioned above (Sect. 1), our goal is not to look at the gain in processing time or storage space of the results, but rather a reduction of the search space by a technique which allows to lighten the procedure of finding a solution for a given case.

From this postulate, we can notice in Table 3 that the rate of concordance (similar delivery) is relatively important for Caesarian and for Normal which indicates that the approach provides hopeful results for computing a delivery close the reality as existing in testing case base $Woman_T$. We notice that our approach tends to recognize the appropriate delivery in case base for Caesarian and Normal or at least that recognition tends to be correctly over 80%. This shows that our approach tends to make a good recognition of delivery.

Table 3. Results with error rate (ER).

Number of Cases tested from Woman$_T$	Delivery	Concordance	Discordance	ER %
20	Caesarian	17	3	15
20	Normal	16	4	20

5   Conclusion and Future Trends

This study provides the theoretical basis of an approach that tends to solve a problem of CBR reasoning by using association rules mining. The advantages gained from using such proposed method, is a reduction case base (search space) to avoid a lengthy and complex processing. Indeed, it becomes interesting to limit by an association rules process the interesting cases, and we locate the best subspace which could contain only the relevant cases and so the relevant solution.

Later, we intend to evolve our approach in another orientation by adding a procedure which allows the user defining the dominant attributes (prevailing attributes) to consider when mining association rules. The Association Rules Mining will be more refined and will reduce the number of rules and at the same time the number of cases or the search space.

References

1. Aamodt, A., Plaza, E.: Case-based reasoning: foundational issues, methodological variations, and system approaches. AI Commun. **7**(1), 39–59 (1994)
2. Begum, S., Ahmed, M.U., Funk, P., Xiong, N., Folke, M.: Case-based reasoning systems in the health sciences: a survey of recent trends and developments. IEEE Trans. Syst. Man Cybern. Part C Appl. Rev. **41**(4), 421–434 (2011)
3. Bichindaritz, I., Marling, C.: Case-based reasoning in the health sciences: foundations and research directions. In: Bichindaritz, I., Vaidya, S., Jain, A., Jain, L.C. (eds.) Computational Intelligence in Healthcare 4, vol. 309, pp. 127–157. Springer, Heidelberg (2010). https://doi.org/10.1007/978-3-642-14464-6_7
4. Montani, S.: Exploring new roles for case-based reasoning in heterogeneous AI systems for medical decision support. Appl. Intell. **28**(3), 275–285 (2008)
5. Pandey, B., Mishra, R.B.: Data mining and CBR integrated methods in medicine: a review. Int. J. Med. Eng. Inform. **2**(2), 205–218 (2010)
6. Benamina, M., Atmani, B., Benbelkacem, S.: Diabetes diagnosis by case-based reasoning and fuzzy logic. IJIMAI **5**(3), 72–80 (2018)
7. Saadi, F., Atmani, B., Henni, F.: Integration of data mining techniques into the CBR cycle to predict the result of immunotherapy treatment. In: 2019 International Conference on Computer and Information Sciences (ICCIS), pp. 1–5. IEEE, April 2019
8. Marling, C., Rissland, E., Aamodt, A.: Integrations with case-based reasoning. Knowl. Eng. Rev. **20**(3), 241–245 (2005)
9. Malathi, D., Logesh, R., Subramaniyaswamy, V., Vijayakumar, V., Sangaiah, A.K.: Hybrid reasoning-based privacy-aware disease prediction support system. Comput. Electr. Eng. **73**, 114–127 (2019)

10. Lee, P.C., Lo, T.P., Tian, M.Y., Long, D.: An efficient design support system based on automatic rule checking and case-based reasoning. KSCE J. Civ. Eng. **23**(5), 1952–1962 (2019)
11. Balakrishnan, V., Shakouri, M.R., Hoodeh, H.: Integrating association rules and case-based reasoning to predict retinopathy. Maejo Int. J. Sci. Technol. **6**(3), 334 (2012)
12. Bichindaritz, I.: Data mining methods for case-based reasoning in health sciences. In: ICCBR (Workshops), pp. 184–198 (2015)
13. Schmidt, R., Montani, S., Bellazzi, R., Portinale, L., Gierl, L.: Cased-based reasoning for medical knowledge-based systems. Int. J. Med. Inform. **64**(2), 355–367 (2001)
14. Mansoul, A., Atmani, B.: Clustering to enhance case-based reasoning. In: Chikhi, S., Amine, A., Chaoui, A., Kholladi, M.K., Saidouni, D.E. (eds.) Modelling and Implementation of Complex Systems. LNNS, vol. 1, pp. 137–151. Springer, Cham (2016). https://doi.org/10. 1007/978-3-319-33410-3_10
15. Xu, L.D.: An integrated rule and case-based approach to AIDS initial assessment. Int. J. Biomed. Comput. **40**(3), 197–207 (1996)
16. Kumar, K.A., Singh, Y., Sanyal, S.: Hybrid approach using case-based reasoning and rule-based reasoning for domain independent clinical decision support in ICU. Expert Syst. Appl. **36**(1), 65–71 (2009)
17. Saraiva, R., Perkusich, M., Silva, L., Siebra, C., Perkusich, A.: Early diagnosis of gastrointestinal cancer by using case-based and rule-based reasoning. Expert Syst. Appl. **61**, 192–202 (2016)
18. Agrawal, R., Imielinski, T., Swami, A.: Mining associations between sets of items in large databases. Acm Sigmod Rec. **22**(2), 207–216 (1993)
19. Bello-Tomás, J.J., González-Calero, P.A., Díaz-Agudo, B.: JColibri: an object-oriented framework for building CBR systems. In: Funk, P., González Calero, P.A. (eds.) ECCBR 2004. LNCS (LNAI), vol. 3155, pp. 32–46. Springer, Heidelberg (2004). https://doi.org/10. 1007/978-3-540-28631-8_4
20. Holmes, G., Donkin, A., Witten, I.H.: WEKA: a machine learning workbench. In: Proceedings of the 1994 Second Australian and New Zealand Conference on Intelligent Information Systems, pp. 357–361. IEEE (1994)
21. UciHomepage.   https://archive.ics.uci.edu/ml/datasets/Caesarian+Section+Classification +Dataset

Stochastic Local Search Based Feature Selection Combined with K-means for Clients' Segmentation in Credit Scoring

Dalila Boughaci[1]([✉])[iD] and Abdullah A. K. Alkhawaldeh[2]

[1] Computer Science Department, LRIA-FEI- USTHB,
BP 32 El-Alia Bab-Ezzouar, 16111 Algiers, Algeria
dboughaci@usthb.dz, dalila_info@yahoo.fr
[2] Department of Accounting, Faculty of Economics and Administrative Sciences,
The Hashemite University, Zarqa, Jordan
alkwaldhh@yahoo.com

Abstract. Segmentation also called clustering is the most important means of data mining. It is an unsupervised learning technique that may be used to split a large dataset into groups. In this work, we propose a new clustering technique that combines the well-known k-means clustering technique with a stochastic local search meta-heuristic. The proposed method is applied to cluster creditworthy customers/companies against non-credit worthy ones in credit scoring. Empirical studies are conducted on five financial datasets. The numerical results are interesting and show the benefits of the proposed technique for banks and clients segmentation.

Keywords: Clustering · Credit scoring · K-means · Stochastic local search · Feature selection

1 Introduction

Data mining is the process that permits to discover patterns in large datasets by using a set of techniques and algorithms. Clustering is the most important means of data mining. Clustering also called segmentation is an unsupervised learning algorithm that may be used to split a large dataset into clusters. In this work, we are interested in clustering for credit scoring in banking and finance. We use clustering to cluster creditworthy customers against non-credit worthy ones.

The clustering technique is an interesting tool that can help banks and managers in decision-making. The process is to split a large dataset (a set of clients or companies in our case) into groups (or clusters) according to a certain common characteristic. The clustering techniques have been used in several areas in particular for credit scoring (CS) in banking and finance. The CS process is used to distinguish between good and bad clients in terms of their creditworthiness.

© Springer Nature Switzerland AG 2019
A. Alfaries et al. (Eds.): ICC 2019, CCIS 1097, pp. 119–131, 2019.
https://doi.org/10.1007/978-3-030-36365-9_10

Each client is evaluated according to its profile in order to predict the probability that such client will default or become delinquent [1,21].

The profile of the client can be defined as a set of descriptive variables or features such as: the age of client, his salary, his historical payments, the guarantees, and default rates. CS is then the evaluation function that takes as input the client's profile and returns a decision whether accepting or rejecting the client's credit [2,13,20].

Several CS models have been developed. Among them, we cite the following ones: the statistical techniques such as: the discriminant analysis and logistic regression [11,14,24], the support vector machines [4], the decision trees [23], the Random Decision Forests [16], the evolution strategy [18], the ensemble classifier [3], the classification and regression trees [9], the neural networks [10], the Bayesian networks [12], the k-nearest neighbor classifier [15], the genetic programming [2], the cooperative agent technology [6], the local search methods [7] and the variable selection method for CS [8].

In this paper, we propose a new clustering technique to classify clients into two categories: "bad" and "good". First we consider k-means algorithm to partition data into clusters. We note that a popular performance function for measuring goodness of the k-clustering is the total within-cluster variance. The centroid of a cluster is defined as the average of all points in the cluster. The clustering algorithm attempts to minimize the intra-cluster variance. However in the classical version of the k-means algorithm the initial starting centroids are chosen randomly which can lead to local optima. In order to enhance the performance and attempt to find a good k-clustering minimizing the cluster variance, we propose to use a stochastic local search method (SLS) to generate a good initial centroid for k-means. We use SLS for feature selection as a prepressing step before starting the k-means algorithm.

Experiments are conducted on five well-known financial datasets which are: German, Australian, Polish, Indian and Taiwan default of credit card clients' datasets available on UCI (University of California at Irvine) Machine Learning Repository [25]. The performance of the proposed technique is then evaluated by using the sum squared error (SSE) standard metric. The numerical results are interesting and show the benefits of the considered technique for banks and customers segmentation.

The rest of this paper is organized as follows: Sect. 2 describes the CS formalization. Section 3 gives a background on both stochastic local search and clustering concepts. Section 4 details the proposed approach. The considered datasets used in this study, the experiments and some numerical results are given in Sect. 5. Finally Sect. 6 concludes and gives some future work.

2   Problem Formalization

Credit scoring (CS) is an important problem in banking and finance. CS can be modeled as a classification problem where the aim is to classify data into classes. This can be done by separating data of similar nature to obtain class or group of each data [19].

Given a set of clients or companies to be partitioned into two main groups, the credit data can be organized as a matrix Data of m rows and n columns where n is the number of features representing the profile of clients/companies and m is the number of clients/companies. Each row of the matrix represents the profile of a client/company. The profile is defined as a set of n values $\{x_{i1}, x_{i2} \ldots x_{in}\}$ where x_{ij} is the value of the feature j related to the client/company numbered as i.

$$\mathbf{Data} = \begin{bmatrix} a_{11} & a_{12} & \cdots & a_{1n} \\ a_{21} & a_{22} & \cdots & a_{2n} \\ \vdots & \vdots & \ddots & \vdots \\ a_{m1} & a_{m2} & \cdots & a_{mn} \end{bmatrix}$$

The aim is to split the data into two main clusters by separating clients into two categories. The decision is whether accepting or rejecting the client's credit. The accepted clients/companies are put in class or cluster number 1 (good clients/companies) and the rejected one are classed in cluster number 0 (bad clients/companies). The decision is then represented as a vector Y with m elements where each element y_i has two possible values 0 or 1.

When the client/company i is accepted the element y_i receives the value 1, 0 otherwise.

$$\mathbf{Y} = \begin{bmatrix} y_1 \\ y_2 \\ y_3 \\ \vdots \\ y_n \end{bmatrix}$$

3   Background

Both classification and clustering are one of the common techniques used in data mining [22]. Classification is used to classify data into classes while clustering is used to separate data of similar nature into groups. In this section, we explain the concepts of k-means the clustering method which we used to partition data. Then we present the stochastic local search method. The latter will be combined with k-means to enhance the goodness of the k-clustering.

3.1   K-means Clustering

A cluster is a set of instances (called also objects or points) such that an instance in a cluster is closer to the "center" of a cluster, than to the center of any other cluster. The k-means clustering algorithm is an unsupervised learning, which is used when we have unlabeled data without defined categories. The aim is to form clusters in the data where k is the number of the clusters to be created [17]. When the value of k is equal to 2, the data will be portioned into two clusters or groups. The instances are assigned to the cluster with the nearest mean.

The classical k-means algorithm is based mainly on Euclidean distance measure that computes distances between instances and clusters. The k-means algorithm starts with an initial partition by taking two furthest instances apart. We obtain two initial clusters. For each cluster, we compute the mean Vector (called cluster centroid) according to the features values of each instance in the cluster and by using the Euclidean distance measure. Then, we examine iteratively the rest of instances to be allocated to the cluster to which they are closest, in terms of Euclidean distance to the cluster mean. The cluster centroid is recomputed each time a new instance is added. In order to verify that each instance has been assigned to the right cluster, we must ensure that the distance of each instance to its own cluster is smaller than the distance to the opposite cluster. When an instance is nearer to the mean of the opposite cluster than its own, the instance should be reallocated to the opposite cluster. This process is repeated until no more reallocations occur or for a certain number of iterations fixed empirically. The basic code of k-means is sketched in Algorithm 1.

Algorithm 1. k-means clustering

1: Select randomly k instances as the initial centroids
2: **repeat**
3:    From k clusters by assigning all instances to the closest centroid
4:    Compute the centroid of each cluster
5: **until** the centroids don't change.

3.2   Stochastic Local Search (SLS)

The stochastic local search (SLS) is a local search meta-heuristic which has been already studied for several optimization problem such as satisfiability and optimal winner determination problem (WDP) in combinatorial auctions [5]. SLS starts with an initial solution generated randomly. Then, it performs a certain number of local steps that combines diversification and intensification strategies to locate good solutions in the search space. The diversification phase selects a random neighbor solution. The intensification phase selects a best neighbor solution according to the accuracy measure. The diversification phase is applied with a fixed probability $wp > 0$ and the intensification phase with a probability $1 - wp$. The wp is a probability fixed empirically. SLS is an iterative process that should be repeated until a certain number of iterations or a criterion is reached [5].

In this work, we use SLS as a feature selection method. The objective is then to find the optimal subsets of features by finding optimal combinations of features from the dataset. The selected potential features can increase the goodness of k-clustering.

4   Proposed Approach

In this section, we propose to combine the stochastic local search (SLS) with k-means. The aim is to obtain good clusters. As depicted in Fig. 1, SLS is used as a pre-processing step before the k-clustering task. SLS is launched in order to select the most significant features to be used to form the centroids and create good clusters. More precisely, SLS is used for feature selection. It removes the redundant features that are deemed irrelevant to the data clustering task. The different components of our approach will be detailed in the next subsections.

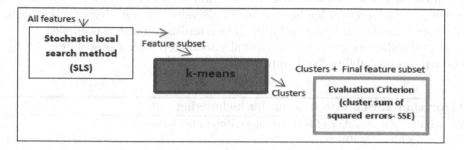

Fig. 1. SLS for k-means unsupervised learning

4.1   The Feature Vector Representation

The feature selection is a pre-processing step where the aim is to select a set of significant feature to be used in the classification or the clustering tasks. We have already studied the effect of feature selection on the classification task [8]. In this work, we are interested in data clustering.

We propose to enhance the k-clustering performance by using the stochastic local search method as a feature selection method. We use a binary vector to represent the features. This binary vector denotes the features presented in the dataset, with the length of the vector equal to n, where n is the number of features of the data. When a feature is selected, the value 1 is assigned to it, a value 0 is assigned to it otherwise. For example, Fig. 2 represents an assignment. We have a dataset of seven features where the second, the third and the sixth features are selected.

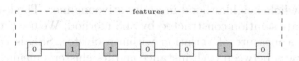

Fig. 2. The feature vector representation

4.2   The Proposed SLS for Feature Selection

We propose to use SLS as a feature selection method. SLS starts with an initial solution considering all the features. Then neighbors' solutions are generated by randomly adding or deleting a feature. We use both intensification and diversification strategies to generate good solutions and avoiding local optima. In the intensification step, the neighbor solution x' of a current solution x is obtained by modifying one bit. For example, if n the number of features equals to 6 and x = 111111 is a current solution vector, then the set of possible neighbor solutions can be represented as: **0**11111, 1**0**1111, 11**0**111, 111**0**11, 1111**0**1, 11111**0**. The intensification consists in selecting the best neighbor solution among the set of the possible solution having the best SSE value. In the diversification step, we select a random neighbor solution. The intensification step is applied with a fixed probability wp > 0 and the diversification step with a probability (1-wp). The wp is a probability fixed empirically.

Algorithm 2. SLS with k-means for k-clustering

Require: :n the number of features, max_iterations, wp.

 1: Start with all features.
 2: Apply k-means on the current data
 3: Evaluate the fitness of x noted f(x) by using the secured error function
 4: **for** $I = 1$ to $max\_iterations$ **do**
 5:     r ← random number between 0 and1.
 6:     **if** $(r < wp)$ **then**
 7:         $xnewi$ = a random neighbor solution
 8:     **else**
 9:         Generate the neighborhood solutions of x;
10:         Evaluate the fitness of each neighbor x by using the secured error function
11:         $xnewi$ = pick a best neighbor solution according to the fitness value
12:     **end if**
13:     **if** $(f(xnewi) < f(x))$ **then**
14:         $x = xnewi$
15:     **end if**
16: **end for**
17: **return** A set of selected features xbest, clusters with minimum of SSE.

The proposed SLS is combined with k-means. The overall method starts with an initial solution considering all the features and then tries to find a good solution in the whole neighborhood in an iterative manner. The k-means is built for each candidate solution constructed by SLS method. We use the sum squared error (SSE) as a measure of variation within a cluster. SSE is the sum of the squared differences between each instance and its cluster's mean.

$$SSE = \sum_{i}^{k} \sum_{x \in C_i} dist^2(m_i, x)$$

where x is a data point in cluster C_i and m_i is the representative point of the cluster.

This means that the solution quality is measured by using an objective function given as: $f(x) = $ SSE where the aim is to minimize this value. The SLS process is repeated for a certain number of iterations (max_iterations) fixed empirically. The overall SLS with k-means algorithm is sketched in Algorithm 2.

5 Empirical Study

In this section, we start with the description of the five financial datasets used in this study. Then, we give some numerical results found by the proposed approaches.

5.1 Considered Datasets

We evaluate our methods on five financial datasets which are: German, Australian, Polish, Indian Qualitative Bankruptcy and Taiwan default of credit card clients' datasets available on UCI (University of California at Irvine) Machine Learning Repository [25]. Table 1 gives details about datasets related to customers' applicants. For instance, German dataset consists of 1000 instances of loan applicants dived into two main classes worthy, 700 instances unworthy, 300 instances. The number of features characterized each customer is equals to 21. Another example is the Polish dataset of Table 2 that consists of 5910 instances of loan applicants in the case of companies. There are two classes: Bankruptcy, 410 instances and non- bankruptcy 5500 instances. The number of feature characterized a company is equals to 64.

Table 1. Description of the datasets (case of customers) used in the study

Dataset	#Loans	#Good loans	#Bad loans	#features
Australian	690	307	383	15
German	1000	700	300	21
Taiwan	30000	6636	23364	24

Table 2. Description of the datasets (case of companies) used in the study

Dataset	#Companies	Non-bankruptcy	Bankruptcy	#features
Polish	5910	410	5500	65
Indian	250	143	107	7

5.2 Numerical Results

All experiments were run on an Intel Core(TM) i5-2217U CPU@1.70 GHz with 6 GB of RAM under Windows 8 64 bits, processor x64. The SLS parameters are fixed as follows: The maximum number of iterations is set to 50. The wp is set to 0.6. In the following, we give the numerical results obtained in this study.

Tables 4 ad 3 give the numerical results found by both k-means and SLS with k-means (the proposed approach). For each method, we give the clustered instances, the number of features and the SSE. From the experiments, we can see that the proposed approach succeeds in finding good results. The SLS succeeds in reducing the number of the features.

Table 3. K-means versus SLS with k-means on German and Australian datasets

Dataset		Australian dataset	German dataset
Full dataset		690 instances	1000 instances
k-means	Clustered	0 323 (47%)	0 786 (79%)
	Instances	1 367 (53%)	1 214 (21%)
	Number of features (without class)	14	20
	Sum of squared errors (SSE)	2863.0	5589.0
SLS with k-means	Clustered	0 374 (54%)	0 836 (84%)
	Instances	1 316 (46%)	1 164 (16%)
	Number of selected features	**4**	**7**
	Sum of squared errors (SSE)	**439.0**	**520.0**

The k-means with SLS permits to enhance the goodness of the k-clustering with a reduced SSE. This is done for all the considered datasets. For example for German dataset the SSE was 5589.0 when we used k-means alone. However the SSE is equal to **520.0** with the proposed method SLS with k-means and the number of the considered features is reduced to **7**.

The same remark is with the Australian dataset. The SSE was 2863.0 with k-means while SLS with k-means gives a SSE equals to **439.0** with only **4** selected features.

For the Indian dataset, the SSE was 583.0 when using only k-means. The SSE is reduced to **167.0** when using SLS combined with k-means with only **2** selected features.

For the Polish dataset, the SSE was 89431.0 when using the pure k-means. The SSE is enhanced when we have used the SLS with k-means. The SSE is reduced to **39654.0** with only **32** selected features.

Table 4. K-means versus SLS with k-means on Taiwan, Polish and Indian datasets.

Dataset		Taiwan dataset		Polish dataset		Indian dataset	
Full dataset		3000 instances		5910 instances		250 instances	
k-means	Clustered	0	20436 (68 %)	0	4589 (78%)	0	119 (48%)
	Instances	1	9564 (32%)	1	1321 (22%)	1	131 (52%)
	Number of features (without class)	23		64		6	
	Sum of squared errors (SSE)	180013.0		89431.0		583.0	
SLS with k-means	Clustered	0	23305 (78%)	0	1814 (31%)	0	151 (60%)
	Instances	1	6695 (22%)	1	4096 (69%)	1	99 (40%)
	Number of selected features	**11**		**32**		**2**	
	Sum of squared errors (SSE)	**93448.0**		**39654.0**		**167.0**	

For the Taiwan dataset, k-means gives a SSE equals to 180013.0 while the proposed approach succeeds to form clusters with an enhanced SSE equals to **93448.0** with only **11** features.

For further comparison, we give information about the obtained centroids. As already said, the centroid is the main characteristic of a cluster. As shown in Table 5, we give an example of the centroid of each cluster computed with k-means for the German dataset. For example, the centroid for cluster 1 of the German dataset shows that this is a segment of customers with middle feature 1(*checking_status*) value of (<0) with an average value of feature 4 (purpose) value of (new car) and average feature 7 (employment) of value (≥7), etc.

We give also an example of the centroid of each cluster computed with SLS combined with k-means for the German dataset. In this case, we consider only the seven potential features obtained by SLS as shown in Table 6.

As shown in Table 7, we give an example of the centroid of each cluster computed with k-means for the Indian dataset. For example, the centroid for cluster 1 of the Indian dataset shows that this is a segment of companies with middle feature 1(IR) value of (N) with an average value of feature 2 (MR) value of (N) and average feature 3 (FF) of value (N), etc.

We give also an example of the centroid of each cluster computed with SLS combined with k-means for the Indian dataset. In this case, we consider only the two potential features obtained by SLS as shown in Table 8.

According to the numerical results, we can say that the proposed k-clustering technique succeeds in improving the goodness of the obtained clusters. For German, Australian, Taiwan, Indian and Polish datasets, SLS with k-means gives high quality results compared to the pure k-means. This is due to the SLS search

Table 5. Final cluster centroids for German dataset with k-means clustering

Feature (mean value)	Full Data (1000)	Cluster 0 (786)	Cluster 1 (214)
checking_status	no checking	no checking	<0
duration	'(15.5-inf)'	'(15.5-inf)'	'(15.5-inf)'
credit_history	existing paid	existing paid	existing paid
purpose	radio/tv	radio/tv	new car
credit_amount	'(-inf-3913.5]'	'(-inf-3913.5]'	'(-inf-3913.5]'
savings_status	<100	<100	<100
employment	$1 \leq X < 4$	$1 \leq X < 4$	≥ 7
installment_commitment	'All'	'All'	'All'
other_parties	none	None	None
residence_since	'All'	'All'	'All'
personal_status	male single	male single	male single
property_magnitude	car	Car	no known property
Age	'All'	'All'	'All'
other_payment_plans	none	None	None
housing	own	Own	Own
existing_credits	'All'	'All'	'All'
Job	skilled	skilled	high qualif/ /self emp/mgmt
num_dependents	'All'	'All'	'All'
own_telephone	none	none	Yes
foreign_worker	yes	yes	Yes

Table 6. Final cluster centroids for German dataset with SLS combined with k-means clustering

Feature (mean value)	Full Data (1000)	Cluster 0 (836)	Cluster 1 (164)
residence_since	'All'	'All'	'All'
Age	'All'	'All'	'All'
existing_credits	'All'	'All'	'All'
Job	skilled	skilled	high qualif/ /self emp/mgmt.
num_dependents	'All'	'All'	'All'
own_telephone	none	None	Yes
foreign_worker	yes	yes	Yes

Table 7. Final cluster centroids for Indian dataset with k-means clustering

Feature (mean value)	Full Data (250)	Cluster 0 (119)	Cluster 1 (131)
IR (mean value)	N	A	N
MR (mean value)	N	P	N
FF (mean value)	N	A	N
CR (mean value)	N	P	N
CO (mean value)	N	P	N
OP (mean value)	N	P	N

Table 8. Final cluster centroids for Indian dataset with SLS combined with k-means clustering

Feature (mean value)	Full Data (250)	Cluster 0 (151)	Cluster 1 (99)
CO	N	P	N
OP	N	P	N

method that permits to reduce the SSE error and select only a set of potential features to use in the clustering task.

6   Conclusion

Clustering is the most important means of data mining. In this paper we proposed an enhanced k-clustering technique for credit scoring and bankruptcy prediction in banking and finance. We proposed a stochastic local search method (SLS) as a feature selection to select only potential features to be used in the clustering task. SLS is combined with k-means to create good clusters. We used SLS with k-means to cluster data. We considered five well-known financial datasets. The numerical results are encouraging and show the benefits of the considered technique for loans segmentation. When SLS is used with k-means clustering the results are interesting. The SSE is reduced and the goodness of clusters is enhanced. The SLS improved highly the data clustering for credit scoring for all the considered datasets. It would be nice to evaluate other clustering techniques on CS. On other hand, it would be interesting to study the impact of other meta-heuristics on k-clustering.

References

1. Abdou, H., Pointon, J.: Credit scoring, statistical techniques and evaluation criteria: a review of the literature. Intell. Syst. Account. Financ. Manag. **18**(2–3), 59–88 (2011)
2. Abdou, H.: Genetic programming for credit scoring: the case of Egyptian public sector banks. Expert Syst. Appl. **36**, 11402–11417 (2009)

3. Abelln, J., Mantas, C.J.: Improving experimental studies about ensembles of classifiers for bankruptcy prediction and credit scoring. Expert Syst. Appl. **41**, 3825–3830 (2014)
4. Bellotti, T., Crook, J.: Support vector machines for credit scoring and discovery of significant features. Expert Syst. Appl. **2009**(36), 3302–3308 (2009)
5. Boughaci, D.: Metaheuristic approaches for the winner determination problem in combinatorial auction. In: Yang, X.S. (ed.) Artificial Intelligence, Evolutionary Computing and Metaheuristics. SCI, vol. 427, pp. 775–791. Springer, Heidelberg (2013). https://doi.org/10.1007/978-3-642-29694-9_29
6. Boughaci, D., Alkhawaldeh, A.A.K.: A cooperative classification system for credit scoring. In: Al-Masri, A., Curran, K. (eds.) Smart Technologies and Innovation for a Sustainable Future. Advances in Science, Technology and Innovation (IEREK Interdisciplinary Series for Sustainable Development), pp. 11–20. Springer, Cham (2019). https://doi.org/10.1007/978-3-030-01659-3_2
7. Boughaci, D., Alkhawaldeh, A.A.K.: Three local search based methods for feature selection in credit scoring. Vietnam. J. Comput. Sci. **5**(2), 107–121 (2018)
8. Boughaci, D., Alkhawaldeh, A.A.K.: A new variable selection method applied to credit scoring. Algorithmic Finance **7**(1–2), 43–52 (2018)
9. Breiman, L., Friedman, J., Olshen, R., Stone, C.: Classification and Regression Trees, p. 1984. Wadsworth, Belmont (1984)
10. Desay, V., Crook, J.N., Overstreet, G.A.: A comparison of neural networks and linear scoring models in the credit union environment. Eur. J. Oper. Res. **95**(1996), 24–37 (1996)
11. Friedman, J., Hastie, T., Tibshirani, R.: Additive logistic regression: a statistical view of boosting. Ann. Stat. **28**(2), 337–407 (2000)
12. Friedman, N., Geiger, D., Goldszmidt, M.: Bayesian network classifiers. Mach. Learn. **29**, 131–163 (1997)
13. Gonzales, F., et al.: Market dynamics associated with credit ratings: a literature review. Banque de France in Financial Stability Review **4**, 53–76 (2004)
14. Hand, D.J., Henley, W.E.: Statistical classification methods in consumer credit scoring. J. R. Stat. Soc. Ser. (Stat. Soc.) **160**, 523–541 (1997)
15. Henley, W.E., Hand, D.J.: A k-nearest neighbour classifier for assessing consumer credit risk. Statistician **45**, 77–95 (1996)
16. Ho, T.K.: Random decision forests. In: Proceedings of the 3rd International Conference on Document Analysis and Recognition, Montreal, QC, 14–16 August 1995, pp. 278–282 (1995)
17. Kanungo, T., Mount, D., Netanyahu, N.S., Piatko, C.D., Silverman, R., Wu, A.Y.: An efficient k-means clustering algorithm: analysis and implementation. IEEE Trans. Pattern Anal. Mach. Intell. **24**, 881–892 (2002)
18. Li, J., Wei, L., Li, G., Xu, W.: An evolution strategy-based multiple kernels multi-criteria programming approach: the case of credit decision making. Decis. Support Syst. **51**, 292–298 (2011)
19. Milne, A., Rounds, M., Goddard, P.: Optimal feature selection in credit scoring and classification using a quantum annealer (2017). https://1qbit.com/whitepaper/optimal-feature-selection-in-credit-scoring-classification-using-quantum-annealer/
20. Mester, L.J.: What's the point of credit scoring? Bus. Rev. **3**(September), 3–16 (1997)
21. Miller, M.: Research confirms value of credit scoring. Natl. Underwrit. **107**(42), 30 (2003)

22. Phyu, T.N.: Survey of classification techniques in data mining. In: Proceedings of the International Multi Conference of Engineers and Computer Scientists, IMECS 2009, Hong Kong, 18–20 March 2009, vol. I (2009)
23. Quinlan, J.R.: Simplifying decision trees. Int. J. Man-Mach. Stud. **27**, 221–234 (1987)
24. Wiginton, J.C.: A note on the comparison of logit and discriminant models of consumer credit behavior. J. Financ. Quant. Anal. **15**, 757–770 (1980)
25. Web site of the considered datasets. https://archive.ics.uci.edu/ml/datasets

Real Time Search Technique for Distributed Massive Data Using Grid Computing

Mohammed Bakri Bashir[1(✉)], Adil Yousif[2],
and Muhammad Shafie Abd Latiff[3]

[1] Department of Computer Science, Turabah University College,
Taif University, Turabah, Saudi Arabia
mhmdbakri@gmail.com
[2] Department of Computer Science, Najran University, Najran, Saudi Arabia
Adiluofk@gmail.com
[3] Faculty of Computing, Universiti Teknologi Malaysia,
Johor Bahru, Johor, Malaysia
shafie@utm.my

Abstract. The development of the grid-based searching techniques for distributed large scale has recently become the trend and it is applied in different type of domains such as information retrieval, digital libraries, and spatial domain. Several techniques were proposed to provide flexible methods for searching a vast distributed data by harnessing grid computing capabilities. Despite these remarkable efforts, the technique's performance remains major challenge in the field of data file search systems. This paper proposes Grid-enabler Search Technique (GST) for massive datasets. GST is implemented as interconnected grid services to provide a means to interact among different virtual organizations. The experiments were conducted to evaluate the performance of GST by measuring the response time, speed up, and efficiency. The result shows that GST has reasonable response time by increasing the speed up and the efficiency of the GST as well as enhancing the performance of the system.

Keywords: Grid computing · Large-scale dataset · Search technique · Data-intensive applications · Big data

1 Introduction

In many scientific and business sectors, massive data collections of gigabyte and terabyte scale need to be accessed. Moreover, in several cases datasets must be shared by large communities of users that pool their resources from different sites location or from a large number of institutions [1]. For these reasons, distributed data sharing is the vital part of a distributed community, and an efficient data sharing infrastructure is crucial to make the distributed information available to users in a timely and reliable manner. However, data sharing in large-scale communities are very challenging due to the potential large amounts of data, diverseness, distributed arrangement, and dynamic nature [2]. These challenges are in the form of providing suitable infrastructures and

© Springer Nature Switzerland AG 2019
A. Alfaries et al. (Eds.): ICC 2019, CCIS 1097, pp. 132–147, 2019.
https://doi.org/10.1007/978-3-030-36365-9_11

techniques to address issues regarding computation power such as (i) The data centers produce large number of data every day, in which the information content needs to be analyzed and extracted. (ii) Continuous increase of the data size requires more resources to store the new produced data. (iii) Distributed dataset among several sites in different geographically locations requires the search to be disseminated across these sites. (iv) Unpredictable execution time of the search. The execution time depends on the number of the site involved in the search tasks and the number of query requires simultaneous processing. (v) To monitor and manage several search tasks at the same. (vi) To collect the result from sites and merge the results in one file.

Nonetheless, the aforementioned issues can be addressed by using grid technology, which provides a means to access, manage, control, and store the distributed data [3]. The grid technology provides big organizations and scientific centers a computing power in order to solve complex problems [4]. The implementation of grid is spread among scientific research to retrieve information from unstructured data that requires high preprocessing tasks [5]. The grid-based data sources have several features such as decentralization, heterogeneous, and dynamic, in which searching these data sources are a type of distributed query [6]. The addition of large-scale feature to the grid-based data source makes the search of these data a complex task [7]. Grid computing can handle the dynamicity of the organizations resources that joins or leaves the system at any time. Furthermore, grid computing presents the distribution of the data and resources for the end user as one big computer contains all the datasets. The searching process is performed as grid job, which monitors and is distributed over the datasets sites by the grid scheduler. This issue can be solved by designing and developing a new comprehensive search technique without the need of Gridification of a search technique. Gridification is the term used in grid community to identify the existing non-grid applications that have been adapted and transferred to run on the grid environment [8].

The paper describes and explains in details the design and implementation of the Grid-based Search Technique (GSA). The paper starts with the review of the related search techniques by using grid computing. The GST components as well as their functions are explained in details. The GST implements Distributed Data Balancer (DDB) algorithm and Result Streaming (RS) mechanism are illustrated in this paper. Moreover, the justification of the implementation of DDB algorithm and RS mechanism is explained. Subsequently, the experiments and the evaluation section are conducted to validate the search technique. This paper ends with a conclusion section.

2 Related Work

The distributed shared datasets will be beneficial if supported with access and search mechanism. The current sharing systems provide diverse ways to implement the search techniques for distributed dataset based on the grid infrastructure. Furthermore, the majority of the datasets is not in the form of database management system rather it is in a file form (documents, HTML, image, video, etc....), that means the query processing will not be useful to search these files. Several researches have proposed various search techniques to handle huge data by using grid technology. The techniques such as proposed by Maly, et al. [9], Meij and De Rijke [10], Nakashole and Suleman [11],

Nakashole [12], and Chihli Hung [13] used Lucene search engine to search the data. The MIFAS technique was used by Yang, et al. [14] and Yang, et al. [15], Grid Information Retrieval GIR was proposed by Shih, et al. [16], Ontology-based semantic search was proposed by Shih, et al. [17], finally, WIR technique was proposed by Trnkoczy, et al. [18], and Trnkoczy and Stankovski [19].

The performance of the search process is based on the factors such as fast response time and relevant results. The search systems as proposed by Maly, et al. [9], Robles, et al. [20], Larson and Sanderson [21], Sanderson and Larson [22], Trnkoczy, et al. [18], Shih, et al. [16], Trnkoczy and Stankovski [19], Shih, et al. [17], Nakashole [12], Toharia, et al. [23], Yang, et al. [15], and Chihli Hung [13] have fast response time, thus it is considered as a real time search technique. However, these systems search indexed data instead of the direct source of the data, which reduce the response time of the search system. Consequently, the search result in the high dynamic datasets will not be up to date because the search is based on the index, and index datasets are updated periodically not immediately. On the other hand, the systems proposed by Haya, et al. [24], Meij and De Rijke [10], Cambazoglu, et al. [25], and Chihli Hung [13] are considered as real time search techniques because these systems either use small dataset or the data search is performed on the indexed data. Additionally, the Online Data represented the search data directly instead of searching the index of the dataset. Bashir, et al. [26] provide a review for all the techniques for searching data over grid computing.

3 The Issues of Data Search Processes

The run of the search tasks over grid infrastructure requires addressing of many challenges and issues. However, the selection strategies of the data sources and grid resources will improve the search execution over the grid and enhance the system performance. The performance of the search is affected by node capabilities such as CPU speed and free memory; in addition, other issues are related to grid computing. Gounaris, et al. [27], Liu and Karimi [28], and Hameurlain [29] outlined the main issues of grid based search processes as follows:

1. The resources in traditional distributed computing are located in one location or distributed among several locations with similar capabilities. Nevertheless, grid computing resources are heterogeneous and they face the problem of resources selection. The problem is that the criteria applied to select the resources will be involved in the search process from unlimited and heterogeneous resources. Additionally, the scheduling of the search jobs to be run over the different nodes should be handled. Consequently, the space of the search task will be very large and the time consumes to distribute and map the nodes will be longer than the execution time for the applications themselves, as also reported by Singh, et al. [30].

2. The grid resources change dynamically by joining the grid or leaving the grid in an unpredictable manner. Additionally, the resources belong to several administrative organizations, which will increase the dynamicity of the resources. The capabilities of the resources such as free storage space and available computing resources are altered periodically. As a result, search jobs need to be evaluated depending on the

available resources at the runtime of the search besides considering the current capabilities of the resources.

3. The grid computing stores the data over distributed locations that are connected through network of the Internet are uncontrollable and cannot guarantee high bandwidth. Furthermore, the data grid is a data intensive application that spends most of the time processing the data as well as the requirement of transferring this data. Consequently, the bandwidth of the network and the transferred data size affect the search response time and may cause bottleneck problem.

4. The dynamicity of the resources makes the information about grid resources in the runtime inaccurate and may produce an error when submitting the jobs, thus affecting the performance of the system.

The aforementioned issues must be considered when designing and developing search technique based on grid computing.

4 Grid-Based Search Technique

The Grid-Based Search Technique (GST) is a group of modules that communicates with each other to provide a means to search for the distributed data as illustrated in Fig. 1. The technique is implemented as modules distributed over grid architecture to provide a mechanism to interaction among the VOs. The GST is implemented and integrated as grid services to enabled data search to run over Grid-based Sharing Architecture (GSA) proposed in [31] and to orchestrate the interaction over the grid nodes. The Local search engine module is a Java program installed in each worker node in the grid architecture and is responsible to perform the search process in the local dataset. Additionally, the other modules are implemented on the head node (broker) of every VO.

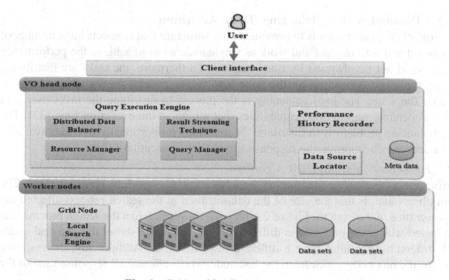

Fig. 1. Grid-enabler Search components.

4.1 GST Components

The study integrates two fields namely data search operations and grid services. On one hand, grid is required to provide platform to facilitate all the grid services such as data transfer, data location, and data replication. On the other hand, the search operations have been determined after studying different search applications and after identifying the nature of these searches techniques as well as the requirement of the grid to work under these techniques. The design and the functionality of the search components will be discussed in the following sections.

4.1.1 Query Search Engine (QEE)

QEE is the component that orchestrates and coordinates the query execution over the grid nodes. Additionally, the QEE has several instances distributed among VOs, in which each VO have instance of the QEE. This distribution of the services provides a decentralized search execution, which prevents the system from bottleneck and scalability problems. It means that each VO is equipped with one QEE service and each node in the VO deploys a copy of the local search engine. The QEE determines the nodes that will perform the search at run time by utilizing its internal modules. After the user submits the search text, the QEE will request the resources information from the Resource Manager who stores the status and all information about system resources. The lists of the data sources that are involved in the search task are gathered from the Data Source Locator component. The list of available resources and data sources are submitted to the DDB to produce the execution plan of the search jobs. The execution plan that distributes the datasets over the nodes depends on the previous performance and produces the best combination to handle the query. The results from the DDB are list of the resources and nodes that participate besides the text parameter which is submitted to the QM. The QM executes the search tasks and returns the result of the search to the end user.

4.1.2 Distributed Data Balancing (DDB) Algorithm

The goal of the grid system is to provide an infrastructure that connects huge number of distributed nodes to interact and work as single node so as to achieve the performance which could not be obtained by one computer. Furthermore, the tasks are distributed among grid node depending on the node load that represents the initial capability to execute the work. The load balancing is the process to distribute the tasks over grid nodes depending on the node capabilities that minimize the execution time [32]. The load balancing problem is to distribute the workload proportionally over the available grid nodes which improve the response time of jobs execution [33].

4.1.2.1 Justification of the DDB Algorithm

During the testing and evaluating of the GSA some observations were recorded. The main observation is that the size of the datasets used in the search process affected the response time of the system. Figure 2 represents the result when the search process was conducted with equal data size in different nodes. The figure shows that the grid nodes with different capabilities have a different response times. Additionally, the response time for the first node varies from the last node, which affected all response time of the users search. Furthermore, the response time is increased when the data size increases, even with the increasing number of grid nodes.

These observations have led the search technique to design and develop a new algorithm that balances the data distribution over the grid node. The algorithm is proposed because the number of records computed and the capabilities of the grid nodes determine the execution time of the job. Consequently, the response time relies on balancing the execution time over the grid and the number of data record on each node. The data balancing requires multiple executions with a change of datasets size until it reaches the optimal data distribution. The minimum and maximum execution time for running the query is calculated for each round. Additionally, the maximum and minimum time of the grid node are used to execute the job. Consequently, the time of the node with maximum execution time should have less number of records than the node with minimum execution time. With this situation, a number of data records should moved from the higher loaded node to the lower loaded node.

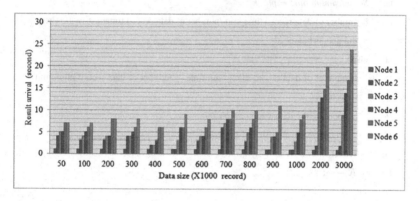

Fig. 2. Response time of each node for the same query

4.1.2.2 The DDB Algorithm Design

The DDB algorithm keeps the record sizes per datasets proportional to execution time, which is determined based on the prior execution results stored in the Performance History Record database. Thus, the data size is determined based on the predicate feature, which affects the execution time if big numbers of records are assigned to slower node. The DDB algorithm uses the previously assigned dataset size to anticipate the execution time for the next execution by adjusting the workload of the data size. The DDB divides the data set into p disjoint partitions, corresponding to n grid nodes. Each node k, where $k \leq n$, has predicated execution time T_k which is the total execution time T achieved by all nodes is $\sum_{k=1}^{n} T_k$. Thus, the partitioning of data size S to p partitions for each node n is calculated with $S_i = \frac{T_k}{T} \times s$ as explained in Algorithm 1.

Algorithm 1 Distributed Data Balancing algorithm

1: **N[]:** the nodes that will used to execute jobs.

2: **D[]:** the new distribution of data.

3: **Function** DDB(n[])

4: **Phr[]**=Read the previous performance record form PHR

5: **for** each node not exist in *phr* list **do**

6:    Data size for node= $\dfrac{All\ data\ size}{No\ of\ nodes}$

7: **end for**

8: Sort-ascending the list of performance history recorder;

9:

10: **for** $i = 1$ **to** round($n/2$) **do**

11:    *set minimum tim = phr[i]*;

12:    *Set maximum time = phr[k]*;

13:    **if** number of data record time min /number of data record timemax $= .05$ **then**

       the data is balanced

14:    **else**

15:       **if** number of data record maximum time $\geq$ number of data record minimum

          time **then**

16:          Increase the data size in $node_i 5\%$

17:          Decrease the data size of $node_k 5\%$

18:       **end if**

19:       $K--$;

20:    **end if**

21: **end for**

4.1.3 Query Manager (QM)

QM is the component that involves several functions to execute the user query in grid nodes and returns the best result relevant for the query to the user. One of the QM functions is to receive the list of all available resources in the grid that can be used to perform the query. The list of resources is assigned with the suitable data source that provides a better performance. Additionally, the QM creates the Job Description File (JDF) with all jobs that will be distributed over grid nodes and determined by the DDB module. The JDF contains the location of all data sources and the local search services that will participate on the search process. Additionally, the JDF includes the user query text as well as the location that should receive the result of the search. The QM is supported by the Result Streaming technique to enhance the system performance and reduce the response time. Furthermore, the QM keeps track of all job execution in the architecture by keeping the job information in the PHR. After the search task is completed, the QM sends the information about resource performance to the PHR to be used in the future search tasks. The query execution that passes several phases begins by receiving the user search text from the QEE which contains all the parameters selected by the user. The QEE submits to the QM a list with candidate resources and data source to perform the search. The QM creates JDF for each data sources separately from the other data source that contains the required information to accomplish the search. A thread is created for each JDF and is submitted to the destination nodes. When the node completes the search task, the result returns to the QM. Since the QM utilizes the SR technique, the result that arrives at the QM is immediately forwarded to the user client and the thread is released. The result streaming will continue until the last job is completed so that the resources used to accomplish the search will be cleared.

4.1.4   Result Streaming Technique

The observations were recorded during the experiments. The experiment was conducted by using six nodes and different size of datasets. The experiments show that the node with high capabilities computing (CPU, RAM,…) is faster than the node with low capabilities. Additionally, the differences of result arrival time between the first and last node vary from 6 s in small data set (50,000 records) to 20 s in large data sets (1,000,000 records). Consequently, the user that submits the query will receive the result after all nodes have completed their job and the result is submitted as one unit, which delays the response time.

QM has proposed solution for this problem by implementing the RS technique as explained in Fig. 3. The main goal of RS is to enhance query response time by streaming the result instead of waiting for all nodes to complete their jobs. RS utilizes the thread technology to enable the isolation of the jobs from each other and to run each job as separate thread. By applying this technique, the response time from every thread will not depend on the other threads. The RS allows the GST to utilize grid nodes and provide more resources to other jobs in order to perform in the released nodes. Furthermore, the RS speeds up the search response time and improves the real time search response.

4.1.5   Local Search Engine (LSE)

The distributed data sources are difficult to be accessed and to be searched by centralized search application. Instead, a centralized application that enables the local search applications to be run on each node have data source and will collect the result of the search. The GST implements the LSE service that runs on each node that participated in the search tasks. The LSE is implemented as a grid service and is installed to be run with the globus container. The globus container is run once the node starts and it continues to run until the node shuts down. By applying this method, the LSE does not need waiting time to load on the memory when the node receives search job request. Additionally, running the LSE as grid service saves the time required to starts the LSE every time the search is performed. The LSE is designed and developed based of the object-oriented technology, which allows a new component to be added easily. This feature offers the LSE the ability to support more dataset types.

1: **Data[]**: the list of data source locations.

2: **node[]**: the list of computing nodes.

3: **JDF[]**: the list of the Job Description Files.

4: **thread[]**: the list of thread objects.

5: **query**: the user search text.

6: **client**: the name of the client node.

7: **for** $i = 1$ **to** No-of-nodes **do**

　　JDF[i]=createfile(Data[i], Resource[i], client, query)

8: **end for**

9: **for** $k = 1$ **to** No-of-nodes **do**

　　Thread thread[k]=new Thread.create(JDF[k]); thread[k].run();

10: **end for**

11: **while** search no finish **do**

12:　　info=thread.getresult;

13:　　id=info.threadid();

14:　　result[id]=info.result;

15:　　send-result(result[id],client);

16:　　thread[id].release;

17: **end while**

Fig. 3. The QM phases pseudo code

The LSE is implemented as grid service to search XML structure files by using some XML API functions. The LSE utilizes the Simple API for XML (SAX) to access and manipulate the XML files. The search technique is implemented to deal with a large dataset size that may exceed the memory size. The SAX does not require a large memory size, instead small memory is enough to perform the search processes. The SAX does not load the entire file on the memory to handles the search tasks. The SAX reads the file based on the event (record by record) from the hard disk. The LSE is equipped with the search of the exact keyword and the search for part of the keyword.

4.1.6   Performance History Recorder (PHR)

The enhancement of the search technique relies on the previous response time of execution. So, saving the performance information of previous search execution will improve the performance of future search because it will help to predict the performance, and provide expectation for the next search response time. The GST technique employs a separate component in order to keep the performance of each search execution which is called the PHR. The main function of this component is to help other components to enhance the performance of the system. The PHR provides two functions for the search task; one before running the search and another after completing the search. Before submitting the search task, PHR provides for DDB service information about the previous search executions performance. The DDB service uses the information to prepare execution plan to obtain the best performance. The execution plan is prepared by selecting the resources with a good history in which it produced better performance from the previous execution. The second function is performed after the search execution is completed. The PHR stores the current execution performance information to be used in the future prediction.

5 Experiment and Evaluation

The evaluation of the search technique depends on the response time of the user query. The search technique via grid computing is evaluated based on the speed up of the search processes. The goal of this experiment is to investigate the usage of grid computing to search large and the distributed dataset in order to enhance the performance of the search processes. The GST is evaluated by using the response time, the speed up, and the efficiency of the search technique. The experiment conducted in the grid testbed contains 12 computer nodes distributed among three Virtual Organizations (VO) and each VO contains four nodes. One of four nodes has two roles as grid broker equipped with CA server and as a computing node. The grid nodes have different specifications by using Red Hat Enterprise Linux 3 as OS. The Globus toolkit 4.0.2 is installed in each broker node beforehand because the broker is considered as a Certificate Authority sever. The datasets used are articles collected from different academic repositories, which contain the open access information about the articles. The worker is equipped with datasets files of different sizes as illustrated in Table 1.

Table 1. The dataset description.

No	File Name	No of records	Size on HD
1	File-50.XML	50,000	43 MB
2	File-100.XML	100,000	87 MB
3	File-200.XML	200,000	174 MB
4	File-500.XML	500,000	453 MB
5	File-1000.XML	1,000,000	985 MB
6	File-2000.XML	2,000,000	2019 MB
7	File-4000.XML	4,000,000	4157 MB

5.1 Response Time

The response time is the search answering time that starts from the sending of query until the receiving of result. The experiments use the Grid User Interface proposed in [34] to execute the query and to calculates the response time starting from the time when the decision is made to distribute the queries over the selected grid nodes until the collected results are received and merged. The components that involve search response time are the grid overhead to orchestrate and run the search operations, and the search processing time required by all the nodes to perform the search.

This experiment is conducted to measure the search response time by increasing both the data size and the computing nodes. The goal of the experiment is to identify the effect of the GST in searching large scale datasets and to measure the enhancement achieved by using the GST. The experiment was conducted by using the GST to search the data as compared to the manual search and to measure the performance enhancement by the GST technique.

The response time is calculates by fixing data size used in the search process. Then, the number of nodes participated in the search is increased and the same data size are distributed among all nodes. The scenario is repeated by increasing the fixed data size and it continues to increase the number of nodes. Figure 4 shows the response time of search which increases as the level of parallelism used to execute the search increases. A comparison between the command line search and the GST search shows that the GST is 100% faster than the manual search when the number of node is small. Furthermore, the GST is 33% faster than the manual search when the number of nodes scales to 11 nodes.

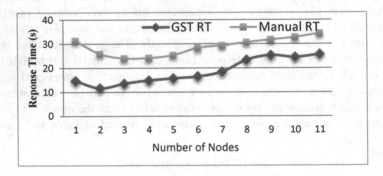

Fig. 4. Response time scales as the increase of size for small dataset.

5.2 Speed Up

The speed up is used to measure the performance of the search techniques. The speed up is defined as the ratio of the time to execute job on small system until the time to execute the same job on large systems. The experiment is conducted to measure the speed up of the GST when the number of nodes is increased. The speed up is defined by Fishburn [35] as:

$$Speedup = Serial\,execution\ time/Parallel\,execution\ time \tag{1}$$

Figure 5 shows that the speed up reduces when the number of the nodes increases which scale from 1.2 down to 0.48. The manual speed up starts with 1.15 then it decreases with the increased number of nodes until it reaches 0.88 when 11 nodes participated. However, the manual search still provides better performance even with the decrease of speed up. This results shows that the GST is not suitable for small datasets size.

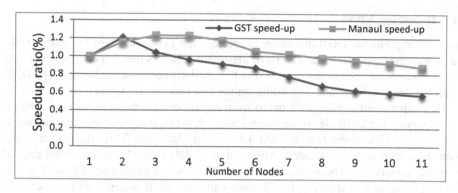

Fig. 5. Speedup scales as the increase of size for small dataset.

5.3   Efficiency

The efficient search technique is a technique that utilizes the resource in a good manner. This experiment is conducted to calculate the GST efficiency and to compare its performance with the manual search by using command line. The efficiency is calculated by dividing the speed up by the number of nodes used in the test, which produce an amount of less than 1.0. The perfect and the best efficiency is equal to or very close to 1.0 [36].

$$\text{Efficiency} = \text{Speedup}/\text{Number of used nodes} \qquad (2)$$

Figure 6 shows that the GST efficiency starts from 0.60 with 2 computing nodes and eventually decreases until it reaches 0.09 when 11 computing nodes are used. The manual search has better efficiency, in which it starts with 0.58 and decreases to obtain 0.07 when the number of nodes is 11. However, the result reported that the manual search and the GST have almost equal efficiency with small size of datasets.

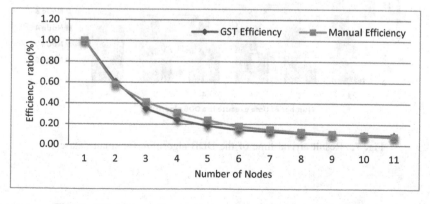

Fig. 6. Efficiency scales as the increase of size for small dataset.

5.4   Balancing Effect

The GST implements DDB algorithm to increase the performance of the search tasks and reduce the response time. The DDB algorithm balances the data distribution every time the search was conducted by utilizing the previous performance history. The DDB obtain the best performance depending on the last tasks performance.

This experiment conducted aims to measure the enhancement of the performance when applying the DDB algorithm several times. The test starts by executing the search query for first time using 6 nodes and 3 M records data size. Then, the arrival of the result from each node is recorded. After that, the DDB applied and the arrival time of the result is recorded. These steps are repeated 6 times as illustrated in Figs. 7 and 8. The first scenario as explain in Fig. 7, shows that the DDB balances of the execution time for small dataset is not significance. The arrival time is reduce from 7 s in first iteration to 5 on the last 4 iteration. This result reported that the effect of the DDB algorithm for small dataset is not significant.

On the other hand, the second scenario is conducted using large dataset to measure the effect of the DDB. The result shows that the DDB balances the execution time for all the nodes in which the difference between the arrival time is less than 2 s for all nodes. Moreover, the DDB reduces the response time from 24 s on the first execution down to 12 s on the sixth execution of the DDB as depicted in Fig. 8. The result reported that the DDB reduce the arrival time of the GST with 49% when using huge dataset. this result a proved the efficiency of the DDB in response time when dealing with large datasets.

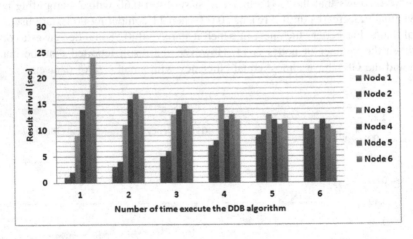

Fig. 7. Result arrival time of the DDB algorithm for small dataset

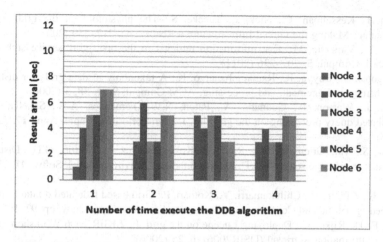

Fig. 8. Result arrival time of the DDB algorithm for large dataset

6 Conclusion

The techniques of large distributed data searching involve the combination of 2 distinct fields, namely grid technology and large datasets. There are many issues that need to be considered in order to implement an effective and efficient system. The paper highlighted the issues of the large scale distributed data and the issues related to the grid data search processes. The Grid-based Search Technique GST was proposed in order to allow the end user to search and access huge datasets distributed over a number of organizations. The GST enhances the search performance by implementing Distributed Data balancing algorithm and the Result Streaming mechanisms. The experiment was performed to measure the performance of the GST techniques and the suitability of using grid computing as the data sharing infrastructure. The experiment results show that the distribution of the data over the grid and the nodes' capabilities are the key issues that reduce the search performance. Moreover, the results show that the implementation of DDB and RS enhances the performance of the system. Additionally, the GST remains the good performance when the system and the data sources grow for large scale and it also shows good performance with the increase of data size.

References

1. Wang, L., Lin, J., Metzler, D.: Learning to efficiently rank. In: Proceedings of the 33rd International ACM SIGIR Conference on Research and Development in Information Retrieval, pp. 138–145 (2010)
2. Foster, I., Zhao, Y., Raicu, I., Lu, S.Y.: Cloud computing and grid computing 360-degree compared. In: GCE: 2008 Grid Computing Environments Workshop, pp. 60–69 (2008)
3. Nicolae, B., Antoniu, G., Bougé, L., Moise, D., Carpen-Amarie, A.: BlobSeer: next-generation data management for large scale infrastructures. J. Parallel Distrib. Comput. **71**, 169–184 (2011)

4. Foster, I., Kesselman, C., Nick, J., Tuecke, S.: The physiology of the grid. In: Grid Computing: Making the Global Infrastructure a Reality, pp. 217–250 (2003)
5. Berka, T., Vajteršic, M.: Fast information retrieval in the open grid service architecture. Serdica J. Comput. **5**, 207–236 (2011)
6. Venugopal, S., Buyya, R., Ramamohanarao, K.: A taxonomy of data grids for distributed data sharing, management, and processing. ACM Comput. Surv. **38**, 3 (2006)
7. Smith, J., Watson, P., Gounaris, A., Paton, N.W., Fernandes, A.A., Sakellariou, R.: Distributed query processing on the grid. Int. J. High Perform. Comput. Appl. **17**, 353–367 (2003)
8. Yalew, S., van Griensven, A., Ray, N., Kokoszkiewicz, L., Betrie, G.D.: Distributed computation of large scale SWAT models on the grid. Environ. Model. Softw. **41**, 223–230 (2013)
9. Maly, K., Zubair, M., Chilukamarri, V., Kothari, P.: Grid based federated digital library. In: Proceedings of the 2nd Conference on Computing Frontiers, Ischia, Italy, pp. 97–105 (2005)
10. Meij, E., De Rijke, M.: Deploying Lucene on the grid. In: SIGIR 2006 Workshop on Open Source Information Retrieval (OSIR2006), p. 25 (2006)
11. Nakashole, N., Suleman, H.: A hybrid distributed architecture for indexing. In: Agosti, M., Borbinha, J., Kapidakis, S., Papatheodorou, C., Tsakonas, G. (eds.) ECDL 2009. LNCS, vol. 5714, pp. 250–260. Springer, Heidelberg (2009). https://doi.org/10.1007/978-3-642-04346-8_25
12. Nakashole, N.: A hybrid scavenger grid approach to intranet search, Ph.D., University of Cape Town (2009)
13. Chihli Hung, C.-F.T., Hung, S.-Y., Chang-Jiang, K.: OGIR: an ontology-based grid information retrieval framework. Online Inf. Rev. **36**, 807–827 (2012)
14. Yang, C.-T., Chen, C.-H., Yang, M.-F., Chiang, W.-C.: MIFAS: medical image file accessing system in co-allocation data grids. In: 2008 Asia-Pacific Services Computing Conference, APSCC 2008, pp. 769–774. IEEE (2008)
15. Yang, C.-T., Chen, C.-H., Yang, M.-F.: Implementation of a medical image file accessing system in co-allocation data grids. Futur. Gener. Comput. Syst. **26**, 1127–1140 (2010)
16. Shih, W.-C., Tseng, S.-S., Yang, C.-T.: Using taxonomic indexing trees to efficiently retrieve SCORM-compliant documents in e-learning grids. Educ. Technol. Soc. **11**, 206–226 (2008)
17. Shih, W.-C., Yang, C.-T., Tseng, S.-S.: Ontology-based content organization and retrieval for SCORM-compliant teaching materials in data grids. Futur. Gener. Comput. Syst. **25**, 687–694 (2009)
18. Trnkoczy, J., Turk, Z., Stankovski, V.: A grid-based architecture for personalized federation of digital libraries. Libr. Collect. Acquis. Tech. Serv. **30**, 139–153 (2006)
19. Trnkoczy, J., Stankovski, V.: Improving the performance of Federated Digital Library services. Futur. Gener. Comput. Syst. **24**, 824–832 (2008)
20. Robles, O.D., Bosque, J.L., Pastor, L., Rodríguez, Á.: CBIR on grids. In: Meersman, R., Tari, Z. (eds.) OTM 2006. LNCS, vol. 4276, pp. 1412–1421. Springer, Heidelberg (2006). https://doi.org/10.1007/11914952_27
21. Larson, R.R., Sanderson, R.: Grid-based digital libraries: Cheshire3 and distributed retrieval, pp. 112–113 (2005)
22. Sanderson, R., Larson, R.R.: Indexing and searching tera-scale grid-based digital libraries, p. 3 (2006)
23. Toharia, P., Sánchez, A., Bosque, J.L., Robles, O.D.: GCViR: grid content-based video retrieval with work allocation brokering. Concurr. Comput.: Pract. Exp. **22**, 1450–1475 (2010)
24. Haya, G., Scholze, F., Vigen, J.: Developing a grid-based search and categorization tool. In: High Energy Physics Libraries Webzine, vol. 8 (2003)

25. Cambazoglu, B.B., Karaca, E., Kucukyilmaz, T., Turk, A., Aykanat, C.: Architecture of a grid-enabled Web search engine. Inf. Process. Manag. **43**, 609–623 (2007)
26. Bashir, M.B., Latiff, M.S.B.A., Coulibaly, Y., Yousif, A.: A survey of grid-based searching techniques for large scale distributed data. J. Netw. Comput. Appl. **60**, 170–179 (2016)
27. Gounaris, A., Smith, J., Paton, N.W., Sakellariou, R., Fernandes, A.A.A., Watson, P.: Adapting to changing resource performance in grid query processing. In: Pierson, J.-M. (ed.) DMG 2005. LNCS, vol. 3836, pp. 30–44. Springer, Heidelberg (2006). https://doi.org/10.1007/11611950_4
28. Liu, S., Karimi, H.A.: Grid query optimizer to improve query processing in grids. Futur. Gener. Comput. Syst. **24**, 342–353 (2008)
29. Hameurlain, A.: Evolution of query optimization methods: from centralized database systems to data grid systems. In: Bhowmick, S.S., Küng, J., Wagner, R. (eds.) DEXA 2009. LNCS, vol. 5690, pp. 460–470. Springer, Heidelberg (2009). https://doi.org/10.1007/978-3-642-03573-9_40
30. Singh, G., Kesselman, C., Deelman, E.: Optimizing grid-based workflow execution. J. Grid Comput. **3**, 201–219 (2005)
31. Bashir, M.B., Latiff, M.S.A., Yousif, A.: Grid-based architecture for sharing distributed massive datasets. Int. J. Commun. Netw. Distrib. Syst. **15**, 248–264 (2015)
32. Hota, A., Mohapatra, S., Mohanty, S.: Survey of different load balancing approach-based algorithms in cloud computing: a comprehensive review. In: Behera, H.S., Nayak, J., Naik, B., Abraham, A. (eds.) Computational Intelligence in Data Mining. AISC, vol. 711, pp. 99–110. Springer, Singapore (2019). https://doi.org/10.1007/978-981-10-8055-5_10
33. Dharmik, R., Sathe, S.: A sender initiated dynamic and decentralized load balancing algorithm for computational grid environment using variable CPU usage. Int. J. Appl. Eng. Res. **13**, 189–194 (2018)
34. Bashir, M., Latiff, M.S.A., Yousif, A.: An efficient and secured grid-enabler interface for large-scale systems. In: 2015 International Conference on Cloud Computing (ICCC), pp. 1–7 (2015)
35. Fishburn, J.P.: Analysis of speedup in distributed algorithms. University Microfilms International (UMI) (1984)
36. Han, S.H., Heo, J., Sohn, H.G., Yu, K.: Parallel processing method for airborne laser scanning data using a PC cluster and a virtual grid. Sensors **9**, 2555–2573 (2009)

Analytical Experiments on the Utilization of Data Visualizations

Sara M. Shaheen[✉], Sawsan Alhalawani, Nuha Alnabet, and Dana Alhenaki

Prince Sultan University, Riyadh, Kingdom of Saudi Arabia
sshaheen@pnu.edu.sa

Abstract. Visualizing data has been well known and widely used to facilitate better understanding of data. Using the right type of visualization enables people to interpret data in a more accurate and correct way and would support decision makers in taking the right decisions. Many researchers have proposed the best types of charts and graphs to visualize data. They recommend certain types of charts based on the data type and the purpose of the visualization. However and up to our knowledge, there has not been studies which would experiment the righteous of such selection of the visualization charts. The main purpose of this research is to survey a large group of people to study the effect of selecting certain chart types on people's comprehension of the visualized data. We conduct a user study to validate the theoretical assumptions on the selection of the best chart types. We evaluated the use of column chart to visualize categorical single variable data and line chart to visualize temporal data against other charts. We analyzed the user study participants' performance according to their response time, accuracy of the results and overall satisfaction.

Keywords: Data visualization · Chart types · Perception analysis · Visual learning · Chart design

1   Introduction

Modern world is now evolving based on data-driven decisions and solutions [22]. Intuitively, the better the data is utilized in a certain field, the smarter the decisions that can be made to serve that field. One important aspect of utilizing data is through data visualization that makes it possible to understand, gather insights and derive conclusions from a given data. Data visualization is one of the most important techniques to convey the maximum possible understanding. It has been addressed in many early researches proposing different guidelines for best practices for visualizing data [26]. Interestingly, data visualization simplifies data analysis and increases data readability [5] through a rapid and instant comprehension of large volume of data [7].

However, this is only possible if the visualizations are designed to be aligned with the nature of the data and through following certain design principles as discussed in [6]. Data comes in different dimensions, categories, nature and serves

© Springer Nature Switzerland AG 2019
A. Alfaries et al. (Eds.): ICC 2019, CCIS 1097, pp. 148–161, 2019.
https://doi.org/10.1007/978-3-030-36365-9_12

various purposes. In terms of dimensionality, data can represent one variable, two variables or more. Moreover, data can represent static information which does not change over time, temporal information that evolves over time or categorical data which represents multiple information categories. Visualizing data is also used to serve a number of purposes depending on what one would like to know about the data. These categories include comparison, distribution, relationship and composition. All of these data categories and the recommended visualizations depending on the nature of the data is summarized in the 'Chart Suggestions A Thought Starter' [2]. It presents a decision tree with a maximum depth of 4 choices as a diagram, one can select the chart that suits the data of interest.

Given all of that, we surrender to the fact that visualizations should be designed and selected carefully in order to convey the information correctly. As will be discussed later, the literature is rich with guidance on how to nominate and select the best visualizations for certain data. However, and up to our knowledge, most of the work in the literature don't validate the theoretical assumptions by conducting real experiments. In this work, we contribute an experiment based analysis on charts selection through conducting a couple of user experiments to assess two types of charts, column charts and line charts. Data is gathered and is visualized through different chart type. Following that, a number of user surveys are conducted to collect information related to how fast, accurate and satisfied are the participants when answering questions using one type of charts in comparison with the other charts. All of this was done through administering certain experimental setup as discussed in details later. After that, a thorough analysis and interesting results are presented in the analysis part of this work.

2   Literature Review

Data visualization is widely used in different domains. Many researchers have studied and proposed the best ways to visualize the different kinds of data such as textual data [11], traffic data [5], search query results [17], educational data [30], business data [29], research data [10] and many others. Choosing the visualization properly is very crucial to convey the correct insights about the data. Khan and Khan [12] presented a document that collects and summarizes the different visualization techniques with their definitions. They also described the aspects, steps and problems which concerns the process of visualization. Many other researchers have proposed different ways on defining the effect of information visualization on people's comprehension. In theory, most of the work have focused on the clarity, the efficiency and the accuracy of performing specific tasks when given the visualization [1, 15, 25].

In order to analyze the importance of the different types of visualizations, Mogull and Stanfield [19] analyzed 43 research articles to revise the use of different types of inscriptions in scientific documentation. The authors concluded that graphs and diagrams are the highest used among other types of inscriptions including Photographs, Tables and equations. The authors also observed that among the different types of charts, conventional bar graph are most common one while pie graphs are relatively uncommon.

Many researchers have studied and proposed different ways for selecting the best types of visualization. Knaflic [14] presented a data visualization guide with the main target of how to tell stories with data by visualizing it in the right way. Mittal [18] proposed a theoretical comparison of charts by using the same data and visualizing it differently. However, he indicated that the study was theoretical and he did not conduct user studies. In the context of business information, Tegarden [29] provided guidelines to designing information visualizations and choosing visualization representations to support decision makers but they did not validate their guidelines with used studies. Raghav et al. [24] discussed different types of the data visualization and analyzed the most used ones by businesses. However, they did not analyze the efficiency of selecting the types of visualization with respect to the visualized data.

Lately, analyzing the effects of changing the presentation and visualization of the information on peoples' perception have gained researchers interest. For example, Majooni et al. [16] investigated the effect of presenting different layouts of visual and textual elements in the information graphics on the comprehension and cognitive load of the viewers. They provided quantitative evidence that changing the layout in each story affects the comprehension of participants and their cognitive load. Afify [3] conducted a study to analyze the effect of using static versus animated infographic design types on developing the skills of designing and producing visual learning materials, and the recognition of the design elements and its principles. Quispel and Maes [23] studied the preferences of professional graphic designers and laypeople when presented with different visualizations using pie and bar chart. They visualized the data using pie and bar chart in a stand way i.e. without any deviation from the standard charts against the non-standard visualization which deviates from the standard charts. They quantified their analysis by measuring the attractiveness, information retrieval, clarity, and overall rating. They concluded that there is a clear difference in the preference of the visualization type based on the audience.

In [27], Skau, Harrison and Kosara studied the effect of charts visual embellishments on data communication. The paper conducted a user study on 100 online participants that were shown seven different charts and asked to answer related questions to evaluate the chart accurate data communication. The paper concluded that generally any small changes on the standard chart visual designs might lead to higher error rate. Similarly, Talbit Setlur and Anand [28] aimed to understand the source interpretation error in different vibration of bar charts. Hence, they conducted four experiments on 50 participants recruited by Amazon Mechanical Turk tool and reported their performance in terms of confidence intervals (CIs). As a result, the author proposed new hypotheses on the bar charts' perception indicating that any small change in the bar charts design could significantly effect its perception.

As it is clear in the literature that researchers have gained interest in proposing the best types of visualizations, especially charts, to facilitate better understanding and comprehension of data. However, there have not been conducted adequate user studies to validate the theoretical assumptions on the best visualization chart which is the main purpose of this research.

3 Experiments Objectives and Overview

In this work, we conduct a number of experiments to analyze the efficiency of selected visualizations. To do that, we create and administer a number of user studies where participants are requested to answer a set of multiple-choice questions given a chart of some data. For each experiment, we select a data category and refer to the literature as in [2] to look up the most suitable chart to visualize that category of data. After that, we select a number of other chart types to compare and assess how effectively people can comprehend the information when presented with the recommended chart in comparison with the other types of charts. A user study is then created for each of these charts and participants performance is gathered for each user study. In designing the user studies, the focus is on assessing clarity, comprehension, efficiency and overall satisfaction of the presented visualizations. We base our hypothesis on what is presented in the literature regarding the recommended chart type for every data specification. In other words, our expectation is that participants performance will be faster or more accurate or both when answering the questions presented using the recommended chart type in comparison with the other charts. The visualizations that are selected for analysis are column charts and line charts. In what follows, we present in more details each of the these experiments.

3.1 First Experiment - Column Chart

Column charts are recommended to be used when visualizing categorical data with a single variable and a limited number of categories, such as the data of the number of kids per school or the number of studying hours per course...etc. [2]. In this experiment, the aim is to evaluate how effective are column charts in comparison with other chart types in visualizing categorical data with few categories. To do that, we design a total of 5 charts, a column chart, a scatter plot chart, a line chart, a bar chart and a pie chart. These charts represent different one variable categorical data as shown in Fig. 1. After that, a set of multiple-choice questions concerning each chart are asked in a separate user study. As participants answer the questions related to the chart, their answers' accuracy is recorded and the time taken to complete every study is also considered. In addition, participants are presented with a qualitative question asking them to rate how happy they are with the chart that was given to them.

Hypothesis: Participants are expected to have either a higher accuracy or faster answering time or both in the user study that includes the column chart over the other charts. In terms of the overall satisfaction, we expect participants to rank the column chart the highest in comparison with the other considered charts.

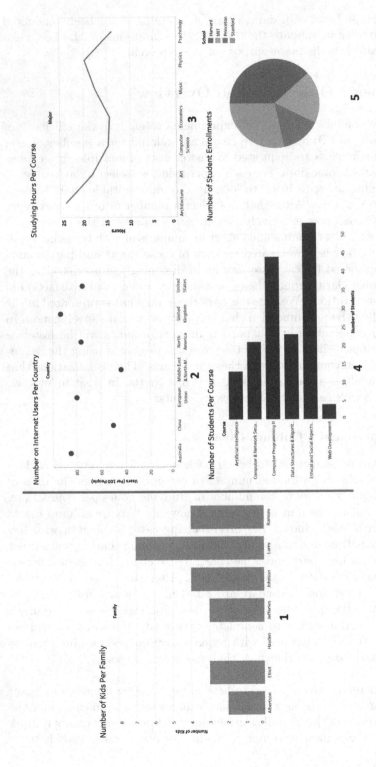

Fig. 1. The charts that are used in the first experiment. Different charts are used to visualize categorical data. The chart on the left (1) is the column chart that is according to the literature is the best to be used in visualizing categorical data while the remaining charts are included to compare against and enrich the analysis. The charts selected are: (2) scatter chart, (3) line chart, (4) bar chart and (5) pie chart. Each chart is used in a separate user study where participants are asked to answer questions related to the given chart.

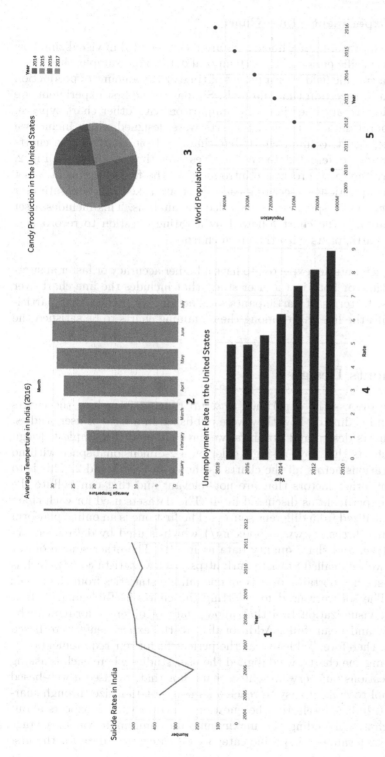

Fig. 2. The charts that are used in the second experiment. Different charts are used to visualize temporal data. The chart on the left (1) is the line chart that is recommended in visualizing data that evolves over time while the remaining charts are included to experiment with. The charts selected are: (2) column chart, (3) pie chart, (4) bar chart and (5) scatter chart. Each chart is used in a separate user study where participants are asked to answer questions related to the given chart.

3.2   Second Experiment - Line Chart

According to the literature [2,5], line charts are recommended in visualizing how data evolves in a specific period of time (temporal data). For example, the rate of enrollment into a specific field over a period of time or the amount of production of a specific item over certain time intervals. Similar to the first experiment, we evaluate how effective are line charts in comparison with other chart types in visualizing temporal data. A total of 5 charts were designed which includes a line chart, scatter chart, column chart, bar chart and pie chart. These charts are used to represent different data that evolves over time as shown in Fig. 2. Following exactly the same procedure introduced in the first experiment, a set of multiple-choice questions concerning each chart are asked in a separate user study and participants responses are recorded for analysis. This includes a set of questions related to the chart followed by a rating question to record how satisfied are the participants with the given charts.

Hypothesis: Participants are expected to have a higher accuracy or faster answering completion time or both in the user study that includes the line chart over the other charts. In terms of participants satisfaction, we predict that participants dealing with the line chart among the remaining charts to be satisfied the most.

4   Experiments Design

In this part, we discuss the experimental setup ranging from how the charts were designed and ending on how they were published in a form of user studies. Starting with charts design and graphics, we have adopted the simplest design approach with charts that have a single color on a 2-dimensional space with no additional decorations across all the charts as shown in Figs. 1 and 2. This is to avoid adding any other factors that are not relevant and that can pollute the outcome of the experiment as discussed in [4]. The datasets used for each chart are all real data utilized from different sources. The first one is an online platform called Kaggle (url: https://www.kaggle.com/) which is used by data scientists to explore, analyze, and share quality data as in [21]. The other source of our data is another website called Statista (url: https://www.statista.com/)which is a statistics and studies portal of over than one million statistics from thousands of sources [8]. The software used for plotting the charts is Tableau [20]. It is a powerful data visualization tool that allows data of different formats to be visualized easily, and beautifully. Additionally, all the experiments were based on static charts, therefore, Tableau was the perfect fit for our requirements.

After designing the charts, we designed the user studies where each is asking a number of questions on every presented chart. For that, we used a web-based online survey tool to make it easy to reach a large population size through sharing a single URL link. We selected the questions to cover various aspects about the presented charts, including the maximum value, minimum value, average value and the exact value of a specific category on categorical data for the first experiment. For the second experiment, we asked questions related to time such as the overall trend of the chart. Questions were generated in a random ordering and the choices for every question were shuffled every time the survey is accessed. This makes it impossible to expect questions and memorize answers ahead of starting the survey. Towards the end of every survey, we have also added a rating questions to enable the collection of the participants overall satisfaction of the presented chart. In addition to that and as it is usually the case in well designed user experiments, we have added a control question which includes a very simple arithmetic question. Upon answering that question correctly, participants contribution is used in our analysis otherwise the participation is marked as terminated and is not recorded. This ensures that no contributions which involve random answering of the questions are included and that only participants who are paying attention are part of the analysis population. In addition to that, no duplicate contributions are allowed or in other word a participant can attempt the set of user studies for each experiment only once (this is through not allowing access from the same IP address twice). All of these above precautions, targeting obtaining authentic population samples for our experiments and thus produce reliable results.

Another aspect we considered, as the users are moving on the chain of the user studies for one experiment, participant will get familiar with the setup of the question and as such it will be easier for them to answer the last chart over the first chart which is not aligned with what we are aiming to experiment. To avoid that, we randomize the sequence of these studies every time they are accessed so that every participant will be given a different sequence of these studies.

Out of every user study, the time taken to complete every survey in seconds is recorded to assess efficiency and the answers of every question along with the overall score of correct answers are recorded to assess participants accuracy. This is along with the rating of every survey to assess the satisfaction for every chart.

After designing the studies for every experiment, we published the survey links. To reach a large number of reliable participants, we published our user studies on Amazon Mechanical Turk (AMT) [9], an internet based platform for sourcing work for any scale of human intelligence tasks. Mechanical Turk have proven to be a reliable platform for studies on perception and visual decisions [13]. The scalability, and relatively automated process that it enables makes it an attractive platform for running browser-based user studies. Through this platform more than 100 unique participants of every experiment were involved. In the next section, a detailed analysis of the outcomes of the two experiments is presented.

5 Analysis and Results

After conducting both experiments, data were retrieved and analyzed in order to examine the purposed hypotheses. The analysis examined the data from three different perspectives which are time efficiency, accuracy and user satisfaction.

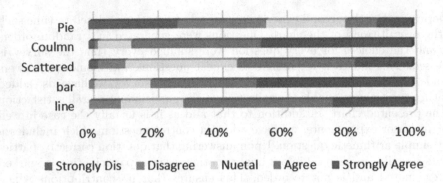

Fig. 3. The chart illustrate the responses regarding the level of satisfaction on the chart clarity and presentation. It is noted that bar chart and column chart received the highest feedback

5.1   First Experiment Analysis

The first experiment intended to investigate the use of different charts with categorical data. Since, and as discussed earlier, column charts are usually recommended in representing categorical data with few categories, we designed our hypothesis accordingly. Our hypothesis for this experiment states that column chart is predicted to perform best in either efficiency or accuracy or both. Moreover, we expect column chart to be the most favorite chart among participants through their satisfaction rating. Next, we discuss the summary statistics of participants in terms of the time taken, accuracy in attempting the questions and finally the overall satisfaction. We will evaluate if our findings are aligned with our hypothesis and attempt to find reasonable answers when not. A summary of the obtained statistics is shown in Table 1.

When evaluating the time required to complete the survey, the median time is considered rather than the average to avoid any skewed results caused by possible outliers. Looking at the results, the column charts required the least time with the 56 s which is typically aligned with our hypothesis. Coming second is the pie chart with median time of 57 s which could result due to the simple nature of the pie chart so that participants needed not much time on it but as shown later the accuracy of participants responses was the lowest. On the other hand, line chart surveys took the highest time as the participants took a median of 117 s to complete the survey.

Looking at the accuracy of the participants' answers, the results indicate that participants performed best using bar chart with an accuracy of 81%. This is not totally aligned with our hypothesis and we will elaborate on this shortly. On the other hand, pie chart and scatter chart performed the worst with an accuracy of 40%.

Coming to the satisfaction rate results which assess the participants' satisfaction with the chart clarity and presentation, column chart received the highest results with 87% of participants satisfaction. The bar chart was next with a satisfaction rate of 81%. On the other hand, pie chart scored the lowest with only 21% were satisfied with the use of pie chart. The low satisfaction rate with the pie chart can be also corelated with the low comprehension as the participants recorded low weighted score when answering the pie chart questions (as shown in Fig. 3).

Aligning with the hypothesis, the column chart performed the best in terms of time efficiency and user satisfaction. Yet, it is interesting to observe that bar chart exceeded the column chart in terms of accuracy. This is accepted given their similar nature. While their purposes might vary, in terms of visual representation the difference between bar chart and column chart are the bars orientation.

Table 1. The table shows participants performance when responding to each chart survey for the categorical data. The time is presented in Seconds.

Chart	Time (sec)	Accuracy	Satisfaction
Line chart	117	69%	71%
Bar chart	75.5	81%	81%
Scatter chart	69	40%	54%
Column chart	56	70%	87%
Pie chart	57	40%	21%

5.2 Second Experiment Analysis

The main purpose of the second experiment is to investigate the effectiveness of using different charts for temporal data which varies over time. According to the literature, temporal data is best visualized using line charts. Accordingly, our hypothesis for this experiment was that line chart is expected to perform the best in terms of the completion time, accuracy rate and user satisfaction rate when compared against other chart types. The other considered charts were the scatter chart, column chart, bar chart and pie chart. A summary of the obtained results is shown in Table 2.

The results of this study were conforming with our hypothesis in terms of the time taken to complete the surveys of the line charts. The participants took the least amount of time to respond to the questions of the line chart surveys with a median of 38 s. In the contrary, participants required a median of 67 s to complete the survey through the pie chart which should be obvious as pie charts are not ideal for the temporal data visualization.

The second perceptive to consider is the accuracy rate. Although the accuracy was %83 for the Line chart surveys, they did not perform as expected in this study. The best accuracy was %93 which was achieved by the scatter chart surveys. We believe that the scatter plot performed better than the line chart due to the nature of the distribution of data. The data used for the line chart is

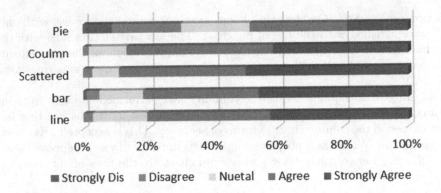

Fig. 4. The chart illustrates the participants' responses on the temporal data survey regarding the level of satisfaction on the chart clarity and presentation. It is noted that the column chart and bar chart received the highest feedback.

fluctuating which made it harder for the participants to comprehend the values while the scatter plot data is linear and it was easier to understand. Therefore, we believe this is an interesting factor which should be addressed in future studies.

Similar to the accuracy, the participants were more satisfied with the scatter chart rather than the line chart. Participants rated the clarity and presentation of the scatter plot to be %89 while they rated the line chart as %81 (as shown in Fig. 4). We believe this is also due to the simplicity of the data visualized in the scatter plot compared to the fluctuating data in the line chart.

The stated hypothesis anticipated line chart to score the best in the three different perspectives. The time taken by the participants to answer the line chart surveys was the least which agrees with our hypothesis. However, the accuracy and satisfaction were not the best in the case of the line chart surveys. It is expected that the scatter plot would perform well considering its similarity to the line chart in terms of recording individual data as marks (Dots) on the graph. The difference is that line chart connects the marks (Dots) which makes it easy to trace the changes over time. The survey results illustrated another factor that might affect the line chart survey results which is the data fluctuation. The line

Table 2. The table shows participants performance when responding to each chart for the temporal data. The time is presented in Seconds.

Chart	Time (sec)	Accuracy	Satisfaction
Line chart	38	83%	81%
Bar chart	42	87%	82%
Scatter chart	39.5	93%	89%
Column chart	47	87%	87%
Pie chart	67	40%	67%

chart represented a fluctuated curved data unlike the steadily increasing plot in the scatter chart. Therefore, a further investigation needs to be conducted where both charts represent the same data distribution to study its effect on the efficiency of the charts.

6   Conclusion and Future Work

Data visualization importance is rapidly increasing to process the huge amount of data we encounter every day. In order to optimize the use of visualization techniques including charts, these techniques must consider the different types of data to present. Therefore in this research, two hypothesis were purposed after being driven from the literature reviews. The evaluation of these experiments indicated that column chart is the most effective chart to use when representing categorical data. This finding confirm the first purposed hypothesis yet a further study needs to be conducted on the column chart performance with different type of data needs to be retrieved. Moreover, while the second hypothesis expected the line chart to perform the best, the scatter chart result exceeded the line chart. This observation draws the attention to the possible effect of visual data distribution on chart performance.

Future Work: The work presented on this paper is just the first seed in considering experimental studies in the selection of data visualizations. For future work, we aim to include more extensive user studies to experiment on various chart types. In addition, we aim to investigate the influence of using different design aspects of the same chart.

Acknowledgement. We would like to acknowledge the Artificial Intelligence and Data Analytics (AIDA) Lab, Prince Sultan University, Riyadh, Saudi Arabia for supporting this work.

References

1. Preface. In: Ware, C. (ed.) Visual Thinking. Morgan Kaufmann, San Francisco (2008)
2. Abela, A.: Chart suggestions-a thought-starter. In: Extreme Presentation (2009)
3. Afify, M.K.: The effect of the difference between infographic designing types (static vs animated) on developing visual learning designing skills and recognition of its elements and principles. Int. J. Emerg. Technol. Learn. **13**, 204–223 (2018)
4. Chen, C.h.: Handbook of Data Visualization
5. Chen, W., Guo, F., Wang, F.Y.: A survey of traffic data visualization. IEEE Trans. Intell. Transp. Syst. **16**(6), 2970–2984 (2015)
6. Cleveland, W.S.: Visualizing Data. Hobart Press (1993)
7. Gao, T., Dontcheva, M., Adar, E., Liu, Z., Karahalios, K.G.: Datatone: managing ambiguity in natural language interfaces for data visualization. In: Proceedings of the 28th Annual ACM Symposium on User Interface Software & Technology, pp. 489–500. ACM (2015)

8. Gullen, A., Plungis, J.: Statista. Charleston Advisor **15**(2), 43–47 (2013)
9. Heer, J., Bostock, M.: Crowdsourcing graphical perception: using mechanical turk to assess visualization design. In: Proceedings of the SIGCHI Conference on Human Factors in Computing Systems, pp. 203–212. ACM (2010)
10. Hicks, A., Lloyd, A.: Seeing information: visual methods as entry points to information practices. J. Librarianship Inf. Sci. **50**(3), 229–238 (2018)
11. Jänicke, S., Blumenstein, J., Rücker, M., Zeckzer, D., Scheuermann, G.: TagPies: comparative visualization of textual data. In: 3(Visigrapp) (2018)
12. Khan, M., Khan, S.S.: Data and information visualization methods, and interactive mechanisms: a survey (2011)
13. Kim, S.H., Li, S., Kwon, B.c., Yi, J.S.: Investigating the efficacy of crowdsourcing on evaluating visual decision supporting system. In: Proceedings of the Human Factors and Ergonomics Society Annual Meeting, vol. 55, pp. 1090–1094. SAGE Publications, Los Angeles (2011)
14. Knaflic, C.: Storytelling with Data: A Data Visualization Guide for Business Professionals. Wiley, Hoboken (2015)
15. Mackinlay, J.: Automating the design of graphical presentations of relational information. ACM Trans. Graph. **5**(2), 110–141 (1986)
16. Majooni, A., Masood, M., Akhavan, A.: An eye-tracking study on the effect of infographic structures on viewerâ^{TM}s comprehension and cognitive load. Inf. Vis. **17**(3), 257–266 (2018)
17. Mazurek, M., Waldner, M.: Visualizing expanded query results. Comput. Graph. Forum **37**(3), 87–98 (2018)
18. Mittal, V.: Visual prompts and graphical exploring design: a framework for the design space of 2-D charts and graphs. Interface (1997)
19. Mogull, S.A., Stanfield, C.T.: Current use of visuals in scientific communication. In: 2015 IEEE International Professional Communication Conference (IPCC), pp. 1–6. IEEE (2015)
20. Murray, D.G.: Tableau Your Data! Fast and Easy Visual Analysis with Tableau Software. Wiley, Hoboken (2013)
21. Narayanan, A., Shi, E., Rubinstein, B.I.P.: Link prediction by de-anonymization: how we won the kaggle social network challenge. In: The 2011 International Joint Conference on Neural Networks, pp. 1825–1834 (2011)
22. Provost, F., Fawcett, T.: Data science and its relationship to big data and data-driven decision making. Big Data **1**(1), 51–59 (2013)
23. Quispel, A., Maes, A.: Would you prefer pie or cupcakes? preferences for data visualization designs of professionals and laypeople in graphic design. J. Vis. Lang. Comput. **25**(2), 107–116 (2014)
24. Raghav, R.S., Pothula, S., Vengattaraman, T., Ponnurangam, D.: A survey of data visualization tools for analyzing large volume of data in big data platform. In: 2016 International Conference on Communication and Electronics Systems (ICCES), pp. 1–6, October 2016
25. Scaife, M., Rogers, Y.: External cognition: how do graphical representations work? Int. J. Hum.-Comput. Stud. **45**, 185–213 (1996)
26. Schmid, C.: Handbook of Graphic Presentation. Ronald Press Co., New York (1954)
27. Skau, D., Harrison, L., Kosara, R.: An evaluation of the impact of visual embellishments in bar charts. In: Computer Graphics Forum, vol. 34, pp. 221–230. Wiley Online Library (2015)
28. Talbot, J., Setlur, V., Anand, A.: Four experiments on the perception of bar charts. IEEE Trans. Vis. Comput. Graph. **20**(12), 2152–2160 (2014)

29. Tegarden, D.P.: Business information visualization. Commun. Assoc. Inf. Syst. **1**(January), 4 (2018)
30. Williamson, B.: Digital education governance: data visualization, predictive analytics. J. Educ. Policy **31**(2), 123–141 (2016)

A Tweet-Ranking System Using Sentiment Scores and Popularity Measures

Sumaya Aleidi, Dalia Alsuhaibani, Nora Alrajebah[(✉)],
and Heba Kurdi

Computer Science, King Saud University, Riyadh, Saudi Arabia
{nrajebah, hkurdi}@ksu.edu.sa

Abstract. Various fields look to Twitter as a marvelous repository of users' opinions. Decision-makers rely on Twitter to examine tweets about various topics of interest. In doing so, they can determine the nature, context, and accompanying emotions of what people are discussing. The topics taken up in such discussions include current affairs, events, and products, and tweets can indicate both the intensity of discussions and how people react to them. In this paper, we propose a system that collects tweets and applies sentiment analysis to them. It allows users and decision-makers to browse an ordered and categorized list of tweets based on their sentiment and popularity measures, such as retweet and favorite. An essential advantage of our system is that it can be used more generally to explore any topic of interest with which the public is engaging on Twitter. Our findings show that using the number of retweets and the number of favorites enhances the sentiment scores and enables the highlighting of tweets' most common opinion on a given topic.

Keywords: Twitter · Sentiment analysis · Retweet · favorite

1 Introduction

The evolution of microblogging services and social media platforms has opened up new horizons for individuals and organizations to share thoughts and opinions about various topics, products, and events. Often, when businesses need to gain an understanding of the public's or consumers' views, they conduct surveys or opinion polls. However, with the surge of activity on social media, individuals and organizations are increasingly using the content on these platforms as a repository of opinions from a variety of users to facilitate decision-making [1]. Twitter has been recognized as ideal for this purpose due to the large number of Twitter users and of tweets exchanged on a daily basis. This has encouraged researchers and decision-makers to mine Twitter for valuable information. Hence, the popularity of Twitter as a source of information has led to the development of numerous applications for analyzing its content.

Tweet sentiment has been utilized for various purposes, including measuring users' reactions to a particular topic. However, the sentiment alone measures only how the public feels about a product or particular topic; it does not offer insights into the extent to which the content of particular tweets is interesting to or influential over others. Twitter provides a number of useful functions, including retweet and like. When a user

© Springer Nature Switzerland AG 2019
A. Alfaries et al. (Eds.): ICC 2019, CCIS 1097, pp. 162–169, 2019.
https://doi.org/10.1007/978-3-030-36365-9_13

finds a tweet interesting, s/he can retweet it to make it visible to all his/her followers. The reposted tweet (retweet) may contain a short comment [2]. Research has shown that tweets with interesting information receive an overwhelming number of retweets [3]. Thus, the number of retweets serves as a proxy with which to estimate users' engagement with the tweet's content, because it allows us to measure how information is disseminated among users. The like function, on the other hand, enables a user to add a tweet s/he likes to his/her list of likes. In contrast to retweeting, users typically like a tweet for several reasons, such as broadcasting the tweet, bookmarking the tweet for future reference, or using the tweet as a way to represent him/herself, that is, to indicate that s/he likes or approves of it [4]. Moreover, Twitter statistics show that mobile Twitter users are 76% more likely to favorite and 66% more likely to retweet [5].

In this paper, we propose a system that enhances tweet sentiment by adding two popularity-estimation measures to the sentiment score of each tweet. These measures are the number of retweets and the number of likes (favorites). The system will show the raw data (tweets) ordered by their sentiment strength, retweet and likes count as far as we are aware has not been explored before. Tweet sentiment shows how people react to a particular topic, whereas retweet reveals the degree to which this tweet is relevant or interesting. However, retweet functionality may account only for certain kinds of tweet relevance and interestingness [6]; thus, incorporating favorite can provide a complementary source of data on implicit user interests and tweet relevance. By focusing on tweets collected from specific hashtags, our system enables decision-makers to apply their knowledge and reasoning skills to explore and understand the tweets.

To compute tweet sentiment, we followed the lexicon-based approach. Because Twitter language tends to be informal, with many abbreviations, misspelled words, and grammatical errors and a great deal of slang, we compared three available lexicons and selected the one that achieved the best performance. We incorporated the resulting sentiment scores into the popularity measures and then ranked the tweets based on the combined score for each sentiment category (positive, negative, and neutral). Our findings show that the ordered list of tweets both provides insight into the nature of the topics discussed in these tweets and enhances their visibility. This pair of outcomes can facilitate the process of further inspection by decision-makers. The remainder of this paper proceeds as follows. Section 2 summarizes the related research, highlighting previous studies of sentiment analysis and Twitter's popularity measures. Section 3 discusses the methodology we used to implement the system, including the stages followed and the formulas used to compute tweets' scores. Section 4 discusses the results, and Sect. 5 offers a conclusion.

2 Related Work

This section provides an overview of related research on Twitter as a source of information, focusing on studies involving tweet-sentiment analysis and indicating what tweet aspects were considered.

A comprehensive overview of the existing studies of opinion mining and sentiment analysis was presented by Pang et al. [1] and Liu [2]. Both provided a thorough introduction to this problem and discussed the techniques used to solve each problem in sentiment analysis.

Go et al. [3] were among the first to explore sentiment analysis on Twitter. They used a variety of machine-learning models to classify tweets into binary classes, that is, negative or positive sentiment for a query term. They extracted tweets through Twitter Search APIs and used the emoticons in tweets to generate a labeled dataset as positive, with positive emoticons ":)", and as negative, with negative emoticons ":(". By adopting the same approach, Pak et al. [4] investigated the validity of Twitter as a corpus for sentiment analysis. They collected a corpus of 300,000 tweets evenly split automatically between three classes: positive and negative tweets using emoticons and neutral tweets acquired from newspapers and magazine accounts. The authors applied a machine-learning process for tweet polarity classification and tested the performance using the test dataset established by [3]. By contrast, we followed the lexicon-based approach and considered tweet aspects other than sentiment. The studies discussed below used this approach as well.

Arslan et al. [5] applied sentiment analysis using a small-scale dataset that contain popular tweets. Our study stresses the importance of retweets as well, but instead of using a dataset of popular tweets, we incorporate the retweet score into the calculation of the combined score with sentiment.

Guevara et al. [6] considered sentiment analysis to provide information about tweets belonging to different domains using a statistical lexicon approach. They developed a mobile app to obtain the polarity of topics discussed, represented by the polarity of the total tweet in terms of positive, negative, and neutral values.

Researchers have also examined the effect of tweet characteristics such as retweets, favorites, replies, mentions, followers, and URLs. The impact of these features on sentiment analysis and opinion mining have been analyzed by considering their presence/absence or their frequency in a tweet. For instance, Lashari et al. [7] monitored Twitter users' opinions by measuring the influence of users' retweet activity for particular search keywords. They classified retweets as endorsing, opposing, or reporting the original tweet according to a sentiment analysis in which retweets were classified as positive, negative, or neutral. Tsugawa1 et al. [8] used the retweet function to investigate the relationship between the sentiment of a tweet and its virality in order to determine what sentiment polarity is more likely to undergo diffusion. Regarding the favorite function, Erzikova et al. [9] analyzed the topmost retweeted tweets shared during the 2014 domestic abuse case of NFL player Ray Rice and found that the number of favorites and followers of the originating tweets could be considered indicators of tweet popularity.

Considering the unique role of retweet and favorite in determining which tweets draw users' attention, in this paper, we combine the tweet popularity scores with their sentiment strength to rank tweets and situate the most interesting ones at the top in order to facilitate the process of decision-making.

3 Methodology

The system design is shown in Fig. 1. The user specifies his/her query and chooses the number of tweets to be retrieved; the system then obtains the number of tweets that match a user-specified query. After a collection of tweets is retrieved from Twitter, the preprocessing steps are applied to the collected data. Then, sentiment classification is automatically performed on tweets using the lexicon-based approach, and the count of retweets and favorites for each tweet is considered. The output of this process is a classification of the sentiment of each tweet in the collection as either positive, neutral, or negative. Tweets are then grouped into a list and ordered according to their combined score. Finally, the system generates a word-cloud visualization and histogram chart to aid in identifying trends and patterns that would be difficult to identify from tweets alone.

The system has been implemented using the R language on Rstudio, an open source data analysis software package, with the help of the Shiny app to make interactive web applications for visualizing data.

We hypothesize that tweets ordered at the top are the most relevant to decision-makers. To summarize, the system consists of five main functions: (1) collecting data, (2) data preprocessing, (3) applying sentiment analysis and classifying tweets into categories of sentiment (positive, negative, or neutral), (4) combining the sentiment score with the retweet and favorite counts, and (5) ordering and visualizing the overall results.

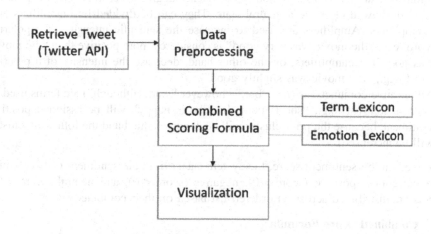

Fig. 1. Proposed system design.

3.1 Data Collection and Preprocessing

Twitter Search API enables developers to retrieve tweets to their systems. We used the Twitter Search API to retrieve tweets in English relevant to the topic using the hashtag symbol (#). A user of our system can decide what hashtag to collect from. The text is then cleaned by applying a series of preprocessing steps, such as removing the following: hashtags (e.g., #apple), Twitter usernames (e.g., @sara, where the symbol @ indicates a username), Twitter special words (such as "RT"), numbers, irrelevant tweets, any additional spaces, duplicate tweets, and tokenization; in addition, emoticons were replaced with their equivalent word.

3.2   Sentiment Analysis

To calculate the sentiment scores for tweets, we utilized sentimentr package [10]. The sentiment words in each sentence are compared to a lexicon of polarized words (pw). Positive and negative words are tagged with "+1" and "−1," respectively (depending on the lexicon default weight). The sentences of tweets are then summed and divided by the square root of the word count (n), as expressed by Eq. (1) [10].

$$\delta = \sum \frac{pw}{\sqrt{n}} \tag{1}$$

Valence shifters [11] are augmented with the previous method to enhance the scoring; the following are lexical phenomena that can affect the valence of a word.

- Negations are terms, such as "not," "never," and "none," that can reverse the polarity of the lexical word next to a negator. Combining positive words with a negation flips the positive valence to a negative valence (e.g., "the movie is not good"), whereas the combination of a negative word with a negation turns the whole into a positive evaluation (e.g., "the movie is not bad").
- Intensifiers are terms used to modify the valence degree to reach an extreme polarity level or draw it closer to a neutral state. They can be divided into amplifiers and deamplifiers. Amplifiers are used to increase the semantic intensity of a polarity word (e.g., "the movie was very good" is considered more positive than "the movie was good"). Deamplifiers, on the other hand, decrease the intensity of a polarity word (e.g., "the movie was slightly good").
- Adversative conjunctions (i.e., "but," "however," and "although") are terms used to express contrast (e.g., "she is poor, but she is happy" will be assigned positive sentiment, because the prior cluster will be downweighted and the following cluster will be increased).

Based on the sentiment score, the system categorizes the sentiment of tweets into three categories: positive (score > 0), negative (score < 0), and neutral (score = 0). Tweets are distributed across an ordered list based on their combined score.

3.3   Combined Score Formula

After the sentiment scoring, the system combines the score with a retweet and favorite count, as follows.

- For the positive and neutral category, the system applies Eq. (2):

$$\text{Final score} = \log_{10} f + \log_{10} r + \delta \tag{2}$$

- For the negative category, noting that the sentiment score is negative, the system subtracts the counts to get the final score as applied in Eq. (3):

$$\text{Final score} = (-\log_{10}(f)) + (-\log_{10}(r)) + \delta, \tag{3}$$

where f and r refer to the count of favorites and retweets, respectively, and δ denotes the sentiment score. The $\log_{10}$ is used to normalize large values.

3.4 Visualization

The data are visualized using an ordered list of tweets that shows the top ten tweets with their favorite and retweet counts, the sentiment score, and the combined score per page for each category, word cloud, and histogram. A word cloud is a visual representation of text data, typically used to represent keywords on websites or to visualize free-form text. This format is useful for quickly perceiving the highest-trending keywords from tweets. Histograms graphically represent the positivity or negativity of peoples' opinions about the topic.

4 Results and Discussion

4.1 Lexicon Evaluation

We evaluated a number of lexicons and then incorporated the best-performing lexicon with valence shifters and replaced the emoticons appearing in a tweet to increase the classification accuracy. We used the Stanford test dataset, which is appropriate for evaluation of the classification models' performance, because it is manually collected and labelled. The dataset contains 177 negative, 182 positive, and 139 neutral manually labelled tweets [3].

We used three freely available, manually created, general-domain sentiment lexicons to identify the lexicon most suitable for the Twitter environment. The lexicons are the Hu and Liu lexicon [12], the SemEval-2015 English Twitter sentiment lexicon [13], and the NRC emotion lexicon [14]. We used precision, recall, and F1 score to evaluate the lexicons. Because the Hue and Liu lexicon exhibited higher performance than the others, we incorporated it with valence shifters and replaced the emoticons, as shown in Table 1.

Table 1. Evaluation measures for English Twitter, NRC, and Hue & Liu lexicons.

Lexicon	Precision	Recall	F1
English Twitter lexicon	0.60	0.54	0.52
NRC lexicon	0.57	0.52	0.52
Hue & Liu lexicon	0.72	0.68	0.69
Augmented Hue & Liu lexicon	0.71	0.70	0.70

4.2 System Results and Discussion

To show the system results in the dashboard, we used the hashtag "GalaxyNote8" as a query, and we specified 500 tweets to be retrieved. After the tweets are collected and preprocessed, the system computes the estimated sentiment of each tweet, considers the number of retweets and favorites associated with each tweet (if any), and then ranks the tweets according to three distinct categories based on their polarity as positive, negative, or neutral, as shown in Table 2.

The case study demonstrated by the system shows that the tweet that attracts the user's interest is the one that is being retweeted and favorited. Therefore, the system raises the tweet score. Table 2 shows how retweets and favorites can affect the sentiment and help product providers find what they seek for, such as the impact of their product. For the positive tweet, we can observe that the Galaxy Note 8 camera is a positive aspect of the product and that a large number of users agree with the tweet author on this. Consequently, the system increases the strength of the sentiment score based on this evidence. The same goes for the negative tweet: the system increases the strength of negativity. As for the neutral tweets, the example shows how a tweet turns from neutral to positive when it has retweets and favorites.

Table 2. Sample of categorized tweets.

Category	Tweet	#Favorite	#Retweet	Sentiment score	Combined score
Positive	Think I'll get a #GalaxyNote8 the camera is nice. No more #iphone for me	28	34	0.1818	3.1883
Neutral	What makes the #GalaxyNote8 S Pen so special? You can pop it out at any time to easily take notes, even if your pho.... https://t.co/7bb6npG0rp	15	6	0	2.0492
Negative	Face Recognition Stopped Working on #GalaxyNote8? Solutions to Fix the Issue #indiedev #AndroidDev... https://t.co/a3I9X3Qplh	2	3	−0.1929	−1.2721

5 Conclusion

In this paper, we proposed a system that obtains tweets from Twitter and then classifies them as positive, negative, or neutral based on their sentiment scores. The results are visualized as ranked categories based on combined sentiment score, with retweet and favorite counts, a histogram chart, and a word cloud. A key advantage of the system is that it can be used more generally to explore any topic of interest with which the public is engaging on Twitter. For example, when a company releases a new product, it can monitor how the product is being discussed as well as gain knowledge about the effect of social media campaigns. In future studies, we plan to improve the system in terms of sentiment classification and to consider other ranking measures, such as the credibility of tweets and users. Regarding sentiment classification, we plan to improve the pre-processing by using abbreviation and slang dictionaries; moreover, interpreting emojis instead of only the emoticon will strengthen the sentiment analysis.

References

1. Pang, B., Lee, L.: Opinion mining and sentiment analysis. Found. Trends® Inf. Retrieval **2** (1–2), 1–135 (2008)
2. Liu, B.: Sentiment Analysis and Opinion Mining. Morgan & Claypool, San Rafael (2012)
3. Go, A., Bhayani, R., Huang, L.: Twitter Sentiment Classification using Distant Supervision (2009)
4. Pak, A., Paroubek, P.: Twitter as a corpus for sentiment analysis and opinion mining. In: Proceedings of the Seventh conference on International Language Resources and Evaluation (LREC 2010), Valletta, Malta (2010)
5. Arslan, Y., Birturk, A., Djumabaev, B., Kucuk, D.: Real-time Lexicon-based sentiment analysis experiments on Twitter with a mild (more information, less data) approach. In: 2017 IEEE International Conference on Big Data (Big Data), Boston, MA, pp. 1892–1897 (2017)
6. Guevara, J., Costa, J., Arroba, J., Silva, C.: Harvesting opinions in Twitter for sentiment analysis. In: 2018 13th Iberian Conference on Information Systems and Technologies (CISTI), Caceres, pp. 1–7 (2018)
7. Lashari, I.A., Wiil, U.K.: Monitoring public opinion by measuring the sentiment of retweets on Twitter. In: Proceedings of the 3rd European Conference on Social Media Research, Caen, France (2016)
8. Tsugawa, S., Ohsaki, H.: On the relation between message sentiment and its virality on social media. Soc. Netw. Anal. Min. **7**(1), 19 (2017)
9. Erzikova, E., Gandy, L.M., Hall, A., Kuntz, K.: The 2014 NFL player ray rice domestic abuse case: an analysis of factors that contributed to tweet popularity during the scandal. In: Proceedings of the 3rd European Conference on Social Media Research, Caen, France (2016)
10. Rinker, T.: sentimentr: Calculate Text Polarity Sentiment (2019)
11. Polanyi, L., Zaenen, A.: Contextual valence shifters. In: Shanahan, J.G., Qu, Y., Wiebe, J. (eds.) Computing Attitude and Affect in Text: Theory and Applications. The Information Retrieval Series, vol. 20, pp. 1–10. Springer, Dordrecht (2006). https://doi.org/10.1007/1-4020-4102-0_1
12. Hu, M., Liu, B.: Mining and summarizing customer reviews. In: Proceedings of the 2004 ACM SIGKDD International Conference on Knowledge Discovery and Data Mining - KDD 2004, Seattle, WA, USA, p. 168 (2004)
13. Kiritchenko, S., Zhu, X., Mohammad, S.M.: Sentiment analysis of short informal texts. J. Artif. Intell. Res. **50**, 723–762 (2014)
14. Mohammad, S.M., Turney, P.D.: Crowdsourcing a word-emotion association lexicon. Comput. Intell. **29**(3), 436–465 (2013)

Event-Based Driving Style Analysis

Zubaydh Kenkar[⊠] and Sawsan AlHalawani

Prince Sultan University, Riyadh, Saudi Arabia
zkenkar@gmail.com, sawsan.halawani@gmail.com

Abstract. Driving styles have been analyzed for different purposes, such as building intelligent road systems, ensuring fuel economy, improving road congestion, vehicle automation, and road safety. Nevertheless, driving analysis is an exciting and evolving topic to study in terms of enhancing Driver Assistance Systems (DAS) and mitigating vehicle accidents. Therefore, the primary goal of this paper aims to develop a model that can classify the drivers based on their driving styles given the behavioural events that the drivers make while driving. Hence, we used an open source UAH-DriveSet dataset; the data were logged by many drivers who performed several trips on motorways and secondary roads with different driving styles (aggressive, normal, drowsy) in a real experiment. Furthermore, we propose the extraction of statistical and behavioural features that are used to represent different driving trips based on the driving events which occur during these trips. Then, we used these features to create a supervised learning model, i.e. using Support Vector Machines (SVM), to classify the trips according to the driver's style. Moreover, the developed model can better classify the styles for different drivers, especially after selecting the best features that clearly distinguish between the different styles. One further application of the proposed features and methodology is to classify the road type according to the driver's style.

Keywords: Driving styles · Classification algorithms · Machine learning · Feature extraction · Feature selection

1 Introduction

Driving cars is an essential transportation medium. It is usually clear that drivers have different driving styles and attitudes while driving. Indeed, you can notice the different driving styles of other people when you drive. The variety of driving styles has various causes, such as driver age: for example, most young drivers tend to go faster than older drivers, who drive at a steady speed [4]. Also, drivers have different attitudes towards obeying the speed limit as some drive within the limit while others exceed the maximum allowed driving speed which of course has an impact on the driving style [18]. Moreover, traffic can be a reason for having different driving styles as drivers are exposed to stop-and-go traffic or congestion [6]. In the literature, researchers have categorized drivers styles into many categories, like Aggressive, Drowsy, Normal [17]. Other works classify the

© Springer Nature Switzerland AG 2019
A. Alfaries et al. (Eds.): ICC 2019, CCIS 1097, pp. 170–182, 2019.
https://doi.org/10.1007/978-3-030-36365-9_14

driving styles into: Calm, Average, Moderate and Aggressive [8,21] compliant or violating [2]. Moreover various factors could impact the driving style, e.g. workload, communication, use of mobile devices, driving on different road types. For instance, driving on an on-ramp could increase the workload more than driving on exit roads, as studied in [20]. Based on that, drivers could adopt various styles while driving on a motorway or a secondary road [17]. The researchers in [19] explored how an autonomous vehicle can learn about an individual's driving style in different scenarios, such as braking. Hence, the autonomous vehicle can react to the human driver based on their style [10]. Classifying driver styles can significantly enhance the lifestyles of individuals. The main goal of the work in this paper is to create a supervised learning model that classifies driving styles in a real-world driving dataset. The dataset already labels the driving trips according to their driver's style as aggressive, drowsy and normal categories. The drivers performed several trips (about six trips per driver) on two types of roads: (Motorway, Secondary). Both roads from the Community of Madrid (Spain), close to the city of Alcal'a de Henares. Further, In this paper we propose an event-based model to analyse driving styles. We extract two categories of features: statistical and behavioural features. The proposed behavioural features capture the pattern of driving in a novel way that was not addressed earlier in the literature as its combining the essence of different events together. Moreover, the combination of the statistical and behavioural features makes the model more robust in identifying the driving styles for individuals. Finally, we introduce the impact of road types (motorway and secondary roads) on different driving styles. So we contribute to represent the different driving trips based on events and extract the features by utilizing the driving events such as braking, turning and acceleration. Also, to create a robust model that can classify the driving styles of individuals based on the proposed features: Statistical and behavioural features. Further, to create a model that is able to classify the driving styles of individuals based on the road type such as: Motorway and Secondary roads. Finally, to select the discriminant and strongest features to identify the styles of the drivers.

2   Related Work

We review the related work in driving styles classification based on events and features.

2.1   Events Detection

We assumed that extracting the event and extracting the event's intensity or level have been already completed in [17], and based on those events; we extracted the features that used to represent the trips in our classification model. Hence, the authors in [3] developed a mobile application (DriveSafe app) that can observe the driving styles under real-time scenarios and alert the driver based on safety scoring sensors. Moreover, In [10], the spectral features were extracted using the Discrete Wavelet Transform (DWT) implemented in [11]. In [5], the harsh braking events were extracted from GPS data. Likewise, the authors in [14], they analysed the braking events and bumps in the road by using accelerometer, GPS and magnetometer sensor data. Following this, the researchers in [3] detected lane drifting by using an indicator called Lanex which is a (fraction of given time interval spent outside a virtual Lane exits), and it measures the driver's tendency to exit the lane [9].

2.2 Road Type Analysis

To answer the ask whether the road type can affect the style of driving; we consider the experiment performed in [17] where drivers drove on different road types. Further, this paper approach tried to state that the change of the road type affects the driving style respectively. The researchers in [2] studied safety improvements to road intersections, noting that drivers' styles classifications such as (compliant, violating) can be applied for an advanced Driver Assistance System (DAS) to alert the driver by providing feedback and balancing their performance under unsafe conditions. In [1], researchers analysed how cities do look by using their topological and geometric features to label their physical layouts. In order to classify diverse cities. The authors suggested network-level descriptors because of their reliability and accuracy. Their research involved determining how cities function and look without studying their visual appearances, instead of using topological features to determine street connectivity and geometric features.

2.3 Driving Styles Analysis

Defining these styles could enhance autonomous driving through the application of intelligent vehicle systems [14]. The analysis also facilitates many DAS [10], to better mitigate risks and adapt the driver's style. Further, driving styles such as aggressive, normal and defensive are having an impact on fuel consumption especially for aggressive drivers who consume fuel at a higher rate [22]. The approach in [16] is to enhance drivers' safety by analyzing the driving styles. Numerous approaches are provided in the literature for implementing driver styles classification. We included the most relevant approaches to this paper. In [2], the researchers classified driver styles at signalized intersections. They concluded with a set of observations of drivers stopped at a traffic signal, and they used two common algorithms in an ML approach: a discriminative approach based on SVM, and a generative approach based on hidden Markov models (HMMs). To combine the features extracted from the sensor observations, such as distance to the intersection, speed, and longitudinal acceleration, accordingly, they used Gaussian radial basis function.

3   Event-Based Classification Model for Driving Behaviours

In this paper we used supervised Machine Learning algorithms to implement an event-based driver styles classification model.

3.1   Features Extraction for Classifying the Driving Styles

Events and features can be extracted in many ways, discussed in details in the literature. Further, we assume that the driving events have been already detected and extracted. In order to prepare for our features extraction, the extracted events are represented using three values based on the event types (T_i) such as: braking $= 1$, turning $= 2$, acceleration $= 3$. In the other hand, the event intensity (L_i) which represents the strength of the occurrence of the respective event are also represented as follows: low $= 1$, medium $= 2$, high $= 3$. Given the events and their intensity, we will represent each of the 40 trips as a vector of 13 features we extracted in this work, see Fig. (1).

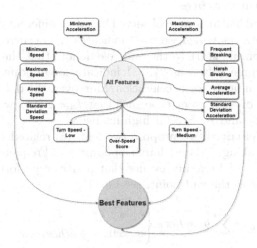

Fig. 1. Features extraction

3.1.1   Statistical Features

These features are determined based on the vehicle speed and its related accelerometers. For **The Speed Features**, the following features are calculated: Minimum Speed f_{ns}: This represents the minimum speed that a driver adopts during a trip from the start point to the end point. Maximum Speed f_{xs}: This represents the maximum speed that a driver adopts during a trip from the start point to the end. Average Speed f_{avs}: This represents the average speed that a driver adopts during a trip from the start point to the end point. Standard Deviation for Speed f_{sds}: This represents the dispersion of the mean speed during a trip from the start point to the end point. On the other hand, for **The Acceleration Features**, the following features are calculated: Minimum acceleration f_{na}: This represents the minimum acceleration that a driver reaches during a trip from the start point to the end point. Maximum acceleration f_{xa}: This represents the maximum acceleration that a driver reaches during a trip from the start point to the end point. Average acceleration f_{ava}: This represents the average acceleration of a driver during a trip from the start point to the end point. Standard deviation for acceleration f_{sda}: This represents the dispersion of the mean acceleration during a trip from the start point to the end point. Harsh acceleration f_{ha}: This is the count of how many times a driver accelerates with a high-intensity acceleration that a driver achieves during a trip from the start point to the end point. The intensity (L_i) acceleration is $= 3$, which is (high). We proposed it as one of the behavioural features, but its value was zeros for all trips in our dataset based on acceleration $L_i = 3$ (high), as no trips included any high acceleration. Therefore, no harsh acceleration occurred.

3.1.2 Behavioural Features

Different behavioural features were observed based on different driving styles and road types. The data set which we used indicates the occurrence of the events thought the trip from its start to the end. We denote that the event type as T_i which could have three values as $T_i = 1$ indicate for braking, $T_i = 2$ indicate for turning, $T_i = 3$ indicate for acceleration. Moreover, the data provides details about the intensity of each event type such that $L_i = 1$ for low intensity, $L_i = 2$ for medium intensity and $L_i = 3$ for high intensity.

For **Braking Features**, we propose two features related to braking as following: frequent braking f_{fb} and harsh braking f_{hb}. Frequent braking f_{fb}: It represents the count of breaking events that a driver performs during a trip from the start point to the end point, see Eq. (1).

$$f_{fb} = \sum_{i=1}^{n} b_i, where \begin{cases} b_i = 1, if & T_i = 1 \\ b_i = 0, & otherwise \end{cases} \tag{1}$$

T_i = Event Type, b_i = Braking Counter, n = number of timestamp in the trip

While, Harsh Braking f_{hb}: braking events have been labeled in the dataset [17] based on the intensity of braking as Low, Medium, High. Indeed, it will indicate the hesitation in the driver style. Therefore, we utilized knowing the intensity of braking to propose the Harsh Braking f_{hb} which represents the high level of braking events, see Eq. (2).

$$f_{hb} = \sum_{i=1}^{n} b_i, where \begin{cases} b_i = 1, & if & T_i = 1 & L_i = 3 \\ b_i = 0, & & otherwise \end{cases} \tag{2}$$

T_i = Event Type, b_i = Braking Counter, n = number of timestamp in the trip, L_i = Event level

for **Turning Speed Features**, we measured how a driver behave while turning (event) in terms of speed. Numerous researchers have studied turning behaviours for their effects on people and road safety [23]. However, none has associated the turning with speed at the occurrence of turning. Therefore, we combined the turning event with each GPS speed and level of that turn. The level of turning event was also categorized in [17] as low, medium or high. So, Low turning speed f_{lt}: This represents the lowest average speed that a driver takes when he/she turns the car with a (low) level turning during the trip from the start point to the end point. The intensity of turning level (low) was already labeled in [17], see Eq. (3)).

$$TurningSpeed f_{lt} = \frac{\sum_{i=1}^{n} S_i}{c_{Low}}, \quad T = 2, \quad L = 1 \tag{3}$$

T_i = Event Type , n = Number of Timestamp in the trip, c = Turning Counter, L_i = Event level, S_i = Turning Speed

While, Medium turning speed f_{mt}: This represents the medium average speed that a driver takes when he/she turns the car with a (medium) level turning during the trip from the start point to the end point. The intensity of turning level (medium) was already labeled in [17], (see Eq. (4).

$$TurningSpeed f_{mt} = \frac{\sum_{i=1}^{n} S_i}{c_{Medium}}, \quad T = 2, \quad L = 2 \tag{4}$$

T_i = Event Type, n = Number of Timestamp in the trip, c = Turning Counter, L_i = Event level, S_i = Turning Speed

However, Harsh turning speed f_{ht}: This represents the high average speed that a driver takes when he/she turns the car with a (high) level turning during the trip from the start point to the end point. The intensity of turning level (high) was already labeled in [17], (see Eq. (5)). While developing this feature, we found out that none of the drivers executed a harsh turning speed f_{ht} on any of the trips, and this feature resulted in zero for each trip. Hence, it was ignored for the given data set in this study.

$$TurningSpeed f_{ht} = \frac{\sum_{i=1}^{n} S_i}{c_{High}}, \quad T = 2, \quad L = 3 \tag{5}$$

T_i = Event Type , n = Number of Timestamp in the trip , c = Turning Counter , L_i = Event level, S_i = Turning Speed

Finally, the last feature is **Over-speeding** f_{ov}, this is evaluate the driver style when the driver is not allowed to exceed the maximum speed limit, see Eqs. (4) and (5). We have calculated the over-speeding values based on the GPS speed, and the maximum allowed speed taken from Open Street Map (OSM) [17], see Eq. (6).

$$Overspeed f_{ov} = \sum_{i=1}^{n} c, where \begin{cases} c = 1 & if \quad S_i > maxS_i \\ c = 0 & if \quad S_i \leq maxS_i \end{cases} \tag{6}$$

c = Speeding Counter , n = Number of Timestamp in the trip , S_i = Speed at timestamp i, $maxS_i$ = Maximum Allowed speed at Timestamp i

3.2   Description of the Drivers Dataset

We utilized the public UAH-DriveSet have been extracted by [17] based on
the driving control application called "DrievSafe" since DriveSafe application
is taking many raw data during the trips. It has also processed signals which
is semantic information. All the data are collected to create UAH-DriveSet for
six different drivers vehicles, behaving three different styles (normal, drowsy and
aggressive) during 40 trips. The experiment took place on two road types: motorways and secondary roads. Both roads were located in the community of Madrid
(Spain) around the city of Alcal'a de Henares. Resulting in a total of 500 min
in real-time data. Researchers in UAH-DriveSet-DriveSet divided the data into
three sections; first, is the Row real-time data which contain two files for the
measurements extracted by the phone-inertial sensors (accelerometers and gyro-
scopes) and the GPS. Second is the processed data as continuous variables and
contains three files; each file has many variables that are processed continuously
by DriveSafe application. Also, DriveSafe processes maneuvers with respect to
the driving lane and the ahead vehicles from the rear camera as well as it processes the road information based on road APIs such as OpenStreetMap (OSM)
from the internet connection, which we utilized to detect the location of the
routes (GPS Latitude degrees and GPS Longitude degrees). The third is the
processed data as events, which we utilized some of these events to extract the
proposed features used in the model's classification.

4   Classifier Implementation for Driving Styles Analysis

Given the richness of the data drawn from many drivers' trips, which are labeled
based on their driving styles. We utilized the "timestamp" and the "GPS data"
to calculate most of the features since "timestamp" presents the seconds from
the start point of the route, in order to synchronize between the different files.
Then, the 13 Statistical and Behavioural features extracted based on the assumed
events in [17] have been normalized to be ready for classification. The classification considers 40 observations for 40 trips among six drivers. We have divided the
classification classes into two groups. The first classification was implemented for
the drivers' behaviours while the second classification implemented for the road
type. The choice of the learning model was to be a supervised learning model
since we have labeled data based on the driver's driving style. We decided to
use Supervised Vector Machine (SVM) [15], because of its simplicity and widely
used. Since the difference between Aggressive and Normal classes, SVM should
works efficiently with a clear margin of separation. Also, SVM can represent the
model using only a few examples. Furthermore, based on the learning algorithm,
we trained the model with 70% as training data and 30% for testing.

4.1   Features Selection

A common practice is to select the best features among all the proposed features. We noticed that most of the best features which were identified are the

behavioural features. It indicates that considering such type of features that capture the essence of the driving style behaviour could significantly improve the identification of the driver's styles in driving. We found the following features: Maximum Speed f_{xs}, Frequent Braking f_{f_b}, Turning speed Medium f_{mt}, Over-speeding f_{ov}, are the ones which are very discriminant. These features were identified as the best features for the multi-classifier and most of the binary classifiers, which indicates the strengthens of these features.

4.2 Building the Classification Model

To train the application model, we used some Support Vector Machine SVM learning algorithms. SVM are mostly used in classification challenges because they provide higher accuracy and work well on kind of smaller datasets. Therefore, we have applied SVM both of multi-class and binary classifications. We classify the model using various SVM kernels, such as linear SVM (LSVM), which makes linear segregation between classes, and we used quadratic SVM (QSVM) and cubic SVM (CSVM), which, both have medium flexibility on the model. Finally, we used medium Gaussian SVM (GSVM) which has a kernel scale and medium distinctions on the model. We use MATLAB [13] to classify the data. Hence, classification learner in MATLAB is useful since we can choose many SVMs parameters at once during classification. Because of the simplicity and the accurate performance estimation of the model [1,12], we used cross-validation for estimating the performance of the model to better evaluate the performance of the model and hyper-parameters [7]. To avoid the model overfitting or underfitting the data, we started by experimenting with the most recommended k-fold CV [1,12]. Since the number of folds depends on the data size, our dataset comprised 40 data instances. We experimented based on $k = 2$, $k = 5$ and $k = 10$ validation. Hence, we considered k-fold $= 5$ as the best fit iteration.

4.3 Driving Styles Multi-classifier

We aimed to construct the model with trips which correctly identifies the class to which the new feature belonged. Moreover, we observed 40 trips for six drivers. The data were labeled based on the driving styles, with 17 instances of data belonging to the normal category, 12 for drowsy and 11 for aggressive. The dataset have total 40 trips, and the distribution of trips based on driving styles is: (11: Aggressive, 12: Drowsy, 17: Normal). After we trained the model with all the features, we received different accuracy's. However, the accuracy results in Fig. (2) show the multi-classifier along with their accuracy based on SVM kernel's algorithm using all extracted features and best-selected features, however, the LSVM outperforms the QSVM when classifying based on the best feature which are determined to be: Maximum Speed f_{ms}, Frequent Braking f_{f_b}, Turning speed Medium f_{mt}, Over-speeding f_{ov}. The performance of Medium GSVM is the lowest. We observe that the model classifies Drowsy instances as Aggressive or Normal trips. Although the model should be able to classify based on the

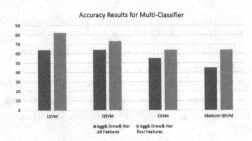

Fig. 2. Accuracy results for multi-classifier with all and selected features. Based on SVM Kernels Algorithm: Linear SVM (LSVM), Quadratic SVM (QSVM), Cubic SVM (CSVM) and Medium Gaussian SVM (GSVM) using k-fold = 5 cross-validation

multi-classes, therefore, we conclude that the Drowsy style is misleading for the classifier. Likewise, when the model classifies the data using the best features and considered to be the most robust features, we notice that accuracy gets higher. We have included the Random Classifier which gives 33% accuracy for the multi-classifier between the Aggressive, Drowsy, Normal classes.

4.4   Driving Styles Binary Classifier

We classify the behaviours as binary classes as the following: Aggressive against (Normal and Drowsy), Normal against (Drowsy and Aggressive), Drowsy against (Normal and Aggressive) and Aggressive against Normal. The primary purpose of this classification is to identify if there are any similarities between the driving styles classes. The reason behind this is to analyze the drowsy class which could be a misleading class and is not very distinctive compared to the aggressive and normal driving. The performance for LSVM and QSVM are the same although the performance of Medium GSVM is the lowest, see the results in Fig. (3). Hence, we noticed that the accuracy overall is improved when the model classifies the data using the best features. We have included the Random Classifier which gives 50% accuracy for the binary classifier to classify one class against all the other classes. Moreover, comparing the binary classifier between the Aggressive and Normal classes with the multi-classifier, we notice that this binary classifier performs better which emphasizes our assumption that the drowsy class is misleading and the classifier could confuse it with the other classes.

5   Results and Application

We proposed a classification model to classify the different driving styles based on the driver's behaviours. We employed different SVM kernels in order to attain a higher accuracy percentage. We noted that each SVM classifier performed differently according to the used kernels from a driving behaviours perspective. Drowsy driving is close to normal driving; accordingly, we assumed that the drowsy class could be misleading. Therefore, we decided to do a binary classification by combining the Aggressive and Normal classes as a single class to get

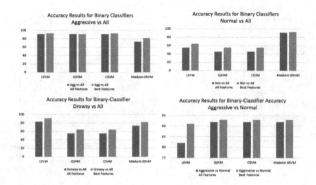

Fig. 3. Accuracy results for binary-classifier with all and selected features. Based on SVM Kernels Algorithm: Linear SVM (LSVM), Quadratic SVM (QSVM), Cubic SVM (CSVM) and Medium Gaussian SVM (GSVM) using k-fold = 5 cross-validation

more clarity about the difference in classification-based. Overall, we found that the accuracy of the binary class is doing better than multi-class whether with all features or best features.

5.1   Confusion Matrix

We used a confusion matrix to describe the performance of the driving behaviours classification model on the test data for which the true values are known. See Fig. (4a) plots confusion matrix for the multi-classifier using (LSVM) with K-Fold = 5. Following this, the total accuracy of this model is 81.8% when we used 70% of the data as training data and tested it on the other 30% of the data, based on all the extracted features. Besides, we experiment our model with less training data, so we built the same model with the same kernel and k-fold = 5 once again by using 50% of the data as training data and tested it on the other 50% of the data. The total accuracy of this model is 73.7% as in Fig. (4b). This proofs the robustness of the proposed model.

5.2   Precision Recall

The Precision-Recall Curve says that multi-classifier performs better when using all the extracted features especially when we used the discriminate features. Although, we expected the binary classifier between the aggressive and normal classes is outperform the multi-classifier because drowsy class is misleading. However, see Fig. (5a), the binary classifier between the aggressive driving against the drowsy and normal classes has the highest Area Under Curve (AUC), while the lowest AUC for the Drowsy driving against the Aggressive and Normal classes. Likewise, the multi-classifier classification performance has improved when we used the best features. So, the multi-class classifier, see Fig. (5b) between the aggressive, drowsy and normal classes have the highest AUC because the behaviours of the drivers in this class are very distinct. So the

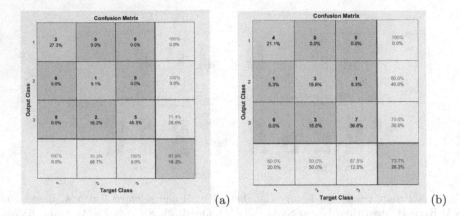

(a)   (b)

Fig. 4. Confusion Matrix for Agg and Drow and Nor Multi-Class and classified by using (LSVM) kernel using k-Fold = 5 cross validation; the Testing Data for each is (Agg = 3, Drow = 3, Nor = 5)

model can distinguish them and classified them correctly. While the lowest AUC for the Drowsy driving against the Aggressive and Normal classes, since Drowsy can still have some features that could classify it in Normal class.

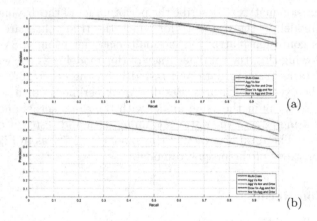

(a)

(b)

Fig. 5. Precision Recall for the classes: Agg& and Drow& and Nor, AggNor, AggAll, DrowAll, NorAll)

5.3   Conclusion

In this paper we aim to learn a model that can classify the different styles of drivers. In summary, Introducing the co-relation between the statistical and behavioural features enables having a robust model that can classify the driving styles, especially to differentiate the Aggressive driving style from the Normal driving style. As noted, these features where identified as the strongest features which improved the accuracy of the classification model. We recommend to consider more co-relations between other features which would be expected to capture the driving style better than the trivial features. One application for understanding the various driving styles is to enable improving the intelligent road systems to enhance the overall safety. As was concluded that driving styles vary depending on the road type, we recommend to consider more differences in road type and analyze the impact on the driving styles. Also, understating the driving styles can be implemented in a training tool for drivers to use and simulate the different behaviours in order to assist the learners to learn a better and safer driving style. It can be also used to evaluate the safety of the driver's driving style by comparing their driving style with the learned driving classes. In future work, we could enhance the proposed model by detecting new events. Also, we believe that features such as Slow driving, Frequent Stopping, Fatigued driving, also, finding the correlation between features such as braking and changing lane or car-following and distance to ahead vehicle are promising features to be included in the future model that classify driving styles.

Acknowledgement. We would like to acknowledge the Artificial Intelligence and Data Analytics (AIDA) Lab, Prince Sultan University, Riyadh, Saudi Arabia for supporting this work.

References

1. AlHalawani, S., Yang, Y.L., Wonka, P., Mitra, N.J.: What makes London work like London? Comput. Graph. Forum (2014). https://doi.org/10.1111/cgf.12441
2. Aoude, G.S., Desaraju, V.R., Stephens, L.H., How, J.P.: Behavior classification algorithms at intersections and validation using naturalistic data. In: 2011 IEEE Intelligent Vehicles Symposium (IV) (2011). https://doi.org/10.1109/ivs.2011.5940569
3. Bergasa, L.M., Almeria, D., Almazan, J., Yebes, J.J., Arroyo, R.: DriveSafe: an app for alerting inattentive drivers and scoring driving behaviors. In: 2014 IEEE Intelligent Vehicles Symposium Proceedings (2014). https://doi.org/10.1109/ivs.2014.6856461
4. Bhoraskar, R., Vankadhara, N., Raman, B., Kulkarni, P.: Wolverine: Traffic and road condition estimation using smartphone sensors. In: 2012 Fourth International Conference on Communication Systems and Networks (COMSNETS 2012) (2012). https://doi.org/10.1109/comsnets.2012.6151382
5. Bijman, J.: Cluster driving behaviour and assigning clusters to safe and unsafe driving behaviour through raw GPS trajectory data. Cluster Driving Behav. 1–53 (2017). https://doi.org/10.1002/9781444301342.ch14
6. BMW-Website: International driving styles: how the world drives, December 2018. https://www.bmw.com/en/automotive-life/driver-types-worldwide.html
7. Brownlee, J.: A gentle introduction to k-fold cross-validation, May 2018. https://machinelearningmastery.com/k-fold-cross-validation/. Accessed 30 Mar 2019
8. Castignani, G., Frank, R., Engel, T.: An evaluation study of driver profiling fuzzy algorithms using smartphones. In: 2013 21st IEEE International Conference on Network Protocols (ICNP), pp. 1–6. IEEE (2013)

9. Daza, I., Bergasa, L., Bronte, S., Yebes, J., Almazán, J., Arroyo, R.: Fusion of optimized indicators from advanced driver assistance systems (ADAS) for driver drowsiness detection. Sensors **14**(1), 1106–1131 (2014)
10. Feng, Y., Pickering, S., Chappell, E., Iravani, P., Brace, C.: Driving style analysis by classifying real-world data with support vector clustering. In: 2018 3rd IEEE International Conference on Intelligent Transportation Engineering (ICITE), pp. 264–268. IEEE (2018)
11. Hallac, D., et al.: Driver identification using automobile sensor data from a single turn. In: 2016 IEEE 19th International Conference on Intelligent Transportation Systems (ITSC) (2016). https://doi.org/10.1109/itsc.2016.7795670
12. Kohavi, R., et al.: A study of cross-validation and bootstrap for accuracy estimation and model selection. In: IJCAI, Montreal, Canada, vol. 14, pp. 1137–1145 (1995)
13. MATLAB: Version number for MATLAB and libraries. https://www.mathworks.com/help/matlab/ref/version.html. Accessed 30 Mar 2019
14. Meiring, G., Myburgh, H.: A review of intelligent driving style analysis systems and related artificial intelligence algorithms. Sensors **15**(12), 30653–30682 (2015). https://doi.org/10.3390/s151229822
15. Mo, W., Gao, Y., Zhao, Q.: Confusable vehicle feature extraction and recognition based on cascaded SVM. In: 2017 3rd IEEE International Conference on Computer and Communications (ICCC) (2017). https://doi.org/10.1109/compcomm.2017.8322918
16. Pathane, P., Pimple, J.: Driving pattern recognition using dataset. Int. J. Recent Innov. Trends Comput. Commun. **4**(5), 71–72 (2016)
17. Romera, E., Bergasa, L.M., Arroyo, R.: Need data for driver behaviour analysis? Presenting the public UAH-DriveSet. In: 2016 IEEE 19th International Conference on Intelligent Transportation Systems (ITSC), pp. 387–392. IEEE (2016)
18. Rygula, A.: Driving style identification method based on speed graph analysis. In: 2009 International Conference on Biometrics and Kansei Engineering (2009). https://doi.org/10.1109/icbake.2009.51
19. Sadigh, D., Sastry, S.S., Seshia, S.A., Dragan, A.: Information gathering actions over human internal state. In: 2016 IEEE/RSJ International Conference on Intelligent Robots and Systems (IROS) (2016). https://doi.org/10.1109/iros.2016.7759036
20. Schneegass, S., Pfleging, B., Broy, N., Heinrich, F., Schmidt, A.: A data set of real world driving to assess driver workload. In: Proceedings of the 5th International Conference on Automotive User Interfaces and Interactive Vehicular Applications, pp. 150–157. ACM (2013)
21. Wang, W., Xi, J.: A rapid pattern-recognition method for driving styles using clustering-based support vector machines. In: 2016 American Control Conference (ACC), pp. 5270–5275. IEEE (2016)
22. Wang, W., Xi, J., Chong, A., Li, L.: Driving style classification using a semisupervised support vector machine. IEEE Trans. Hum.-Mach. Syst. **5**, 650–660 (2017)
23. Zhao, Y., Yamamoto, T., Morikawa, T.: An analysis on older drivers driving behavior by gps tracking data: road selection, left/right turn, and driving speed. J. Traffic Transp. Eng. (Engl. Edn.) **5**(1), 56–65 (2018). https://doi.org/10.1016/j.jtte.2017.05.013

Swarm Intelligence and ICA for Blind Source Separation

Monia Hamdi[1,2]([✉]), Hela ElMannai[1,3], and Abeer AlGarni[1]

[1] College of Computer and Information Sciences,
Princess Nourah bint Abdulrahman University, Riyadh, Kingdom of Saudi Arabia
Monia.Hamdi@isimg.rnu.tn, Hela.Elmannai@gmail.com
[2] RTIM Research Group, Gabès University, Gabès, Tunisia
[3] Institut Supérieur des Etudes Technologiques de Radès, Radès, Tunisia
adalqarni@pnu.edu.sa

Abstract. Source separation is to retrieve the origin signals from mixed signals. For linear mixture, the problem consists in generating the separating matrix, having only the observations. In the blind source separation, no prior information about the transformation is available. In our model, the sources are supposed non gaussian and thus independent. Based on the Independent Component Analysis, we proposed an iterative swarm intelligence algorithm. The Flower Pollination Algorithm has the advantage of separating at each iteration, the exploration and the exploitation. Compared to the well known Particle Swarm Optimization algorithm, the proposed method presents better results in terms of similarity between the origin sources and the estimated sources.

Keywords: Blind source separation · Independent Component Analysis · Particle Swarm Optimization · Flower Pollination Algorithm

1 Introduction

The *cocktail-party* problem is to retrieve the original voice signals emitted by the speakers using only the recorded signals. In order to recover the underlying signals, with no prior information about the linear transformations, many assumptions are made [3]. Statistical independence of the sources leads to the separation by Independent Component Analysis (ICA) [6]. In this paper, we considered a linear mixing of the sources, which means that each observation is a linear combination of the original inputs. This model can be found for example in the electrical recordings of the brain activity, biomedical signals, biological data analysis, acoustics applications and image processing [2]. Principal component analysis, factor analysis and projection pursuit represent some examples of linear transformation methods.

ICA has proved its efficiency for linear blind source separation. The ICA methods tends to minimize the statistical independence between retrieved components. ICA have been widely investigated in the context of blind source separation. Many approaches exist to approximate the underlaying sources. These

© Springer Nature Switzerland AG 2019
A. Alfaries et al. (Eds.): ICC 2019, CCIS 1097, pp. 183–192, 2019.
https://doi.org/10.1007/978-3-030-36365-9_15

approaches tend to maximize the non-gaussianity of the recovered sources, to minimize the mutual information or use the Maximum likelihood [12]. Many non-gaussian maximization methods were based on the negative entropy since it provides better results than kurtosis. Therefore, the ICA is viewed as an optimization model of the misfit function [10]. Several optimization techniques exist int he literature among them, we find the metaheuristics methods.

The metaheuristics based on swarm intelligence mimic the animals behaviour in the nature. From local information emerges a global behaviour where all the individuals cooperate in order to find the optimal path or/and the optimal position. Many algorithms were developed in the literature among them the Particle Swarm Optimization. It is a well established and well studied algorithm. Recently, more advanced approaches were proposed. The Flower Pollination Algorithm is characterized by explicit reformulation of the exploration and the exploitation. The exploration is the process of discovering the research space following large steps. The exploitation is searching around a limited portion of the research space.

The remainder of this paper is organized as follows. Section 2 presents the related works. Section 3 describes the problem model. Section 4 presents the proposed ICA based on FPA. The simulation results will be presented in Sect. 5.

2   Related Works

Jain et al. [7] proposed a blind source separation (BSS) scheme for super and sub-Gaussian speech signals using the Artificial Bee Colony (ABC). The objective function is to minimize the dependence among the estimated signals. Thus, the signals can be separated successfully. Through the repetition of the employee bee, the onlooker bee and the scout bee phases, the coefficients of separating matrices in the population travel toward the best solution. The proposed scheme is demonstrated to outperform the genetic algorithm (GA).

Swarm intelligence was also used by Li et al. [9] where the Dynamic Niching Particle Swarm Optimization (DNPSO) is proposed to solve linear blind separation problem for speech signals. Both the ICA, the traditional method of linear BSS, and the standard PSO are likely to be trapped into local optimum and also suffer from slow convergence rate. In DNPSO, the search space is partitioned and each partition is occupied by a set of sub-swarms or a group of free particles. The sub-swarms can change dynamically at each generation and form niching search areas near potential solutions. The free particles contribute to protecting the algorithm from being trapped into a local optimum by searching around the extreme value points. The ICA uses the negative entropy as a cost function.

The authors in [11] proposed an hybridation of the competitive learning and the simulated annealing (SA) in order to solve the source separation problem for both linear and non-linear mixtures. The SA allows to speed up the convergence of the weights around the maximum density points in the search space during the starting phase in which the optimization of the neural network by competitive learning is still inactive. The energy in the SA is derived from the fourth-order cumulant of the original sources and their expectations. Similar to the other evolutionary algorithms, this fitness function reflects the hypothesis of statistical independence between the mixture sources.

The convergence of the PSO algorithm was analyzed in [8] where it was applied to the learning of the radial-basis function (RBF) parameters. The RBF function approximates the nonlinear mapping. The unmixing is therefore performed by learning the RBF parameters using PSO algorithm. The authors focused on the inter-particle communication and the network structure of the swarm in order to highlight the relationship between the average path length and the algorithm search performance.

In [13], the authors treated the source separation problem for noisy and blurred images. The main target is to restore the original image while removing any source of degradation that can be misfocus or motion, for example. The Genetic algorithm is used to estimate the parameters of the point spread function. The cost function used to differentiate between blurred image and the original image is the non-gaussianity measure, kurtosis.

3   Problem Model

Let us denote by $\mathbf{x}$ the random vector whose elements are the observations $x_1, ..., x_n$ and likewise by $\mathbf{s}$ the random vector with elements $s_1, ..., s_n$. Let us denote by $\mathbf{A}$ the matrix with elements a_{ij}. The mixing model is written as:

$$\mathbf{x} = \mathbf{As} \tag{1}$$

$\mathbf{A}$, the mixing matrix, is supposed unknown. However, we can make a simple but practical assumption that the sources are statistically independent and must have nongaussian distributions. The idea is to compute the matrix $\mathbf{W}$, the inverse of the matrix $\mathbf{A}$. We can then obtain the independent component by:

$$\mathbf{s} = \mathbf{Wx}. \tag{2}$$

Based on the nongaussianity maximization for the ICA implementation, the negentropy has proved to be more reliable for local minima then the kurtosis. In this study, we will use the negentropy, as a non gaussianity measurement. The related method is known as FastICA and was introduced by Hyvärinen and Oja in [5]. Negentropy J is defined as follows:

$$J(\mathbf{y}) = H(\mathbf{y}_{gauss}) - H(\mathbf{y}) \tag{3}$$

where $\mathbf{y}_{gauss}$ is a Gaussian random variable of the same covariance matrix as $\mathbf{y}$. Negentropy is always non-negative, and it is zero if and only if $\mathbf{y}$ has a Gaussian distribution. Computing the exact value of the negentropy is very difficult and requires an estimate of the pdf. Thus, the definition of approximate expression of negentropy is necessary. Hyvärinen [4] proposed the following approximation:

$$J(\mathbf{y}) \approx \sum_{i=1}^{p} k_i [E\{G_i(y)\} - E\{G_i(v)\}]^2 \tag{4}$$

where k_i are positive constants, and v is a Gaussian variable of zero mean and unit variance. G_i are nonquadratic functions. The following choices of G have proved their efficiency in the litterature:

$$G_1(x) = \frac{1}{a} log(cosh(a \times x)), G_2(x) = -exp(-x^2/2) \tag{5}$$

where $1 < a < 2$ is a constant.

4   Proposed Solution

In this paper, we proposed to compare the performance of two Swarm Intelligence metaheuristics: FPA and PSO in solving the source separation problem. The pseudo-codes of these two methods are given in Algorithms 1 and 2.

4.1   FPA

Actually, FPA is inspired from the reproduction of flowering plants through pollination process and it is designed for the global optimization issues. In nature, flowers pollination process ensue from the transfer of pollen by the pollinators like birds, insects, bats. Pollination process can be generally classified into two types: Self-pollination and Cross-pollination. The former can be achieved by the pollen of the same flower, the latter can take place by pollen of a flower of a other plant.

The global pollination process is started by generating a random number r, where r $\in$ [0,1], for each solution x_i. If $r < p$, where p is a switch probability, the new solution is generated by a Levy distribution as follows:

$$x_i(t+1) = x_i(t) + L(x_i(t) - gbest) \tag{6}$$

where $x_i(t)$ is the solution vector at iteration t, and *gbest* is the current best solution found among all solutions at the current iteration. The parameter L is the strength of the pollination, which essentially is a step size. Since insects may move over a long distance with various distance steps, we can use a Lévy flight to mimic this characteristic efficiently. That is, we draw L from a Lévy distribution:

$$L = \frac{\lambda \Gamma(\lambda) sin(\pi\lambda/2)}{\pi} \frac{1}{s^{1+\lambda}} \tag{7}$$

where $\Gamma(\lambda)$ is the standard gamma function.

$$s = \frac{U}{|V|^{1/\lambda}}, U \sim N(0, \sigma^2) \text{ and } V \sim N(0,1) \tag{8}$$

$$\sigma^2 = \{\frac{\Gamma(\lambda+1) sin(\pi\lambda/2)}{\lambda \Gamma(\frac{\lambda+1}{2})} 2^{\frac{\lambda-1}{2}}\}^{1/\lambda} \tag{9}$$

Otherwise, the local pollination process is started by generating a random number $\epsilon \in [0,1]$. It can be represented as follows:

$$x_i(t+1) = x_i(t) + \epsilon(x_j(t) - x_k(t)) \tag{10}$$

where j and k are randomly selected.

Algorithm 1. Pseudo-code for the FPA.

1: Generate the initial random population of n particles
2: Generate the initial random separation matrix for each particle
3: Find the best solution **gbest** in the initial population
4: Define a switch probability $p \in [0, 1]$
5: **for** j=1:1:numberIterations **do**
6:     **for** each particle i **do**
7:         **if** $random \leq p$ **then**
8:             Draw a 4-dimensional step vector L
9:             which obeys a Levy Flight
10:           Global pollination via
11:           $x_i(t+1) = x_i(t) + L(x_i(t) - gbest)$
12:         **else**
13:           Generate $\epsilon \in [0,1]$
14:           Local Pollination via
15:           $x_i(t+1) = x_i(t) + \epsilon(x_j(t) - x_k(t))$
16:         **end if**
17:     **end for**
18:     Evaluate new solutions
19:     If new solutions are better,
20:     update them in the population
21:     Find the current best global solution **gbest**
22: **end for**
23: **Output: Separation matrix**

4.2 PSO

Contrary to FPA, the PSO algorithm defines the exploitation and the exploration in a single equation. At each iteration t, the velocity of each particle is updated according to the best local position and the global position ever found. The velocity is updated according to following equation:

$$\mathbf{v}_i(t+1) = \mathbf{v}_i(t) + c1 \times r1 \times (\mathbf{pbest}_i - \mathbf{x}_i(t)) + c2 \times r2 \times (\mathbf{gbest} - \mathbf{x}_i(t)) \tag{11}$$

where $r1$ and $r2$ are random numbers

Algorithm 2. Pseudo-code for the PSO.

1: Generate the initial random population of n particles
2: **for** each particle i **do**
3:     Initialize velocity vector x_i randomly within permissible range
4:     Initialize position vector randomly v_i within permissible range
5: **end for**
6: **for** j=1:1:numberIterations **do**
7:     **for** each particle i **do**
8:         Calculate fitness function
9:         **if** the fitness value is better than **pbest then**
10:             update **pbest**
11:         **end if**
12:     **end for**
13:     Choose the particle having the best fitness value as **gbest**
14:     **for** each particle i **do**
15:         Calculate the velocity:
16:         $\mathbf{v}_i = \mathbf{v}_i + c1 \times r1 \times (\mathbf{pbest}_i - \mathbf{x}_i)+$
17:         $c2 \times r2 \times (\mathbf{gbest} - \mathbf{x}_i)$
18:         update the position: $\mathbf{x}_i = \mathbf{x}_i + \mathbf{v}_i$
19:     **end for**
20:     Evaluate new solutions
21:     If new solutions are better, update them in the population
22:     Find the curren best global solution **gbest**
23: **end for**
24: **Output: Separation matrix**

The position of the particle is updated according to following equation:

$$\mathbf{x}_i(t+1) = \mathbf{x}_i(t) + \mathbf{v}_i(t) \tag{12}$$

5   Simulation Results

We focus in this paper on speech separation. Two speakers were recorded talking in English. The first counts digits from one to ten and the second pronounces the word *why*. We took a portion of 2000 samples. For the FPA, the switch probability is set to 0.5, which means equivalent statistical weights are given to both the exploration and the exploitation. For the PSO, the intertia weight is set to 1. The Personal Learning Coefficient $c1 = 1.5$ and the Global Learning Coefficient $c2 = 2.0$. The population size and the number of iterations for both algorithms are set to 50 and 1000, respectively. FPA and PSO are stochastic algorithms. In order to obtain statistically significant results, each algorithm was run 30 times. We also implemented the PowerICA method presented in [1].

We used measurement index of similarities between signals to estimate the results quantitatively. **y** are the estimated signals and **s** are the source signals.

$$\phi_{ij} = \phi(y_i, s_j) = \frac{\sum_{t=1}^{T} y_i(t)s_j(t)}{\sqrt{\sum_{t=1}^{T} y_i^2(t) \sum_{t=1}^{T} s_j^2(t)}} \tag{13}$$

The Fig. 1 represents the two source signals and the two estimated (separated) sources, using FPA. The Fig. 2 represents the two source signals and the two estimated (separated) sources, using PSO. It can be observed that the estimated signals by the FPA are more similar to the origin signals than those estimated using the PSO algorithm.

Before presenting the performance comparison, we need to show that the two algorithms converge. It means that the number of iterations is long enough to obtain the optimal solution at the end of the execution and the algorithm itself succeeds to find a near-optimal solution. The Figs. 3 and 4 display the evolution of the fitness function in a logarithmic scale for the y-axis, for the FPA and the PSO algorithm, respectively. We can observe that FPA achieves better fitness function and also it converges faster than the PSO algorithm.

The Table 1 presents the simulation results in terms of the index of similarities. We analyzed the mean, best and worst index for the two source signals. We can observe that the FPA presents better results than the PSO algorithm, in terms of average and worst similarities. Another interesting result in this paper, is that the FPA is able to find a better optimal point in the search space. Compared the powerICA proposed in [], both the FPA and the PSO algorithms are able to find better approximation of the mixing matrix and that better approximation of the origin sources. in fact, the best result achieved by the powerICA is

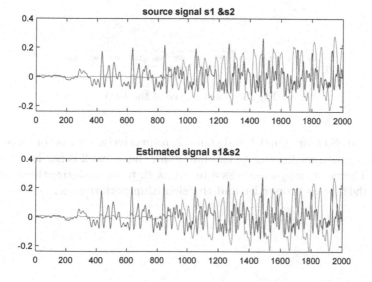

Fig. 1. Source and separated signals using the FPA.

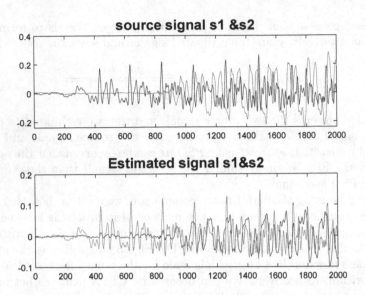

Fig. 2. Source and separated signals using the PSO algorithm.

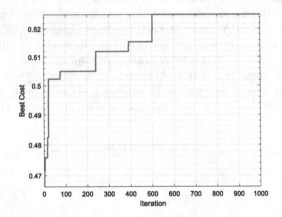

Fig. 3. Convergence of the FPA.

0.9906 and 0.9842 for signal 1 and signal 2, respectively. We also observe that for the three algorithms, finding an estimation for the signal 2 is harder that for the signal 1. Therefore, we propose as a future work to characterize the relationship between the signals properties and the algorithm performance.

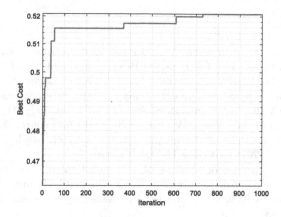

Fig. 4. Convergence of the PSO algorithm.

Table 1. Performance comparison between the FPA and the PSO: the index of similarities.

Methods		FPA	PSO
Similarity with the original signal 1	Average	0.9568	0.93815
	Best	0.9999	0.9993
	Worst	0.9003	0.7797
Similarity with the original signal 2	Average	0.9452	0.8868
	Best	0.9997	1
	Worst	0.8370	0.7194

6 Conclusion and Future Works

In this work, we examined the blind source separation where the transformation model is linear. Based on the fact that nongaussian signals are independent, we applied the Independent Component Analysis. We particularly used an approximation of the negentropy as a cost function of the two swarm intelligence metaheuristics FPA and PSO. We compared the performance of these two algorithms in terms of similarity index. The simulations results showed that the FPA outperforms the PSO algorithm, previously suggested in the literature to solve the BSS problem. The parameter setting in our implementation suggests that the parameters such as switch probability and intertia weights remain the same during the execution time. As a future work, we propose to investigate dynamic parameter control where the exploitation can be for example preferred to exploitation at the later phase of the process.

References

1. Basiri, S., Ollila, E., Koivunen, V.: Alternative derivation of fastica with novel power iteration algorithm. IEEE Signal Process. Lett. **24**(9), 1378–1382 (2017)
2. Elmannai, H., Loghmari, M., Naceur, M.S.: A new classification approach based on source separation and feature extraction. In: 2016 International Symposium on Signal, Image, Video and Communications (ISIVC), pp. 137–141, November 2016
3. He, P., She, T., Li, W., Yuan, W.: Single channel blind source separation on the instantaneous mixed signal of multiple dynamic sources. Mech. Syst. Signal Process. **113**, 22–35 (2018). SI: IMETI-MechElectro
4. Hyvärinen, A.: New approximations of differential entropy for independent component analysis and projection pursuit. In: Jordan, M.I., Kearns, M.J., Solla, S.A. (eds.) Advances in Neural Information Processing Systems, vol. 10, pp. 273–279. MIT Press (1998)
5. Hyvärinen, A., Oja, E.: A fast fixed-point algorithm for independent component analysis. Neural Comput. **9**(7), 1483–1492 (1997)
6. Hyvärinen, A., Oja, E.: Independent component analysis: algorithms and applications. Neural Netw. **13**(4), 411–430 (2000)
7. Jain, S., Rai, D.: Blind source separation of super and sub-gaussian signals with ABC algorithm. vol. 5 (2014)
8. Kurihara, T., Jin'no, K.: Analysis of convergence property of PSO and its application to nonlinear blind source separation. In: 2013 IEEE Congress on Evolutionary Computation, pp. 976–981, June 2013
9. Li, H., Li, Z., Li, H.: A blind source separation algorithm based on dynamic niching particle swarm optimization. In: MATEC Web of Conferences, vol. 61, p. 03008 (2016)
10. Pati, R., Kumar, V., Pujari, A.K.: Gradient-based swarm optimization for ICA. In: Pati, B., Panigrahi, C.R., Misra, S., Pujari, A.K., Bakshi, S. (eds.) Progress in Advanced Computing and Intelligent Engineering. AISC, vol. 713, pp. 225–235. Springer, Singapore (2019). https://doi.org/10.1007/978-981-13-1708-8_21
11. Puntonet, C.G., Mansour, A., Bauer, C., Lang, E.: Separation of sources using simulated annealing and competitive learning. Neurocomputing **49**(1), 39–60 (2002)
12. Tharwat, A.: Independent component analysis: an introduction. Appl. Comput. Inf. (2018). https://www.sciencedirect.com/science/article/pii/S2210832718301819
13. Yin, H., Hussain, I.: Blind source separation and genetic algorithm for image restoration. In: 2006 International Conference on Advances in Space Technologies, pp. 167–172, September 2006

Shiny Framework Based Visualization and Analytics Tool for Middle East Respiratory Syndrome

Maya John[1] and Hadil Shaiba[2(✉)]

[1] Sree Buddha College of Engineering, Pathanamthitta, Kerala, India
maya.j.mail@gmail.com
[2] Princess Nourah Bint Abdulrahman University, Riyadh, Kingdom of Saudi Arabia
hashaiba@pnu.edu.sa

Abstract. People in the Middle East have been affected by the Middle East Respiratory Syndrome CoronaVirus (MERS Co-V) since 2012. New cases are continuously reported especially in the Kingdom of Saudi Arabia, and the risk of exposure remains an issue. Data visualization plays a vital role in effective analysis of the data. In this paper, we introduce an interactive visualization application for MERS data collected from the Control and Command Centre, Ministry of Health website of Saudi Arabia. The data corresponding to the period from January 1, 2019 to February 28, 2019 was used in the present work. The attributes considered include gender, age, date of reporting, city, region, camel contact, description and status of the patient. The visualization tool has been developed using Shiny framework of R programming language. The application presents information in the form of interactive plots, maps and tables. The salient feature of the tool is that users can view and download data corresponding to the period of their choice. This tool can help decision makers in the detailed analysis of data and hence devise measures to prevent the spread of the disease.

Keywords: MERS · Data visualization · Shiny framework · Coronavirus · Location-based analysis

1 Introduction

MERS is a viral disease that was first discovered in 2012 when a patient in Saudi Arabia was diagnosed with critical respiratory distress and kidney trouble [1]. The infection can either be asymptomatic or show symptoms such as cough, fever etc. along with difficulty in breathing [2]. The disease has been brought under control in all Middle Eastern countries except Saudi Arabia where each month, new cases are still reported. Studies have confirmed that this disease is zoonotic and camels are its significant reservoir [3,4]. People in close contact with infected camels and health care professionals who care for infected patients have a high risk of acquiring the infection. Many cases of community and household

© Springer Nature Switzerland AG 2019
A. Alfaries et al. (Eds.): ICC 2019, CCIS 1097, pp. 193–202, 2019.
https://doi.org/10.1007/978-3-030-36365-9_16

acquired infections have been reported from Saudi Arabia [5]. The Ministry of Health, Saudi Arabia has issued guidelines for infection prevention, control and management.

To the best of our knowledge, there is a lack of interactive visualization tools for MERS data visualization in Saudi Arabia. This work deals with developing an application where users can interactively view information about the infection in the form of plots, tables and maps. The data used in this study was obtained from the Saudi Ministry of Health website and it includes the cases reported in Saudi Arabia from January 1, 2019 to February 28, 2019. By viewing the data visualizations, users can analyze MERS cases better, find trends, monitor the disease and help authorities set detection and prevention guidelines.

2   Data and Methods

2.1   Data Description

The MERS data analyzed consists of 82 cases reported during the first two months of the year 2019. The information is present in the form of a pdf file corresponding to the cases reported each week. The cases reported contains details which include the date of reporting and patient information such as personal information, demographic information, camel contact details, description of infection and status of the disease. The latitude and longitude of the regions and cities are stored in separate .csv files. The details of the attributes present in the database are shown in Table 1.

Table 1. Description of data used.

Attribute	Description
Date	Date of reporting
Gender	Male or female
Age	Age of patient
City	Patient city
Region	Region corresponding to patient city
Camel Contact	Yes or no
Description1	Primary or secondary
Description2	Community acquired, household contact, healthcare acquired or unknown
Status	Dead, recovered or hospitalized

2.2   Shiny Framework

Shiny is an R package used to create interactive web applications [6]. The Shiny framework is a reactive programming model where browser refreshing is not required to instantiate the output changes when the user modifies the input. It can be used to build web applications without using Javascript coding. Shiny combines the computational power of R programming language with the highly interactive nature of the web.

2.3   Leaflet Package

Leaflet package is used to create interactive maps in R based on the Javascript library leaflet [7]. These interactive maps can be rendered in R markdown, Shiny apps, RStudioIDE and R console as it was developed in association with html-widgets. The leaflet( ) function is used to create the map widget. The different types of layers which can be included in the map widget are map tile, markers, lines, polygon, popups, raster images, color legends, layer groups, layer control etc. The maps created can be zoomed or downsized interactively.

2.4   Googleviz Package

The googleviz package in R facilitates the use of Google Chart APIs [8]. Interactive charts can be incorporated into web pages using Google Charts. The data stored in R data frames can be visualized in the form of Google Charts without uploading the information to Google. An internet connection is required to view the output rendered by this package.

3   Results and Discussion

The MERS data visualization tool was developed using R programming language. The tool consists of three sections (tabs) namely "Different Cases Analysis", "Miscellaneous Analysis" and "Summary" section. The users can choose the period for which they would like to visualize the MERS data.

3.1   Different Cases Analysis

In the case of different cases analysis, the user can view the information as pie charts and maps, or tables. The users can view details about either all the cases together or recovered cases, death cases or hospitalized cases separately. The details regarding the cases can be viewed with respect to all cities, all regions or cities within a region. In the case of the option "cities within a region", the user has to choose a region from the drop down list provided. Unlike conventional pie charts, the pie charts created using googleviz package are interactive in nature. By pointing the cursor over a portion in the pie chart, one can understand the actual number of cases in that particular part of the chart. In the map, places are marked based on longitude and latitude of that place. On clicking the marker displayed in the map, the name and number of cases in that place will be displayed as a pop-up. Based on the number of cases, markers are assigned colors such as red, orange or yellow. The colors red, orange and yellow represent "large number of cases", "moderate number of cases" and "few number of cases" respectively.

The information in Figs. 1 and 2 is presented in the form of pie chart and map. The screen shot of the page corresponding to different cases analysis is shown in Fig. 1. The figure depicts the analysis of all MERS cases reported for the first two months of the year 2019 with regard to cities. It can be inferred from Fig. 1 that during that period 76.8% of the patients recovered from the disease and the maximum number of cases (61%) were reported from the city of Wadi Aldawasir. The analysis based on all cases reported in "all cities within Riyadh region" during January to February 2019 is shown in Fig. 2. It can be observed from the figure that majority of cases in Riyadh region were reported from the city of Wadi Aldawasir. Nearly 78% of the infected people in Riyadh region recovered from the disease.

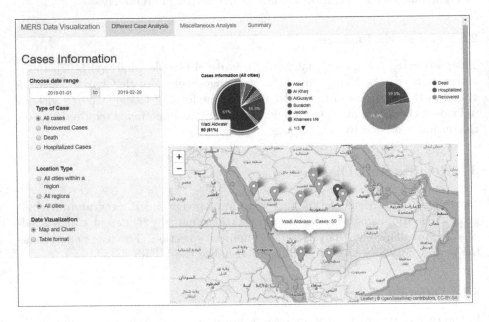

Fig. 1. Application page corresponding to Different Cases Analysis

The application page with table output is shown in Fig. 3. It can be observed from the table that 12 people died due to MERS in Riyadh region during the first two months of the year 2019. The table which displays the information is interactive in nature. When the user clicks a column name in the table, the records in the table are sorted based on values in the clicked column and displayed accordingly. The table also has provision for searching values and selecting the number

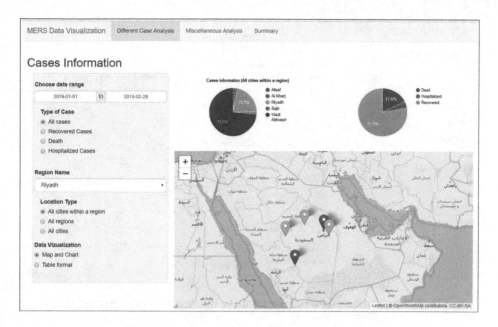

Fig. 2. Application page corresponding to "Different Cases Analysis" tab for cities within a region

of records to be displayed in a page. The users can also download the details contained in the table. The different cases analysis will help decision makers in gathering information regarding the cases reported in different places. This type of analysis is essential to identify disease prone areas and hence take measures to curtail the spread of infection.

3.2 Miscellaneous Analysis

The miscellaneous analysis consists of analysis based on age, camel contact and months. The users can analyze the data for all cases, death cases or recovered cases. Depending on the user's choice, the analysis corresponding to all cities, all regions or cities within a region are displayed.

Analysis Based on Age. The infected people are divided into three age categories namely below 25 years, 26–60 years and greater than 60 years. In the case of age based analysis, the information is displayed both in the form of pie chart and stacked bar chart. The pie chart represents the number of cases corresponding to each age group. The stacked bar chart depicts the number of cases in each age group corresponding to the location type selected. The screen shot corresponding to age category wise analysis is shown in Fig. 4. The figure corresponds to the analysis corresponding to all cases reported with respect to cities for the first two months of the year 2019. It is evident from the pie chart

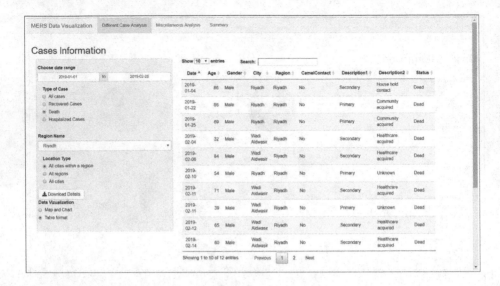

Fig. 3. Application page corresponding to information displayed as table

in Fig. 4 that the percentage of cases reported is 4.9%, 65.9% and 29.3% for the age group below 25 years, 26–60 years and above 60 years respectively. The age category wise helps in understanding the number of cases reported among people of different age groups. This type of analysis will help in identifying which group has more mortality rate and health authorities may conduct extensive analysis of causes leading to death.

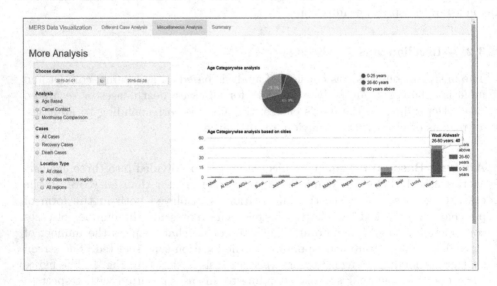

Fig. 4. Data visualization on the basis of age category

Analysis Based on Camel Contact. Camels have been identified as a carrier of the disease, and hence it is essential to perform analysis of patient cases involving camel contact. Depending on the choice of the user, the information is displayed for "all cases", "death cases" or "recovery cases". The analysis is carried out for "all cities", "all regions" or "cities within a region". The details are displayed as pie chart, map and table. The pie chart represents the numbers of cases corresponding to the location type selected by the user. The places where camel contact cases are reported are marked in the map. This can help in analyzing whether the cases pertaining to people with camel contact are clustered in a region or not. The table displays the details of infected people who had contact with camels. The data visualization based on camel contact is shown in Fig. 5. The figure depicts the analysis corresponding to all cases with regard to cities in Saudi Arabia. It can be observed from Fig. 5 that 56% of the camel contact based cases were reported from the city of Wadi Aldawasir. Camel contact based analysis of MERS patients is highly essential to identify places where people in contact with camels have been infected with the disease. This will help health authorities in taking more measures to spread awareness about the precautionary methods to be taken when handling camels. The infected camels in such regions may be identified and isolated to prevent the spread of the disease.

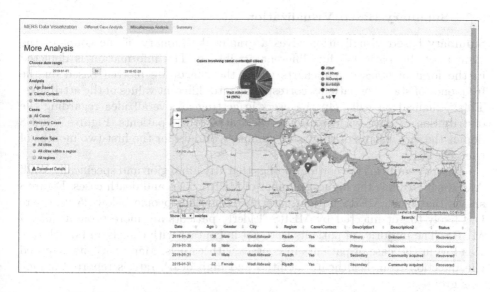

Fig. 5. Data visualization based on cases involving camel contact

Analysis Based on Month-Wise Comparison. Month-wise comparison of the data can be carried out for "all cases", "death cases" and "recovery cases". The stacked bar chart for cases reported in different months is plotted based on the location type specified by the user. When the cursor is moved to a region in the bar chart, the number of cases in the particular month will be displayed

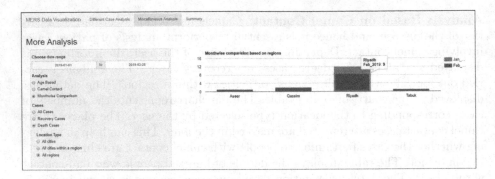

Fig. 6. Application page corresponding to month-wise comparison of cases

corresponding to the location. The screenshot corresponding to month-wise comparison is shown in Fig. 6. The figure portrays the analysis corresponding to death cases reported in various regions. The maximum number of death cases were reported in Riyadh region during February. Monthwise analysis is useful in identifying whether the infection is related to climate.

3.3   Summary-Based Visualization

Summary based visualization gives a graphical summary of the count of the "status of the patients" for different attributes. The information is depicted in the form of stacked bar charts where the charts are plotted based on the frequency of status of patients corresponding to different values of the attributes. This visualization will help the users in getting an overall idea regarding the distribution of data with regard to the status of the patients. Figures 7 and 8 depict the screenshots of the visual summary of data for the first two months of the year 2019.

Figure 7 confirms the earlier findings that Riyadh region and specifically Wadi Aldawasir city has the highest number of MERS cases and death cases. Figure 8 shows that most MERS patients are male and that people below 25 years are less likely to get infected by MERS. Elderly patients are more prone to die of MERS. The majority of patients were not in contact with camels and death rate was low in the case of patients in contact with camels. Many patients acquired the infection from healthcare facilities and high death rate is reported among this group.

3.4   Benefits of the Application

The users can view information corresponding to their period of interest. The interactive feature of the pie chart prevents the chart from being cluttered with description. The use of maps to represent the information will give an idea regarding the spatial distribution of MERS cases. These maps will help the health authorities to identify the areas with large number of cases and hence

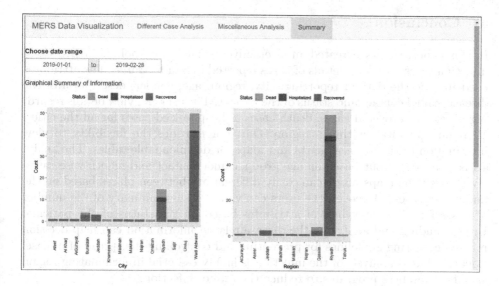

Fig. 7. Summary of attributes based on status of patients

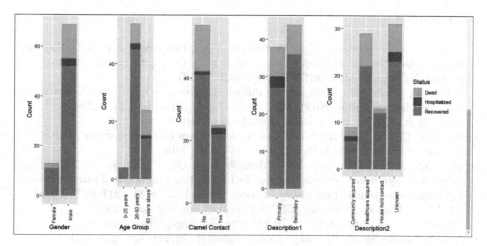

Fig. 8. Summary of attributes based on status of patients

alert the hospitals and the general public regarding that. The interactive nature of the table helps the users in analyzing the data as per their requirement. A salient feature of the application is that the users can easily download details corresponding to the period of their choice. Analyzing the data based on camel contact will aid health authorities to identify the areas where many such cases are present and hence intensify the awareness programs to reduce the rate of infection.

4 Conclusion

In this paper, we have created an interactive visualization tool for MERS Co-V infection cases based on details of cases reported in Saudi Arabia. The attributes used include the date of reporting, city, region, age, gender, description of the disease, camel contact and status of the patient. The user can view details regarding all cases, recovered cases, death cases or hospitalized cases for all the cities, all regions or cities within a region. Our tool provides the flexibility to view information in the form of charts and maps, or downloadable tables. The analysis is also carried out based on age group, camel contact and month-wise cases. By viewing the maps, users can easily differentiate between places based on the number of cases. Moreover, the users can view a visual summary of the number of cases for different values of attributes based on the status of the patients. Understanding and analyzing the disease related information can help decision makers in setting guidelines for preventing and controlling the spread of disease. Location-based analysis of the infection is highly essential in formulating region specific awareness programs to reduce the rate of infection.

References

1. Zaki, A.M., Van Boheemen, S., Bestebroer, T.M., Osterhaus, A.D.M.E., Fouchier, R.A.M.: Isolation of a novel coronavirus from a man with pneumonia in Saudi Arabia. N. Engl. J. Med. **367**(19), 1814–1820 (2012)
2. John, M., Shaiba, H.: Main factors influencing recovery in MERS Co-V patients using machine learning (2019). https://doi.org/10.1016/j.jiph.2019.03.020
3. Memish, A.: MERS. Int. J. Infect. Dis. **53**, 23 (2016)
4. Reusken, C.B., et al.: MERS-CoV infection of alpaca in a region where MERS-CoV is endemic. Emerg. Infect. Dis. **22**(6), 1129–1131 (2016)
5. Hui, D.S., Azhar, E.I., Kim, Y.-J., Memish, Z.A., Oh, M., Zumla, A.: Middle east respiratory syndrome coronavirus: risk factors and determinants of primary, household, and nosocomial transmission. Lancet Infect. Dis. **18**(8), e217–e227 (2018)
6. CRAN-Package shiny. https://CRAN.R-project.org/package=shiny
7. CRAN-Package leaflet. https://CRAN.R-project.org/package=leaflet
8. CRAN-Package googleVis. https://cran.r-project.org/package=googleVis

Ensemble Learning Sentiment Classification for Un-labeled Arabic Text

Amal Alkabkabi and Mounira Taileb[✉]

King Abdulaziz University, Jeddah, Kingdom of Saudi Arabia
{aalkabkabi,mtaileb}@kau.edu.sa

Abstract. Sentiment classification has become one of the most trending research topics, due to the rapid growth of social media platforms and applications. It is the process of determining the opinion or the feeling of a piece of text and assigning a label to it (positive, negative or neutral). One of the issues in sentiment classification is the need for labeled data – that is often carried out manually - in order to train the classifiers which is a time consuming task. In this paper we consider the lexicon-based classification as labeling technique instead of the manual labeling. In addition, for an effective sentiment classification we investigate the using of multiple ensemble learning methods - where multiple classifiers are combined - in order to improve the performance of the classification. Experiments have been run on datasets of reviews written in Modern Standard Arabic. Results show that the labeling technique is effective and promising and the use of ensemble learning has clearly improved the accuracy for the sentiment classification compared to the traditional methods.

Keywords: Sentiment analysis · Lexicon-based classification · Ensemble learning · Unlabeled Arabic text

1 Introduction

It has become apparent in the last ten years that social media has changed drastically the way how people communicate and socialize with each other in social networking sites such as: Facebook, twitter, whats-app and blogs, etc. People nowadays can express their feelings, views and opinions regarding many topics without boundaries, thus enrich those platforms with enormous amount of data that can be of great help for many people such as: customer services in companies or simply individuals seeking a review on some product. Thus, the need for automated system or model to extract readable information from those sites arise. Sentiment analysis (SA), also known as opinion mining, is the use of natural language processing or text analysis to identify and extract opinion, sentiment and subjective information from text [8]. SA models as stated by [11], consists of the following steps: data pre-processing, features extraction and applying machine learning algorithms. Sentiment analysis can be utilized using

© Springer Nature Switzerland AG 2019
A. Alfaries et al. (Eds.): ICC 2019, CCIS 1097, pp. 203–210, 2019.
https://doi.org/10.1007/978-3-030-36365-9_17

two main approaches: machine learning classification and lexicon-based classification. One of the challenging issues in SA is labeling the dataset for training (usually done manually by human which may be considered as a burden and time consuming task) as well as choosing the best classifier for the dataset. In this paper, we took advantage of some approaches and methods to handle those challenges; Lexicon-based approach has been used for data labeling. And the ensemble learning method has been used to improve the classification performance. The remainder of the paper is organized as follows. In Sect. 2, a review of the ensemble learning approaches is presented, in Sect. 3 the proposed model is described in details, in Sect. 4 we presented the experiments and evaluation of the model. Finally, in Sect. 5 we conclude the paper.

2   Ensemble Learning

Ensemble learning (EL) is a scheme in which multiple machine learning algorithms are combined in a single model in order to improve the performance of a single classifier and achieve better performance [17]. EL uses machine learning algorithms such as: SVM, Decision Tree, etc. to train a specific dataset, then EL produces either a homogeneous algorithm (learner) from combining a single type of algorithm also called "base algorithm", or it produces a heterogeneous algorithm (learner) from combining multiple types of algorithms called "component algorithm" (see Fig. 1) [3]. There are several methods for combining the algorithms: bagging, boosting, stacking and voting [13]. Ensemble learning has been applied in many fields, for example, Malware detection [7,16], voice recognition [2,15], decision-making [9] and last but not least in sentiment analysis.

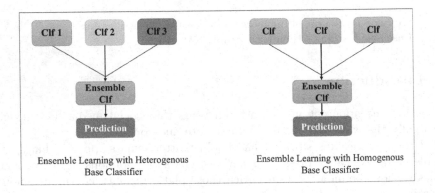

Ensemble Learning with Heterogenous Base Classifier

Ensemble Learning with Homogenous Base Classifier

Fig. 1. Ensemble learning types

2.1   Bagging

Bagging, also known as Bootstrap Aggregation, where the same base algorithm is trained multiple times in parallel using a bootstrapped samples from the original dataset. The classifier algorithms are then aggregated using either averaging or majority voting technique and the most voted class is predicted. Bagging is used to minimize the prediction variance by producing additional data for training from the original dataset (see Fig. 2). The variance is linked directly to over-fitting and the performance improvement in ensembles is the direct result when reducing variance [5].

2.2 Boosting

Boosting is a technique where the base algorithm is trained multiple times in series using the same dataset but with more focus on difficult instances each time [12]. The main goal in boosting is to convert a weak classifier algorithm (learner) into a strong one [17]. The previous model is used in order to adjust the weight of observation for the next model according to the model's error rates-better models are given better weights. The aim in this method is to decrease the bias error and produce better model (see Fig. 2).

2.3 Stacking

Stacking, also known as stacked generalization, has two level structure in which multiple component algorithms are trained using the same dataset in level 1, then the output of the level 1 is used as training data for level 2 classifier algorithm, also called meta classifier, as shown in Fig. 2. This technique can either reduce bias or variance error depending on the algorithms used [14].

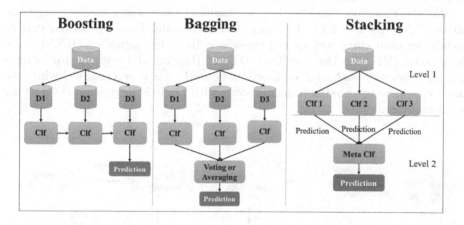

Fig. 2. Ensemble learning combining methods

3 Proposed Model

Our proposed model consists of four stages: data pre-processing, lexicon labeling, feature extraction and ensemble classification as shown in Fig. 3. For the data pre-processing, each review in the dataset goes through cleaning - where characters and symbols are removed such as: $ % # @ : , etc - and stop words removal - in which a predefined list of Arabic stop words are used to eliminate connecting words that has no sentiment meanings.

In the lexicon labeling, each review is labeled to either positive (+1) or negative (−1). An Arabic lexicon is needed for the labeling process, and by the end of this stage the whole dataset would be labeled for further processing as shown in Fig. 4. A lexicon is a special dictionary that contains words with their sentiment label (+1 for positive, −1 for negative and 0 for neutral).

The most common feature extraction technique is bag of words (BOWs), in which the counts of the words appearance in a document (text) is more significant than the order of the words. BOW converts the dataset into a matrix with one row per document (text or review) and one column per word occurring in the dataset. If the word appears in the document, "1" is assigned to it, otherwise "0" is assigned to the word.

For our experiments, the dataset (labeled Arabic reviews) is represented using bag of words (BOWs) and N-gram model. Two n-gram models will be considered: uni-gram (individual words), bi-gram (two consecutive words), uni-gram provides full text converge while bi-gram captured some phrases and dependencies between the words [1,6,10]. After feature extraction stage, the labeled dataset is split into a training-validation set (80%), and a testing set (20%), which is used to evaluate the model.

For the ensemble classification, we examine three ensemble learning techniques - described in Sect. 2. Bagging, Boosting and Stacking. In our experiments, we used three well-known classifiers: K-nearest neighbor (KNN), Random Forest (RF) and Decision Tree (DT). In Bagging and Boosting for increasing the efficiency each of the classifiers is used as a base classifier, while the three classifiers are used in Stacking along with Logistic Regression (LG) as the meta-classifier.

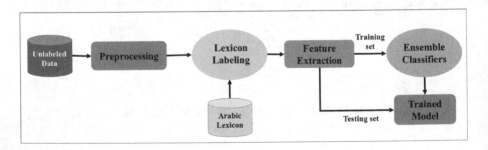

Fig. 3. The proposed model

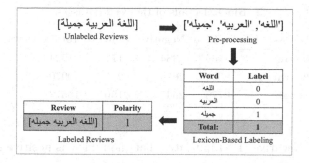

Fig. 4. Lexicon-based labeling

4 Experiments and Evaluation

The following sections describe the proposed model, the data set used in the experiment, the metrics used to evaluate the proposed model and the experimental results.

4.1 Dataset

Lack of Arabic datasets may be considered as a challenge in the field of text mining. It is clearly noted that Arabic resources are not as rich as in English language. We considered the dataset proposed by El-Sahar and El-Beltag [4], it consists of 33k labeled reviews written in Modern Standard Arabic (MSA)[1]. This dataset one of the largest Arabic dataset available and it contains multi-domain reviews for movies, hotels, restaurants and products. It also consists of multi-domain lexicon of 2K entries extracted from the datasets. The Restaurant, Movie and Hotel reviews are used in this paper from the dataset along with their multi-domain lexicons [4]. We only processed positive and negative reviews (the neutral reviews was omitted beforehand). The reviews were processed without their respective labels (as un-labeled dataset) and then the labels are used for evaluation (validation) purposes to measure the accuracy of the model. The dataset also contains multi-domain lexicon (1912 words with their respective labels). The dataset details are provided in Table 1.

4.2 Evaluation Metrics

The accuracy rate is used as a metric for the performance evaluation, it is given in Eq. (1). True Positive (TP) indicates that the review is positive and classified successfully by the model as positive. True Negative (TN) indicates that the review is negative and classified successfully by the model as negative. False Positive (FP) indicates that the review is negative and classified by the model as

---

[1] https://github.com/hadyelsahar/large-arabic-sentiment-analysis-resouces/tree/master/datasets.

Table 1. Details of the used datasets.

Dataset	Positive	Negative	Neutral	Total reviews
Movie	969	384	171	1524
Restaurant	8030	2675	265	10970
Hotel	10775	2647	2150	15572

positive. False Negative (FN) indicates that the review is positive and classified by the model as negative.

$$Accuracy = \frac{TP + TN}{TP + FP + FN + TN} \tag{1}$$

4.3 Experimental Results

The three classifiers (KNN, DT and RF) were run as stand-alone and ensemble classifier on three different datasets (Restaurant, Movie and Hotel reviews). The results shown in Table 3 represent a comparative analysis of each classifier along with their ensemble classifiers based on accuracy.

The un-labeled dataset, as explained in Sect. 3, goes through data pre-processing then data labeling in which the lexicon-based reviews labeling process takes place. The lexicon-based labeling was able to label the reviews with an accuracy of **76%** for the Movies dataset, **83%** for the Restaurant dataset and **90%** for the Hotel dataset (see Table 2).

Table 2. Accuracy values for lexicon-based labeling.

Dataset	Labeling accuracy
Movie reviews	76.71%
Restuarant reviews	83.55%
Hotel reviews	90.85%

In general, all the ensemble learning algorithms achieved good results, with the highest accuracy equal to 92.10% and the lowest is 85.56%. As shown in Table 3, all the ensemble classifiers have better accuracy compared to the stand-alone classifiers. Boosting algorithm outperforms Bagging in most cases, both methods are homogeneous algorithms. The highest improvement in accuracy for Bagging was in the case of RF classifier with the Movie reviews by 1.22% (compared to the RF when used as a stand-alone classifier). While in Boosting, the highest accuracy is achieved when using KNN classifier with the Hotel reviews by 2.69% (compared to the KNN when used as a stand-alone classifier). While Stacking, which is a heterogeneous algorithm, has achieved the highest accuracy 92.10% for the Hotel reviews, the improvement is equal to 3.77%.

Table 3. Accuracy of ensemble learning methods

Classifier		Accuracy for each dataset		
		Movie	Restaurant	Hotel
RF	Single	84.34%	86.22%	87.75%
	Bagging	**85.56%**	**87.11%**	88.08%
	Boosting	84.59%	86.76%	**88.33%**
DT	Single	87.32%	89.12%	90.73%
	Bagging	86.66%	89.25%	**91.74%**
	Boosting	**88.56%**	**90.26%**	90.31%
KNN	Single	86.10%	87.61%	88.33%
	Bagging	86.89%	87.32%	88.66%
	Boosting	**87.78%**	**88.76%**	**91.02%**
All	Stacking	**87.75%**	**91.35%**	**92.10%**

5   Conclusion

Sentiment Analysis is the process of extracting subjective information from texts SA applications are very broad, it is very useful in many areas such as: marketing and customer services. Arabic Sentiment analysis has gained considerable inter-est in re-cent years, which may be considered challenging due to the natural of the Arabic language. Another challenging issue in SA is labeling the dataset for training and the fact that this process is usually done manually by humans. In addition, choosing the most appropriate ML classification algorithm is con-sidered a challenging task. In this paper, we developed a model for classifying unlabeled Arabic text to either positive or negative. We used lexicon-based tech-nique to label the dataset and the results obtained from the experimental results show that the labeling process has performed well with high accuracy values. In addition, we investigated the possibility of increasing the accuracy for some of well-known ML algorithms using ensemble learning methods (Bagging, Boosting and Stacking). The results show that the use of ensemble learning methods has improved the classification accuracy. As future work, the enrichment of the lexi-con is necessary by adding more word along with their polarity, this will improve the labeling phase.

References

1. Assiri, A., Emam, A., Aldossari, H.: Arabic sentiment analysis: a survey. Int. J. Adv. Comput. Sci. Appl. **6**(12), 75–85 (2015). https://doi.org/10.14569/IJACSA. 2015.061211
2. Deng, L., Platt, J.C.: Ensemble deep learning for speech recognition. In: Fifteenth Annual Conference of the International Speech Communication Association (2014)

3. Dong, Y.S., Han, K.S.: A comparison of several ensemble methods for text categorization. In: Proceedings of IEEE International Conference on Services Computing (SCC 2004), pp. 419–422. IEEE (2004)

4. ElSahar, H., El-Beltagy, S.R.: Building large arabic multi-domain resources for sentiment analysis. In: Gelbukh, A. (ed.) CICLing 2015. LNCS, vol. 9042, pp. 23–34. Springer, Cham (2015). https://doi.org/10.1007/978-3-319-18117-2_2

5. Galar, M., Fernandez, A., Barrenechea, E., Bustince, H., Herrera, F.: A review on ensembles for the class imbalance problem: bagging-, boosting-, and hybrid-based approaches. IEEE Trans. Syst. Man Cybern. Part C (Appl. Rev.) **42**(4), 463–484 (2012). https://doi.org/10.1109/TSMCC.2011.2161285

6. Mejova, Y., Srinivasan, P.: Exploring feature definition and selection for sentiment classifiers. In: Proceedings of the Fifth International AAAI Conference on Weblogs and Social Media, January 2011

7. Menahem, E., Shabtai, A., Rokach, L., Elovici, Y.: Improving malware detection by applying multi-inducer ensemble. Comput. Stat. Data Anal. **53**(4), 1483–1494 (2009)

8. Pang, B., Lee, L.: Opinion mining and sentiment analysis. Found. Trends Inf. Retr. **2**(1–2), 1–135 (2008). https://doi.org/10.1561/1500000011

9. Polikar, R.: Ensemble based systems in decision making. IEEE Circ. Syst. Mag. **6**(3), 21–45 (2006)

10. Alowaidi, S., Saleh, M., Abulnaja, O.: Semantic sentiment analysis of Arabic texts. Int. J. Adv. Comput. Sci. Appl. **8**(2), 256–262 (2017). https://doi.org/10.14569/IJACSA.2017.080234

11. Saxena, D., Gupta, S., Joseph, J., Mehra, R.: Sentiment analysis. Journal Homepage http://www.ijesm.co. in **8**(3) (2019)

12. Schapire, R.E.: The boosting approach to machine learning: an overview. In: Denison, D.D., Hansen, M.H., Holmes, C.C., Mallick, B., Yu, B. (eds.) Nonlinear Estimation and Classification. Lecture Notes in Statistics, vol. 171, pp. 149–171. Springer, New York (2003). https://doi.org/10.1007/978-0-387-21579-2_9

13. Seijo-Pardo, B., Porto-Díaz, I., Bolón-Canedo, V., Alonso-Betanzos, A.: Ensemble feature selection: homogeneous and heterogeneous approaches. Knowl.-Based Syst. **118**, 124–139 (2017)

14. Su, Y., Zhang, Y., Ji, D., Wang, Y., Wu, H.: Ensemble learning for sentiment classification. In: Ji, D., Xiao, G. (eds.) CLSW 2012. LNCS (LNAI), vol. 7717, pp. 84–93. Springer, Heidelberg (2013). https://doi.org/10.1007/978-3-642-36337-5_10

15. Tao, F., Liu, G., Zhao, Q.: An ensemble framework of voice-based emotion recognition system for films and TV programs. In: 2018 IEEE International Conference on Acoustics, Speech and Signal Processing (ICASSP), pp. 6209–6213. IEEE (2018)

16. Zhang, B., Yin, J., Hao, J., Zhang, D., Wang, S.: Malicious codes detection based on ensemble learning. In: Xiao, B., Yang, L.T., Ma, J., Muller-Schloer, C., Hua, Y. (eds.) ATC 2007. LNCS, vol. 4610, pp. 468–477. Springer, Heidelberg (2007). https://doi.org/10.1007/978-3-540-73547-2_48

17. Zhang, C., Ma, Y.: Ensemble Machine Learning: Methods and Applications. Springer, Heidelberg (2012). https://doi.org/10.1007/978-1-4419-9326-7

Predicting No-show Medical Appointments Using Machine Learning

Sara Alshaya[1]($\boxtimes$), Andrew McCarren[2]($\boxtimes$), and Amal Al-Rasheed[3]($\boxtimes$)

[1] Dublin City University, Dublin, Ireland
sara.alshaya4@mail.dcu.ie
[2] Insight Center for Data Analytics, Dublin City University, Dublin, Ireland
andrew.mccarren@dcu.ie
[3] Princess Nourah University, Riyadh, Kingdom of Saudi Arabia
aaalrasheed@pnu.edu.sa

Abstract. Health care centers face many issues due to the limited availability of resources, such as funds, equipment, beds, physicians, and nurses. Appointment absences lead to a waste of hospital resources as well as endangering patient health. This fact makes unattended medical appointments both socially expensive and economically costly. This research aimed to build a predictive model to identify whether an appointment would be a no-show or not in order to reduce its consequences. This paper proposes a multi-stage framework to build an accurate predictor that also tackles the imbalanced property that the data exhibits. The first stage includes dimensionality reduction to compress the data into its most important components. The second stage deals with the imbalanced nature of the data. Different machine learning algorithms were used to build the classifiers in the third stage. Various evaluation metrics are also discussed and an evaluation scheme that fits the problem at hand is described. The work presented in this paper will help decision makers at health care centers to implement effective strategies to reduce the number of no-shows.

Keywords: Machine learning · Deep learning · No-show · Data imbalance · Dimensionality reduction

1 Introduction

Hospitals suffer from a number of different problems that affect their services in many ways. The total budget reserved for health care in the U.S. for the 2013 fiscal year was 3.8 trillion dollars, this represented 23.3% of the total gross domestic product (GDP) [1]. The limited resources available for health care in terms of funds, equipment, beds, physicians, and nurses could lead to various consequences depending on how they are allocated [5]. In addition, the early discharge of patients to admit other patients with more critical conditions [20] is common due to a lack of beds. Inefficient human resources management can

© Springer Nature Switzerland AG 2019
A. Alfaries et al. (Eds.): ICC 2019, CCIS 1097, pp. 211–223, 2019.
https://doi.org/10.1007/978-3-030-36365-9_18

also lead to an insufficient number of available staff members to handle emergencies and disasters [30]. One of the important problems that face health care centers is when patients miss their scheduled medical appointments without cancellation, i.e., a no-show. The reservation of an appointment involves the allocation of health care providers' time, medical equipment, room, etc. Therefore, an increased ratio of no-show appointments could cause a severe waste of already scarce resources. This in turn could potentially endanger the lives of many who need timely interventions. This research aims to build a classifier to predict whether a scheduled appointment will be attended or not. This in turn could help hospital and clinic administrators to define effective strategies to mitigate the no-show problem. Overbooking could be an effective strategy which involves booking extra appointments on the days of high predicted no-shows [15,23]. Also, sending SMS reminders to patients who are likely to miss their appointments [3] could be an option. Reservation fees at the time of booking have also been found to be an effective deterrent [2]. Due to the nature of the data, a sub-problem arises, namely data imbalance. Most of the available datasets for this problem are imbalanced, as the percentage of missed appointments is naturally lower than the percentage of those attended. Data imbalance in the training and validation sets could cause the resulting models to be biased towards the majority class (i.e., those who do not miss their appointments). Therefore, the approach proposed in this paper addresses this issue [19,22,26].

2   Related Work

2.1   Machine Learning Methods for Missed Appointments

A relevant work [16] used stepwise logistic regression on a dataset obtained from Kaggle[1], which included information about medical appointments in Brazil. The researchers divided the dataset into four independent populations, depending on age group, above-18 or under-18 (adults, children), and whether they visited the clinic once or many times (non-recurrent, recurrent). Stepwise logistic regression was used to train a classifier for each population. Area under the receiver operator characteristic curve (AUC ROC) and prediction accuracy were reported to evaluate the models. Table 1 shows the results obtained on the test sets for the four predictors. Another work by [27] also utilized stepwise logistic regression. They introduced an insightful variable calculated for each patient using an empirical Markov model based on up to 10 previous appointments. Variables were selected based on a likelihood ratio according to the following criteria: (1) the p-value to enter was set at 0.05, and (2) the p-value for removal was set at 0.10. The variables that were found significant in all 24 models were: the natural log of appointment age, multiple appointments per day, and the empirical Markov model value based on past attendance history. The probability that a patient will miss his/her appointments decreased as he/she got older and that effect was present in all 24 models. The area under the ROC curve was used to

---

[1] https://www.kaggle.com/joniarroba/noshowappointments.

assess the model's performance. The average test accuracy was 0.762. While the average test AUC ROC score was 0.713.

Table 1. Results summary of the method proposed by [16]

Population	ROC	Prediction accuracy
No-recurrent children	0.7564	79.05%
Recurrent children	0.6893	76.35%
Non-recurrent adults	0.7503	81.88%
Recurrent adults	0.7030	79.54%

A method to calculate the threshold of stepwise logistic regression has been proposed by [14] by minimizing the misclassification count. The authors assumed a higher cost for a show misclassified as a no-show than for a no-show misclassified as a show. They designed the cost function as given in (1). They assume that c_{show} is greater than $c_{no-show}$. Given these assumptions, they investigated two values $\frac{c_{show}}{c_{no-show}}$, 2 and 3, to determine their impact on minimizing show errors at the expense of additional no-show errors.

$$c_{show}[\sum E_{show}/N_{show}] + c_{no-show}[\sum E_{no-show}/N_{no-show}] \qquad (1)$$

Using the cost function given by (1) for the training, they optimized the probability threshold. Given a cost ratio of 2, the error is minimized at the threshold of 0.86. For a cost ratio of 3, the threshold is 0.74. Applying a threshold of 0.74 gave a better accuracy on the training set as illustrated in Table 2. The model test accuracy was 86.1%. The overall error rate was 13.9%, which consisted of 3.9% show errors and 87.2% no-show errors.

Table 2. Error percentages on training set for the method proposed by [14]

Threshold	Show error	No-show error
0.86	11.3%	68.1 %
0.74	1.8%	91.9 %

A different study by [21] considered three different machine learning algorithms and compared their performance. In addition to the variables that were already represented in the data, the authors derived three more variables: (1) lead time, which is the time difference (in days) between the date of visit and the reservation date, (2) prior no-show rate, which is the portion of no-shows for a given patient prior to the last appointment, and (3) days since the last appointment, which is the number of days between the date of the last visit and the date of appointment. The authors reported that smoking was one of the most significant factors related to missing medical appointments. They found that lower income and unemployment were associated with more missed medical appointments. The results also showed that patients without insurance for medical services were at risk for not adhering to their appointments and consequently, their care plans. The three machine learning algorithms included in the study were, stepwise logistic regression, feed-forward neural net, and naïve Bayes. A multilayer perceptron structure was used as a neural net with a hidden layer of 25 nodes. A smoothing value of 0.1 provided the best performance for the naïve Bayes classifier. Table 3 shows the results on both the training and test sets using all the prediction models as reported by the authors. As determined by the experiments, naïve Bayes had the better performance.

Table 3. Summary of the results by [21] on Both Training and Testing Sets

Model	Training set		Test set	
	AUC	Accuracy (%)	AUC	Accuracy (%)
Logistic regression	0.91	80%	0.81	73%
Neural net	0.77	79%	0.66	71%
Naive Bayes	**0.96**	**92%**	**0.86**	**82%**

2.2 Methods Used for the Data Imbalance Problem

Different methods can be utilized to tackle a data imbalance problem. Some can be performed at the data level, while others can be performed at the algorithm level. A hybridization of both is also possible. Methods for addressing this problem can be categorized into three major groups [11, 19]: (1) data sampling, which includes either undersampling the majority class (eliminating some observations) or oversampling the minority class (replicating some observations), (2) algorithmic modifications, which modify the learning algorithms using techniques that account for the imbalanced nature of the data, such as a balanced random forest, and (3) cost-sensitive learning in which a higher misclassification cost for the samples from the minority class is assumed.

In the method proposed by [12], the authors tackled data imbalance in a medical diagnosis dataset by introducing a distribution sensitive oversampling approach. In the proposed method, the minority samples were divided into noise samples, unstable samples, boundary samples, and stable samples according to their location in the distribution. Depending on a minority sample's distance from other surrounding minority samples, different replication methods were applied. This was performed to ensure that newly created samples had the same characteristics as the original ones. In the replication process, minority noise and unstable samples were excluded. For each minority sample not characterized as noise or unstable, the accumulative distance between it and its k neighbors was calculated. If the distance was less than or equal to a defined threshold, then a few samples were generated using this sample. If the cumulative distance was greater than the threshold, then as many samples as possible were created using it. Testing on real medical diagnosis data showed that compared to existing sampling algorithms, the classification learning algorithm was more accurate when using the proposed method, especially in terms of the precision and recall rate of minority classes.

A hybridization of undersampling and algorithmic modifications was proposed by [18]. The authors proposed two methods, EasyEnsemble and Balance-Cascade. The EasyEnsemble method includes subsetting the data at random to ensure that the number of majority and minority samples are equal. Then, a number of sub-classifiers are trained using these subsets. The final decision is the result of combining all the sub-classifiers after each is trained using the AdaBoost [24] algorithm. In the second method, BalanceCascade, after every classifier is trained the majority samples that were classified correctly are eliminated from the training set and are then fed to the next sub-classifier, so that every classifier uses a balanced dataset. In BalanceCascade, the final classifier is different from the EasyEnsemble classifier. While EasyEnsemble's final prediction is created by forming an ensemble classifier that combines all sub-classifier predictions, BalanceCascade predicts a positive value if and only if all sub-classifiers predict a positive value. The two methods were tested using datasets suffering from a high imbalance ratio, referred to as "hard" datasets, and "easy" datasets with lower imbalance ratios. The results showed that for easy tasks, most of the class imbalance learning methods had lower AUC ROC scores than Ada. On the other hand, for hard tasks, class imbalance learning methods generally had higher AUC ROC scores than Ada, including SMOTE, Chan [7], Cascade, and Easy. The authors reported that for tasks on which ordinary methods could have high AUC scores, class-imbalance learning was unhelpful. However, Easy and Cascade reduced training time (3.50 and 5.50 for Easy and Cascade vs. 19.83 and 18.63 for Ada and Asym [28]), while their average AUC ROCs were similar to that of Ada and Asym. Therefore, class-imbalance learning was particularly helpful for hard tasks. In this paper, different machine learning algorithms were studied and compared, such as random forest, support vector classifier, and stochastic gradient descent. To tackle data imbalance, the effect of using an ensemble classifier was studied. The ensemble classifier used was balanced random forest, which performed competitively.

3   Proposed Framework

In order to achieve the objective of this research, represented in designing and training a high-performing predictive model for no-show appointments, the framework used is introduced. Figure 1 illustrates the general framework used to build the proposed solution. At each phase, different techniques that were applied in order to generate various combinations of techniques. In the following section, the purpose of each phase is highlighted along with the summarization of all techniques used in each phase.

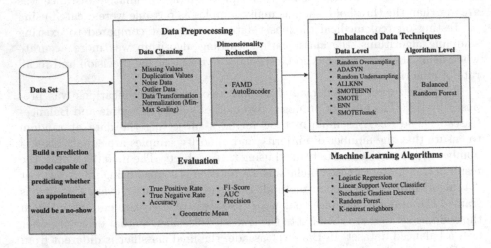

Fig. 1. The general framework followed to perform this study.

3.1 Data Collection and Preprocessing

The dataset used for this study was obtained from the Kaggle (See footnote 1) medical appointment no-show dataset. This dataset contained information about scheduled medical appointments in Brazil. This dataset is available in different versions, and the one used here was the version released in May 2016. The dataset contained 14 variables. These variables were used to derive seven more that were used in initially building the predictive model. These variables were: lead days, on same day, day of week, patient's visits count, patient's no-show rate, no-show last appointment, and appointments count at same day. All derived variables are described in Table 4. Since the weather is believed to affect appointment status, a weather dataset was studied and merged with the original dataset. The no-show appointments dataset provider indicated that all the hospital neighborhoods in the data were located in the city of Vitoria. Therefore, a dataset was obtained from the weather website[2] for the months (April, May, and June) included in the appointment dataset.

A check for missing values was performed with the appointment dataset, and none were found. Also, no duplicate records were observed. However, some problematic values were observed when analyzing the attributes to check for potential noise or outliers. For example, one appointment was scheduled for a patient whose age was recorded as −1. Since there are no negative ages, this case was considered as noise and was dropped. Also, there were seven appointments for patients older than 100 years old. There were five appointment records with

---

[2] https://www.tutiempo.net.

Table 4. Derived variables description.

Lead days	The number of days between the reservation day and the actual appointment day
On same day	An indication as to whether the appointment takes place on the same day it was reserved, i.e. lead days = 0
Day of week	It is represented as integer numbers (0 for Monday, 1 for Tuesday etc.)
Patient's visits count	The number of appointments the patient has in the entire dataset
Patient's no-show rate	The number of no-show appointments divided by the patient's total number of past appointments
No-show last appointment	An indication to whether the patient's last appointment was a no-show or not
Appointments count at same day	This indicates the number of appointments the patient has on the same day of the appointment under consideration

a patient age of 115 and there were two unique appointment records for patients of age 102. Since these cases were extremely rare, they were considered outliers and were removed from the analysis.

For the weather dataset, a check for missing values was performed, and total precipitation of rain and/or the melted snow indicator had four missing values. Since there was no known relationship between these missing values, they were considered to be missing completely at random. The mean of precipitation of rain and/or melted snow over the respective month was used to impute the missing values.

To enable the different algorithms and techniques in the framework to use the data, the categorical variables were encoded into numerical form. For this purpose, one-hot encoding was performed by creating a separate variable for each category of a given variable.

In datasets, where variables have disparate distribution characteristics, feature scaling is usually recommended [25]. Such characteristics can slow the learning rate, thus preventing convergence. In this research, a min-max scaling approach was performed as the variables were not normally distributed. Min-max scaling is performed by subtracting the minimum value of each variable from its respective variable's values and dividing the result by the difference between the maximum and the minimum.

3.2 Dimensionality Reduction

In this study, two methods for dimensionality reduction were applied. Since the dataset contained both categorical and numerical variables, a factor analysis of mixed data (FAMD) [4] was used, also a deep-learning-based method that performs dimensionality reduction in an unsupervised manner, namely AutoEncoder (AE) [29], was applied. AE was implemented as a fully-connected three-layered neural network with one hidden layer and a sigmoid activation function for all nodes. The input data was split in a 80:20 ratio of training to test data. The autoencoder was trained using AdaDelta optimization to minimize the binary cross-entropy loss function. For both methods, the number of resulting components was set to 10 which represents 10% of all features after the one-hot encoding.

3.3   Data Balancing

Data balancing techniques were performed to avoid bias in the learned models. A number of balancing techniques at both the data and algorithm level were explored in this research. The techniques utilized in this paper included: oversampling balancing (random oversampling [10], adaptive synthetic (ADASYN) [10], and SMOTE [8]), undersampling balancing (random undersampling [10], AllKNN, edited nearest neighbors [13]), and hybrid techniques (SMOTEENN, SMOTETomek).

3.4   Machine Learning Algorithms

The logistic regression [6], random forest, k-nearest neighbors, support vector classifier [9], and stochastic gradient descent algorithms were implemented and evaluated. Logistic regression is a commonly used algorithm for binary classification problems similar to the one at hand. In addition, random forest is used to build a strong classifier using an ensemble of weaker ones, therefore, it yields high scores for many problems. The support vector classifier algorithm is a kernel-based method that deals with non-linearity by transforming the data points into a higher dimension space where there is a separating hyperplane. Due to its simplicity, the k-nearest-neighbors algorithm was also included in the experiments. Since most real-life datasets are linearly inseparable, the support vector classifier was included in the study. The stochastic gradient descent was also studied to speed up the training of the support vector machine. For the experiments, the number of trees in the random forest (RF) was set to 100. The number of features considered in data splitting was identified as the square root of the total number of features. The criterion selected for measuring the quality of data splits was set to the Gini index. To find the weights of the logistic regression that corresponded to the least error, liblinear was used as an optimization method, which is indicated as suitable for small datasets. The support vector classifier (SVC) with a linear kernel was built, the loss (i.e., the error function) was set to hinge. The maximum number of iterations was set to 15 000, since it did not converge using the default value of 100, and more than 15 000 was computationally expensive in terms of training time. In order to speed up the training of the linear support vector classifier and to be able to set the maximum number of iterations to a higher value, the stochastic gradient descent (SGD) method with a hinge loss function was used to fit a support vector classifier with a maximum number of iterations set to 50 000. The number of neighbors for k-nearest neighbors was specified to be five, and the algorithm used to specify the nearest neighbors was KDTree. The implementation of the balanced random forest (BRF) [18] was performed as a technique for tackling the data imbalance issue on the algorithm level. Being a type of random forest, it was a collection of decision trees, and was similarly set to 100 trees. The criterion used to measure the data splits quality was also set to the Gini index.

4 Experimental Settings

In order to organize the experiments and to facilitate the training and cross-validation of each setting, the suggested framework was implemented as a pipeline. Feature scaling was included as the first step of the pipeline. The second step was the dimensionality reduction technique utilized (FAMD (n = 10), AE, or no reduction). The data sampling balancing technique was then included, where a technique was chosen from those described earlier, or no balancing was performed. Finally, the machine learning algorithm used for training the model was executed. It was chosen from the algorithms defined for this research. If the learning algorithm was a balanced algorithm, this meant that no data sampling step was needed.

4.1 Evaluation

For each experimental setting, a 10-fold cross-validation was performed by dividing the dataset into ten splits, each one was used once for testing while the remaining nine were used for training at each step. The process was performed 10 times and performance metrics were calculated for each. Finally, the average of every evaluation metric was reported. Accuracy, training time, F1-score, precision, and the AUC ROC obtained on the test set were used as evaluation metrics. True positive and true negative rates were implemented by utilizing the true positive, true negative, false positive, and false negative results from the confusion matrix. Additionally, the geometric mean (G-mean) was used since it is recommended for problems with imbalanced data [17]. G-mean can be calculated in terms of both (TPR) and (TNR) as in (2).

$$G - mean = \sqrt{TPR \times TNR} \tag{2}$$

5 Experimental Results

Table 5 details the best results obtained by the different machine learning algorithms (i.e., logistic regression, random forest, linear SVC, stochastic gradient descent, and KNN). Each machine learning algorithm was studied by combining it with the different dimensionality reduction and data balancing techniques included in this research. The best results were determined using G-mean as the primary evaluation metric; if there was more than one setting that had the top G-mean score, the F1-score was considered; and if there was still a tie, then the AUC ROC was used.

Five different settings of logistic regression obtained the best results according to the evaluation scheme described. All of these five settings used AE with 10 components as a dimensionality reduction method in combination with ADASYN, SMOTE, random undersampling, SMOTEENN, and SMORETomek.

The random forest algorithm scored the best when used in combination with FAMD with 10 components and SMOTEENN.

The support vector classifier obtained the best results on five different settings, four of them used AE and one of the balancing techniques: ADASYN, random oversampling, random undersampling, or SMOTEENN. The fifth used FAMD with AllKNN as a balancing technique.

Six different settings yielded the best results in the case of SGD, four of these settings used AE and the remaining two used no dimensionality reduction. For the settings that used AE, either RandomOverSampler, SMOTE, SMOTEENN, or SMOTETomek were used.

Since the training of the k-nearest-neighbors algorithm when applied on all features without dimensionality reduction was very time-consuming, it was only used with dimensionality reduction. This emphasizes the importance of dimensionality reduction in some cases when using all features is computationally expensive. K-nearest neighbors performed the best when used with ENN as a balancing technique and FAMD with 10 components as a dimensionality reduction method.

Lastly, the best performance obtained by balanced random forest was when combined with AE for dimensionality reduction.

The results show that according to the evaluation scheme, SGD and SVM had the top performance in terms of G-mean, F1-score, and AUC ROC. Although logistic regression had the same G-mean and AUC ROC scores, it was slightly outperformed in terms of F1-score by both SGD and SVM. Best performances were mostly obtained using AE for dimensionality reduction.

6   Contribution

This paper contributes in solving the problem of no-show medical appointments. It proposes a framework for building a prediction model using different machine learning algorithms, various balancing techniques, and dimensionality reduction methods. It tackles the problem of data imbalance to avoid the bias in the trained models. It also introduced AE and FAMD as possible options for dimensionality reduction in the no-show prediction. The effectiveness of using dimensionality reduction to enhance the performance in general and reduce the time for training time-consuming models has been empirically demonstrated. A number of derived attributes were also calculated to increase the expressive power of the data. Since weather is believed to affect the no-show, a weather dataset was collected and merged with the original data to enhance the performance.

Table 5. Best experimental results as obtained by all included algorithms combined with all dimensionality reduction and balancing techniques.

ML algorithm	Balancing	Dimensionality reduction	AUC ROC	Acc.	PR	F1-score	TPR	TNR	G-mean	Fitting time (sec.)
Logistic regression	ADASYN	AE (n=10)	**0.68**	0.54	0.61	0.43	0.84	0.47	**0.62**	8.65
	SMOTE	AE (n = 10)	**0.68**	0.55	0.60	0.43	0.81	0.49	**0.62**	9.55
	RandomUnderSampler	AE (n = 10)	**0.68**	0.56	0.60	0.43	0.81	0.49	**0.62**	9.25
	SMOTEENN	AE (n = 10)	**0.68**	0.53	0.61	0.43	0.88	0.44	**0.62**	14.21
	SMOTETomek	AE (n = 10)	**0.68**	0.55	0.60	0.43	0.82	0.49	**0.62**	14.99
Random forest	SMOTEENN	FAMD (n = 10)	0.65	0.62	0.57	0.36	0.57	0.63	0.57	29.72
Support vector classifier	ADASYN	AE (n = 10)	**0.68**	0.52	0.62	**0.44**	0.91	0.42	**0.62**	10.48
	RandomOverSampler	AE (n = 10)	**0.68**	0.52	0.62	**0.44**	0.91	0.42	**0.62**	9.99
	RandomUnderSampler	AE (n = 10)	**0.68**	0.52	0.62	**0.44**	0.91	0.42	**0.62**	5.29
	SMOTEENN	AE (n = 10)	**0.68**	0.52	0.62	**0.44**	0.91	0.42	**0.62**	11.37
	AllKNN	FAMD (n = 10)	**0.68**	0.52	0.62	**0.44**	0.92	0.41	**0.62**	11.81
Stochastic gradient descent	RandomOverSampler	AE (n = 10)	**0.68**	0.52	0.62	**0.44**	0.91	0.42	**0.62**	13.57
	SMOTE	AE (n = 10)	**0.68**	0.52	0.62	**0.44**	0.91	0.42	**0.62**	14.83
	SMOTEENN	AE (n = 10)	**0.68**	0.52	0.62	**0.44**	0.91	0.42	**0.62**	20.37
	SMOTETomek	AE (n = 10)	**0.68**	0.52	0.62	**0.44**	0.91	0.42	**0.62**	20.58
	RandomOverSampler	None	**0.68**	0.52	0.62	**0.44**	0.92	0.42	**0.62**	2.05
	SMOTEENN	None	**0.68**	0.52	0.62	**0.44**	0.92	0.42	**0.62**	648.85
K-nearest neighbors	ENN	FAMD (n = 10)	0.67	0.58	0.60	0.40	0.72	0.55	0.60	7.94
Balanced random forest		AE (n = 10)	0.58	0.52	0.55	0.36	0.65	0.49	0.56	17.05

7 Conclusion

In this work, a framework for building a high-performing balanced predictor for no-show medical appointments has been proposed. Logistic regression, random forest, stochastic gradient descent, k-nearest neighbors, and linear support vector classifier have been explored as possible machine learning algorithms to apply. To avoid the consequences of data imbalance, various data balancing techniques on both data and algorithmic levels have been tested. Two different dimensionality reduction techniques, AE and FAMD, as they both fit data of a mixed nature (i.e., that includes a mixture of categorical and numerical variables) have been implemented. Geometric mean (G-mean) was used as the primary evaluation metric, while F1-score and AUC ROC were considered when G-mean scores were equal for different settings. The best performance according to the described evaluation scheme was obtained by both SGD and SVM in combination with different dimensionality reduction and balancing techniques. The results also showed that the best scores were mostly obtained using AE for dimensionality reduction which emphasizes the usefulness of using novel unsupervised dimensionality reduction based on deep learning.

References

1. United states office of management and budget: fiscal year 2013 budget of the U.S. government. https://www.govinfo.gov/content/pkg/BUDGET-2013-BUD/pdf/BUDGET-2013-BUD.pdf#page=214
2. Aggarwal, A., Davies, J., Sullivan, R.: "nudge" and the epidemic of missed appointments: can behavioural policies provide a solution for missed appointments in the health service? J. Health Organ. Manag. **30**(4), 558–564 (2016)
3. Arora, S., et al.: Improving attendance at post-emergency department follow-up via automated text message appointment reminders: a randomized controlled trial. Acad. Emerg. Med. **22**(1), 31–37 (2015)
4. Bécue-Bertaut, M., Pagès, J.: Multiple factor analysis and clustering of a mixture of quantitative, categorical and frequency data. Comput. Stat. Data Anal. **52**(6), 3255–3268 (2008)
5. Belciug, S., Gorunescu, F.: Improving hospital bed occupancy and resource utilization through queuing modeling and evolutionary computation. J. Biomed. Inform. **53**, 261–269 (2015)
6. Branco, P., Torgo, L., Ribeiro, R.P.: A survey of predictive modeling on imbalanced domains. ACM Comput. Surv. (CSUR) **49**(2), 31 (2016)
7. Chan, P.K., Stolfo, S.J.: Toward scalable learning with non-uniform class and cost distributions: a case study in credit card fraud detection. In: KDD 1998, pp. 164–168 (1998)
8. Chawla, N.V., Bowyer, K.W., Hall, L.O., Kegelmeyer, W.P.: SMOTE: synthetic minority over-sampling technique. J. Artif. Intell. Res. **16**, 321–357 (2002)
9. Cortes, C., Vapnik, V.: Support-vector networks. Mach. Learn. **20**(3), 273–297 (1995)
10. Estabrooks, A., Jo, T., Japkowicz, N.: A multiple resampling method for learning from imbalanced data sets. Comput. Intell. **20**(1), 18–36 (2004)
11. Haixiang, G., Yijing, L., Shang, J., Mingyun, G., Yuanyue, H., Bing, G.: Learning from class-imbalanced data: review of methods and applications. Expert Syst. Appl. **73**, 220–239 (2017)
12. Han, W., Huang, Z., Li, S., Jia, Y.: Distribution-sensitive unbalanced data oversampling method for medical diagnosis. J. Med. Syst. **43**(2), 39 (2019)
13. He, H., Ma, Y.: Imbalanced lEarning: Foundations, Algorithms, Andapplications. Wiley, Hoboken (2013)
14. Huang, Y., Hanauer, D.A.: Patient no-show predictive model development using multiple data sources for an effective overbooking approach. Appl. Clin. Inform. **5**(03), 836–860 (2014)
15. Huang, Y., Zuniga, P.: Dynamic overbooking scheduling system to improve patient access. J. Oper. Res. Soc. **63**(6), 810–820 (2012)
16. Kheirkhah, P., Feng, Q., Travis, L.M., Tavakoli-Tabasi, S., Sharafkhaneh, A.: Prevalence, predictors and economic consequences of no-shows. BMC Health Serv. Res. **16**(1), 13 (2015)
17. Kubat, M., Matwin, S., et al.: Addressing the curse of imbalanced training sets: one-sided selection. In: ICML, Nashville, USA, vol. 97, pp. 179–186 (1997)
18. Liu, X.Y., Wu, J., Zhou, Z.H.: Exploratory undersampling for class-imbalance learning. IEEE Trans. Syst. Man Cybern. Part B (Cybern.) **39**(2), 539–550 (2008)
19. López, V., Fernández, A., García, S., Palade, V., Herrera, F.: An insight into classification with imbalanced data: empirical results and current trends on using data intrinsic characteristics. Inf. Sci. **250**, 113–141 (2013)

20. Mallor, F., Azcárate, C., Barado, J.: Control problems and management policies in health systems: application to intensive care units. Flexible Serv. Manuf. J. **28**(1–2), 62–89 (2016)
21. Mohammadi, I., Wu, H., Turkcan, A., Toscos, T., Doebbeling, B.N.: Data analytics and modeling for appointment no-show in community health centers. J. Primary Care Commun. Health **9**, 2150132718811692 (2018)
22. Nanni, L., Fantozzi, C., Lazzarini, N.: Coupling different methods for overcoming the class imbalance problem. Neurocomputing **158**, 48–61 (2015)
23. Nuti, L.A., et al.: No-shows to primary care appointments: subsequent acute care utilization among diabetic patients. BMC Health Serv. Res. **12**(1), 304 (2012)
24. Schapire, R.E.: A brief introduction to boosting. In: IJCAI, vol. 99, pp. 1401–1406 (1999)
25. Singh, B.K., Verma, K., Thoke, A.: Investigations on impact of feature normalization techniques on classifier's performance in breast tumor classification. Int. J. Comput. Appl. **116**(19) (2015)
26. Sun, Y., Wong, A.K., Kamel, M.S.: Classification of imbalanced data: a review. Int. J. Pattern Recognit. Artif. Intell. **23**(04), 687–719 (2009)
27. Vargas, D.L., et al.: Modeling patient no-show history and predicting future outpatient appointment behavior in the veterans health administration. Mil. Med. **182**(5/6), E1708 (2017)
28. Viola, P., Jones, M.: Fast and robust classification using asymmetric adaboost and a detector cascade. In: Advances in Neural Information Processing Systems, pp. 1311–1318 (2002)
29. Wang, Y., Yao, H., Zhao, S.: Auto-encoder based dimensionality reduction. Neurocomputing **184**, 232–242 (2016)
30. Xiang, Y., Zhuang, J.: A medical resource allocation model for serving emergency victims with deteriorating health conditions. Ann. Oper. Res. **236**(1), 177–196 (2016)

Cancer Incidence Prediction Using a Hybrid Model of Wavelet Transform and LSTM Networks

Amani Alrobai[1]([✉]) and Musfira Jilani[2]([✉])

[1] College of Computer and Information Sciences,
Princess Nourah Bint Abdulrahman University, Riyadh, Saudi Arabia
aalrabaie@pnu.edu.sa
[2] School of Computing, Dublin City University, Dublin, Ireland
musfira.jilani@dcu.ie

Abstract. Cancer is a major public health concern. Being able to predict the number of future cancer incidences is vital to allocate appropriate healthcare resources and research funding. Real data, such as cancer incidences, exhibit non-linear characteristics along with a high degree of fluctuations, which makes the modelling process difficult. This study explores the potential of time series modelling, especially the long short-term memory (LSTM) recurrent neural networks, to predict the number of cancer incidences. A novel hybrid model of the wavelet transform and LSTM is proposed with the goal of increasing forecasting accuracy. The evaluation of the proposed models for the three most common types of cancer in the Kingdom of Saudi Arabia shows that the proposed hybrid model has better accuracy than the original LSTM model.

Keywords: Long short-term memory · Wavelet transform · Time series prediction

1 Introduction

Cancer is rated as the second-most common cause of death in many countries. It is expected that it will become the number-one killer in many parts of the world, thus constituting a critical barrier to the ability to increase life expectancy [1]. Even in the Kingdom of Saudi Arabia (KSA), cancer statistics are a cause of concern. The total number of new cancer cases was 16,210 in the latest report of the National Cancer Registry for 2015 [2]. Meanwhile, in 2010 the total reported cancer cases was 13,706 [3], suggesting an increase of 3.41% per year. The KSA needs to be ready to cope with the challenge of a foreseeable increase in cancer burden mainly associated with the population growth and ageing.

Currently, 30–50% of cancers could be prevented by averting risks and implementing evidence-based prevention strategies [4]. To enable policymakers planning to address future challenges and promote national cancer control policies, the proposed plans must be tailored to the local disease burden. Therefore, accurate modelling to forecast the future cancer burden is necessary to aid public health officials' decision-making.

© Springer Nature Switzerland AG 2019
A. Alfaries et al. (Eds.): ICC 2019, CCIS 1097, pp. 224–235, 2019.
https://doi.org/10.1007/978-3-030-36365-9_19

Over the past several decades, many researchers in the field of cancer incidence prediction have proposed different statistical analyses – such as age-period-cohort analysis [5, 6], Bayesian analysis [7, 8] and regression analysis [9, 10]. They either conduct cancer trends analysis to inform the public health authorities of the latest trends or forecast the burden of cancer in terms of incidences and mortality. It appears that an adaption of a time series model for cancer burden forecasting utilising long short-term memory (LSTM) has not been widely conducted. However, real data such as cancer incidences exhibit non-linear characteristics as well as a high degree of fluctuations due to time-varying behaviours, which makes the modelling process difficult. Therefore, the goal of this study is to explore the potential of a hybrid model of wavelet transform and LSTM to capture non-linear attributes in the number of new cancer incidences.

The rest of this paper is organised as follows: The background and related literature is examined in Sect. 2; an overview of the methodology that underpins this research and the design of the proposed models is presented in Sect. 3, while the experiments and results are explained in Sect. 4. This is followed by the discussion and conclusion in Sect. 5.

2 Background and Related Work

2.1 Cancer Incidence Studies

In an attempt to monitor the growth of cancer incidence and mortality in Saudi Arabia, many researchers in the field of cancer incidence have proposed different studies. Ibrahim et al. [11] designed a study to estimate the future cancer burden, using the most recent sources of cancer data available at that time. The authors concluded that there will be a notable increase in future cancer burden, which will require enormous health care resources. Also, an analysis of cancer incidence in Saudi Arabia for 2012, which was aimed at minimising the health care burden associated with cancer, showed notable differences according to gender, age and region of Saudi Arabia [12]. Other studies attempted to predict the future burden for a specific type of cancer [13–15] – such as liver and kidney cancer and leukaemia, respectively.

2.2 Wavelet Transform Studies

Predicting future cancer burden, either in terms of the number of new cases or deaths, is a challenging exercise [16]. The fluctuation in the number of new cancer incidences is not easy to predict. To overcome the high degree of fluctuation, signals need to be separated from noise, which can be done using wavelet transform. Wavelet transform [17] is a time-frequency decomposition technique that provides a useful basis of time series for both time and frequency. Wavelet transform can be used in two ways: for time series analysis [18] and signal processing [19]. Many researchers have developed hybrid models that combine wavelet denoising with forecasting methods to improve forecasting accuracy. For instance, Lotric et al. [20] proposed two denoising layers based on wavelet transform analysis. Those layers were integrated into feedforward and recurrent neural networks. The proposed models were validated using three time series prediction problems. The results showed that the use of the denoising layers improved the prediction accuracy in both cases. Li et al. [21] proposed a novel model that combines real-time wavelet denoising with LSTM to predict East Asian stock indexes. The empirical results showed that the proposed prediction model's performance was significantly improved compared to the original LSTM model. Liang et al. [22] proposed LSTM and wavelet threshold-denoising method to pre-process stock price data, as there is high noise in the data. They also reduced the degree of distortion in signal reconstruction by proposing a new multioptimal combination wavelet transform (MOCWT) method. The results showed that the proposed MOCWT had better a prediction accuracy than the traditional methods.

2.3 Long Short-Term Memory Networks Studies

LSTM [23] is a particular type of recurrent neural network (RNN) model that is explicitly designed to avoid the short-term dependency problem of RNN. LSTM is a popular time series model that has been used in many domains, such as emergency event prediction [24] and infectious disease prediction [25]. The LSTM models proposed in the previous studies have the ability to make accurate predictions when forecasting. Yunpeng et al. [26] attempted to model different data patterns using LSTM for multistep-ahead prediction. The results showed that LSTM had a higher accuracy than the conventional statistical-based models.

In this paper, a novel hybrid model that combines wavelet transform and LSTM is introduced. The proposed method was applied to predicting the number of cancer incidences. The wavelet transform denoised the original signals of the historical number of cancer incidences into a better series pattern for prediction. Meanwhile, LSTM was used as a non-linear pattern recognition device to identify cancer incidence data patterns.

3 Methodology

This section describes the techniques used in our proposed models by describing the mathematical theories behind wavelet transform and LSTM.

A univariate time series $X = \{x_1, x_2, \ldots \ldots x_t\}$ is a finite set of sequential data points recorded at evenly spaced intervals in which each $x_i \in X$ represents the value of observation at time i.

3.1 LSTM Networks

LSTM is a successful RNN architecture that can learn long-term dependencies in time series data [23] as opposed to RNN, which lack the ability to remember a long sequence of data. To explain what the LSTM model is and how it works, artificial neural network (ANN) and RNN need to be understood.

An ANN [27] is a brain-inspired system intended to replicate the way that humans learn. An ANN uses different layers of mathematical processing to make sense of information. It is a collection of basic computational elements (nodes) arranged in a series of layers. Each node is connected by a weighted edge. The higher the number of weights, the more significant influence one unit has on another. Each node receives multiple inputs from other nodes or external sources. Then, the node updates its current state by computing the internal activation function to produce the output.

An RNN [28] is a type of ANN with the dynamic ability to incorporate past experience due to internal recurrence. Therefore, the node can store information from the current step to make predictions for the next steps. RNN is only suitable for remembering a few recent steps.

The ability of LSTM comes from a unit in the hidden recurrent layer called a memory block [23]. The memory block typically has a memory cell, which is the key to LSTM RNN. An LSTM memory block is shown in Fig. 1. Inside each memory block there are three different types of gates:

- The forget gate is applied to decide which information should be kept or thrown away from the cell state.
- The input gate determines the flow of the new inputs and if they should be stored in the cell state.
- The output gate determines which parts of the cell state are going to be in the output.

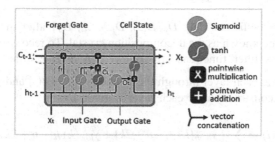

Fig. 1. An LSTM memory block (Source: adapted from Energies 10, p. 1168)

Where x_t is the input x at time t, h_t is the output with respect to x_t. In addition, h_{t-1} is the output of the previous memory cell, and C_t is the cell state, while C_{t-1} is the previous cell state. Therefore, LSTM RNN can store the temporal state of the current step or remove or add information to the memory cell to be used in the following steps.

3.2 Discrete Wavelet Transform (DWT) and Wavelet Denoising

A wavelet transform is a mathematical tool that provides a useful basis of time series for both time and frequency. There are two kinds of wavelet transformations: continuous wavelet transformation and discrete wavelet transformation (DWT) [29]. DWT works on two main functions, the scaling function (father ϕ) and wavelet function (mother Ψ), which characterises the basic wavelet shape. There are many different families of wavelets. The types of wavelet used in this study are the Haar and Daubechies of order 4(db4) [29]. The Haar is a special case of the Daubechies wavelet. It is also known as Db1 and is suitable to detect time-localised information and increase the performance of the prediction technique [30]. The basic Haar mother and father wavelet functions can be described using:

$$\phi(t) = \begin{cases} 1, & 0 < t < 1 \\ 0, & otherwise \end{cases} \quad \Psi(t) = \begin{cases} 1, & 0 \le t < 0.5 \\ -1, & 0.5 \le t < 1 \\ 0, & otherwise \end{cases} \tag{1}$$

The decomposition process can be done at one or more levels [31]. At each level, the signal can be divided into two parts: the low-frequency part, or approximated series (cA_j), and the high-frequency part, or detail series (cD_j). The decomposition for each layer is represented by:

$$y_{low}(k) = \sum_i x(i)h(2k - i) \tag{2}$$

$$y_{high}(k) = \sum_i x(i)g(2k - i) \tag{3}$$

Where y_{low} and y_{high} refer to low-pass and high-pass filters, respectively, both subsampling by two. The symbol k refers to the time decomposition, and $x(i)$ is the original signal data, which is passed through to a high-pass filter $g(.)$ and a low-pass filter $h(.)$.

The set of the coefficients $\{A_j, D_j, D_{j-1}, D_{j-2}, ..., D_1\}$ after the wavelet decomposition at level j are known as the decomposition crystal. To reconstruct the signal, the high- and low-pass filter functions are followed in reverse order. The signals are upsampled by two at each layer through the synthesis filters $g'(\cdot)$ and $h'(\cdot)$ and added to each other. The reconstruction for each layer is given by:

$$x(i) = \sum_k y_{high}(k) g'(-n + 2k) + y_{low}(k) h'(-n + 2k) \tag{4}$$

Denoising is the process used to reconstruct a signal from a noisy one without distorting the quality of the processed signal. Wavelet transformation is a powerful tool for removing noise from a variety of signals. A signal that contains noise is difficult to model. Removing the noise from the signal facilitates the modelling process [32]. A signal that is corrupted by additive noise can be represented by:

$$y(i) = x(i) + \sigma\varepsilon(i)i = 0, 1, ...n - 1 \tag{5}$$

Where $y(i)$ is the noisy signal, $x(i)$ is a noise-free signal, σ represents the intensity of the noise and $\varepsilon(i)$ is an independent normal random variable [32]. The signal denoising procedure based on DWT has three steps: signal decomposition, thresholding and signal reconstruction. One crucial point in the thresholding method is to find the appropriate value for the threshold, which requires the estimation of the noise level. In [33], the researchers proposed an estimator σ for wavelet denoising, which is generally calculated from the standard deviation of the detail coefficient:

$$\sigma = median\left(d_{l-1,k}\right), \; k = 0, 1, \dots 2^{l-1} - 1 \tag{6}$$

Where l refers to the number of decomposition levels. The estimated noise level σ is used to threshold the small coefficient assumed as noise. The most well-known threshold selection algorithms are minimax, universal and rigorous sure threshold estimation techniques [32]. The universal technique uses a fixed threshold form given as:

$$\lambda_u = \sigma\sqrt{2\log{(n)}} \tag{7}$$

Where n refers to the length of the analysed signal, and σ is given by Eq. 6. The advantage of the universal threshold is that it ensures that every sample in which the underlying function is exactly zero will be estimated as zero. Additionally, this threshold estimator is easy for software implementation. In [33], the researchers also proposed a non-linear strategy for thresholding, which can be implemented either by a soft or hard thresholding method. In hard thresholding, the wavelet coefficient below a given value is set to zero; meanwhile in soft thresholding, the wavelet coefficient above the threshold are reduced in absolute value [32]. The soft thresholding can be expressed as:

$$\text{Hard threshold} = \begin{cases} y = x, & if \; |x| > \lambda \\ y = 0, & if \; |x| < \lambda \end{cases} \tag{8}$$

$$\text{Soft threshold} = \{y = sign(x)(|x| - \lambda) \tag{9}$$

Where x refers to the input signal, λ is the threshold value and y is the signal after threshold.

3.3 Design of the Proposed Models

Persistence Model. A persistence model is a point of reference to measure the relative prediction improvements for all other modelling techniques on the problem. The persistence forecast is defined as the uses of the value of the prior time step (x_t) as a prediction outcome for the next time step ($t + 1$).

LSTM Model. In this study, an LSTM model was used to identify data patterns and forecast the number of future incidences of each cancer type. The following points elaborate the general design of the proposed LSTM model.

- **Phase 1: Normalisation:** All $x_i \in X$ time series are normalised such that all values lie in the interval $[-1; 1]$. This avoids local minima and improves convergence rates [34]. The technique used is called min-mix normalisation.
- **Phase 2: Dividing the dataset into training and testing:** In order to create a model and evaluate it, the entire dataset is divided into training and testing.
- **Phase 3: Converting a time series to supervised learning:** To fit the network, the time series needs to be transformed into feature spaces $\tilde{X}$ and target spaces Y. In the

one-node input layer, the previous observation is used to predict the current, as shown in Eq. 10, where $\tilde{X}$ is the normalised training and testing time series:

$$\tilde{X} = \{x_t, x_{t+1}, x_{t+2}, \ldots, x_n\} Y = \{x_{t+1}, x_{t+2}, \ldots\} \tag{10}$$

- **Phase 4: Data training and testing with an LSTM model:** Two LSTM topologies are implemented: a one-node and a five-node LSTM hidden layer. Both topologies have one node in the input layer and one node in the output layer. The network is trained on the normalised train set for 2000 epochs and 52 batch size. Testing is done on the normalised test set to produce the forecasted values by the LSTM.
- **Phase 5: Denormalisation:** This process is conducted on the forecasted values to set the normalised value to the original value.

Wave LSTM. This is a hybrid time series model of wavelet transform and LSTM. This model is proposed to improve the forecasting accuracy by denoising time series X for each cancer type using wavelet transform. Prediction using wave LSTM can be done in four phases:

- **Phase 1: Selecting a wavelet and a level of decomposition:** The Haar and db4 wavelets are used to decompose the signal. The time series signal X is decomposed into one level to produce the set of coefficients $\{A_1, D_1\}$. This allows for smoothing the noise time series signal without making a significant change to the signal value.
- **Phase 2: Selecting an appropriate threshold value:** The threshold selection algorithm used is the universal threshold estimation technique, implemented by the soft thresholding method shown in Sect. 3.2. Thresholding is applied to the detailed part of coefficient $D1$.
- **Phase 3: Reconstructing the denoised coefficients:** After applying soft thresholding, denoised detailed coefficients $D'1$ and approximation coefficients $A1$ are reconstructed to form the denoised series.
- **Phase 4: Forecasting using LSTM:** The network topologies implemented are the same as the LSTM models, as are most of the steps for producing forecasts. The main difference lies in the input series for the LSTM model, which is the denoised time series signal.

4   Experiments and Results

4.1   Data Description and Pre-processing

Cancer incident data used in this study were provided by Saudi Cancer Registry [35], which is an established organisation working under the Saudi Health Council, KSA. The data were collected over ten years (2006–2015) from multiple hospitals in the KSA following the international regulations for cancer registries. The data covers 140,272 cases of cancer, each of which is described according to hospital registration number, age, gender, address, cancer type and date of diagnosis.

Exploratory Data Analysis will be conducted first to understand the data. Analysing cancer type reveals that the dataset includes 69 types of cancer. The three most common cancers shared by men and women are cancers of the blood, colon and lymph nodes. Thus, this study focuses on modelling these types of cancers.

Data cleaning will remove errors and double/multiple entry cases. The cancer cases were extracted for each of the three common cancer types (blood, colon, lymph nodes) and aggregated on a weekly basis to apply time series modelling. It is more interesting to predict cancer incidences on a yearly basis, but deep learning is more accurate with more data points. However, the weekly forecasted incidents can be aggregated into a yearly basis after time series modelling. The incidences from 2006–2012 were used for training, and the rest were used for testing. Figure 2 plots the weekly cancer incidents for each of the cancer types.

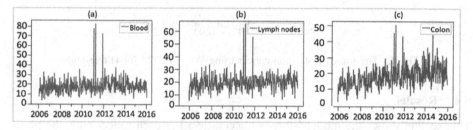

Fig. 2. Weekly cancer incidents for (a) blood, (b) lymph nodes and (c) colon cancer from 2006 to 2015

4.2 Experiments

Several analyses were conducted based on the model implementations from the previous section. The persistence model was applied to each type of cancer (blood, colon and lymph nodes). The persistence model forecast accuracy was used as a baseline for comparison with the developed time series models' accuracies.

This study is primarily interested in evaluating the effect of the wavelet transform on the forecast accuracy of the number of cancer incidences. This is done by comparing the performance of the LSTM and hybrid model of the wavelet transform and LSTM. First, the two LSTM topologies were applied to each series, for the Wave LSTM, applying one level of decomposition using the Haar and db4 wavelets to each series. In total, there were six models for each type of cancer.

4.3 Evaluation Metrics

In this study, root mean square error (RMSE) [36] was used as a metric to evaluate the prediction accuracy of the proposed models. Figure 3 displays the forecast of colon cancer using Wave LSTM db4 five-nodes. RMSE measures the quality of the fit between the observed data and the values predicted by a model. A lower RMSE value means better accuracy. RMSE is calculated by:

$$RMSE = \sqrt{\frac{1}{n}\sum_{i=1}^{n}(y_i - \widetilde{y}_i)^2} \qquad (11)$$

Where n is the number of samples, y_i is the observed values and $\widetilde{y}_i$ is the predicted values.

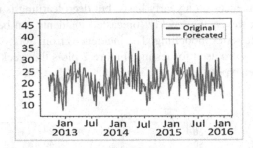

Fig. 3. The forecast of colon cancer using Wave LSTM (db4) five-nodes

4.4 Results

This section shows the models' forecast accuracies. For each cancer type, the persistence model RMSE was used to calculate the uplift in accuracy for the proposed time series models. Additionally, the calculation of the uplift accuracy is the percentage of the improvement in RMSE. The improvement in accuracy resulting from the wavelet transform can be presented as the difference between the two uplifts. The summary of the results for each proposed model with uplifts is shown in Table 1, with only the best performing Wave LSTM displayed. The results of Wave LSTM using the Haar and db4 wavelets are shown in Table 2.

Table 1. Summary of the results for each proposed model with uplifts

Model RMSE	Blood		Colon		Lymph nodes	
	LSTM (5 node)	LSTM (1 node)	LSTM (5 node)	LSTM (1 node)	LSTM (5 node)	LSTM (1 node)
Persistence	7.539	7.539	8.445	8.445	6.080	6.080
LSTM	5.678	5.687	6.995	7.025	4.833	4.869
% LSTM uplift	24.685%	24.566%	17.170%	16.815%	20.510%	19.918%
Wave LSTM	4.874	4.870	5.538	5.532	4.249	4.224
% Wave LSTM uplift	35.350%	35.403%	34.423%	34.494%	30.115%	30.526%
Difference	10.665%	10.837%	17.253%	17.679%	9.605%	10.608%

Table 2. The results of wave LSTM using the haar and db4 wavelets

Model RMSE	Blood		Colon		Lymph nodes	
	LSTM (5 node)	LSTM (1 node)	LSTM (5 node)	LSTM (1 node)	LSTM (5 node)	LSTM (1 node)
Haar wavelet LSTM	5.017	5.013	5.851	5.844	4.423	4.419
Db4 wavelet LSTM	4.874	4.870	5.538	5.532	4.249	4.224

5 Discussion and Conclusion

5.1 Discussion

Both the LSTM and Wave LSTM significantly outperformed the persistence forecasts in all cancer implementations, providing around 16–35% uplift in forecast accuracy.

LSTM with a five-node hidden layer had slightly better performance than LSTM with a one-node hidden layer. Meanwhile, Wave LSTM with a one-node hidden layer had slightly better performance than Wave LSTM with a five-node hidden layer. The improvement between the two topologies was negligible ($\leq 1\%$ increase) in uplift. This demonstrates that an increase in model complexity does not always lead to an improvement in model performance.

The db4 Wave LSTM had better performance than the Haar Wave LSTM. The db4 Wave LSTM provided around 30–35% uplift in forecast accuracy. Meanwhile, the Haar Wave LSTM provided around 27–30% uplift in forecast accuracy. The results demonstrate that the db4 wavelet is more suitable than the Haar wavelet to decompose and denoise the cancer data time series. The selection of the Haar wavelet and db4 wavelet was arbitrary, and further studies can investigate the models using different kinds of mother wavelets.

The differences in uplift between the LSTM and Wave LSTM models were notable, around 9–17% in all cancer implementations. To sum up, the results showed significant improvement in forecast accuracy resulting from the Wave LSTM models compared to regular LSTM.

5.2 Conclusion

This study is primarily focused on predicting cancer incidences, specifically in evaluating the effect of the wavelet transform on the forecast accuracy of the number of cancer incidences. Cancer incidences data exhibit non-linear characteristics along with a high degree of fluctuation. Therefore, a novel hybrid model that combines wavelet transform and LSTM was proposed to increase forecasting accuracy. The wavelet algorithm denoised the original signals of the historical number of cancer incidences into better series pattern for prediction. Meanwhile, LSTM was used as a non-linear pattern recognition to identify cancer incidence data patterns.

The proposed models were applied to each type of cancer (blood, colon and lymph nodes). The predicted outcome of the proposed hybrid model was compared to the original LSTM. The evaluation of the proposed models showed that the hybrid model of the wavelet transform and LSTM has better performance in terms of forecast accuracy than the original LSTM, which does not utilize wavelet denoising function.

References

1. Bray, F., Ferlay, J., Soerjomataram, I., Siegel, R.L., Torre, L.A., Jemal, A.: Global cancer statistics 2018: GLOBOCAN estimates of incidence and mortality worldwide for 36 cancers in 185 countries. CA Cancer J. Clin. **68**(6), 394–424 (2018)
2. Saudi Cancer Registry: Cancer Incidence Report Saudi Arabia 2015. Saudi Health Council, Riyadh (2015)
3. Saudi Cancer Registry: Cancer Incidence Report Saudi Arabia 2010. Saudi Health Council, Riyadh (2010)
4. World Health Organization. https://www.who.int/cancer/en/
5. Smittenaar, C.R., Petersen, K.A., Stewart, K., Moitt, N.: Cancer incidence and mortality projections in the UK until 2035. Br. J. Cancer **115**(9), 1147 (2016)
6. Rosso, T., Malvezzi, M., Bosetti, C., Bertuccio, P., Negri, E., La Vecchia, C.: Cancer mortality in Europe, 1970–2009: an age, period, and cohort analysis. Eur. J. Cancer Prev. **27** (1), 88–102 (2018)
7. Martín-Sánchez, J.C., et al.: Projections in breast and lung cancer mortality among women: a bayesian analysis of 52 countries worldwide. Cancer Res. **78**(15), 4436–4442 (2018)
8. Botta, L., et al.: Bayesian estimates of the incidence of rare cancers in Europe. Cancer Epidemiol. **54**, 95–100 (2018)
9. Jung, K.W., Won, Y.J., Kong, H.J., Lee, E.S.: Prediction of cancer Incidence and mortality in Korea 2019. Cancer Res. Treat. Off. J. Korean Cancer Assoc. **51**(2), 431 (2019)
10. Leiter, U., et al.: Incidence, mortality, and trends of nonmelanoma skin cancer in Germany. J. Invest Dermatol. **137**(9), 1860–1867 (2017)
11. Ibrahim, E., Bin Sadiq, B.M., Banjar, L., Awadalla, S., Abomelha, M.S.: Current and future cancer burden in Saudi Arabia: meeting the challenge. Hematol. Oncol. Stem Cell Ther. **1** (4), 210–215 (2008)
12. Bazarbashi, S., Al Eid, H., Minguet, J.: Cancer incidence in Saudi Arabia: 2012 data from the Saudi cancer registry. Asian Pac. J. Cancer Prev. APJCP **18**(9), 2437 (2017)
13. Shoukri, M.M., Elsiesy, H.A., Khafaga, Y., Bazarbashi, S., Al-Sebayel, M.: Predictive models for incidence and economic burden of liver cancer in Saudi Arabia. Epidemiology **5** (193), 1165–2161 (2015)
14. Alkhateeb, S.S., Alothman, A.S., Addar, A.M., Alqahtani, R.A., Mansi, T.M., Masuadi, E. M.: Kidney cancer in Saudi Arabia: a 25-year analysis of epidemiology and risk factors in a tertiary center. Saudi Med. J. **39**(5), 495 (2018)
15. Bawazir, A., Al-Zamel, N., Amen, A., Akiel, M.A., Alhawiti, N.M., Alshehri, A.: The burden of leukemia in the Kingdom of Saudi Arabia: 15 years period (1999–2013). BMC Cancer **19**(1), 703 (2019)
16. Bray, F., Møller, B.: Predicting the future burden of cancer. Nat. Rev. Cancer **6**(1), 63–74 (2006)
17. Joo, T.W., Kim, S.B.: Time series forecasting based on wavelet filtering. Expert Syst. Appl. **42**(8), 3868–3874 (2015)

18. Conlon, T., Crane, M., Ruskin, H.J.: Wavelet multiscale analysis for hedge funds: scaling and strategies. Phys. A: Stat. Mech. Appl. **387**(21), 5197–5204 (2008)
19. Rioul, O., Vetterli, M.: Wavelets and signal processing. IEEE Signal Process. Mag. **8**, 14–38 (1991)
20. Lotric, U., Dobnikar, A.: Predicting time series using neural networks with wavelet-based denoising layers. Neural Comput. Appl. **14**(1), 11–17 (2005)
21. Li, Z., Tam, V.: Combining the real-time wavelet denoising and long-short-term-memory neural network for predicting stock indexes. In: 2017 IEEE Symposium Series on Computational Intelligence (SSCI), pp. 1–8. IEEE, Honolulu (2017)
22. Liang, X., Ge, Z., Sun, L., He, M., Chen, H.: LSTM with wavelet transform based data preprocessing for stock price prediction. Math. Probl. Eng. (2019)
23. Hochreiter, S., Schmidhuber, J.: Long short-term memory. Neural Comput. **9**(8), 1735–1780 (1997)
24. Cortez, B., Carrera, B., Kim, Y.J., Jung, J.Y.: An architecture for emergency event prediction using LSTM recurrent neural networks. Expert Syst. Appl. **97**, 315–324 (2018)
25. Chae, S., Kwon, S., Lee, D.: Predicting infectious disease using deep learning and big data. Int. J. Environ. Res. Public Health **15**(8), 1596 (2018)
26. Yunpeng, L., Di, H., Junpeng, B., Yong, Q.: Multi-step ahead time series forecasting for different data patterns based on LSTM recurrent neural network. In: 2017 14th Web Information Systems and Applications Conference (WISA), pp. 305–310. IEEE, Liuzhou (2017)
27. Shanmuganathan, S., Samarasinghe, S.: Artificial neural network modelling: an introduction. In: Shanmuganathan, S., Samarasinghe, S. (eds.) Artificial Neural network modelling, vol. 628, pp. 1–14. Springer, Cham (2016). https://doi.org/10.1007/978-3-319-28495-8_1
28. Williams, R.J., Zipser, D.: A learning algorithm for continually running fully recurrent neural networks. Neural Comput. **1**(2), 270–280 (1989)
29. Percival, D.B., Walden, A.T.: Wavelet Methods for Time Series Analysis, vol. 4. Cambridge University Press, New York (2006)
30. Stolojescu, C., Railean, I., Moga, I., Lenca, P., Isar, A.: A wavelet-based prediction method for time series. In: Proceedings of Stochastic Modeling Techniques and Data Analysis (SMTDA2010) International Conference, Chania, Greece, pp. 767–774 (2010)
31. Sripathi, D.: Efficient implementations of discrete wavelet transforms using FPGAs. Florida State University, New York (2003)
32. Ergen, B.: Signal and Image Denoising Using Wavelet Transform. INTECH Open Access Publisher, Rijeka (2012)
33. Donoho, D.L., Johnstone, I.M.: Adapting to unknown smoothness via wavelet shrinkage. J. Am. Stat. Assoc. **90**(432), 1200–1224 (1995)
34. Laurent, C., Pereyra, G., Brakel, P., Zhang, Y., Bengio, Y.: Batch normalized recurrent neural networks. In: 2016 IEEE International Conference on Acoustics, Speech and Signal Processing (ICASSP), pp. 2657–2661. IEEE, Shanghai (2016)
35. Saudi Cancer Registry. https://chs.gov.sa/AR/NCC/Pages/default.aspx
36. Hyndman, R.J., Athanasopoulos, G.: Forecasting: Principles and Practice. OTexts (2018)

Enhanced Support Vector Machine Applied to Land-Use Classification

Hela ElMannai[1,2(✉)], Monia Hamdi[1], and Abeer AlGarni[1]

[1] College of Computer and Information Sciences, Princess Nourah Bint Abdulrahman University, Riyadh, Kingdom of Saudi Arabia
monia.hamdi@isimg.rnu.tn, adalqarni@pnu.edu.sa
[2] Laboratoire de Tledetectionet Remote Sensing LTSIRS, ENIT, Tunis, Tunisia

Abstract. It is very important to track the current status of land. Many applications like geology and ecology are based on collecting information from sensors about land surfaces. These sensors are either airborne or on satellite. Thus, image processing has prominent importance for the land classification and analysis. Taking advantages from feature extraction methods and classification algorithm may improve the results and the leaded analysis. In this work, we performed feature extraction methods related to the color and multiresolution transform. After that, we propose an improved Support Vector Machine (SVM) model based on a modified kernel. The new model introduces weights on features that determined from the training data. The new model will be compared to the usual SVM model. The classification results show that the reached accuracy is better with the enhanced SVM classifier than the basic SVM. The number of false negative is notably reduced.

Keywords: Remote sensing · Support Vector Machine · Classification · Enhanced SVM

1 Introduction

Remote sensing sciences aim to detect and monitor the land characteristics by measuring reflected and emitted radiation. Related applications help researchers to identify the imaged land cover type, physical composition and temporal variation. Classification systems using these data depend on the data type, the application outcomes and the user's need. Suitable classification system will include well-chosen classification algorithm. Also, good image resolution and training samples are determinant to reach accurate classification. Currently, machine learning is gaining ground in the remote sensing researches. Problem of non-linearity of the classification is solved using kernel-based approaches such us SVM. In fact, presenting the data in higher dimension provides a linear problem [1]. Thus, the data presentation is determinant for the classification problem resolution.

This paper starts in Sect. 2 by presenting the related works of image classification such as feature extraction and classification algorithms. In Sect. 3, we detail the proposed approach based on an enhanced SVM model. In Sect. 4, we explore the

© Springer Nature Switzerland AG 2019
A. Alfaries et al. (Eds.): ICC 2019, CCIS 1097, pp. 236–244, 2019.
https://doi.org/10.1007/978-3-030-36365-9_20

experimentations results on a land use data base. Section 5 concludes and presents eventual feature works.

2 Image Classification Frameworks

Remote sensing applications are based on recognizing the land ground truth and land cover composition. Related applications are various such as environment studies, resources planning, urban area plan, geological studies, fire detection and inundation detection.

For a complex study area that contains heterogenous land categories, the feature selection and extraction is determinant to achieve optimum classification performance. Many feature extraction techniques have been applied over the years for classification workflows development. Features extraction methods can be classified by levels. Low level operators includs edge operators. High level features are dealing with shape matching and are based on image transform (Fourier, Hough, snakes, etc.) [2]. Information fusion like image and feature fusion have proven their efficiency to improve the classification accuracy [3]. In the next paragraphs, we will present the feature extraction and classification approaches.

2.1 Feature Extraction and Selection

The use of not suitable data presentation in a classifier framework may decrease classification accuracy. In fact, feature selection is a critical step for a trustworthy classification framework. For remote sending classification, the features include the spectral signature, the image transform, the texture and the fusion of multitemporal or multisensory images. Some approaches associate different characteristics presentation. Using data transform allows a new presentation for data in frequency domain for example. As a result, the obtained feature space determines specific characteristics of land surfaces like orientations, scale, multiresolution and textural information's. Mainly used transformations are based on Principal component analysis [4], Gaussian mixture [5] and Wavelet transform [6].

Textural features are extracted by computing different statistics in the spatial domain as presented in [7, 8] or by the gray level co-occurrence matrices [9]. Gabor filters have been also widely used for textural characterization [10].

2.2 Classification Methods

Based on the type of the data to process and the considered knowledges, we can group the classification approaches as: pixel based, subpixel based, field based, contextual based, knowledge based, and a combination of multiple classifiers. These approaches can be supervised or unsupervised, parametric or non-parametric and fuzzy or hard.

Frequently used approaches for remote sensing data classification are maximum likelihood classifier, neural network [11, 12] and machine learning approaches [13–15]. However, maximum likelihood method has the drawbacks to have the assumption of data normally distributed. Artificial networks have the drawbacks of over fitting and local minima. Machine learning has the advantage to recognize complex patterns and to determine a decision function based on training data. In this context, SVM is a supervised method based on kernel transformation. Data is transformed into high dimension space to find a linear separability by maximum margin [16].

In [17] the authors focus on the SVM parameter selection for optimal classification results. In fact, most SVM applications don't investigate the SVM model. The authors conclude that the obtained results based on SVM model are better when using the optimal parameters. For crop land use classification, the authors in [18] use a cross-validation process in a range of log2 for C and γ parameters. After that a detailed research is processed more precisely in the range of C and γ values. In [19], the polynomial and Radial Basis kernel (RBF) functions were applied to remote send data with the correspondent optimal parameters. The experimentations show when the SVM kernel is the RBF kernel, the classification results outperforms the maximum likelihood approach.

3   Methodology Presentation

Remote sensing data have many characteristics. These information's provide the image characterization related to the spatial presentation, spectral presentation, radiometric information. Tacking advantages of these characteristics is an effective way to improve classification accuracy. We propose a classification system based on an enhanced radial based kernel. We identify thee mains stages which are:

- Feature extraction
- Kernel parameters and the weights determination
- Classification results.

3.1   Feature Extraction

To improve the recognition performance, we performs three feature extraction methods related to the color, the texture and the multiresolution properties.

Color Feature Extraction. In content-based retrieval systems, the color has great importance to represent the information related to the pixels. In our project, the color features are determined from color moments. The three first moments which are the mean, the variance and the skewness have been proved to present efficiently the color distribution. For a three-dimension color space like RGB, the i-th color moment is defined bellow in Eqs. 1, 2 and 3 for respectively the first, the second and the third moment. p_{ij} is the value of the j-th pixel in the image in the i-th color component.

$$m_i^1 = \frac{1}{M} \sum_{j=1}^{M} p_{ij} \tag{1}$$

$$m_i^2 = \sqrt{\frac{1}{M} \sum_{j=1}^{M} \left(p_{ij} - m_i^1\right)^2} \tag{2}$$

$$m_i^3 = \sqrt[3]{\frac{1}{M}\sum_{j=1}^{M}\left(p_{ij} - m_i^1\right)^3} \qquad (3)$$

Texture Feature Extraction. Texture identification is an important characterization when the image contains texture propriety. Texture feature provides a strong tool to identify the pattern present in texture. Gaussian filters offer different scale frequencies and directions. In a Fourier domain, the Gabor filters are given by a Gaussian centered about the central frequency (U, V) is given by Eq. 4 [10]. θ presents the orientation in the spatial domain. θ is defined in Eq. 5.

$$H(u, v) = e^{-2\pi^2\sigma^2(u-U) + (v-V)^2} \qquad (4)$$

$$\theta = \tan^{-1}\left(\frac{V}{U}\right) \qquad (5)$$

Image Transform Feature Extraction. Multiresolution analysis was developed to process non-stationary signals of finite energy [6, 20]. Remote sensed images are within this constraint. Wavelet transform decomposes the image into structures at different scales [21]. The values of wavelet coefficients in a given position and a given scale measures the intensity of the local variations at this position and provide therefore a characterization of the location.

3.2 Calculation of the Weights

The idea behind finding weights for the feature vector components is to find a linear transform of the feature space that enhance the classification accuracy [22]. Inherently the classification performance depends on the feature space. Let consider a general linear feature fusion scheme given by Eq. 6 where α_i denotes the weight assigned to the feature v_i.

$$V = \sum_{k=1}^{N} \alpha_i \, v_i \qquad (6)$$

The weights are presented by the vector $W = \{w_k\}_{k\in[1,N_f]}$ where w_k is the weight associated to the feature k. The weight are constrained by $\sum_{K=1}^{k=N_f} w_k = 1$. The best weights are obtained by cross validation performed to the training data.

3.3 Classification Using Enhanced SVM Kernel

To develop more reliable classification methods, the SVM was introduced in [20] based on statistical learning theories. The classification process is done by finding an optimal hyperplane that lies on the support vectors. The chosen separator is selected with maximum margin which is the distance to the support vectors [21]. The classification can be linear or nonlinear. A kernel function denoted k is used for nonlinear data to project the original training data into a higher dimensional space where the classification is linear [22, 23]. The support vectors are a subset of the training data. The discriminant function is given by $f(x)$. For a set of L training samples (x_i, y_i) where $y_i = f(x_i)$, the decision function is given by $f(x) = sgn(w.x - b)$ where $w.x - b = 0$ is a separating hyperplane.

$(w.x - b) = 0$ presents a hyperplane. The discriminant function can be expressed as $f(x) = sgn\left(\sum_{i=1}^{i=L} \varepsilon_i y_i (x.x_i - b)\right)$. y_i is the class label. In a two-class problem, y_i is 1 or -1. x_i is a support vector, $0 \leq \varepsilon_i \leq C$. C is a positive constant. The decision function is given in Eq. 7.

$$f(x) = sgn\left(\sum_{i=1}^{i=N} y_i \varepsilon_i K(x, x_i) + b\right) \tag{7}$$

Considering relative contribution for each feature could enhance the classification accuracy. We propose to determine the importance for each feature by adding the vector of weights W to the kernel model. The enhanced decision function is provided by adding the weights to the decision function as given in Eq. 8. Therefore, the features will not be treated equally. The selected best weights are obtained from the learning data set.

$$f(x) = sgn\left(\sum_{i=1}^{i=N} y_i \varepsilon_i K(Wx, Wx_i) + b\right) \tag{8}$$

3.4 Classification Evaluation Based on Measurements

Evaluation of classification results is an important process in the classification framework. Different approaches may be based on the qualitative evaluation or the quantitative evaluation. The first one is based on expert while the second one is based on some values computed by data sampling. Mostly used metrics are accuracy, sensitivity, specificity and F-score. True positive and true negatives are the observations that are correctly predicted by the classification process. True Positives (TP) are the correctly predicted positive. True Negatives (TN) are the correctly predicted negative values by the classifier. In a one-class problem, TP are $+1$ class and the value of predicted class is also $+1$. TN are samples with the value of class label is -1 and the value of predicted class is also -1 [24]. When real class instances contradict with the predicted class, we introduce False positives (FP) and false negatives (FN) concepts. When FP and FN are almost the same, the dataset is called symmetric. Accuracy is the ratio of correctly predicted data to the total data. High accuracy is an important measure only for a symmetric dataset. The ratio of correctly predicted positive data to the total predicted positive data represents the precision. The recall is the ratio of correctly predicted positive data to all the data in the class labelled as positive. To weight the average of precision and recall, we use the F1-score function. The F1-score uses the recall and precision and is particularly important especially for non-symmetric data.

4 Experimentation Results and Analysis

4.1 Dataset

UC Merced Land Use Dataset is used for research purposes. The dataset contains 256 × 256 images for 21 classes. The images were extracted manually from the USGS National Map Urban Area Imagery collection. The classes represent various urban areas in the USA. There are 100 images for each of classes. Figure 1 shows the classes samples.

The image data set is separated in two subs set. The first one represents the learning set. Learning data will be used to obtain optimal SVM parameters and to determine the optimal weights of features. Testing data will be used for the finally classification step assessment. The output of the feature extraction step is the training and test files containing extracted feature vectors. The syntax of the feature vector for each instance is:

    <label> <index1>:<value1> <index2>:<value2>...

    <label> is the class label. The feature number and value are given by the <index>: <value>. For testing data, the label is just used to determine the accuracy.

4.2 Feature Scaling

Scaling before applying SVM is very important to scale features to avoid attributes in greater numeric ranges dominating those in smaller numeric ranges. Other advantage of feature scaling is to avoid numerical difficulties during the calculation. For instance, large feature values might cause numerical problems for the polynomial kernel. We

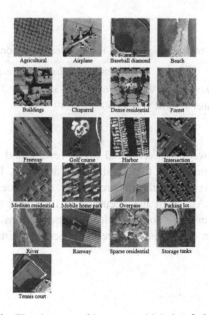

Fig. 1. The data set of images and labels of classes

perform a linear scaling to the range of $[-1, +1]$. The same scaling factor is applied to both the training and testing data.

4.3   Kernel Parameters and Feature Weights Determination

The RBF kernel is defined as $e^{-\gamma\|x-x_i\|^2}$ where γ is the kernel width. There are two parameters to be determined: the kernel width γ and the regularization parameter C. We perform a model selection by parameter search to identify suitable (C, γ) so that the classifier can accurately predict testing data. For that, we use the cross-validation process that could prevent overfitting problem. The process divides the training data into subsets of equal size. Each subset will be tested while the remaining subsets will be used for training. A grid of values with an exponential growing is applied for this purpose [24]. The determined accuracy is the percentage of data which are correctly classified during the process. The best RBF kernel parameters are $C = 8$ and $\gamma = 10^{-2}$.

The determined kernel model will be used to determine the feature weights by the given algorithm. To weights determination has the advantages of deleting unimportant features. After this step the number of features is narrowed down from 54 to 47. This is explained by the null weights corresponding to some features.

4.4   Classification Results Analysis

The classification evaluation is based on extracting the confusion matrix firstly. This one is computed from the test label vector and the predicted label vector. After that, the different classification measures are extracted. Table 1 summarizes the classification results for the usual RBF kernel and for the enhanced SVM model by using the obtained weights.

Table 1. Comparisons of the experimental results for conventional and enhanced SVM

	Accuracy	False negative rate
Conventional SVM	97.86	2.13
Enhanced SVM	98.50	1.49

The comparison between conventional SVM results and enhanced SVM results shows consistent improvements in the classification accuracy. The false negative rate is notably reduced. The new model has the ability to reduce the false negative by weighting the features. Although the accuracy is improved only by 0.63, the false negative reduction is interesting for classification applications. On the other hand, the feature number reduction could also reduce the processing time.

5   Conclusion

Image classification plays a very crucial role in many image processing applications. Machine learning have proven their efficiency for classification especially when data are mapped to the labels with a nonlinear mapping. We propose an enhanced classification model based on features heightening. The features will be considered by taking into account their relevance in the classification process. The results show the method contribution in improving the classification results specially to reduce false negative ad false positive rates. In addition, the method could be used as dimension reduction method and could reduce the processing time.

References

1. Kuo, B.C., Li, C.H., Yang, J.M.: Kernel nonparametric weighted feature extraction for hyperspectral image classification. IEEE Trans. Geosci. Remote Sens. **47**(4), 1139–1155 (2009)
2. Aguado, A.S., Nixon, M.: Feature Extraction and Image Processing for Computer Vision, 3rd edn. Elsivier, Amsterdam (2012)
3. Prabukumar, M.: Comparative study of feature extraction techniques for hyper spectral remote sensing image classification: a survey. In: International Conference on Intelligent Computing and Control Systems (2017)
4. Liebert, J., LaRoche, P., Dared, E., Craig, S.: Chlorophyll-a concentration retrieval in the optically complex waters of the st. Lawrence estuary and Gulf using principal component analysis. Remote Sens. **10**(2), 265 (2018)
5. Yin, S., Zhang, Y., Karim, S.: Large scale remote sensing image segmentation based on fuzzy region competition and gaussian mixture model. IEEE Access **6**, 26069–26080 (2018)
6. Shi, Y., et al.: Wavelet-based rust spectral feature set (WRSFs): a novel spectral feature set based on continuous wavelet transformation for tracking progressive host-pathogen interaction of yellow rust on wheat. Remote Sens. **10**(4), 525 (2018)
7. Gierull, C.H.: On the statistics of coherence estimators for textured clutter plus noise. IEEE Geosoc. Remote Sens. Lett. **14**(5), 679–683 (2017)
8. Deng, X., López-Martínez, C.: Higher order statistics for texture analysis and physical interpretation of polarimetric SAR data. IEEE Geosci. Remote Sens. Lett. **13**(7), 912–916 (2016)
9. Lan, Z., Liu, Y.: Study on multi-scale window determination for GLCM texture description in high-resolution remote sensing image geo-analysis supported by gis and domain knowledge. ISPRS Int. J. Geo-Inform. **7**(5), 175 (2018)
10. Olson, H., Czaja, W., Le Moigne, J.: Registration of textured remote sensing images using directional gabor frames. In: IGARSS 2017, pp. 2585–2588 (2017)
11. Fang, T., Hong, H., Zhou, T., Zhang, Y., Lihong, W., Liu, N.: Exploiting convolutional neural networks with deeply local description for remote. IEEE Access **6**, 11215–11228 (2018)
12. Ferda, O., Sergio, E., Hakan, Ç., Ilyes, L.: Sensing image classification. Recurrent neural networks for remote sensing image classification. IET Comput. Vis. **12**, 1040–1045 (2018)
13. Wen, Y.: Remote sensing image land type data mining based on QUEST decision tree. Cluster Comput. (2018). ISSN:1386-7857

14. Negri, R.G., da Silva, E.A., Casaca, W.: Inducing contextual classifications with kernel functions into support vector machines. IEEE Geosci. Remote Sens. Lett. **15**(6), 962–966 (2018)
15. Eeti, L.N., Buddhiraju, K.M.: Classification of hyperspectral remote sensing images by an ensemble of support vector machines under imbalanced data. In: IGARSS, pp. 2659–2661 (2018)
16. Moorthi, S.M., Misra, I., Kaur, R., Darji, N.P., Ramakrishnan, R.: Kernel based learning approach for satellite image classification using support vector machine. In: 7th International Conference on Agro-geoinformatics (Agro-geoinformatics) (2018)
17. Petrovic, M.S., Dragic, S., Kovačević, M., Bajat, B.: Urban land use changes using support vector machines. Trans. GIS **20**(5), 718–734 (2016)
18. Kang, J., Zhang, H., Yang, H., Zhang, L.: Support vector machine classification of crop lands using sentinel-2 imagery. In: 7th International Conference on Agro-geoinformatics (Agro-geoinformatics) (2018)
19. Kavzoglu, T., Colkesen, I.: A kernel functions analysis for support vector machines for land cover classification. Int. J. Appl. Earth Observ. Geoinform. **11**, 352–359 (2009)
20. Mpysn, Y.: Ondelettes et opérateurs I: Ondelettes. Hermann, paris, p. 215 (1990)
21. Mallat, S.G.: A theory for multiresolution signal decomposition: the wavelet representation. IEEE Trans. Pattern Anal. Màch. Intell. **2**, 674–693 (1989)
22. Elmannai, H., Loghmari, M.A., Naceur, M.S.: Nonlinear separation source and parameterized feature fusion for satelite image patch exemplars. In: IGARSS (2015)
23. Vapnik, V.N.: The Nature of Statistical Learning Theory. Springer, Heidelberg (1995)
24. Hsu, C.W., Chang, C.C., Lin, C.J.: A practical guide to support vector classification (2003)

Predicting Students' Academic Performance and Main Behavioral Features Using Data Mining Techniques

Suad Almutairi[1]([⊠]), Hadil Shaiba[1], and Marija Bezbradica[2]

[1] Princess Nourah Bint Abdulrahman University, Riyadh, Saudi Arabia
{sfalmutairi,hashaiba}@pnu.edu.sa
[2] Dublin City University, Dublin, Ireland
marija.bezbradica@dcu.ie

Abstract. Creating learning environments, where students, parents, and teachers are linked to a learning process, helps study their overall impact on the students' performance. Data mining can analyze these inter-relationships and thus enable the prediction of academic performance to improve the student's academic level. The main factors that affect the student's performance were selected using feature selection methods. An analysis of the crucial features was investigated to better understand the data. One of the main outcomes found is the impact of the behavioral features on the students' academic performance. Moreover, gender and relation demographical features are another important features found. It was evedent that there is an academic disparity between genders, as females constitute the most outstanding students. Furthermore, mothers have a clear role in student academic excellence. Six machine learning methods were used and tested to predict the studnet's performance, namely random forest, logistic regression, XGBoost, MLP, and ensemble learning using bagging and voting. Of all the methods, the random forest got the highest accuracy with 10-best selected features that reached 77%. Overfitting was addressed successfully by tuning the hyper-parameters. The results show that data mining can accurately predict the students' performance level, as well as highlight the most influential features.

Keywords: Educational data mining · Machine learning · Deep learning · Learning Analytics

1 Introduction

Building learning environments, where students have an active interaction in their learning, has become a priority for educational institutions. Learning Analytics (LA) is an emerging area for the collection, analysis, and presentation of learners' data for the purpose of studying the influencing factors on the learning process with the aim of understanding and developing the learning environment [1]. LA provides all parties (parents, teachers, and students) with the appropriate and quick feedback about the educational process. On the other hand, behavior analytics helps us understand the

© Springer Nature Switzerland AG 2019
A. Alfaries et al. (Eds.): ICC 2019, CCIS 1097, pp. 245–259, 2019.
https://doi.org/10.1007/978-3-030-36365-9_21

behavior of students and how they interact during the learning period with contributing influences.

Predicting the performance of students has attracted the attention of several authors due to its importance in helping teachers identify and support their students according to the level of difficulty [2]. Considerable works have been done in recent years to analyze the behavior of students and extract the significant patterns that can be used to predict the students' performance.

This study intends to use data mining methods to: (i) find the strongest features that can help in the prediction of students' performance, (ii) analyze the most important behavior and demographical features to have a better understanding of the features that affect the students' performance level, (iii) predict the students' performance by using data mining techniques and show how feature selection, oversampling, ensemble learning, and parameter tuning can enhance the predictive power of the models and resolve overfitting.

A summary of the previous work has been presented in the literature review section. Explanation of the data used and the data mining methods applied in this resarch have been discussed in the data and methodology sections. In the results section, we show the best selected features, provide a detailed analysis of the main selected features, and evaluate and discuss the results of our prediction models. We finally conclude our research in the conclusion section.

2 Literature Review

2.1 The Use of E-Learning in Education

Online-based learning environments, such as learning management systems (LMSs), allow teachers to study and track students' performance by recording and keeping student information online [2]. E-Learning environments have been used to monitor and record all educational processes and actions done by students, thus it could provide useful information on the progress that each student achieves as mentioned in [3]. In order to achieve the best level of electronic learning, it is necessary to evaluate the processes of learning and teaching continuously by observing all aspects, from the level of interaction between the parties involved in the quality of teaching through the reactions of students and their initiative. In addition to the use of multiple sources, the effect of management, and other aspects, on the development of cognitive skills, should be considered [4].

In recent years, there has been a significant growth of using methods to facilitate the analysis of existing processes related to learners and e-learning systems. In order to provide a more efficient learning environment, data mining techniques have been used in this field, for processing the data and extracting information patterns that can be useful indicators [3].

2.2   Educational Data Mining

Data mining in the educational analysis is described as the process of automatic extraction of a meaningful chain from a large dataset. It is used not only to train the model on the learning process but also to evaluate and develop e-learning systems [3].

The efficiency of machine learning methods has been analyzed in [2] by predicting the difficulty the students will face in the next session to support the students and help them according to the level of difficulty. Five of the well-known machine learning algorithms have been used for the prediction process, namely artificial neural network (ANN), logistic regression (LR), naïve Bayes (NB), support vector machine (SVM), and decision tree (DT). The methods have been selected based on their suitability for the dataset and insensitivity towards overfitting [2]. For evaluation, authors in e.g. [2] used multiple techniques such as root-mean-square error (RMSE) and Cohen's kappa coefficient. Feature selection techniques focus on reducing the dimensionality and avoid unrelated data to the research interest [2]. Alpha-investing feature selection for ranking was used by [2] to minimize the input features to be used in the student prediction model. Their results showed that SVMs and ANNs are the most suitable models to predict student's performance [2].

Two datasets were analyzed in [5] to predict students failing in the early stages, exactly after the first exam in introductory programming courses available from a Brazilian Public University. A noticeable result was shown by using the SVM algorithm and F-measure for evaluation. They claimed that female students had less in-class participation than male students. In addition to that, after the first exam application, the F-measure value reached approximately 0.92 and 0.83 with distance and on-campus datasets, respectively.

Other research [6] focused on a new side of educational analytics called behavioral features. The authors chose ANN, DT, NB and ensemble models (bagging, boosting, and random forest) to build a performance predictive model. The information gain algorithm has been used to build the students' performance model. The results were presented with and without behavioral characteristics using 10-fold cross-validation. The result showed how behavioral characteristics had a strong effect on the students' academic achievement. In addition, the ANN technique overcomes other methods, as its accuracy was around 79.1%. The result and quality of the classifiers were measured by four common measures; Accuracy, Precision, Recall, and F-Measure [6]. The lack in this paper is that it did not predict early enough student performance due to the lack of information about midterm exams and assignments, the prediction was after the finals.

Using data mining to predict the student's dropouts was explored with a dataset of 165, 715 high school students from different schools [7]. The authors [7] selected significant features that were presented by using the random forests model with out of bag (OOB) estimate. The unauthorized absence was the most significant variable in predicting students' dropouts, followed by unauthorized lateness. The random forests model predicts students' dropouts with a high accuracy of 95% using 10 folds cross-validation. AUC score got 97% which represents an outstanding performance. The work in this article was excellent, but they noted some shortcomings with the calculation of the model features, that used inaccuracy weights [7].

The researches which were discussed in this section varied by using data mining techniques to predict at-risk students. Findings cannot be generalized due to their limited domain, but their work is worthy of praise. The following section concentrates on one main stage in data analysis which is feature selection and its effect on the predicted results and data visualization and its importance in better understanding the data.

3 Dataset

A LMS called Kalboard 360 has been used to collect educational dataset. This system gives users (students, teachers and parents) synchronous access to reach the educational resources from all devices by using an internet connection [6]. The original source of the dataset is found in [6]. The dataset is available on Kaggle.com under the name of BStudents' Academic Performance Dataset. In total 480 students with 16 features are analyzed in this project which can be divided into four basic categories. Details of these features and their number of instances have been presented in Table 1.

Table 1. Features' description of the dataset used in this study adapted from [7].

Features category	Feature	Description	Number of instances
Demographical features	Gender	Male/Female	2
	Nationality	Kuwait/Lebanon/Saudi Arabia etc.	14
	Place of birth	Kuwait/Lebanon/Saudi Arabia etc.	14
	Relation	Parent responsible for student (Mother/father)	2
Academic background features	Educational Stages	Lower level/Middle School/High School	3
	Grade Levels	G-01/G-02/.......G-12	10
	Section ID	Classroom student belongs to (A/B/C)	3
	Topic	Course topic (English/Spanish/French/IT etc.	13
	Student Absence Days	above-7/under-7	2
	Semester	First/Second	2
Behavioral features	Raised hand	How many times the student raises his/her hand in classroom (numeric: 0–100)	101
	Visited resources	How many times the student visits a course content (numeric: 0–100)	101
	Viewing announcements	How many times the student checks the new announcements (numeric: 0–100)	101
	Discussion groups	How many times the student participate in discussion groups (numeric: 0–100)	101
Parents participation on learning process	Parent answering survey	Yes/No	2
	Parent school satisfaction	Yes/No	2

The class feature contains the performance level which is the total mark of the student in a subject decided in each record. This performance level is categorized into three levels (High, Medium, and Low). Marks below 70 are belonging to the low level, marks between 70 and 89 are belonging to the medium, and marks higher than 89 considered as a high level [6].

4 Methodology

The process of feature selection is considered as a major step in the classification process. This is due to two great benefits: the first is to reduce the complexity of the computation [16, 17], and the second is to enhance the classifier's generalization to correctly classify unseen instances [17]. In this research, the wrapper method and the filter-based method have been used for feature selection. A subset of features is selected and evaluated based on the predictor's accuracy [16] in a wrapper method which guarantees accurate results [17]. Recursive Feature Elimination (RFE) have been used as a wrapper method.

The filter method requires a lower computational effort [17]. Information Gain algorithm (IG) and K-best feature selection have been used. IG ranks the features separately in decreasing order based on how relevant it is to the class label (student academic performance level). K-best (SelectKBest) is a univariate method that selects features based on the K highest scores. It calculates the Analysis of Variance (ANOVA) F-value between each feature and the class which is the target vector [18].

Four popular classification algorithms are used in this research in addition to ensemble models. The discription of each method is explained in the following:

- **Random forest (RF)** algorithm has its immunity against exaggeration [7]. It is also considered as an effective tool for prediction [8]. Moreover, it is known for its performance and ability to dealing with corrupted data and overfitting [9].
- **Extreme gradient boosting (XGBoost)** is a scalable implementation of gradient boosting framework which works efficiently [10]. Its scalability refers to many algorithmic optimizations, and it is trained in an additive manner [11].
- **Logistic regression** reduces the impact of confounding factors by analyzing multiple explanatory variables at the same time [12]. In addition to that, the allowance of continuous variables has a useful smoothing impact on the model or on the estimates [13].
- **Multilayer perceptron artificial neural network (MLP)** is one type of neural network with a number of neuron layers such that every layer is connected to the following layer. In this way, it can classify data that is not separated linearly [14]. This algorithm is known for reducing the estimation error by calculating and updating the weights in the network in order to acquire the great configuration of the neural network [15].
- **Ensemble models** are the new trend in machine learning, which are based on training multiple classifiers, therefore the choice of the best result. **Bagging** uses one model over various and random sampling (with replacement) of the dataset. Bagging using a decision tree has been applied in this research. **Voting** combines

multiple classifiers and selects the best performance by voting. Soft voting was chosen in this research by Ensemble Vote Classifier function with mixing logistic regression and XGBoost.

The best practices to avoid overfitting were introduced in this paper. Along with feature selection, oversampling, ensemble learning, and parameter tuning were used. This could be as road map to researchers who would like to resolve the problem of their predictive models facing overfitting.

5   Results and Discussion

The result and performance of the model depend on the techniques used in the preprocessing. The original data is converted into a form that is suitable for use with data mining such as data cleaning and data conversion [2]. The whole 480 records in the dataset are clean from any missing values, and outliers. The class feature has three values, High, Medium, and low levels which contain 141, 211, and 127 cases, respectively. This slight difference in the number of cases is not considered as imbalance dataset [19]. Normalization is applied to prevents misleading variance between features' values. After these steps, the dataset is ready to be used with classification methods.

To analyze the features and their relationships, the dataset has been explored using data visualization. Then, evaluation using train/test/split and cross-validation with the feature selection are studied next.

5.1   Evaluation Measures

Four different measures for evaluating the predictive models were used, which are precision, recall, accuracy, and F-measure. Equations of these measures are defined in the following [6]:

$$\text{Precision} = \frac{tp}{tp + fp} \tag{1}$$

$$\text{Recall} = \frac{tp}{tp + fn} \tag{2}$$

$$\text{Accuracy} = \frac{tp + tn}{tp + tn + fp + fn} \tag{3}$$

$$F - \text{measure} = 2 \cdot \frac{\text{precision} \cdot \text{recall}}{\text{precision} + \text{recall}} \tag{4}$$

Those four measures are calculated using the confusion matrix shown in Table 2.

Table 2. Confusion matrix [7].

		Predicted	
		Positive	Negative
Actual	Positive	True Positive (TP)	False Negative (FN)
	Negative	False Positive (FP)	True Negative (TN)

5.2 Feature Analysis

Three feature selection methods have been used in this research. Information gain ranking and 10-best feature selection chose the same features except that information gain selected nationality and place of birth with the most high-ranking features while the 10-best method selected gender and semester as shown in Table 3. On the other hand, RFE has chosen different collection with each classifier and focused on academic background features. Figure 1 shows that students who did more behavioral features have acquired the highest grades. Since this paper attempts to discover which behavioral features have the greatest impact on the class, thus, more focus is presented about these features and their relation to the other features that got higher ranks, which are: **(1)** The parent responsible, **(2)** Parents' involvement, **(3)** Students' absence days and **(4)** The gender of the student.

1. **The parent responsible:** Fig. 2 shows that students were more active when their mother was responsible for them. Fathers make up two-thirds of the dataset, yet the parent responsible for the most excellent students were their mothers. Figure 3 shows that mothers were responsible for the most high-level students.
2. **Parents' involvement:** After addressing the effect of parents' involvement on the behavioral features we found a strong relationship between these features. Most of the students who were active during the learning period; their parents answered the survey and were satisfied with the school.

Table 3. Top 10 features using k-best feature selection (were k = 10) and information gain ranking methods.

Best 10 features using k-best method	Best 10 features using information gain ranking
Visited resources	Visited resources
Student' absence days	Student' absence days
Raised hands	Raised hands
Announcements view	Announcements view
Parent' answering survey	Parent' answering Survey
Gender	Nationality
Semester	Place of birth
Relation	Relation
Discussion	Discussion
Parent' school satisfaction	Parent' school satisfaction

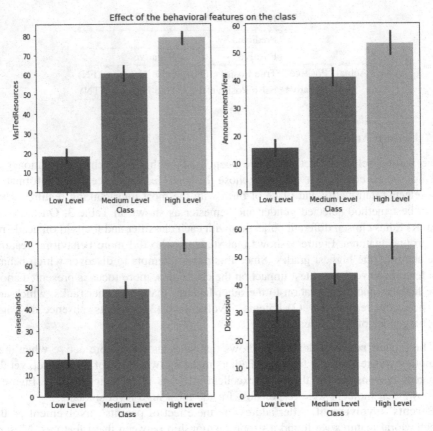

Fig. 1. Comparison between the four behavioral features and the students' academic performance (the class feature).

3. **Student' absence days:** There is clear evidence that the absence of a student negatively affects participation, visiting resources, viewing announcements, and raising hands during class.

4. **The gender of the student:** Most of the students who got the highest grades are females with 52%, compared with male students which are 47%. This means that 42% of the whole female students got high-performance level, while just 21% of the whole male students are excellent. The discussion did not show a significant influence on female students as presented in Fig. 4.

Four of the behavioral features (visited resources, raised hands, discussion and announcements view) were ranked by information gain method as the top features which influenced the students' performance. Showing those behavioral features visually have made a clear vision of the influence of these features on the student's academic success.

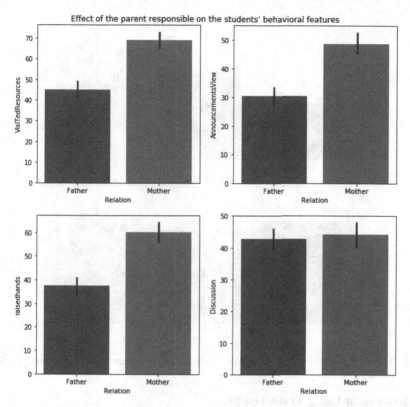

Fig. 2. Effect of the parent responsible of the student on the four behavioral features.

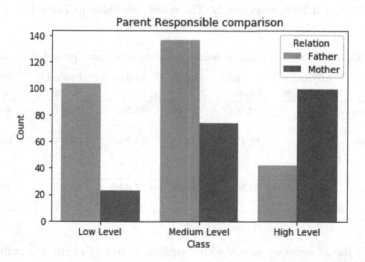

Fig. 3. Influence of the parent responsible of the student on the students' academic performance (the class feature).

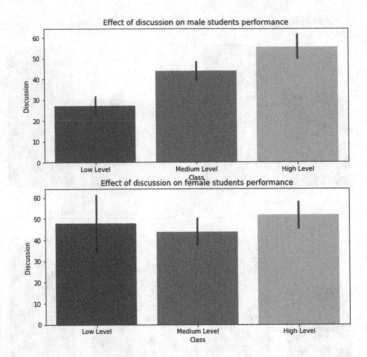

Fig. 4. Effect of discussion feature on the academic performance of both students' genders.

5.3 Evaluation Using Train/Test/Split

For evaluation, the dataset was first split to train, test, and validation such that each part has 60%, 20%, and 20%, respectively. The results are listed in Table 4.

Table 4. Train/test/split evaluation results including all features presented in Table 1.

Accuracy score	Logistic regression	Random forest	MLP	XGBoost	Ensemble voting	Ensemble bagging
Accuracy on training set	78.1%	100%	50.6%	96.5%	78.4%	80.9%
Accuracy on validation set	68.7%	72.9%	54.1%	69.7%	68.7%	64.5%
Accuracy on test set	65.6%	70.8%	56.2%	77.08%	66.6%	70.8%

Table 4 shows accuracy scores with a significant sign of overfitting problem with all classifiers and a slight underfitting with MLP. Overfitting means that the predictive model gives satisfactory results, but when applied with new data, it gave significantly lower results. In other words, the model will not be able to generalize, because it fits much noise while training [7]. Multiple techniques were used to overcome overfitting issues such as: **(1)** Examining the collinearity between features, **(2)** Oversampling to gain more data, **(3)** Fine-tuning of hyperparameters and **(4)** Feature selection. After applying each technique, classification algorithms were used to examine their effect on solving the overfitting problems.

1. **Examining the Collinearity Between Features:** To address the collinearity, two methods have been used which are the heat map and Reduce VIF (variance inflation factor) function. Heat Map showed that there is no significant correlation higher than 0.7 between the features except the correlation between the nationality and the place of birth which shows 0.9 as expected. The VIF measures the collinearity between features in regression analysis [20]. After applying this method, four features have been chosen, one of them was PlaceofBirth feature which we deleted. The remaining three were behavioral features that we combined into one feature. Addressing the collinearity showed a slight improvement with the overfitting problem, but it was not solved completely.

2. **Oversampling with SMOTE:** To oversample the minority class, SMOTE-NC (Synthetic Minority Oversampling Technique Nominal Continuous) algorithm is used with the training part of the original dataset [5]. This technique takes each sample of the minority class and creates synthetic examples based on nearest neighbors [19]. After doing oversampling, classification methods are applied, random forests got 72.9% but the overfitting was not solved with all classifiers.

3. **Hyper-Parameter Tuning:** Each classifier has its hyper-parameters that are used to control the learning process. Choosing a specific set of values for those hyper-parameters will change the performance of the model [7, 21]. The grid search algorithm is used to accelerate the selection of values. Some hyper-parameters proved their effect on solving overfitting such as the maximum depth of the trees, the higher value means the deeper tree, and this will lead to capturing more knowledge about the data. Moreover, the minimum number of samples that need to split an internal node. As increasing its value, each tree will be more constrained because of the growing number of samples that each node needs to consider. In logistic regression, the C parameter (inverse of regularization strength) controls the regularization by adding information to solve problems such as overfitting and increase the accuracy. As the value becomes smaller, the stronger the regularization is. Table 5 shows the hyperparameters that prove to solve the overfitting problem.

Table 5. Hyper-parameter tuning to solve overfitting problem.

Classifier	Random forest	Decision tree	Logistic regression	XGBoost
Parameter	max_depth = 6 min_samples_split = .2	max_depth = 2 min_samples_split = .02	C = .09	max_depth = 2

Table 6 shows the result after tuning the hyper-parameter with information gain as a filter-based feature selection. The score of training for logistic regression improves to

Table 6. The result of train/test/split evaluation with the top 10 features using filter-based information gain ranking and after hyper-parameter tuning.

Accuracy score	Logistic regression	Random forest	MLP	XGBoost	Ensemble voting	Ensemble bagging
Accuracy on training set	80.5%	82.2%	77.7%	79.1%	80.5%	74.6%
Accuracy on validation set	73.9%	72.9%	77.08%	68.7%	72.9%	67.7%
Accuracy on test set	71.8%	75%	68.7%	68.7%	71.8%	67.7%

reach 80.5%. Moreover, the random forest training score decreases to reach 82.2% to solve the overfitting problem. While the test score for ensemble voting increases to 71.8%.

In Table 7 the result of 10-best feature selection which shows that overfitting problem has been solved except that there is a little overfitting with XGBoost. Comparing the result of both feature selection techniques, the k-best shows the best result with random forest which got 77.08%.

Table 7. The result of train/test/split evaluation with filter-based 10-best feature selection method and after hyper-parameter tuning.

Accuracy score	Logistic regression	Random forest	MLP	XGBoost	Ensemble voting	Ensemble bagging
Accuracy on training set	77.08%	82.2%	74.3%	80.2%	77.7%	74.6%
Accuracy on validation set	72.9%	72.9%	68.7%	70.8%	72.9%	64.5%
Accuracy on test set	67.7%	77.08%	68.7%	68.7%	67.7%	68.7%

There is a decrease in the score of training, but this to solve the problem of overfitting, which is more important for the generalization of the models. Random forest shows the highest testing score with train test evaluation using both feature selection methods.

5.4   Evaluation Using Cross Validation

The k-fold cross validation is considered as the most popular technique to avoid overfitting [7]. The results of using 10-fold cross-validation with other techniques are

Table 8. 10-Fold cross validation results scores with all feature selection methods.

Accuracy	Logistic regression	Random forest	MLP	XGBoost	Voting	Bagging
With all features (original dataset)	70%	72.08%	68%	70.8%	71.2%	70.8%
With combining features and removing correlation	70.4%	71.6%	68%	70.6%	70%	70%
With information gain (the best 10 ranks)	74.1%	75%	75%	71.6%	72.5%	68.9%
With 10-best feature selection	73.5%	75.2%	74%	71.8%	72.7%	70.4%
With RFE	72.9%	74.1%	Not used	72.08%	Not used	Not used

shown in Table 8. MLP, ensemble voting, and ensemble bagging algorithms cannot work with RFE, because they do not have any metric for feature importance.

Most classifiers show their best performance with 10-best feature selection. Applying the filter method with information gain for feature selection shows great accuracies for random forest and MLP as they reach 75%. On the other hand, XGBoost got its best score with RFE feature selection. Comparison with other evaluation measures using cross-validation based on 10-best selected features is listed in Table 9.

Table 9. Evaluation scores of 10-fold cross validation based on 10-best selected features.

Scores	Logistic regression	Random forest	MLP	XGBoost	Ensemble voting	Ensemble bagging
Accuracy	73.5%	75.2%	74%	71.8%	72.7%	70.4%
F1	73.2%	71.4%	73.1%	70.9%	73.5%	67.5%
Precision	74.7%	74.3%	75.3%	73.5%	74.91%	72.5%
Recall	73.5%	72.1%	73.6%	71.2%	73.8%	68.3%

Other evaluation metrics are addressed in addition to accuracy which are recall, precision, and F1 measures. Recall means the ratio of the total relevant results that are classified correctly by the classifier. Ensemble Voting showed 73.8% percentage in the recall, while MLP got 73.6%. Moreover, precision expresses the ratio of the instances that the algorithm classifies them as relevant, and they were relevant. Ensemble Voting is precise with 74.9%, while logistic regression got 74.7% in precision.

6 Conclusion

Academic achievement has become widely concerned by academic institutions around the world. With the widespread use of e-learning management system, a lot of hidden knowledge can be extracted and analyzed to improve the students' performance level.

Students' performance prediction model has been presented in this research. Predicting the academic level of students with a small amount of data shows clear evidence of overfitting problems. The best ways that worked better with this research to overcome overfitting and to increase the accuracy of the model is by:

- Tuning the hyperparameters especially the ones that affect overfitting.
- Using feature selection methods such as filter based k-best feature selection.

Data mining techniques proved that they can predict the student academic level which in turn answers the first question of the paper. In this research, six predictive models have been used. Random forest shows the highest testing score with train test evaluation which reaches 77.08% with the k-best feature selection method. With cross-validation, it got 75.2% based on 10-best feature selection. Thus, it confirms what has stated in [9] that it fits the data facing the problem of overfitting.

Visited resources, raised hands, announcements view, and the discussion shows a clear impact on students' final scores which brings us to answer the second question. These behavioral features show a significant relationship with the academic performance of the students. Moreover, they got the highest rank using information gain ranking and was chose by the 10-best method as the most features that influence the academic performance of the students.

Male and female students have the same academic behavior except with discussion which did not show a clear influence on female students' academic performance. An interesting finding has been shown by the parent responsible feature, as fathers make up two-thirds of the dataset, yet for most high-performance students their mother was responsible for them during their studies. Female students in this dataset prove their high academic performance, such that 42% of the whole female students got high-performance level, compared with male students who represent just 21% of them have got high academic performance.

In our future work, more investigation in hyper-parameter tuning will be performed. Moreover, increasing the size of the dataset by merging with other data from another school will make the predictive model more convenient to be generalized. Different academic performance between both genders needs more attention to know beyond this disparity. This is also the case with the parent responsible, is there an education strategy followed by mothers and thus enable students to excel?

References

1. Sin, K., Muthu, L.: Application of big data in education data mining and learning analytics – a literature review. **6956**, 1035–1050 (2015)
2. Hussain, M., Zhu, W., Zhang, W., Muhammad, S., Abidi, R., Ali, S.: Using machine learning to predict student difficulties from learning session data. Artif. Intell. Rev. **52**, 381–407 (2018)
3. Romero, C., Ventura, S.: Educational data mining: a survey from 1995 to 2005. Expert Syst. Appl. **33**, 135–146 (2007)
4. Rodrigues, M.W., Isotani, S., Zárate, L.E.: Educational data mining: a review of evaluation process in the e-learning. Telemat. Inform. **35**, 1701–1717 (2018)

5. Costa, E.B., Fonseca, B., Santana, M.A., De Araújo, F.F., Rego, J.: Evaluating the effectiveness of educational data mining techniques for early prediction of students' academic failure in introductory programming courses. Comput. Hum. Behav. **73**, 247–256 (2017)
6. Amrieh, E.A., Hamtini, T., Aljarah, I.: Mining educational data to predict student's academic performance using ensemble methods. Int. J. Database Theory Appl. **9**, 119–136 (2016)
7. Chung, J.Y., Lee, S.: Dropout early warning systems for high school students using machine learning. Child Youth Serv. Rev. **96**, 346–353 (2018)
8. Hänsch, R., Hellwich, O.: Random forests. Handb. Der Geodäsie. 1–42 (2016)
9. Sandoval, A., Gonzalez, C., Alarcon, R., Pichara, K., Montenegro, M.: Centralized student performance prediction in large courses based on low- cost variables in an institutional context. Internet High. Educ. **37**, 76–89 (2018)
10. Chen, T., He, T.: Xgboost: EXtreme gradient boosting. 1–4 (2019)
11. Krauss, C., Do, X.A., Huck, N.: Deep neural networks, gradient-boosted trees, random forests: statistical arbitrage on the S&P 500. Eur. J. Oper. Res. **259**, 689–702 (2017)
12. Sperandei, S.: Lessons in biostatistics understanding logistic regression analysis (2014)
13. Roalfe, A.K., Holder, R.L., Wilson, S.: Standardisation of rates using logistic regression: a comparison with the direct method. BMC Health Serv. Res. **8**, 1–7 (2008)
14. Latham, A., Crockett, K., Mclean, D.: Profiling student learning styles with multilayer perceptron neural networks. In: 2013 IEEE International Conference on Systems, Man, and Cybernetics, pp. 2510–2515 (2013)
15. Kayri, M.: An intelligent approach to educational data: performance comparison of the multilayer perceptron and the radial basis function artificial neural networks. Educ. Sci.: Theory Pract. **15**, 1247–1256 (2015)
16. Chandrashekar, G., Sahin, F.: A survey on feature selection methods Q. Comput. Electr. Eng. **40**, 16–28 (2014)
17. Maldonado, S., Weber, R.: A wrapper method for feature selection using support vector machines. Inf. Sci. (Ny) **179**, 2208–2217 (2009)
18. Pe, M., Barrag, M.: Feature Engineering based on ANOVA, cluster validity assessment and KNN for fault diagnosis in bearings. J. Intell. Fuzzy Syst. **34**, 3451–3462 (2018)
19. Chawla, N. V, Bowyer, K.W., Hall, L.O., Kegelmeyer, W.P.: SMOTE: synthetic minority over-sampling technique (2002)
20. Robinson, C., Schumacker, R.E.: Interaction effects: centering, variance inflation factor, and interpretation Issues. Multiple Linear Regres. Viewpoints **35**, 6–11 (2009)
21. Mustaffa, Z., Yusof, Y.: LSSVM parameters tuning with enhanced artificial bee colony. Int. Arab J. Inform. Technol. **11**, 236–243 (2014)

Crime Types Prediction

Hanan AL Mansour[1]([⊠]) and Michele Lundy[2]([⊠])

[1] PNU, Riyadh, Kingdom of Saudi Arabia
haalmansur@pnu.edu.sa
[2] DCU, Dublin, Ireland
Michele.Lundy@dcu.ie

Abstract. Crime prevention and resolution strategies depend on having the right crime team available in the right place and at the right time. Therefore, it is important to know where, when and under what conditions a specific crime type typically occurs. The goal of our current research is to identify the spatial, temporal, weather and event features most often associated with specific crime types; using these features, we can compare a number of different machine learning algorithms tasked with crime classifications. The results show that the XGboost algorithm performs best and that spatial, temporal and weather features do indeed play a significant role in crime type classification – for example, drug crimes tend to happen on sidewalks, late in the evening and in cold temperatures, proposing that specific 'drug dealing crime team resources' should be matched according to these specific spatial, temporal and weather forecast details.

Keywords: Crime types · Influence factors · Classification algorithms · Logistic regression · Random forest · Decision tree · XGBoost

1 Introduction

The security of cities and the safety of residents are among the most important social priorities in most nations around the world. Although massive resources and potential are already assigned to this issue [1], fighting crime and providing security require still more mechanisms to increase the effectiveness of law enforcement. For example, an immediate reaction to a crime is not enough to decrease general criminal incidence in the area. The best solutions to fighting crime lie with prevention rather than reaction. When police departments become more capable of anticipating when and where different types of criminal activity occur, they can concentrate resources to fight such activity, establish surveillance rounds, distribute forces according to time and location, and mount a prevention campaign through communication media.

Given this, the current research will classify different types of crime based on spatial, temporal, and weather factors (such as location, day of the week, temperature and humidity), as well as annual events. Research then determines the features associated with the different types of crime. The data used are historical data obtained from the Chicago Data Portal.

© Springer Nature Switzerland AG 2019
A. Alfaries et al. (Eds.): ICC 2019, CCIS 1097, pp. 260–274, 2019.
https://doi.org/10.1007/978-3-030-36365-9_22

2   Previous Work

In this section, we review past crimes and relevant non-crime studies to focus on understanding the results and research gaps in crime prediction and classification.

Previous crime works can be divided into two categories based on the field of research: crime rate prediction and crime type prediction.

2.1   Crime Rate Prediction

Wang et al. [2] predicted crime rates in Chicago from various types of data, such as hyperlinks, points of interest (POI), venue information, taxi flow data, and demographic data using logistic regression (LnR) and negative binomial regression (NBR) algorithms. A general prediction on crime rate was made without considering the potentially characteristics of different crime types. The results emerging just from POI features and taxi flow data alone can reduce crime prediction errors by 17.6%.

Ivanov et al. [3] estimated the street crime rate in St. Petersburg, Russia, by using linear regression, logistic regression (LR) and gradient boosting. This study depends solely on longitude and latitude as the spatial attributes of their predictive model. The gradient boosting model gave the best results. The authors' work also used clustering alongside classification to study spatial patterns of each type of crime in more detail. They applied a features selection technique to each crime category using a chi-squared test to avoid model overfitting. Alghamdi [4] predicted the next-year burglary rate in Chicago based on seven geographical levels: nation, state, census tract, block group, block, place, and 5-digit ZIP code. He implemented prediction using linear regression, ridge regression, random forest, gradient boosting and simple moving average (SMA) models. Dhaifallah tried to understand the significance of the micro-geographical level on crime rates, which plays a critical role in providing information to help police departments better plan their operations. In one instance, approximately 20% of the block groups (the smallest geographical area from the decennial census) [5] were the basis of 50% of the burglary crimes in Chicago. A focus on block groups estimated that the burglary crime rate could be reduced by up to 50%. In terms of the algorithms, the accuracy of the random forest-based model surpassed all other models used. For the burglary crime rate, Dhaifallah examined the impact using multiple geographic levels on but did not take other factors into account. Chen et al. [6] used LnR to predict the future theft incident rate in Chicago through forecasted weather data and sentiment tweets on Twitter. The results suggested that high temperatures increase theft crimes while humidity decreases them. Chen and colleagues also found that the model containing Twitter data improved predictions for most crime types.

2.2   Crime Types Prediction

Lor et al. [7] focused on finding spatial and temporal criminal hotspots and predicting potential crime types in Denver and Los Angeles. This was achieved by extracting common crime patterns using an 'a priori' algorithm applied to spatial factors and a time-period variable. The authors predicted crime types using a decision tree algorithm (DT) and naïve Bayesian classifier (NB) with a 5-fold cross-validation strategy. The NB classifier was the more accurate of the two models.

Pradhan [8] has predicted crime type using a historical San Francisco crime dataset and compared her results with previous findings. She used five algorithms for the classification process: NB, DT, k-nearest neighbor (KNN) and Random Forest (RF). She addressed the imbalance problem by using three techniques: oversampling the minority classes, undersampling the majority class and adjusting weights on the classifiers. The results reveal that using imbalance to correct the technique does not show a significant improvement when measured by the recall or precision metrics. Further, when using demographic information without modification, ensemble techniques such as Random Forest or Gradient Boosting worked best. Alsalman [9] predicted the type of crimes in the City of Chicago using crime data from 2017. She used Twitter data features, including the tweet text and geospatial objects, along with historical crime data features using LnR, NB, KNN, support vector machines (SVM), artificial neural network (ANN) and ensemble learning. Two experiments were applied: The first experiment used only historical features while the second used both historical and Twitter data. The result proved that Twitter data in general improves prediction accuracy. for example, logistic regression model accuracy increased by 20% in the second experiment compared to the first one.

The following section reviews studies not related to crimes related but rather use methodologies with results that may be helpful in crime-type classification. Zhang et al. [10] predicted DNA protein binding sites using the real DNA protein test dataset. The imbalanced data was addressed by ADASYN to oversample positive data and a bootstrap strategy to under sample negative data. They proposed an ensemble convolutional neural network (CNN) as a classifier. The result proved more efficient than the methods previously used and achieved a high prediction performance. Along the same lines but using different techniques, Hu et al. [11] predicted protein-DNA binding residues using SVM and boosting algorithms. These algorithms trained data to address the imbalance problem after applying a random underdamping technique. The results indicated a high prediction performance and outperformed many others.

3   Problem Statement and Contributions

Most previous works have focused on predicting crime rates within a specific crime type rather than on classifying different crime types themselves and have been limited in scope to the examination of spatial and time features only as potential influential factors of crime rates. Moreover, the few studies that did focus on classifying crime types did not focus on the explicit identification of the influential features of each crime type, nor did they take into account the problem of imbalanced data amongst different crime types (although this imbalance problem can affect classification accuracy). Therefore, this work aims to enhance previous crime studies by

- Expanding the set of potentially influential features examined by including weather elements in addition to the spatial and temporal features of previous works.
- Enhancing the knowledge of previous crime type classification studies through the explicit identification of the influential features of each crime type
- Addressing the problem of imbalanced data in crime types.

In other words, the contribution of this research is to examine a wider set of potentially influential features of a crime and to explicitly identify the influential features of each crime type using this wider set of features while also addressing the problem of imbalanced data.

4 Methodology

4.1 Data

The data used for the research in this paper was collected from three public resources: Chicago Crime Data, Historical Hourly Weather Data 2012–2017, and Events in the United States from which 3 datasets were constructed, as detailed below

Crime Dataset: This contains crime data taken from the Chicago Data Portal [12] and was chosen for this research, first of all, because the city was ranked as 24th most dangerous in the United States and, secondly because it has adequate publicly available crime datasets.

The portal contains approximately 900,000 crime instances over the three-year period 2014–2016 with 22 variables for each crime, including information about the date, time, location, and type of crime. Detailed attributes can be seen in Table 1.

Weather Dataset: This contains weather data from Kaggle [13]. It contains three years' worth of high temporal resolution (hourly measurements) data related to various weather variables (temperature, humidity, and weather description) and consisting of 34,000 records from 2014–2016. More attributes can be found in Table 2.

Events Dataset: This contains data taken from the Time and Date website [14]. It contains data on major events – federal holidays, sports events, and religious observances in the United States, particularly in Chicago. It includes dates, event types, and event names from 2014–2016. Details can be seen in Table 3.

Table 1. Crime dataset (bold = related attributes or key features for the study purpose)

Attributes	Description	Attributes	Description
ID	Unique record identification	District	Indicates where the incident occurred in the police district
Case Number	The Chicago Police Department RD Number (Records Division Number), unique to the incident	Ward	Specifies the ward (district of the city council) where the incident took place
Date	Date of the occurrence	Community area	Indicates the area of the community where the incident took place
Block	Where the incident occurred, whether the partially edited address places it on the same block as the actual address	X coordinate	The X location coordinate where the incident took place in the projection of State Plane Illinois East NAD in 1983

(continued)

Table 1. (*continued*)

Attributes	Description	Attributes	Description
FBI code	Specifies the classification of a crime as outlined in the National Incident Reporting System (NIBRS) of the FBI	**Primary type**	The primary description of the IUCR code
Year	Year of the occurrence	Description	Secondary IUCR code description, a primary description subcategory
Location	The location where the incident took place in a format that allows maps and other geographical operations to be created on this data portal	**Location description**	Description of the location of the incident
Updated	Date and time of the last update of the record	IUCR	The IUCR code. This is directly linked to the Primary Type and Description
Arrest	Specifies whether or not an arrest has been made	**Latitude**	The location latitude where the incident took place
Domestic	Indicates whether, as defined by the Illinois Domestic Violence Act, the incident was domestic	**Longitude**	The location longitude where the incident took place. For partial redaction, this location is shifted from the actual location but falls on the same block
Beat	Specifies the beat where the incident took place	Y coordinate	Y coordinate of the site where the incident occurred in the 1983 projection of State Plane Illinois East NAD

Table 2. Weather dataset attributes

Attributes	Description
Date	Date and time of weather attributes
Humidity	Percentage of humidity
Temperature	Temperature using kelvin unit
Weather description	A text description of the weather

Table 3. Events dataset attributes

Attributes	Description
Date	Date of the event
Event name	Name of the event
Event type	Description

4.2 Data Preprocessing

Data Reduction: We applied data reduction for all crime datasets. This study carried out a dimensionality reduction. Among the available 22 features in the crime dataset, we selected six of them. The selected features are related ones or possess key features for the study purpose such as date and location (see boldface features in Table 1). We removed all irrelevant and high correlated features from the dataset.

Data Cleaning: Since missing data can have a major impact on conclusions drawn from a dataset, the missing values were imputed and handled with different methods. Missing humidity data were filled using linear interpolation. This method is based on using linear polynomials to build new data points within a distinct set of known data points. Further, the cases were removed if they were missing values in latitude and longitude.

Data Integration: As described, three different datasets were used in this study – namely Crime Dataset, Weather Dataset, and Events Dataset. In combination, these databases were used to source the variables for subsequent analysis – first, the 'Target Variable' for crime type classification and, second, the 'Feature Variables' (spatial, temporal, weather and event) for association examination with the 'Target Variable'. However, before these key 'Target' and 'Feature Variables' can be constructed, a number of data integration steps were implemented to combine the datasets. This was achieved using the *date variable* as a key merge variable. The final file was saved in CSV format.

This study needs analyses of the date and time information on distinct granularities. Therefore, we used the date features (which contain date and time crime details) to create three more features: day of the week, season and month. Moreover, we considered part of the hour without paying attention to minutes and seconds.

Variables: The two key variable types – 'Target Variable' and 'Feature Variable' – were then sourced as follows:

Target Variables: 'Primary Type' was used to define the target variable for the classification problem of this research. It consisted of 30 types of crime. A large number of types showed skewed data distributions between types, making classifying more complicated. Hence, these types were categorised into four major categories, thereby reducing a potentially large number of target variable categories down to a smaller, more manageable set and making the modelling process easier and faster [15]. The types were reduced based upon categories used in The Bureau of Justice Statistics

(BJS) in the United States; BJS is a primary source of criminal justice statistics [16]. The new four categories are:

- *Violent crimes*: The UCR program defines 'violent crimes' as offences involving force or threat of force [17]. They include assault, battery, homicide, offences involving children, weapons violation, sexual assault and other sexual offences.
- *Property crimes*: This includes burglary, criminal damage, criminal trespass, motor vehicle theft, theft and robbery, and arson.
- *Drug crimes*: These include narcotics violations.
- *Other crimes*: These include all crimes not belonging to the previous categories such as kidnapping, prostitution, concealed carry license violation, deceptive practice, gambling, human trafficking, interference with a public officer, intimidation, liquor law violation, obscenity, other offense, public indecency, public peace violation, stalking.

Feature Variables: A number of preprocessing steps were applied to construct the feature variables described below:

Data Transformation, Discretisation and Normalisation

Data transformation was applied in this research by grouping variable attribute values together. Transformations can reduce data skewing and outliers prominence in the data subsequently increasing model accuracy. The values of the hour feature were transferred into 4-h intervals, the transferred values generate a new variable called 'period'. Table 4 illustrates the values of period variables.

Table 4. Period variable values

Range of hour	Period	Range of hours	Period
00:00–03:59	Late night	12:00–15:59	Afternoon
04:00–7:59	Early Morning	16:00–19:59	Evening
08:00–11:59	Morning	20:00–23:59	Late evening

The normalisation process was applied to numeric features. Normalisation means that scale-attributed values fall within a specified range. The Min-Max normalisation technique was used in this research, which scales data between 0 and 1, as given by

$$Z = x - \min(x)/\max(x) - \min(x) \tag{1}$$

where min and max are the minimum and maximum values in x.

Text Preprocessing: Repeated values and other synonymous words in text features were removed. This study used two versions of the location description feature: the first version contained the original values of the features (78 values). The second was designed to decrease the computational complexity for future analysis and runtime [18] and contained 15 grouped values based on similarities of places and synonyms of words. Table 5 shows the 15 new values of location description features.

Table 5. Location description values after categorisation

Grouped	Raw	Grouped	Raw
Financial sites	Automatic teller machine (ATM), bank	Parking	Airport parking lot, parking lot
Business premises	Factory/manufacturing building, business office	Vehicles	Taxicab, truck
Other	Cemetery, elevator, bridge	Residential	House, apartment
Hotels	Hotel, motel	Street	Sidewalk
Government building	Government building, federal building	Nursing home	
CTA platforms	CTA bus, CTA train	School	
Medical location	Medical/dental office, hospital	Airport	
Retail and shops	Barbershop, cleaning store		

After the preprocessing step described above, 12 features were retained for modelling purposes, as represented in Table 6.

Table 6. Final features used in the modelling stage

Domestic	Period	Humidity	Day of week
Latitude	Day	Description of weather	Temperature
Longitude	Season	Location description (2 versions)	Event name

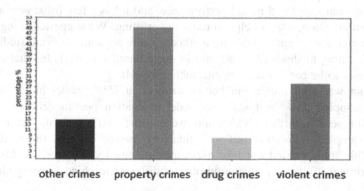

Fig. 1. Crime types distribution.

4.3 Resampling

As can be seen from Fig. 1, the Target Variable instances were imbalanced (e.g. the largest category was property crimes with 49% and the smallest was drug crimes with

10%) and this 'class imbalance' issue is known to adversely affect classification performance and therefore needs to be addressed. *Class imbalance learning* refers to a group of learning algorithms designed to deal with the particular type of classification problem whereby some classes have significantly fewer instances than do others [19]. The study addressed the problem based on a hybrid resampling technique, which combined an adaptive synthetic (ADASYN) and an oversampling approach with random undersampling (RUS).

Oversampling Using ADASYN: This is an improved version of SMOTE (synthetic minority oversampling technique). The main idea of ADASYN is to use a weighted distribution for different minority class instances based on their classification difficulties where most synthetic data is generated for minority class instances that are more difficult to classify when compared to minority class instances that are easier to classify. ADASYN improves data distribution learning by reducing the class imbalance bias [20].

Random Undersampling (RUS): Random undersampling is one of the simplest methods of handling imbalanced data in a dataset. It works by randomly deleting cases from the majority classes to decrease their total number.

5 Modelling

This study has attempted to classify the types of crimes based upon the 12 features listed in Table 5 and using 4 classification methods: multinomial logistic regression (MLR) which is useful for understanding the impact of independent variables on a categorical dependent variable, DT which is simple to understand and visualize, and requires little data preparation, RF, and eXtreme Gradient Boosting (XGboost). XGboost is the implementation of a gradient boosting decision tree algorithm focused on computational speed and model performance, and it has a few frills: new additions such as regularization, which helps to reduce overfitting. We suggested using RF and XGboost which are ensemble learning methods. There are some relevant studies using ensemble learning methods [3, 4, 8], and in using them, we concluded that ensemble learning tends to be better than non-ensemble methods.

The data was split into a number of datasets: a 75% 'model build' set and a randomly sampled 25% 'test set' for model evaluation post-modelling. The 75% 'model build' set was further divided into two subsets: a 60% 'training' set and a 15% randomly sampled 'validation' set to validate the performance of the model while training. This study carried out four experiments using Python (version 3.6.4), with each experiment itself comparing a number of different machine learning algorithms (see Table 7).

Table 7. Experiments setting

Experiments	Setting	Experiments	Setting
Experiment 1	Original dataset + original version of location description feature	Experiment 3	Balanced dataset + original version location description feature
Experiment 2	Original dataset + grouped version location description feature	Experiment 4	Balanced dataset + grouped location description feature

6 Results and Evaluation

Considering that the research dataset in this study was imbalanced, there are two metrics proposed to measure the performance of the algorithms, namely macro_F1 score and geometric mean (G-mean).

These metrics depend upon a number of primary building blocks – as follows:

True Positives (TP) where the model predicts the positive class correctly, *True Negatives (TN)* where the model predicts the negative class correctly, *False Positives (FP)* where the model predicts the positive class incorrectly and *False Negative (FN)* where the model predicts the negative class incorrectly.

Precision – the ratio of correctly predicted positive values to the total number of predicted positive values given:

$$\text{Precision} = \text{TP}/\text{TP} + \text{FP} \tag{2}$$

Recall (aka Sensitivity) – the ratio of correctly predicted positive values to the number of actual positive values:

$$\text{Recall} = \text{TP}/\text{TP} + \text{FN} \tag{3}$$

Specificity – the ratio of actual negative values that are correctly predicted

$$\text{Specificity} = \text{TN}/(\text{TN} + \text{FP}) \tag{4}$$

F1 score – the harmonic mean of recall and precision:

$$\text{F1 score} = 2 \times (\text{Precision} \times \text{Recall})/(\text{Precision} + \text{Recall}) \tag{5}$$

The F1-score involves two averages: micro and macro. The micro F1-score is calculated by computing the global precision and recall values for all classes and then calculating F1-score; therefore, the metric tends to be weighted towards the highest value of classes. The macro F1-score is computed by calculating each class separately and then averaging all classes (therefore, the metric tends to be weighted towards rare categories). The macro F1-score is important when a set of classes is imbalanced, as in the present study, to validate the capacity of the classifier to perform well in smaller categories [21].

G-mean – the square root of the product of sensitivity or recall and specificity:

$$G\text{-mean} = \sqrt{\text{Specificity} \times \text{Sensitivity}} \tag{6}$$

The G-mean has been proposed for classifier assessment of imbalanced datasets in multiple studies [22]. Table 8 presents the model results of the selected algorithms for each experiment obtained using Macro – F1_score, G_mean, Precision and Recall metrics. Experiments demonstrated multiple approaches that addressed or ignored the imbalance problem while at the same time assessing the impact of the grouped location description feature.

The first comparison examined the effect of addressing the data imbalance (Experiment 1 vs. Experiment 3, and Experiment 2 vs. Experiment 4). The results (see Table 8) show that regardless of the proposed algorithm, the balanced training dataset performed better than did the original training dataset (using the macro_F1_score and G-mean metrics).

The second comparison examined the effect of grouping the location description feature (Experiment 1 vs. Experiment 2, and Experiment 3 vs. Experiment 4). The results (see Table 8) show that regardless of the proposed algorithm, grouping the location description feature did not improve the classification.

Based on the aforementioned summary and Table 8, we concluded that the results were more favourable when the imbalance problem was addressed using a hybrid technique combining an adaptive synthetic sampling approach with random under-sampling; this technique demonstrated improvements in recall scores compared with

Table 8. Experimental results of different metrics

	Algorithms	Micro F1_score	Macro F1_score	G_mean	Precision	Recall
Experiment 1	Decision tree	60.29	44.34	59.77	53.70	43.28
	Logistic regression	60.47	39.82	57.62	58.94	40.33
	Random forest	62.08	45.84	60.80	61.95	44.53
	XGboost	62.43	46.93	61.46	61.65	45.37
Experiment 2	Decision tree	58.51	44.13	59.49	51.20	43.18
	Logistic regression	59.14	33.07	53.54	59.59	35.51
	Random forest	61.24	45.38	60.41	62.13	44.25
	XGboost	61.37	45.74	60.57	62.20	44.48
Experiment 3	Decision tree	51.46	**45.68**	**64.93**	46.81	50.87
	Logistic regression	44.92	**42.79**	**64.85**	45.80	51.12
	Random forest	52.82	**47.82**	**66.43**	48.31	52.90
	XGboost	52.62	**48.48**	**67.60**	48.44	54.52
Experiment 4	Decision tree	47.89	44.47	64.84	45.43	51.04
	Logistic regression	41.20	39.91	62.95	44.46	48.71
	Random forest	49.36	45.89	65.87	47.37	52.35
	XGboost	50.57	46.83	66.41	47.51	53.04

those of other methods for addressing imbalanced data, mentioned in a previous study [8]such as oversampling the minority classes (see Table 9). Also, when comparing the recall and precision results of the proposed algorithms in this study in Table 8 with the results of the study [9] in Table 9 (using historical data only and different algorithms such as KNN, SVM, and ANN algorithms), this study gave better results.

Table 9. Results of past works

Algorithms	Recall	Precision	Ref
DT	16.83	18.47	[8]
RF	13.19	17.03	[8]
KNN	31.00	16.00	[9]
SVM	32.00	46.00	[9]
ANN	48.00	50.00	[9]
Ensemble	52.00	56.00	[9]

According to the macro F1_score and G-mean metrics, the most favourable results for all the algorithms were those in Experiment 3. These results see boldface in Table 7. Based on the most favourable results of the four algorithms, XGboost outperformed the other algorithms, with 67.60% for G-mean and 48.48% for macro F1_score. Therefore, XGboost was considered the most suitable algorithm in this research based on all the experimental results.

6.1   Feature Importance

XGBoost algorithm can calculate a 'Feature Importance' score that indicates the usefulness or value of each feature in the construction of the model; the higher the score, the higher the relative importance. This attribute enables features to be ranked and compared with one another.

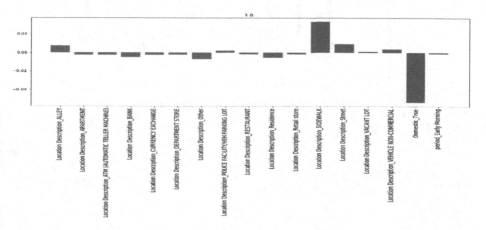

Fig. 2. Features influencing drug crimes.

Figures 1, 2 and 3 show the features that affected each crime type either positively or negatively. Drug crimes (Fig. 2) primarily occurred on sidewalks, in alleys, on streets, in car parks, in non-commercial vehicles and at evening and late evening. By contrast, relatively few drug crimes occurred in banks, in restaurants or in residential buildings.

Violent crimes (Fig. 3) were mostly domestic and primarily occurred in apartments, in schools, and on sidewalks, followed by in nursing homes and residential buildings. Property crimes (Fig. 4) primarily occurred on streets and in department stores, retail stores, restaurants and car parks, as well as in early mornings and on relatively warm days. Also, latitude and longitude features indicate that this type of crime frequently occurs in specific locations.

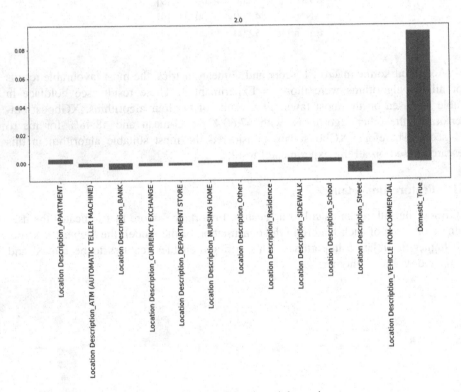

Fig. 3. Features influencing violent crimes.

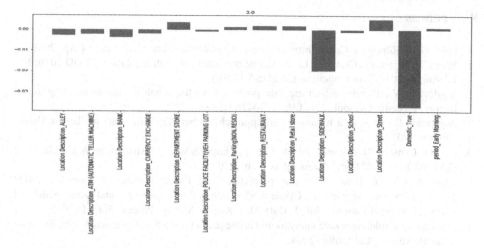

Fig. 4. Features influencing property crime.

7 Conclusion

This research presents evidence indicating that obtaining optimal algorithm performance, requires that we use balanced data for classification to yield more favourable results. The proposed method for addressing the problem of imbalanced data yielded results that were more favourable and more reliable than those obtained from the original data, and the ADASYN method outperformed balancing methods used in past studies. The attribute values of the location description feature were reduced to address large quantities of categorical dummy variables; however, these reductions did not markedly improve performance. Our study shows that the most favourable algorithm for benefitting police departments in Chicago is XGboost, which exhibited prediction accuracy for crime types of up to 67.60%, with a G-mean of approximately 49% when the macro F1_score metric was used. We also concluded that spatial, temporal, and weather-related factors influence the occurrence of crimes. Spatial factors were the most influential, where a particular type of crime can be repeated several times in the same location (for example, drug crimes appear outdoors, especially in streets and alleys, while violent crimes increase indoors such as in apartments, buildings, and schools). Time of day is the most influential temporal factor affecting all crime types. We see the period between 16:00 pm and 1:00 am as the active period for drug crimes, while property and violent crimes occur in the early morning. In terms of weather features, drugs crimes are more prevalent in the cold climate while property crimes increase with high temperatures such as in the summer. These conclusions and analysis can be used to improve and help crime team resourcing – e.g. if drug deals tend to happen during the late evening, on sidewalks and particularly when the temperature is cold, then the 'drug dealing crime team resources' should be matched according to these specific 'drug dealing spatial, temporal and (forecast) weather details'.

References

1. USA GOV Reporting Crime. https://www.usa.gov/report-crime. Accessed 14 Apr 2019
2. Wang, H., Kifer, D., Graif, C., Li, Z.: Crime rate inference with big data. In: KDD 2016, 13–17 August 2016, San Francisco, CA, USA (2016)
3. Ingilevich, V., Ivanov, S.: Crime rate prediction in the urban environment using social factors. Procedia Comput. Sci. **136**, 472–478 (2018)
4. Alghamdi, D.M.: A data mining based approach for burglary crime rate prediction, thesis, Chicago (2017)
5. Ch 11 Census Blocks and Block Groups. https://www2.census.gov/geo/pdfs/reference/GARM/Ch11GARM.pdf. Accessed 10 Feb 2019
6. Chen, X., Cho, Y., Jang, S.Y.: Crime prediction using Twitter sentiment and weather (2015)
7. Lor, E., Mirza, R., Almanie, T.: Crime prediction based on crime types and using spatial and temporal criminal hotspots. Int. J. Data Min. Knowl. Manag. Process **5**(4), 1 (2015)
8. Pradhan, I.: Exploratory data analysis and crime prediction in San Francisco, thesis, San Jose State University, California (2018)
9. Alsalman, A.: Machine Learning Algorithms and Natural Language Processing Techniques. Qassim University, Qassim (2018)
10. Zhang, Y., Qiao, S., Ji, S., Han, N., Liu, D., Zhou, J.: Identification of DNA–protein binding sites by bootstrap multiple convolutional neural networks on sequence information. Eng. Appl. Artif. Intell. **79**, 58–66 (2019)
11. Hu, J., Li, Y., Zhang, M., Yang, X., Bin, H.: Predicting protein-DNA binding residues by weightedly combining sequence-based features and boosting multiple SVMs. IEEE/ACM Trans. Comput. Biol. Bioinform. **14**(6), 1389–1398 (2017)
12. Chicago Data Portal. https://data.cityofchicago.org/Public-Safety/Crimes-2001-to-present/ijzp-q8t2
13. Kaggle. https://www.kaggle.com/selfishgene/historical-hourly-weather-data#weather_description.csv
14. https://www.timeanddate.com/holidays/us/2001
15. Sengupta, A., Kumar, M., Upadhyay, S.: Crime analyses using R. In: Data Mining Applications with R, p. 514. Elsevier (2013)
16. https://bjs.gov/
17. FBI:URC. https://ucr.fbi.gov. Accessed 11 Apr 2019
18. Cui, Y.: Customer Relationship Management. University of Toronto, Toronto (2018)
19. Wang, S., Yao, X.: Multiclass imbalance problems: analysis and potential solutions. EEE Trans. Syst. Man Cybern. **42**, 1119–1130 (2012)
20. He, H., Bai, Y., Garcia, E.A., Li, S.: ADASYN: adaptive synthetic sampling approach for imbalanced learning. In: 2008 IEEE International Joint Conference on Neural Networks (IEEE World Congress on Computational Intelligence), Hong Kong, China (2008)
21. Benevenuto, F., Magno, G., Rodrigu, T.: Detecting spammers on Twitter. Universidade Federal de Minas Gerais, Belo Horizonte, Brazil (2010)
22. Liu, X.-Y., Wu, J., Zhou, Z.-H.: Exploratory undersampling for class-imbalance learning. IEEE Trans. Syst. Man Cybern. Part B (Cybern.) **39**, 539–550 (2008)

Intensive Survey About Road Traffic Signs Preprocessing, Detection and Recognition

Mrouj Almuhajri[1,2]([⊠]) and Ching Suen[1]

[1] Department of Computer Science and Software Engineering, Concordia University, CENPARMI, Montreal, Canada
mr_almuh@encs.concordia.ca, suen@cse.concordia.ca
[2] Department of Computer Science, Saudi Electronic University, Dammam, Kingdom of Saudi Arabia
m.almuhajri@seu.edu.sa

Abstract. Driving is a complex task that needs drivers' attention, cognition, and perception. Many vehicle accidents happened because of driver-related critical reasons, such as failure to notice a stop sign, weather conditions, or personal distractions. Nowadays, technology becomes part of our daily routine in which it is involved in driving aspects either partially (like driving assistance systems) or fully (like self-driving vehicles). In both cases, having Traffic Sign Detection and Recognition TSDR systems is essential. This survey paper, intensively reviews studies proposed in this field considering the three main phases of any TSDR system: preprocessing, detection, and recognition. It also spots the light on the common public datasets and the issues and challenges that TSDR systems may face. Finally, some insight regarding the future work that could be done to improve the field is provided.

Keywords: Traffic Sign · Preprocessing · Dataset · Detection · Recognition · TSDR

1 Introduction

Driving is a complex task that needs drivers' attention, cognition, and perception. Many vehicle accidents happened because of driver-related critical reasons including recognition and decision errors [1]. Some accidents occurred because of driver failure to notice a stop sign due to personal distractions, weather conditions, or environmental causes [31] Technology came to take control of automated tasks and assist drivers in interpreting the perceived information over roads either partially (like driving assistance systems) or fully (like self-driving vehicles) with a consideration to overall safety. For more flexibility, some of these systems can be operated on smartphones with real time process.

© Springer Nature Switzerland AG 2019
A. Alfaries et al. (Eds.): ICC 2019, CCIS 1097, pp. 275–289, 2019.
https://doi.org/10.1007/978-3-030-36365-9_23

1.1   Road Traffic Signs

Road Traffic Signs are signs located at the side or above roads bearing visual symbolic language in order to be interpreted by drivers. Those signs convey information about the road ahead to make driving safe and convenient. Different design styles are used in traffic signs based on shapes and colors with respect to environment. In fact, traffic signs can be categorized into two groups: ideogram-based and text-based signs. The first group expresses the meaning using symbols while the other contains text and symbols [7]. They can also be classified based on their type into one of three main classes (see Fig. 1): danger proclamation signs, regulation signs, and informational signs [30]. The first class contains signs to warn drivers of possible dangers ahead; the second class signs tell drivers about special obligations or restrictions they must conform to; the last class signs give information to help drivers in navigation tasks. Shapes and colors have been chosen carefully in order to make the signs recognizable from the environmental background. Each color and shape indicates different meaning. For example, yellow means danger; triangle is to yield right of way.

Fig. 1. Example of traffic signs classes: (from top to down) danger proclamation signs, regulation signs, and informational signs (Color figure online)

1.2   Traffic Sign Detection and Recognition TSDR Systems

Road Traffic Sign Detection and Recognition TSDR systems have been studied extensively over the past decades. Many techniques and methodologies have been implemented for this purpose. There are three main sequential stages: preprocessing, detection, and recognition. In general, the acquired images/videos have to be enhanced using some preprocessing techniques. Then, detection stage identifies the region of interest RoI of traffic signs. Finally, recognition stage classifies the candidate region into one of road sign groups, or rejects it. Figure 2 illustrates a pipeline of TSDR systems. High accuracy have been achieved in some of the proposed studies under specified but not all possible conditions.

In this paper, an intensive study about road traffic signs detection and recognition TSDR systems is provided. Section 1 provides introduction and abstract

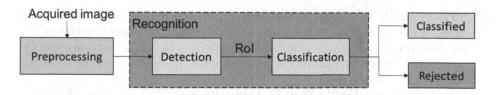

Fig. 2. An overview of TSDR process

information about TSDRs. Section 2 lists and discusses the available common public datasets for traffic signs. Then, Sect. 3 presents preprocessing techniques considering different color spaces. Next, Sects. 4 and 5 go over detection and recognition phases and their used methodology. After that, issues and challenges related to the process of TSDR are explained in Sect. 6. Finally, a conclusion and future work for this field is introduced in Sect. 7.

2 Public Datasets

One of the factor that may assure robustness of TSDR systems is having a good dataset for training and testing. An optimal dataset should have a large number of samples because small sizes have been a serious limitation for many earlier studies. Moreover, samples have to include different variations of signs appearing under several conditions.

Public datasets for traffic signs detection and recognition supply researchers with a fair way to evaluate their models by comparing results with those who used same dataset and similar methodology. Following, the most common used public datasets (Table 1 summarizes the mentioned public datasets):

- **GTSDB – German Traffic Sign Detection Benchmark** [13] is a single-image detection assessment that targets researchers in the related fields. It has 900 images (600 for training and 300 for testing). The images were captured near Bochum, Germany considering different scenarios (urban, rural, high-way) over daytime and dusk time in variations of weather conditions. There are three categories in which each traffic sign is assigned to: prohibitory, danger, and mandatory signs.
- **GTSRB German Traffic Sign Recognition Benchmark** [23] is a multiclass, single-image classification dataset. It is a large and life-like database with more than 50,000 images and 40 classes.
- **BTSDB Belgium Traffic Sign Detection Benchmark and BTSCB Belgium Traffic Sign Classification Benchmark** [3,18,32] are large datasets of traffic signs in Belgium for the purpose of detection and classification. The first one has around 7000 images (4500 for training and 2500 for testing) while the other has 10,000 images which include 13,444 signs with 62 classes. It also has some sign free samples to be used for negative training.

- **STS Swedish Traffic Sign Dataset** [16,17] is a public database for traffic signs. It has more than 20,000 images/frames (only 20% annotated) containing 3488 traffic signs. Annotations contain signs type (i.e. pedestrian crossing, no parking, 50 km/h), visibility status (occluded, blurred, or visible), and road status (main or side road).
- **CTSD Chinese Traffic Sign Dataset** [40] has 1100 images (700 for training and 400 for testing) taken in Beijing and Xiamen, China with different sizes. Many scenarios (highway, urban, rural) and weather conditions (sunny, cloudy, and rainy) were considered.
- **Stereopolis Dataset** [3] from Paris, France has 847 images including 251 annotated ones with 10 classes.
- **LISA Traffic Sign Dataset** [20] contains about 7000 annotated images and frames for United states traffic signs with 49 classes.

Table 1. Public datasets summary.

	GTSDB	GTSRB	BTSDB	BTSCB	STS	CTSD	LISA	Stereopolis
Classes	3	43	-	62	7	3	49	10
Images	900	51,840	7000	10,000	20,000	1100	7000	847
Training	600	75%	4500	-	-	700	-	-
Testing	300	25%	2500	-	-	400	-	-
Annotated?	Yes	Yes	Yes	Yes	20%	Yes	Yes	251 only
Country of Origin	Germany	Germany	Belgium	Belgium	Sweden	China	US	France

3   Preprocessing

Image preprocessing is an essential step for the sake of successful detection. The quality of digital images/frames taken by camera or phone could be easily disturbed by variation of factors like noise and lighting effects. Hence, many techniques and filters have been introduced to enhance the quality of those digital images without alerting any possible information. The less the noise in the image, the less time needed to detect the traffic sign and the more time left over for classification phase [20,38]. So, it is important to understand the main component of images which is color. There are several types of color spaces. The most common ones are: RGB, HSV, HSI, YUV, and YCbCr in which each of them has its own characteristics and peculiarities. Conversion between these types, or sometimes to greyscale, is done depends on the need.

3.1   Color Spaces

- **RGB** (Red, Green, Blue) is the most frequently used format for digital images. Although most cameras use this format, it is extremely sensitive to illumination variations. So, a conversion from RGB to other color spaces is necessary sometimes in order to lessen the lighting effect [5].

- **HSV** (Hue, Saturation, Value) is unlike RGB, it is immune to lighting effects. Hence, it is widely considered for traffic sign color segmentation. In fact, HSV is pretty similar to human perception [24]. Yet, the cost of interconversion RGB to HSV is considerably high as the computations are non-linear. Also, hue component is vulnerable to change considering dust and distance factors [5].
- **HSI** (Hue, Saturation, Intensity) color space is similar to HSV in hue component only. The authors of [11] believed that using HSI color space, hue and saturation in particular, is sufficient to isolate traffic signs from their complex background working with fixed thresholds. Like HSV, it is less sensitive to lighting changes [15].
- **YUV** color model is an analog system that defines color through Luminance Y and two chrominance values U and V. Decoupling color information from luminance is an advantage. The digital version of YUV is **YC$_b$C$_r$**, and the two terms can be used interchangeably. Usually, they are used with videos. A conversion between YC$_b$C$_r$ and RGB could be done however, it is important to know that some conversions might result in invalid RGB values. This is because RGB colors occupy only part of the YC$_b$C$_r$ color space.

3.2 Experimental Preprocessing

As mentioned before, RGB color format is super sensitive to illumination variations, so many researchers convert RGB to other formats. The authors of [40,41] converted RGB images to Ohta color space which was originally developed for image processing as it can give very low probability of errors with color image segmentation and color recognition algorithms [25]. Then, the images were transformed to normalized Ohta space which defines a family of three reduced (two-dimensional) color representation to get an increased color invariance with respect to intensity [34]. Next, they used color information and classes to calculate the probabilities of a color class given some pixel pairs using Bayesian rules. As a result, a number of probability maps were obtained. The maps are gray images with high intensities in which they increase the contrast between traffic signs and background for easier detection. Another study [29] used several preprocessing steps on the input RGB images to enhance them for detection phase. First of all, the images were converted into grayscale and binarized using several threshold levels. Then, to suppress background textures, a Red/Blue Channel Enhancement (RBCE) method was applied. Others [10] converted RGB based on the inner background of the signs. In particular, signs with white background were converted into grayscale, otherwise normalized red/blue formats were extracted.

To avoid illumination influence, some studies like [6,36] used HSV rather than RGB as they can get the color channels (hue and saturation) independent from illumination. Moreover, researchers in [26] used YC$_b$C$_r$ for the input images in order to get color information (blue chroma and red chroma) separated from brightness. Hence, they performed color segmentation based on the colors appear in traffic signs, such as red and blue.

4 Detection

Detection is the action of identifying the region of interest RoI of road traffic signs. Color and shape are the main features that distinguish road traffic signs from their background. Several methods have been proposed on this basis, and hence they are classified into color-based methods and shape-based methods. Some of these methods use learning techniques for better performance.

4.1 Color-Based Techniques

Colors in traffic signs were chosen carefully in order to be visible regardless their complex background. Therefore, color-based methods take this advantage to detect traffic signs using color information. Some researchers tend to use color-based methods over shape-based methods to avoid the influence of background texture. However, the main drawback about color-based methods is lighting inconsistency which affects the robustness of detection. Also, clustering colors may cause issues especially if they are over/under clustered [22].

Many studies rely on techniques that are based on color thresholding. For example, studies [10, 29, 40] used Maximally Stable Extremal Regions MSER method as a first step toward extracting the candidate regions of traffic signs. MSER regions are connected areas in which they are almost uniformed in their intensity and surrounded by contrasting background. The MSER regions are generated through a process of multiple thresholds, and it is robust to changes in illumination and contrast conditions [10] as it depends on the inner background of signs. Unfortunately, there is no clear way for deciding on the optimal color threshold values.

Other studies apply color learning techniques for detection process. Support Vector Machine SVM is one of the most popular algorithms in this field. Nevertheless, before using SVM, most studies implement feature extraction [21] like HOG, Haar extracted from AdaBoost algorithm.

In [32], AdaBoost classifier was used with the 6 Haar-like patterns. So, by cascading AdaBoost then SVM, region of interests were detected coming up with only 0.5% false negative and 0.2% false positive. Moreover, the authors of [40] who used MSER as mentioned above, found that there are lots of false positive. So, they used HOG features to extract color information from the probability maps, and finally feed them to the multi-class SVM model. They achieved recall of 99.47% and 99.51% for GTSDB and CTSD respectively in very costless time.

4.2 Shape-Based Techniques

Shape-based methods can avoid obstacles exist with color-based methods like lighting inconsistency, simply because they do not deal with colors. However, these methods are sensitive to the complexity of the background [42]. Several shape-based approaches have been used for traffic signs detection. Some of the common ones are Hough transform, Template matching, Filtering, Corners, Edges, Contours, and using some of deep learning techniques.

Traffic signs have five main shapes, and they can be classified by the number of lines detected. Hough transform HT is a technique that finds aligned points in images in order to identify lines and shapes. It is important to mention that HT is able to detect those signs with imperfect shapes which are affected by occlusion or noise [5]. Study [28] used HT on the input images to extract triangle (3-lines), square/rectangle/diamond (4-lines), octagon (8-lines), and circle (more than eight lines). Though, only circle, square, and octagon were detected perfectly. Another study [39] used a modified Generalized Hough transform GHT for real-time detection as the original HT could consume too much time for computation. For triangular signs only from GTSDB, accuracy was 97.3%.

Shape can also be detected by applying template matching. Many studies, such as [14,27] first use color segmentation followed by template matching. Hsu and Huang [14] used prior knowledge plus color information to identify RoI. Then, they searched into those RoI for triangular or circular shape regions. Finally, a closer view image is captured and a template matching is applied by using variable-sized template shapes with fixed thickness belt. After moving templates around the image, the shape is selected if it meets a matching threshold condition. The percentage of correctly detected signs was 93 and 95 for triangular and circular respectively.

Despite that template matching technique is time consuming and can not be used for real-time application [5], Qian et al. [27] proposed template matching based on multi-level chain code histogram (MCCH) for real-time purposes with low computational cost. For prohibitory signs, they could achieve a recall of 95% and a precision of 90% in normal conditions. Other studies used edge, corner, and contour descriptors to detect traffic signs with template matching in real time. Authors in [12] for example, detected triangular and circular signs by scanning the input frames with various window sizes depending on shape information. The rectangle pattern matching was also used for circular detection. They achieved perfect detection accuracy of 100% when the sign is close enough as 22×22 px and over.

Last but not least, some researchers implement deep learning techniques for traffic signs detection based on shape information. Abdi and Meddeb [2] used Haar cascade detection algorithm to extract RoI using scanning window. Then, to eliminate false positives, they used convolutional Neural Network CNN with four convolution layers, one fully connected layer, and one output layer. High precision and recall were achieved by 98.81% and 98.22% respectively, and the system is able to run for real-time detection.

In the other hand, studies like [37,43] proposed methods with high performance but with costly time consumption. In particular, [37] introduced CNN after color transformation into grayscale with a fixed layer and mulitple learnable layers running with GTSD dataset. The precision-recall curve AUC achieved 98.68% for the testing set. Similarly, [43] proposed two CNNs one for detection only and another for simultaneous detection and classification. They could achieve impressive results compared to the up-to-date state-of-art as 91% and 88% on recall and accuracy respectively.

Among all the mentioned approaches for road traffic signs detection, there is no best way ever! It looks like that a mixture between those approaches may lead to great performance depending on the purpose and the type of application.

5 Recognition

The final phase of TSDR systems is recognition or classification which either classifies the detected candidate coming from the previous stage into one of road sign classes or rejects it. Several methods are available for recognizing and classifying the detected traffic signs, and they are mainly based onmachine learning/deep learning techniques.

In [10], a comparison study has been conducted to find the best traffic sign classifier among Multilayer Perceptron MLP, SVM, and Random Forest RF. Results showed that RF is the dominant in term of accuracy, time consumption, and dealing with large feature vector. So, a cascade classifier with several trees were used for candidates based on the background color of the signs. Testing results on three filmed videos gave 83.33% precision and 87.72% recall in total.

Shih et al. [29] classified traffic signs using Linear Support Vector Machine LSVM with HOG descriptor. The classifier was trained with GTSRB plus some data augmentation. The system was tested with GTSRB dataset and the classification obtaining 94.48% in recall and 96.12% in precision.

Some studies applied deep learning methods for classification phase of traffic signs. As the number of super classes in traffic signs is small, some studies like [8, 40] built n models in which n equal to the number of super classes. In [40], three CNN models with simple structure have been used for three traffic sign classes (Mandatory, Prohibitory, and Danger). They have been trained with GTSRB dataset. The testing results represent high accuracy with an average of 98.24% for all three traffic sign classes. Likewise, in [8] two backpropagational ANN: one for triangular signs and the other for circular signs, were structured. The authors tested their system on day/night time and on variant weather conditions including rain, and it shows robustness in performance in which the average accuracy for speed limit and warning signs is 97.85%. They referred that to the adaptation methods they applied during detection phase.

Table 2 summarizes and compares the mentioned studies in this paper. It is noticed that using deep learning algorithms, CNN in particular, enhances the performance dramatically. However, results are still fluctuating! From our opinion, there are many factors may affect the final results. First of all, the quality of the dataset used in training would have a great influence on the final results. In particular, some dataset lack the variations of signs, environmental circumstances, and negative samples which contradicts with reality. Furthermore, recognition stage is highly dependent on the previous stages (preprocessing and detection). So, it is important to spend more time on them in order to end up with less time and more accuracy in recognition phase.

6   Issues and Challenges

As was pointed out in the introduction to this paper, traffic signs were designed carefully in a very simple style to appeal human attention quickly while driving. However, it is not the case with machine recognition. In fact, there are many issues and challenges that can be faced during detecting and recognizing traffic signs. The key aspects of those problems can be listed as follows. All the below issues and challenges have caught researchers attention however, they are not fully solved yet.

- **Lighting inconsistency** [4,7,9,19,20,33,35] images are acquired during different time of the day. Sometimes, they get affected by the sun light or any external source of light. This leads to inconsistency in illuminations, especially when shades and reflections appear on signs. Moreover, up to our knowledge, most of the studies in this fields focus on day time detection and recognition only. Very few of them have considered night time.
- **Visibility and weather conditions** [2,7,20,33] different weather conditions, such as rain, snow, and fog make detection and recognition process challenging. Also, signs may be occluded by nature, like trees, or by human sabotage, like placing stickers on signs or scribbling over them which reduce their visibility.
- **Damages** [4,7,9,20,33,35] color of signs could be faded or rusted over time which complicates recognition process especially if the used algorithm is color-oriented. Also, signs can be tilted, rotated, flipped or positioned wrongly as a result of storms and natural effects.
- **Scene complexity and cascading** [4,7,20,33,35] when signs combined with complex background, it becomes hard to recognize them. Sometimes, more than one traffic signs appear in the same image. Also, street signs, such as store and advertisement signs, may appear together with traffic signs which increase the overall complexity. Worse yet, multiple signs are in some cases installed close to each other in which they overlap and appear as one sign. Hence, it becomes an issue as boundaries and edges are not clear enough to be recognized.
- **Motion and blurring** [4,7,33,35] taking pictures/videos while car is moving can cause motion blur effects on images. Add to that, using low resolution camera may result in noisy and blurry data specially with autofocus feature.
- **Different countries, different signs** [20,33] – some detection and recognition algorithms work accurately in some countries, but not in others. The main reason behind that is the differences in signs' shapes/colors among countries. The European traffic systems for example, are based on Vienna convention while American traffic systems are based on Manual on Uniform Traffic Control Devices (MUTCD). As a result, the speed signs in United Kingdom are rounded and red, but in North America they are rectangle and black/white with text on it, see Fig. 3.

Table 2. A comparison table that summarizes the mentioned studies in this paper.

Study	Year	Real time?	Dataset	Methodology			Signs included	Evaluation	
				Preprocessing	Detection	Recognition		Detection	Recognition
[29]	2017	yes	GTSDB GTSRB	RGB-> Grayscale-> RBCE	MSER	HOG + LSVM + voting approach	red & blue	TSD process time: 28.74 ms	TSR process time: 0.35 ms, Recall: 94.48%, Precision: 96.12%
[2]	2017	yes	GTSRB	-	Haar cascade + CNN	Linear SVM + 3D Augmentation	not mentioned	Recall: 98.22% Precession: 98.81%	Accuracy: 99.36%
[40]	2016	yes	GTSDB GTSRB CTSD	RGB-> normalized red Ohta space -> red and blue probability maps	MSER,HOG + multiclass SVM	CNN	red, blue, & yellow	For GTSDB and CTSD: Recall: 99.47%, 99.51% Time: 0.067, 0.090 sec	For GTSDB and CTSD: Accuracy: 98.24%, 98.77%
[43]	2016	no	Tsinghua-Tencent 100K Benchmark	-	CNN	CNN	not mentioned	Accuracy: 84% Recall: 94%	Accuracy: 88% Recall: 91%
[39]	2015	yes	GTSDB	RGB-> HSV and remove noise (using detection and retouching of point-like glares)	Modified Generalized Hough transform	Template Matching	red & triangular	Overall Accuracy of the system: 97.3%	
[27]	2015	yes	Database created by the authors	-	Template matching based on MCCH	No recognition	red, blue, yellow, circle, triangle, inverted triangle, & octagon	For Prohibitory signs: Recall: 95% Precision: 90%	-
[32]	2014	no	BelgiumTS	Normalized RBG	Adjustable extraction methods + cascade of AdaBoost + HOG + SVM	SVM	triangle, inverted triangle, circle-blue, circle-red, rectangle, & diamond	False negative: 0.5% False positive: 0.2%	Accuracy: 97%

(continued)

Table 2. (*continued*)

Study	Year	Real time?	Dataset	Methodology			Signs included	Evaluation	
				Preprocessing	Detection	Recognition		Detection	Recognition
[12]	2014	yes	Database created by the authors	Grayscale noise reduction filter & enhancement filter	Rectangle Pattern Matching (RPM) and circle detection modules	Multi-scan windows	triangle & circle	Not clear	Accuracy: up to 100% when the sign is closer with size over 22 × 22 px
[37]	2013	no	GTSDB	RGB-> extract Y only (Grayscale) via learning threshold using SVM	CNN + bootstrap method	-	triangle-red, circle-blue	AUC (Danger): 99.73% AUC (Mandatory): 97.62%	-
[10]	2012	yes	UK Road Signs DB	RGB-> Grayscale if sign with white background, RGB-> normalized red/blue if sign with colored background	MSER	HOG + Random Forest	all UK road signs	Not available	Recall: 83.33% Precision: 87.72% F-Measure: 0.85
[28]	2010	yes	Malaysian road signs	-	Hough transform	Library templates	circle, square, & octagon *some signs are excluded	Overall Accuracy of the system: 83.67%	
[26]	2009	yes	Database created by the authors	YCbCr	SOM-based neural approach	SOM-based neural approach	red	Processing time: 19–21 fps in normal conditions	Rates do not go below 100% with appropriate lighting
[8]	2006	no	Database created by the authors	-	Canny method + Hough transform	ANN	triangle, & circle	Accuracy (speed limit & warning): 95.75%	Accuracy (speed limit & warning): 97.85%
[14]	2001	no	Database created by the authors	Color segmentation using Ohta space thresholding	Conventional template-matching + Geometrical reasoning	Matching Pursuit (MP) filters	red, circle, & triangle	Accuracy: 94%	Accuracy: 92.5%

UK (mph)   Canada (km/h)   US (mph)

Fig. 3. Speed limit sign in three different countries (Color figure online)

7   Conclusion and Future Work

To conclude, it is important to have reliable TSDR systems as they become part of our life style while driving. This paper has intensively reviewed work have been done in preprocessing, detection, and recognition for road traffic signs. It also provides a list of the common used public datasets for traffic signs. Moreover, it discusses the problems and challenges related to this field.

For future work, we notice that almost all of the common public datasets are taken under different weather conditions during day time only. Non of them up to date have samples taken during night time. It is worth to collect and populate public datasets in which it has this variety between day and night time under different weather conditions.

In addition, most of the studies focus on particular shapes of signs, such as circle or triangle because they are considered as some of the crucial signs (prohibitory or danger) comparing to other types of signs which are less important in term of road safety. Yet, It would be great improvement if all type of signs are considered at once as they provide essential information to the driver, if exists!

Finally, traffic signs detection and recognition methodology are based on shape and colors despite that some signs are rich in text. For instance, a 'no entry' sign may have an extended sign underneath it stating in text some types of exception either in time or in vehicle types. A regular TSDR system will be able to tell the 'no entry' sign, but not the exceptions. Thus, studies in this field may extend their work to include text detection, recognition, and semantic analysis for traffic signs. This would take self-driving into a new level of reliability.

References

1. Critical reasons for crashes investigated in the national motor vehicle crash causation survey. U.S. Department of transportation, National Highway Traffic Safety Administration (2015)
2. Abdi, L., Meddeb, A.: Deep learning traffic sign detection, recognition and augmentation. In: Proceedings of the Symposium on Applied Computing, pp. 131–136. ACM (2017)
3. Belaroussi, R., Foucher, P., Tarel, J.P., Soheilian, B., Charbonnier, P., Paparoditis, N.: Road sign detection in images: a case study. In: 2010 20th International Conference on Pattern Recognition, pp. 484–488. IEEE (2010)

4. Dalve, A., Shiravale, S.: A survey on real time text detection and recognition from traffic panels. Int. J. Res. Appl. Sci. Eng. Technol. (IJRASET) **3**(XII), 2321–9653 (2015)
5. Dewan, P., Vig, R., Shukla, N., Das, B.: An overview of traffic signs recognition methods. Int. J. Comput. Appl. (2017). ISSN 0975–8887
6. de la Escalera, A., Armingol, J., Mata, M.: Traffic sign recognition and analysis for intelligent vehicles. Image Vis. Comput. **21**(3), 247–258 (2003)
7. Fu, M.Y., Huang, Y.S.: A survey of traffic sign recognition. In: 2010 International Conference on Wavelet Analysis and Pattern Recognition (ICWAPR), pp. 119–124. IEEE (2010)
8. Garcia-Garrido, M.A., Sotelo, M.A., Martin-Gorostiza, E.: Fast traffic sign detection and recognition under changing lighting conditions. In: 2006 IEEE Intelligent Transportation Systems Conference, pp. 811–816. IEEE (2006)
9. Gokul, S., Kumar, S.S., Giriprasad, S.: Survey-an exploration of various techniques for sign detection in traffic panels. ARPN J. Eng. Appl. Sci. **10**(9) (2015). ISSN 1819–6608
10. Greenhalgh, J., Mirmehdi, M.: Traffic sign recognition using MSER and random forests. In: 2012 Proceedings of the 20th European Conference on Signal Processing Conference (EUSIPCO), pp. 1935–1939. IEEE (2012)
11. Gudigar, A., Jagadale, B.N., Mahesh, P.K., Raghavendra, U.: Kernel based automatic traffic sign detection and recognition using SVM. In: Mathew, J., Patra, P., Pradhan, D.K., Kuttyamma, A.J. (eds.) ICECCS 2012. CCIS, vol. 305, pp. 153–161. Springer, Heidelberg (2012). https://doi.org/10.1007/978-3-642-32112-2_19
12. Hoang, A.T., Tetsushi, K., Yamamoto, M.: Low cost hardware implementation for traffic sign detection system. In: 2014 IEEE Asia Pacific Conference on Circuits and Systems (APCCAS), pp. 363–366. IEEE, November 2014
13. Houben, S., Stallkamp, J., Salmen, J., Schlipsing, M., Igel, C.: Detection of traffic signs in real-world images: the German traffic sign detection benchmark. In: The 2013 International Joint Conference on Neural Networks (IJCNN), pp. 1–8. IEEE (2013)
14. Hsu, S.H., Huang, C.L.: Road sign detection and recognition using matching pursuit method. Image Vis. Comput. **19**(3), 119–129 (2001)
15. Kuo, W.J., Lin, C.C.: Two-stage road sign detection and recognition. In: 2007 IEEE International Conference on Multimedia and Expo, pp. 1427–1430. IEEE (2007)
16. Larsson, F.: Traffic signs dataset, March 2014. http://www.cvl.isy.liu.se/research/datasets/traffic-signs-dataset/
17. Larsson, F., Felsberg, M.: Using fourier descriptors and spatial models for traffic sign recognition. In: Heyden, A., Kahl, F. (eds.) SCIA 2011. LNCS, vol. 6688, pp. 238–249. Springer, Heidelberg (2011). https://doi.org/10.1007/978-3-642-21227-7_23
18. Mathias, M., Timofte, R., Benenson, R., Van Gool, L.: Traffic sign recognition—how far are we from the solution? In: The 2013 International Joint Conference on Neural Networks (IJCNN), pp. 1–8. IEEE (2013)
19. Messelodi, S., Modena, C.M., Porzi, L., Chippendale, P.: i-Street: detection, identification, augmentation of street plates in a touristic mobile application. In: Murino, V., Puppo, E. (eds.) ICIAP 2015. LNCS, vol. 9280, pp. 194–204. Springer, Cham (2015). https://doi.org/10.1007/978-3-319-23234-8_19
20. Møgelmose, A., Trivedi, M.M., Moeslund, T.B.: Vision-based traffic sign detection and analysis for intelligent driver assistance systems: perspectives and survey. IEEE Trans. Intell. Transp. Syst. **13**(4), 1484–1497 (2012)

21. Mukhometzianov, R., Wang, Y.: Machine learning techniques for traffic sign detection. arXiv preprint arXiv:1712.04391 (2017)
22. Murugan, S., Karthika, R.: A survey on traffic sign detection techniques using text mining. Asian J. Comput. Sci. Technol. **8**(S1), 21–24 (2019)
23. für Neuroinformatik, I.: German traffic signs benchmarks, September 2016. http://benchmark.ini.rub.de/?section=gtsrb&subsection=news
24. Paclík, P., Novovičová, J., Pudil, P., Somol, P.: Road sign classification using laplace kernel classifier. Pattern Recogn. Lett. **21**(13–14), 1165–1173 (2000)
25. Palus, H.: Representations of colour images in different colour spaces. In: Sangwine, S.J., Horne, R.E.N. (eds.) The Colour Image Processing Handbook, pp. 67–90. Springer, Boston (1998). https://doi.org/10.1007/978-1-4615-5779-1_4
26. Prieto, M.S., Allen, A.R.: Using self-organising maps in the detection and recognition of road signs. Image Vis. Comput. **27**(6), 673–683 (2009)
27. Qian, R., Zhang, B., Yue, Y., Coenen, F.: Traffic sign detection by template matching based on multi-level chain code histogram. In: 2015 12th International Conference on Fuzzy Systems and Knowledge Discovery (FSKD), pp. 2400–2404. IEEE (2015)
28. Sallah, S.S.M., Hussin, F.A., Yusoff, M.Z.: Shape-based road sign detection and recognition for embedded application using MATLAB. In: 2010 International Conference on Intelligent and Advanced Systems, pp. 1–5. IEEE (2010)
29. Shih, P.C., Tsai, C.Y., Hsu, C.F.: An efficient automatic traffic sign detection and recognition method for smartphones. In: 2017 10th International Congress on Image and Signal Processing, BioMedical Engineering and Informatics (CISP-BMEI), pp. 1–5. IEEE (2017)
30. Siogkas, G.K., Dermatas, E.S.: Detection, tracking and classification of road signs in adverse conditions. In: 2006 IEEE Mediterranean Electrotechnical Conference, MELECON 2006, pp. 537–540. IEEE (2006)
31. Sumi, K., Arun Kumar, M.: Detection, and recognition of road traffic signs-a survey. Int. J. Comput. Appl. **160**(3) (2017). ISSN 0975–8887
32. Timofte, R., Zimmermann, K., Van Gool, L.: Multi-view traffic sign detection, recognition, and 3D localisation. Mach. Vis. Appl. **25**(3), 633–647 (2014)
33. Toth, Š.: Difficulties of traffic sign recognition. In: 7th Winter School of Mathematics Applied to ICT, MICT 2012, SACHTICKY (2012)
34. Vertan, C., Boujemaa, N.: Color texture classification by normalized color space representation. In: ICPR, p. 3584. IEEE (2000)
35. Wali, S.B., Hannan, M.A., Hussain, A., Samad, S.A.: Comparative survey on traffic sign detection and recognition: a review. Przeglad Elektrotechniczny (2015). ISSN 0033–2097
36. Wu, W.Y., Hsieh, T.C., Lai, C.S.: Extracting road signs using the color information. Int. J. Comput. Electr. Autom. Control Inf. Eng. **1**(8), 2391–2395 (2007). http://waset.org/Publications?p=8
37. Wu, Y., Liu, Y., Li, J., Liu, H., Hu, X.: Traffic sign detection based on convolutional neural networks. In: The 2013 International Joint Conference on Neural Networks (IJCNN), pp. 1–7. IEEE (2013)
38. Yakimov, P.Y.: Preprocessing digital images for quickly and reliably detecting road signs. Pattern Recogn. Image Anal. **25**(4), 729–732 (2015)
39. Yakimov, P., Fursov, V.: Traffic signs detection and tracking using modified Hough transform. In: 2015 12th International Joint Conference on e-Business and Telecommunications (ICETE), vol. 5, pp. 22–28. IEEE (2015)
40. Yang, Y., Luo, H., Xu, H., Wu, F.: Towards real-time traffic sign detection and classification. IEEE Trans. Intell. Transp. Syst. **17**(7), 2022–2031 (2016)

41. Yang, Y., Wu, F.: Real-time traffic sign detection via color probability model and integral channel features. In: Li, S., Liu, C., Wang, Y. (eds.) CCPR 2014. CCIS, vol. 484, pp. 545–554. Springer, Heidelberg (2014). https://doi.org/10.1007/978-3-662-45643-9_58

42. Zhang, S.: Traffic sign detection for vision-based driver's assistance in land-based vehicles. Technical report, School of Aeronautics and Astronautics-Stanford University (2016)

43. Zhu, Z., Liang, D., Zhang, S., Huang, X., Li, B., Hu, S.: Traffic-sign detection and classification in the wild. In: The IEEE Conference on Computer Vision and Pattern Recognition (CVPR), June 2016

Machine Learning for Automobile Driver Identification Using Telematics Data

Hanadi Alhamdan[1(✉)] and Musfira Jilani[2(✉)]

[1] College of Computer and Information Sciences, Princess Nourah bint
Abdulrahman University, Riyadh, Saudi Arabia
halhamdan@pnu.edu.sa
[2] School of Computing, Dublin City University, Dublin, Ireland
musfira.jilani@dcu.ie

Abstract. Recent years have seen rapid developments in the automotive industry
and the Internet of Things (IoT). One such development is the use of onboard
telematic devices that generate data about the car and the driver's behaviour. This
data can be used for identifying drivers through their driving habits. This paper
proposes a novel driver identification methodology for extracting and learning
driving signatures embedded within the telematics data. First, features representatives of driving style are extracted and derived such as longitudinal acceleration,
longitudinal jerk and heading speed from the raw telematics data of GPS coordinates, speed and heading angle. Next, statistical feature matrices are obtained for
these features using sliding windows. Finally, several traditional machine learning
models are trained over these matrices to learn individual drivers. Results show a
driver identification accuracy of 90% for a dataset consisting of only two drivers;
the accuracy falls gradually as the number of drivers increases.

Keywords: Telematics · Driver identification · Machine learning · Signal
processing

1 Introduction

Smart vehicles are spreading rapidly throughout the world. They help to meet a basic
demand of modern society, transportation. However, with increased proliferation of
smart vehicles, there is also a growing concern about the associated safety and security
risks [1]; in light of this, it is reasonable to explore potential ways to reduce these risks.
In this paper we propose to study the problem of driver identification, which can be
defined as the ability to recognise drivers through their individual driving behaviours,
including how the driver controls the vehicle in the driving scene under external
conditions [2]. Driver identification could also be used to authenticate a driver for
security purposes, or to build other types of applications, such as personalising an
automobile's functions to fit the driver's preferred configuration [3]. Moreover, driver
identification could be a key pricing factor for auto insurance companies (e.g., pay-as-
you-drive and pay-how-you-drive). Finally, driver identification can also form the basis
of several applications such as detection of driver fatigue, which might help in reducing
road accidents [4].

© Springer Nature Switzerland AG 2019
A. Alfaries et al. (Eds.): ICC 2019, CCIS 1097, pp. 290–300, 2019.
https://doi.org/10.1007/978-3-030-36365-9_24

Toward the goal of effectively identifying drivers this paper presents a novel methodology that makes use of telematics data generated by on-board devices fitted on vehicles that generate useful data about the vehicle. First, features representatives of driving style are extracted and derived from raw telematics data. These features include longitudinal acceleration, longitudinal jerk and heading speed. Next, statistical feature matrices are obtained for these features using sliding windows. Finally, supervised machine learning models based on Random Forest, Nearest Neighbours, and Support Vector Machines are developed to learn individual drivers. Results show a driver identification accuracy of 90% for a dataset consisting of only two drivers. The accuracy falls gradually as the number of drivers increases.

The rest of the paper is structured as follows. In Sect. 2 we review the background and related works on the topics of driver identification and machine learning methods used. Section 3 describes the proposed methodology. Section 4 presents a set of experiments which evaluate the proposed models. Finally, in Sect. 5 we draw conclusions from the work presented and discuss possible future research directions.

2 Background and Related Work

2.1 Driver Identification

Previous research on driver identification was conducted primarily in a controlled environment or using simulated data. For instance, Zhang et al. [5] and Wakita et al. [6] developed predictive models for driver identification using data collected from a simulation environment. Although these studies provide insights on modelling driver identification, they cannot be compared to natural situations because they do not consider normal conditions, such as weather and traffic.

Van Ly et al. [7] examined the use of mobile-sensor data to distinguish between two drivers. They used one car on a controlled route, which included residential and highway segments, and applied supervised learning. Their results had an accuracy of 60% using the support vector machine (SVM) method.

Ezzin et al. [3] used real driving datasets consisting of measurements taken from in-vehicle sensors to address the problem of driver identification. The study used several models, including decision tree, random forest, extra trees, K-nearest neighbour (KNN), SVM, gradient boosting, and adaptive boosting (AdaBoost). Their results showed that it is possible to identify drivers with high accuracy during the first three minutes of driving, using a reduced volume of sensor data collected from a judiciously chosen set of sensors.

Driver identification using data collected from multiple sensors and cameras was explored using Gaussian mixture models (GMM) by Miyajima et al. [8] and Nishiwaki et al. [9]. These driving-simulator studies differentiated 276 drivers with 77% accuracy. Enev et al. [10] used a controlled and predefined route to investigate the possibility of using in-vehicle sensor data to identify drivers based on their natural driving behaviours. They concluded that a random forest (RF) model outperformed other supervised learning models, achieving 87% accuracy in differentiating between 15 drivers when using only the brake-pedal signal, and 99% accuracy when using five sensor signals.

The most promising study in this area was conducted by Wang et al. [11], who computed new signals from the telematics data, including longitudinal acceleration, longitudinal jerk and steering speed. The new features helped to capture drivers' basic behaviour, such as the harshness or smoothness of their driving. The authors computed the mean, median and standard deviation of the new signals and applied a random forest model to distinguish between 30 drivers, achieving 100% accuracy from six minutes of driving data.

2.2 Machine Learning Methods

Random Forest. The random forest algorithm [12], developed by Leo Breiman, is an ensemble learning method designed for decision tree classifiers. It creates a group of decision trees (Tk) from a bootstrap sample (Lk), and lets them vote for the most popular class, where k is the total number of trees to be constructed. There are two sources of randomness in random forest, bagging and subspace sampling. Each tree is grown using a learning sample that is bootstrapped from the entire dataset (L) with replacement, and each bootstrapped sample uses a randomly selected subset from the pool of all variables [12].

Previous studies have shown random forest to be an effective and powerful model for driver identification, and it has many advantages that make it appropriate for this study: it can build a highly accurate predication model for multiple classes, using categorical and continuous variables with both linear and non-linear relationships; it can be used to rank the importance of variables; and it is a flexible method that requires few preliminary data assumptions and rarely overfits the dataset.

Support Vector Machines. The SVM [13] is a supervised learning method that generates input-output mapping functions from a labelled training dataset. For classification, input data are transformed to a high-dimensional feature space using nonlinear kernel functions, to which the t input data become more separable when compared to the original input space. Hyperplanes of the maximum margin are then created [13].

SVMs have been used with huge datasets encompassing millions of dimensions. They have been especially effective with medical images, text classification, and so forth. The major drawback of SVM is that it provides a kind of black-box model, making it difficult to interpret the model parameters. Also, SVMs do not directly support multi-class classification [13]. Van Ly et al. [7], Enev et al. [10], and Ezzin et al. [3] used SVM for driver identification.

K-Nearest Neighbours. KNN [14] is one of the simplest algorithms and can be used for classification as well as regression predictive problems. Even with such simplicity, it can give highly competitive results. However, it is more widely used in classification problems where a case is classified by a majority vote of its neighbours and assigned to the most common class amongst its nearest neighbours, as measured by a distance function.

To apply KNN we need to choose an appropriate value for k as the performance of classification is highly dependent on this value. Consequently, KNN is often referred to as a *lazy learner*, and it is computationally expensive. Enev et al. [10] and Ezzin et al.

[3] used KNN for driver identification. Previous studies showed that the optimal choice of K depends on the data. For our study, using trial-and-error, K was chosen to be 5.

3   Methodology

The structure of this section is as follows. It begins with an outline of the overall components of the proposed framework in Sect. 3.1, followed in the next sections by a brief explanation of the major processes.

3.1   Framework Outline

As shown in Fig. 1, the proposed framework was composed of five phases: (1) Data gathering; (2) Data pre-processing; (3) Feature engineering; (4) Feature transformation; (5) Modelling; and (6) Evaluation.

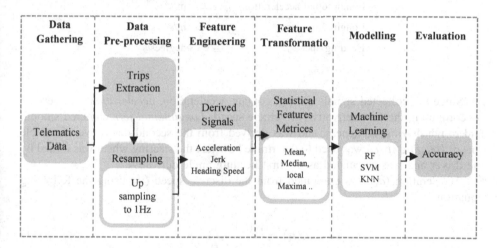

Fig. 1. Framework outline

3.2   Data Pre-processing

The data used in this research were generated in completely naturalistic environment. Hence, the first step is to extract meaningful trips from the data streams. Toward this goal of extracting trips, a sequential procedure was developed by dividing the GPS traces into trips based on an empirical time gap threshold [15]. The start of the trip was recognised when the vehicle's speed changed from zero to some larger value. The trip was considered running until the vehicle's speed went to zero and remained there for more than 120 s. If the time gap was smaller than 120 s, the trip was considered continuing until the trip end point was defined, then the total time for each trip was calculated. Trips longer than 10 min were included in the analyses.

Next, data resampling was performed. Essentially, up-sampling by interpolation was conducted to increase the resolution of the data from 0.1 Hz to 1 Hz. Such up-sampling is shown to improve the performance of machine learning methods [16].

3.3 Feature Engineering

Raw telematics data consisted of features such as *vehicle speed* and *heading angle*. However, previous studies [11] have shown that these features alone cannot help in effectively identifying drivers. Hence, three additional features namely, *Longitudinal Acceleration*, *longitudinal jerk*, and *heading speed* respectively were derived from the raw data as shown in Table 1. These features help in effectively capturing driver's intrinsic behaviour such as harsh or smooth driving [11].

Table 1. Derived signals

Derived signal	Symbol	Unit
Longitudinal acceleration	$a_x = \frac{dv_x}{d_t}$	m/s^2
Longitudinal jerk	$j_x = \frac{d2v_x}{d_t}$	m/s^3
Heading speed	$s_x = \frac{d\theta_x}{d_t}$	degrees/s

Since the collected signals did not contain acceleration, *acceleration* was derived by computing the first derivative of vehicle speed. *Longitudinal jerk* captured smooth and rough driving subtleness, and was derived from the second derivative of vehicle speed. *Heading speed* was used to determine how fast the steering wheel was turned by the driver and was calculated as the first heading angle derivative.

Acceleration (a_x) was computed from the discrete speed (v_x) using the following equation:

$$a_x(t_2) = \frac{v_x(t_2) - v_x(t_1)}{t_2 - t_1} \tag{1}$$

where t_2 is the current time stamp, and t_1 is the previous time stamp.

Successively the longitudinal jerk, (j_x), was computed as:

$$j_x(t_2) = \frac{a_x(t_2) - a_x(t_1)}{t_2 - t_1} \tag{2}$$

The heading speed (s_x) was calculated from the heading angle (θ_x) using the following equation:

$$s_x(t_2) = \frac{\theta_x(t_2) - \theta_x(t_1)}{t_2 - t_1} \tag{3}$$

3.4   Feature Transformation

To build an efficient model using the few signals recorded it was necessary to transform the data into an easily consumable form that captured the driving signature. This data transformation helped to develop a model that was easy to implement and less computationally expensive [11].

Sliding Windows. The data were divided into sliding windows from which the statistical features matrices were extracted. The sliding window length (number of samples) and the percentage of overlap with previous and successive windows were set to default values and subsequently optimised. The sliding window size used in this study was 3 min (180 s) with no overlap.

Data Standardisation. The data were standardised using z-score normalisation as follows:

$$s_i(t) = \frac{s_i(t) - \widehat{s_i}}{\sigma_i} \tag{4}$$

where σ_i is the standard deviation and $\widehat{s_i}$ is the time average of s_i within a time window of size 180, for signals $i = 1, 2, 3, 4, 5$. This normalisation was used to prevent data skewness and to include all signals on the same scale [11].

Statistical Features Matrices. Using the vehicle speed and the heading angle from the raw telematics signals, the longitudinal acceleration, longitudinal jerk, and heading speed from the derived signals, statistical features matrices were constructed from each sliding window to capture most of the driving signature.

For each window, the statistical features computed include *mean, median, variance, standard deviation, skewness, local maxima* and *kurtosis*.

Table 2 provides brief definitions for each of these features. The resulting statistical feature matrix (5 signals $\times$ 7 statistical features = 35 columns) was used as machine learning input.

Table 2. Statistical feature matrix explanation [16, 17]

Feature	Explanation
Mean	The sum of the values divided by the number of values
Median	The middle value that separated the higher half from the lower half of a measure
Variance	The expected squared deviation of a random variable from its mean
Standard deviation	The square root of variance
Skewness	A measure of the asymmetry of the distribution about the mean
Local maxima	The largest value of the function
Kurtosis	A measure of the frequency distribution tails

4 Experiments and Results

4.1 Data Description

We examined the anonymous telematics data from 25 different drivers, provided by MachinesTalk [18], a data analytics company in Saudi Arabia. No personal information on the drivers was recorded.

The data were collected over 24 h from 25 drivers in a natural environment that included regular everyday trips in various regions of Saudi Arabia. Data collection was enabled by OBD-II plug-in devices that transmit a range of signals through the CAN bus at a frequency of 0.1 H (an interval of once every ten seconds). The dataset contained a unique device ID, UTC timestamps, and the GPS-based measurements of the longitude, latitude, vehicle speed, and heading angle. Table 3 presents a list of the data features. Vehicle telematics data signals used for the machine learning application included vehicle speed and heading angle. An illustration of these signals collected from a sample trip is shown in Fig. 2.

4.2 Evaluation Metrics

Previous studies have shown that accuracy is the most important evaluation metric for driver identification methodologies [2, 6–11]. Hence, the main evaluation method used in this research is accuracy. Accuracy provides an overall measure of a classifier's quality and is defined as the proportion of all instances that are correctly classified. It is expressed as:

$$Accuracy = \frac{TP + TN}{TP + TN + FP + FN} \tag{5}$$

where TP, TN, FP, and FN are the true positives, true negatives, false positives and false negatives, respectively [19].

4.3 Results

As a first step, the data set were split into the training set (75% of the data), used to build the models, and testing set (25% of the data), used to evaluate the performance of the developed models. Then, a statistical features matrices representation was obtained for both the training and testing sets.

The models were tested in phases, starting with two drivers as a binary classification problem, and then increasing the number of drivers to five, ten, fifteen and twenty-five. The results of evaluating the models on the testing set for the different subgroups are presented in Table 4, which shows that the random forest model outperformed the other models, achieving a classification accuracy of 90% with two drivers, and 88%, 76% and 72% with 5, 10 and 25 drivers, respectively. Given the complexity of the problem and an analysis of previous work in the area [6–10], these scores can be considered as reasonably good. The hypothesis is that the performance of the model decreases as the number of drivers increases, since the process becomes more complicated. The results in Table 4 confirm this hypothesis.

(a)

Time	Longitude	Latitude	Speed	Heading
18:01	46.643325	24.76196	0	200
18:01	46.643362	24.76023	34	220
18:01	46.643092	24.75992	16	246
18:01	46.643092	24.75992	16	246
...	....	.....	.....	....

(b)

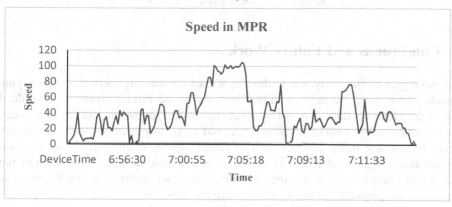

(c)

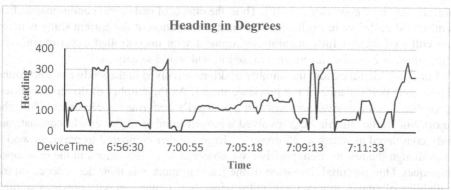

Fig. 2. A sample of telematics data for a trip: (a) raw GPS data, (b) plot of the speed, (c) plot of the heading.

Table 3. Dataset features

Feature	Explanation
Device Id	Unique identifiers for the vehicles
Timestamp	The UTC time for each location
Longitude, Latitude	The GPS coordinates of each location
Vehicle speed	The speed of the vehicle in miles per hour
Heading angle	The vehicle's steering wheel angle in degrees

Table 4. Driver identification accuracy for the traditional machine learning models applied to the statistical-feature matrices for different numbers of drivers

No. of drivers	2	5	10	25
RF	0.90	0.88	0.76	0.72
SVM	0.90	0.85	0.77	0.63
KNN	0.87	0.81	0.77	0.62

5   Conclusions and Future Work

The main goal of this study was to develop a machine learning method for identifying individual drivers by extracting and learning their unique driving signatures embedded within the telematics data. Toward achieving this goal, appropriate data pre-processing, feature engineering, feature transformation and modelling methods were developed. Results show that using features such as vehicle speed, heading angle, longitudinal acceleration, longitudinal jerk, and heading speed; a window size of 180 s, a random forest based model can identify drivers with an accuracy of 90% for two drivers. The accuracy falls gradually as the number of drivers increases.

While driver identification has been actively explored, previous experiments have mostly used simulated data or have been conducted in a controlled environment, under carefully designed conditions [5–10]. Thus, the effects of real-world conditions, such as weather and traffic, were excluded. The main contribution of the current study is using data collected from a fully natural environment with uncontrolled experimental settings. Thus, our results can be generalised to real world situations.

For driver identification, the number of drivers involved in the study has a profound effect on the performance of the proposed model. As the number of drivers increases, the problem's complexity increases and the model's performance decreases. Thus, the majority of studies in this field involved a limited number of drivers. In contrast, our study considered as many as 25 drivers, a large number compared to previous works.

Although the results were positive, we observed some limitations in the developed techniques. One potential limitation of the learning models is their dependence on the availability of signals that can transmit driving style. Compared with previous studies, our data lack many signals that require special sensors, such as brake and gas pedal position. These signals are important for distinguishing one driver from another [10], and their absence might affect the results. While promising results were obtained with the available signals, we believe that datasets containing more signals may improve the model performance.

Acknowledgements. The dataset used in this study was provided by MachinesTalk [18], a data analytics company in Saudi Arabia. The authors are thankful to Mr. Mohammed Alkhoshail of MachinesTalk, who arranged for access to the telematics data and provided us the opportunity to work with it.

References

1. Bishop, R.: Intelligent vehicle applications worldwide. IEEE Intell. Syst. Appl. **15**, 78–81 (2000)
2. Martinez, C.M., Heucke, M., Wang, F.-Y., Gao, B., Cao, D.: Driving style recognition for intelligent vehicle control and advanced driver assistance: a survey. IEEE Trans. Intell. Transp. Syst. **19**, 666–676 (2018)
3. Ezzini, S., Berrada, I., Ghogho, M.: Who is behind the wheel? Driver identification and fingerprinting. J. Big Data. **5**, 9 (2018)
4. Li, Z., Chen, L., Peng, J., Wu, Y.: Automatic detection of driver fatigue using driving operation information for transportation safety. Sensors **17**, 1212 (2017)
5. Zhang, X., Zhao, X., Rong, J.: A study of individual characteristics of driving behavior based on hidden Markov model. Sens. Transducers **167**, 194 (2014)
6. Wakita, T., et al.: Driver identification using driving behavior signals. IEICE Trans. Inf. Syst. **89**, 1188–1194 (2006)
7. Van Ly, M., Martin, S., Trivedi, M.M.: Driver classification and driving style recognition using inertial sensors. In: 2013 IEEE Intelligent Vehicles Symposium (IV), pp. 1040–1045. IEEE Press, New York (2013)
8. Miyajima, C., et al.: Driver modeling based on driving behavior and its evaluation in driver identification. Proc. IEEE **95**, 427–437 (2007)
9. Nishiwaki, Y., Ozawa, K., Wakita, T., Miyajima, C., Itou, K., Takeda, K.: Driver identification based on spectral analysis of driving behavioral signals. In: Abut, H., Hansen, J.H.L., Takeda, K. (eds.) Advances for In-Vehicle and Mobile Systems, pp. 25–34. Springer, Heidelberg (2007). https://doi.org/10.1007/978-0-387-45976-9_3
10. Enev, M., Takakuwa, A., Koscher, K., Kohno, T.: Automobile driver fingerprinting. Proc. Priv. Enhanc. Technol. **2016**, 34–50 (2016)
11. Wang, B., Panigrahi, S., Narsude, M., Mohanty, A.: Driver identification using vehicle telematics data. SAE Technical Paper (2017)
12. Breiman, L.: Random forests. Mach. Learn. **45**, 5–32 (2001)
13. Wang, L.: Support Vector Machines: Theory and Applications, vol. 177. Springer, New York (2005). https://doi.org/10.1007/b95439
14. Cover, T.M., Hart, P.E.: Nearest neighbor pattern classification. IEEE Trans. Inf. Theory **13**, 21–27 (1967)
15. Zhang, L., Dalyot, S., Eggert, D., Sester, M.: Multi-stage approach to travel-mode segmentation and classification of GPS traces. In: International Archives of the Photogrammetry, Remote Sensing and Spatial Information Sciences. [Geospatial Data Infrastructure: From Data Acquisition and Updating to Smarter Services] 38, pp. 87–93 (2011)
16. Rabiner, L.R., Gold, B., Yuen, C.K.: Theory and Application of Digital Signal Processing. Prentice-Hall, Englewood Cliffs (1975). (p. 777)

17. Johnson, R.R., Kuby, P.J.: Elementary Statistics. Cengage Learning, Boston (2011)
18. MachinesTalk. www.machinestalk.com/
19. Sokolova, M., Japkowicz, N., Szpakowicz, S.: Beyond accuracy, F-Score and ROC: a family of discriminant measures for performance evaluation. In: Sattar, A., Kang, B.-H. (eds.) AI 2006. LNCS (LNAI), vol. 4304, pp. 1015–1021. Springer, Heidelberg (2006). https://doi.org/10.1007/11941439_114

Employee Turnover Prediction Using Machine Learning

Lama Alaskar[1]([✉]), Martin Crane[2]([✉]), and Mai Alduailij[3]([✉])

[1] College of Computer and Information Sciences, Princess Nourah bint
Abdulrahman University, Riyadh, Saudi Arabia
lama.m.alaskar@gmail.com
[2] School of Computing, Dublin City University, Dublin, Ireland
martin.crane@dcu.ie
[3] College of Computer and Information Sciences, Princess Nourah bint
Abdulrahman University, Riyadh, Saudi Arabia
MAAlduailij@pnu.edu.sa

Abstract. High employee turnover is a common problem that can affect
organizational performance and growth. The ability to predict employee turnover would be an invaluable tool for any organization seeking to retain
employees and predict their future behavior. This study employed machine
learning (ML) algorithms to predict whether employees would leave a company.
It presented a comparative performance combination of five ML algorithms and
three Feature Selection techniques. In this experiment, the best predictors were
identified using the SelectKBest, Recursive Feature Elimination (RFE) and
Random Forest (RF) model. Different ML algorithms were trained, which
included logistic regression, decision tree (DT), naïve Bayes, support vector
machine (SVM) and AdaBoost with optimal hyperparameters. In the last phase
of the experiment, the predictive models' performance was evaluated using
several critical metrics. The empirical results have demonstrated that two predictive models performed better: DT with SelectKBest and the SVM-polynomial
kernel using RF.

Keywords: Employee turnover · Machine learning · Support vector machine ·
Feature selection · Decision tree

1 Introduction

One of the most valuable assets of any organization is its employees. The key to the
success of any organization is attracting and retaining talent. Human resources
(HR) play an essential role in driving organizational performance and helping develop
a company, and those resources have a substantial influence on company performance.
Further, one of the most common issues affecting organizational performance and
growth is the phenomenon of employee turnover, particularly when it may be unex-
pected, or when a departing employee held an important position within the organization. In any company it is essential to retain skilled employees, as they are considered
a crucial element of HR management (HRM).

© Springer Nature Switzerland AG 2019
A. Alfaries et al. (Eds.): ICC 2019, CCIS 1097, pp. 301–316, 2019.
https://doi.org/10.1007/978-3-030-36365-9_25

Significant growth in the volume of HR data has created a desire to extract meaningful information from those data. Ideally, this large volume of data would be used to identify behavioural patterns, and those patterns would be understood to create the knowledge needed to help decision-makers improve policies that both increase employee performance and maintain high levels of employee satisfaction.

Employee turnover may be one of the biggest challenges facing many companies today. Use of machine-learning (ML) techniques, like those discussed in this study, to develop predictive models can potentially help a company identify staff that are likely considering leaving. Knowing the most important factors that lead to turnover can help provide a crucial element to the HRM system. Talent retention plans and strategies can then be used to address this issue in an effective and timely manner to enhance employee performance and job satisfaction, and in turn, minimize departures.

This study proposed several supervised ML algorithms in order to find the one most suitable for the HR domain. In addition, the study identified the predictors (or features) that contributed most to employee turnover, which could be used to help decision-makers both manage new staff and analyse the departure of existing employees to improve overall employee retention rates. The study also employed a survival analysis technique to determine time-to-turnover within an organization.

The feature selection (FS) technique was applied on proposed models that offered the best prediction results. This resulted in an optimal feature subset that greatly affected the prediction results.

A combination of five ML models and three FS techniques were created, and the experiment was conducted using the train-validate-test and 10-fold cross-validation methods. The proposed models that were developed for predicting employee turnover were a naïve Bayes classifier, a decision tree (DT) classifier, logistic regression (LR), a support vector machine (SVM) and an AdaBoost ensemble classifier. The popular FS techniques were the f_classif function using the SelectKBest method, Recursive Feature Elimination (RFE), and the Random Forest (RF) model.

The performance of the predictive models was studied using the critical metrics for accuracy, sensitivity, precision, specificity, F1-score, misclassification rate, and AUC value.

Experimental comparisons were made to address several key research questions (RQs). However, the results of this study also demonstrated the value of prediction outcomes to decision-makers in their efforts to successfully manage human capital.

This study aims to improve employee retention plans for organizations. Toward that end, it sought to answer the following the RQs:

- RQ1: Can a prediction model determine whether an employee will leave the company (thus, contribute to turnover) or not?
- RQ2: What are the key factors or best predictors that significantly contribute to employee turnover?

The rest of this paper is organized into five sections. Review of the literature is examined in Sect. 2, and an overview of the proposed methods used in the experiment is presented in Sect. 3. Sections 4 and 5 show research methodology and results, respectively. Section 6 is the conclusions of this paper.

2 Literature Review

In recent years, the employee-departure phenomenon has gained considerable attention within the data mining (DM) domain. It is becoming increasingly necessary for organizations to attempt to predict employee turnover and to determine the factors most effective in helping retain employees going forward. In this section, the DM techniques and experiment methodologies are discussed.

In [1], researchers concluded that proper integration between HRM and data mining would improve the recruitment and decision-making processes, which in turn would significantly reduce turnover. Moreover, the researchers showed that the probabilistic neural network (PNN), support vector machine (SVM), and k-nearest neighbours (KNN) models were sensitive to parameters. Conversely, they found that the naïve Bayes classifier is both the most user-friendly and demonstrated high performance in the classification problem. The random forest model outperformed other classifiers with 91% accuracy, followed by the naïve Bayes classifier at 88.8%, while SVM was found to be the least accurate [1]. In [2], researchers employed four prominent models for churn prediction, including decision tree (DT), KNN, artificial neural network (ANN), and SVM models. The authors found that the ANN model slightly outperformed the SVM model. Meanwhile, the proposed hybrid model, which combined four classifiers, was found to be more accurate, at 95% in precision and recall measures than the other four models. In other work, the unsupervised DM method employed by [3] for predicting turnover among technology experts, along with clustering analysis, involved a self-organizing map (SOM) and a hybrid artificial neural network. These data were obtained from surveys of Taiwanese company employees. Three models were used, k-mean, SOM with a backpropagation network algorithm (BPN), and BPN. The SOM–BPN model had the highest accuracy at 92%.

As data mining has a role in selecting candidates in order to limit turnover, empirical research has shown practical benefits from using data-mining processes to create useful rules for companies [4]. This empirical research has shown the viability of using decision trees to create useful rules for HRM within the semiconductor industry. Another study surveyed ML techniques and compared the models used in predicting customer-churn behaviour [5]. The results indicated that ML algorithms, such as SVM could be extended to build accurate predictive models for employee turnover [5]. The comparison revealed that SVM outperformed other classifiers that have higher accuracy score. In [6], two proposed methods, DT and ANN, were examined to both manage and prevent turnover for a Taiwanese telecommunications company. The resulting research revealed that ANN performed better in predicting employee churn [6].

In a practical experiment [7], data extracted from the first two months of an employee contract was used to predict departure in the third month. In this study, an understanding of whether call centre employees would continue through to the third month, thereby earning permanent contracts, was of importance to the human resource manager. The results of various predictive models were shown using 10-fold cross-validations, where the naïve Bayes algorithm slightly outperformed other techniques, with an accuracy of 85%.

A further overview of the recent literature on turnover prediction is provided in [8]. The literature on churn analysis has employed intelligent data analysis in addressing the turnover issue through construction of predictive models (such as SVM).

Another study demonstrated the effectiveness of logistic regression to predict voluntary employee turnover [9]. The data in this research were collected by a private company in Belgium specializing in human resources. The finding was that the AUC of logistic regression was around 74%. The authors concluded that the results of this study helped the HR manager prepare interviews with the at-risk group to prevent and reduce turnover in the company.

Despite other efforts in turnover prediction, no research examined different feature selection techniques. Hence, this paper has attempted to improve performance predictive models. This research has employed various techniques to select important features, and it has compared those techniques with different models. In addition, optimized models by hyperparameters such as grid search are discussed.

3 Methods

3.1 Logistic Regression

Logistic regression (LR) is a kind of classification approach that measures a relationship between the target variable in dichotomies (such as no turnover/turnover) and one or more explanatory variables. The LR calculation is shown in Eq. 1 [9].

$$y = e^{\left(b_0 + \sum_{i=1}^{p} b_i, x_i\right)} / 1 + e^{\left(b_0 + \sum_{i=1}^{p} b_i, x_i\right)} \tag{1}$$

Where b_0 is the intercept and b_i is the regression coefficient for the input value of predictors x_i.

3.2 Decision Tree

One powerful technique commonly used in classification and as a predictor for decision making is a decision tree (DT). DT is a top-to-bottom approach that recursively splits data into smaller subsets, based on the attribute value of some test [10]. The partition is complete when the subsets include instances with pure values (homogenous) [11]. The type of DT algorithm that applied in this study was a classification tree (e.g., classification and regression tree (CART)).

3.3 Naïve Bayes

A Naïve Bayes (NB) is a probabilistic model based on the Bayes Theorem [12]. It assumes that the value of a particular attribute in a class is independent of the presence of another attribute [7]. The Bayes rule computes conditional probabilities of each feature for a given class and class probabilities.

The algorithm predicts by estimating the probability for a particular class by considering the maximum *a posteriori* probability according to Eq. 2 [13], where c is a class and x_j are features of vector x.

$$y = \arg \underset{C=\{0,1\}}{\text{MAX}} \; p(y) \prod_{j=1}^{n} p(x_j|y) \tag{2}$$

3.4 Support Vector Machine

Support vector machine (SVM) algorithm [2] attempts to distinctly separate data points of different classes by finding the optimal hyperplane in a high dimensional space.

The hyperplanes H1 and H2 that separate instances (data points) of the two classes are parallel, where the margin is the distance between them. The instances on the planes are called the support vectors, as illustrated in Fig. 1.

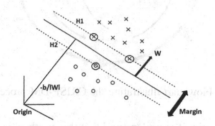

Fig. 1. SVM model [14].

The main benefit of using the SVM is its ability to use a kernel function, which can classify nonlinear data by mapping a space to a higher dimension, as given by Eq. 3 [2].

$$y = \text{sign}\left(\sum_{i=1}^{n} \alpha_i y_i k(x, x_i) + b\right) \tag{3}$$

Where $k(x, x_i)$ is the kernel function; α_i and b are free parameters. The kernel applied in this experiment was polynomial as it was considered the best method for tuning in this type of classification problem [2].

3.5 AdaBoost

AdaBoost is an abbreviation of Adaptive Boosting. AdaBoost is an ensemble method that aims build a strong learning algorithm from multiple, weak classifiers [12].

Initially, the same weight is set for all data points, and after each iteration the weights of the incorrectly classified observations are increased. The focus is on iteratively improving incorrectly classified instances (hard cases) with updated weights in the training set. The resultant model from this process combines the most effective classifiers and creates a stronger classifier, which has high accuracy on the training set and eventually improves prediction power [12].

4   Research Methodology

4.1   CRISP-DM Approach

This study follows the Cross-Industry Standard Process for DM (CRISP-DM) methodology, comprised of six phases, as illustrated in Fig. 2.

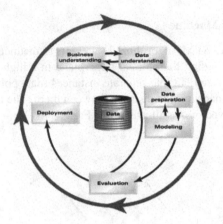

Fig. 2. Flowchart illustrating the CRISP-DM process [14].

In researching this topic, it is understood that this method is considered the *de facto* standard for planning successful DM projects [14]. As such, this methodology was chosen for use in this work.

4.2   Business Understanding

The first step in the CRISP approach is business understanding. This study aims to address the costly issue of employee turnover faced by many organisations. Employee turnover is a significant issue for several reasons, such as the financial losses and the time required to replace, hire and train new employees. This study aims, in part, to predict whether an employee will leave a company. Moreover, the work uncovers key factors, or predictors, that significantly contribute to employee turnover, which can help with developing retention planning strategies within HR management.

Predicting employee departure helps decision makers develop measures to identify areas for improvement, which is a crucial part of an organisational management system.

4.3   Data Understanding

The dataset examined in this paper was collected by Kaggle [15]. The dataset contains 14,999 data points and ten attributes. Class label is the 'Left' attribute; whether the employee departs the company or not. The ten attributes and their descriptions are provided in Table 1.

Table 1. Attribute description

Attributes	Description
Satisfaction level	Satisfaction level of employee; ranges from 0 to 1
Average monthly hours	Average numbers of hours worked by the employee in a month
Last evaluation	Evaluated performance of the employee by the company; ranges from 0 to 1
Number projects	The number of projects assigned to the worker
Promotion last 5 years	Whether the employee has had a promotion during the last five years
Time spent company	The number of years the staff member has worked at the company
Department	Employee's department/division
Work accident	Whether the employee has had an accident or not at work
Salary	Salary levels: low, medium or high relative to employees the company
Left	Whether the employee has left the job or not

Exploratory Data Analysis (EDA). EDA was employed for the goal of exploring potentially meaningful patterns determine the reasons for turnover, and the relationships between variables. This was done using graphical techniques. It enabled to examine the factors affecting staff so as to identify either the main causes of departure or any pre-existing symptoms of a problem. Another objective was defining the factors that would be useful for distinguishing between employees who leave their organisations and those who do not [6].

The dataset showed that the percentage of employees who remained in their jobs was much higher than those who left, at 76% and 24%, respectively. This indicated the class imbalance problem, which was addressed with the synthetic minority oversampling technique (SMOTE) in the data-preparation step.

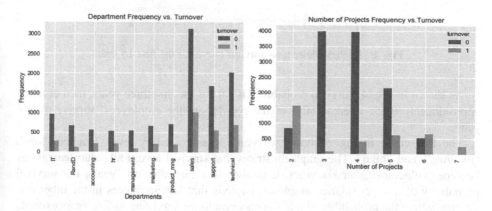

Fig. 3. Exploratory data analysis plots for the Department (a) and Number of Projects (b) features

Examining the graphs of the different variables, Fig. 3(b) shows that the employees with two, six and seven projects were more likely to leave the organisation, while the employees with three, four and five projects tended to stay with the company. A plot of various company departments is shown in Fig. 3(a), which clearly illustrates that the departments with the highest employee turnover were sales, technical, and support. In contrast, the management and research and development (R&D) departments experienced less turnover.

Survival Analysis. Survival analysis is a statistical technique used for analysis of time to event variables. It indicates the time until the occurrence of an event of interest; in this case, the event of interest is employee turnover [16]. The Kaplan–Meier (KM) approach [17] is one of the most important quantitative measures in survival analysis for estimating the survival curve. The survival function, $S(t)$, estimates the probability of survival at a certain time, t. It is defined as [17]:

$$S(t) = \prod_{j:t_j \leq t} \frac{n_j - d_j}{n_j} \qquad (4)$$

Where n_j represents individuals at risk just before time t_j, and d_j is the number of turnover events at time t_j.

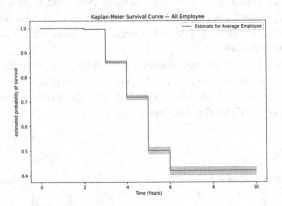

Fig. 4. Kaplan–Meier total survival curve for the first 10 years

As shown in Fig. 4, survival probability is 1.0 for the first three years, then drops to approximately 0.85, whereas 50% of the population, the employees, survive at five years.

The KM curve in Fig. 5 shows survival curves by salary level, labelled "low", "medium", and "high". The graph illustrates that survival across all salary categories becomes vulnerable after six years. It is also clear that after two years, the survival probability of a lower-salaried employee exceeds that for employees in the other categories, where the probability of a low-salary employee surviving to five years exceeds 85%; for high-salary staff, the survival rate is about 78%, while for medium-salary staff,

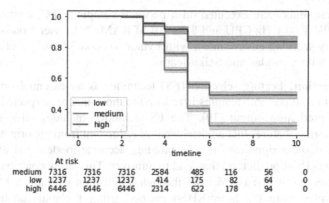

Fig. 5. Survival curve for different groups of employees based on salary level

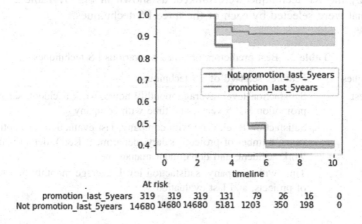

Fig. 6. Survival curve based on promotions variable for different groups of employees

the rate is approximately 60%. The curve in Fig. 6 illustrates the survival proportion of the group that had received promotions in the last 5 years, which was much higher than that of the no-promotion group. It can be observed that the promotion factor signifi- cantly extended the time until the employee's departure.

4.4 Data Preparation

Data preparation is an important step that is executed before modelling in order to maximize the chances of achieving accurate results. This experiment started with the application of a pre-processing phase on the HR dataset, which included checking for missing values, identifying outliers, feature correlation, data transformation and nor- malization. The employee dataset was considered imbalanced, as only 24% of the employees in the dataset left the company. The SMOTE approach was applied to address the class imbalance problem and was used only in the training set [18].

The experiments were executed on a personal computer (PC) containing an Intel Core i7-8550U 1.80 GHz CPU and 8.00 GB of RAM. A Jupyter Notebook was used as the primary working environment, with Python version 3.6 and its libraries such as matplotlib, lifeline, pandas and Scikit-learn.

Feature Selection. Feature selection (FS) technique is an essential process in ML, where the set of all possible features is reduced to those that are expected to contribute most to the prediction output [19]. The FS technique includes selecting a features subset by ignoring features that are irrelevant or redundant from the original feature set. FS therefore plays a significant role in building accurate models and identifying the critical features (best predictors) that lead to turnover. This study contributed to finding effective predictors in the HR dataset through application of various FS techniques; these techniques were the SelectKBest method using f_classif function based on analysis of variance (ANOVA) F-Test, the RFE-based logistic regression model and the RF technique based on training the RF algorithm. The five most important features obtained by the RF technique were ranked, as shown in Fig. 7. Table 2 defines the features that were selected by each of the three FS techniques.

Table 2. Best predictors obtained by various FS techniques

FS techniques	Features selected of FS techniques
SelectKBest (f_classif)	Satisfaction level, average monthly hours, work accident, salary promotion last 5 years, and time with company
RFE	Satisfaction level, time with company, last evaluation, promotion last 5 years, number of projects, salary, department R&D, department HR, work accident, and department management
RF model	Time with company, satisfaction level, average monthly hours, number of projects, and last evaluation

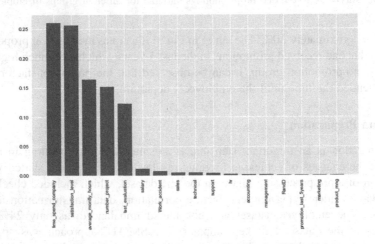

Fig. 7. Features importance as ranked by the RF model

4.5 Modelling

In this phase, a set of candidate models has been prepared to find the best performance. The literature suggests that no single classifier achieves the best results in all contexts, therefore it is necessary to investigate which classifiers are more suited to the specific data being analysed. Several classifiers can be applied to predict employee attrition, such as the SVM, naïve Bayes, Logistic Regression, DT and AdaBoost ensemble classifiers.

Moreover, each model can be applied to three different feature sets, as established by the different FS techniques to determine the best combination of model and feature set. In this work, each candidate model was tuned with hyperparameters using the GridSearchCV function. Grid Search [20] is an approach to find the optimal parameters to models that trained. The values of the hyperparameters obtained via Grid Search were: {'C': 0.5, 'gamma': 1.0, 'kernel': 'poly'} for SVM, and {'criterion': 'entropy', 'max_depth': 8, 'max_features': 0.5} for DT. AdaBoost used {'learning_rate': 0.1, 'n_estimators': 500}.{'C': 1.0, 'fit_intercept': True, 'penalty': 'l1'} was used for the LR model.

4.6 Evaluation

To determine the performance of each model, the classifier was evaluated by use of the appropriate metrics. In the experiment, the performance of the predictive models was evaluated using several critical metrics that included accuracy, sensitivity, precision, specificity, F1-score, misclassification rate, and AUC value.

5 Results

5.1 The Train-Validate-Test Split

In this experiment, the dataset was divided into three subsets: training, validating and testing. The training set was used to train the classifier, while the validating set was applied to optimize the model. Finally, the testing set was used to evaluate the ability of a classifier to predict given new, unseen data [21]. Generalization on testing data indicates how well the models perform to new data. The generalization refers to the ability of the ML model that trained to perform well on new unseen data (e.g., testing data). The results in Table 3 show the performance of each of the five models paired with the different FS techniques.

Overall, SVM with RF (feature importance) achieved the best performance by most metrics as compared with the other models, with an accuracy of 0.97. Decision Tree-RFE followed in performance, with an accuracy score of 0.967, and the DT-RF model was next, with an accuracy of 0.96. The AdaBoost-RF classifier followed, with an accuracy score of 0.95. The LR and naïve Bayes classifiers were the weakest performers by all measures.

SVM-RF performed better than the other models by most metrics, including accuracy, precision, specificity, F1-score, misclassification rate and AUC value. The only metric by which SVM-RF was not superior was the sensitivity score, where the

Table 3. Algorithm performance results using various feature selection techniques

Classifier	FS methods	Accuracy	Precision	Sensitivity	Specificity	F1	Mis-classification	AUC
LR	SelectKBest	0.75	0.702	0.785	0.739	0.71	0.25	0.76
	RFE	0.751	0.687	0.687	0.771	0.698	0.25	0.73
	RF	0.737	0.687	0.753	0.732	0.694	0.26	0.74
NB	SelectKBest	0.737	0.688	0.758	0.73	0.695	0.26	0.74
	REF	0.711	0.674	0.771	0.692	0.674	0.29	0.73
	RF	0.816	0.754	0.49	0.919	0.722	0.18	0.70
SVM	SelectKBest	0.942	0.916	0.90	0.955	0.922	0.6	0.93
	REF	0.959	0.945	0.911	0.974	0.944	0.4	0.94
	RF	**0.971**	**0.964**	0.922	**0.986**	**0.961**	**0.3**	**0.95**
DT	SelectKBest	0.954	0.932	**0.931**	0.962	0.939	0.5	0.95
	REF	0.967	0.959	0.916	0.983	0.954	0.3	0.95
	RF	0.964	0.949	0.927	0.975	0.95	0.4	0.95
AdaBoost	SelectKBest	0.948	0.936	0.87	0.973	0.928	0.5	0.92
	REF	0.944	0.932	0.853	0.973	0.922	0.6	0.91
	RF	0.951	0.941	0.872	0.977	0.932	0.5	0.92

DT model using SelectKBest feature selection performed better, with a score of 0.93 versus 0.92.

5.2 10-Fold Cross-Validation

10-fold cross-validation was applied to the dataset to attempt to determine if the model results would improve. The dataset was divided into ten equal subsets [7]. Nine subsets were used to train the model, validating the model with the remaining fold (one of the subsets). Then, the average of all 10 trials were computed for a final estimation of performance [7]. 10-fold cross-validation was used this research due to its powerful method to prevent overfitting by splitting the data into two parts (train and test), applying the cross-validation only to the training set and leaving out the testing set to evaluate the model's ability to predict the unseen dataset.

The experimental results using cross-validation identified the two best models, as illustrated in Table 4. The SVM-RF model achieved the highest accuracy (0.97), precision (0.94), specificity (0.98), F1-score (0.93) and lowest misclassification rate (0.3). DT using SelectKBest performed best in sensitivity (0.92) and AUC value (0.96). In general, model performance was little changed between the train-validate-test and cross-validation methods. However, the logistic regression classifier did produce better results using cross-validation; the accuracy of LR-RF increased from 73% to 83%. Also, misclassification of LR improved from 25% to 17% across all feature sets.

Table 4. Algorithm results using 10-fold cross-validation and FS methods

Classifier	FS methods	Accuracy	Precision	Sensitivity	Specificity	F1	Mis-classification	AUC
LR	SelectKBest	0.830	0.596	0.886	0.812	0.713	0.17	0.75
	RFE	0.830	0.596	0.886	0.812	0.713	0.17	0.75
	RF	0.833	0.593	0.940	0.797	0.730	0.17	0.77
NB	SelectKBest	0.803	0.567	0.739	0.824	0.642	0.20	0.74
	REF	0.794	0.541	0.878	0.768	0.670	0.21	0.73
	RF	0.749	0.458	0.816	0.892	0.356	0.25	0.71
SVM	SelectKBest	0.938	0.853	0.891	0.952	0.872	0.6	0.94
	REF	0.951	0.897	0.899	0.968	0.898	0.5	0.95
	RF	**0.966**	**0.944**	0.913	**0.983**	**0.928**	**0.3**	0.95
DT	SelectKBest	0.948	0.870	**0.918**	0.957	0.894	0.5	**0.96**
	REF	0.962	0.930	0.909	0.979	0.920	0.4	0.95
	RF	0.947	0.873	0.913	0.958	0.892	0.5	0.96
AdaBoost	SelectKBest	0.945	0.902	0.862	0.971	0.882	0.6	0.93
	REF	0.944	0.912	0.848	0.974	0.879	0.6	0.92
	RF	0.954	0.918	0.888	0.975	0.903	0.5	0.93

5.3 Decision Tree Result

Figure 8 illustrates the constructed DT model, built with the five most important features, as defined through RF feature selection. This representation can facilitate the decision-making process by organizing features in order of condition [10]. The condition represents a subset of values for a given attribute in order to classify the chance of turnover as a series of if-then-else decision rules. According to the results of the DT classifier, the following rules can be extracted:

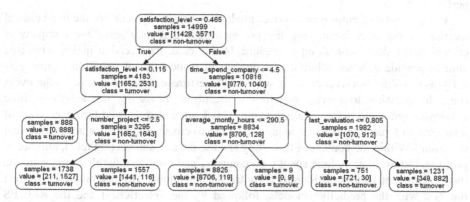

Fig. 8. Decision tree result

Rule 1: If (satisfaction_level <= 0.115), THEN Class = Turnover

Rule 2: If (satisfaction_level <= 0.465 and satisfaction_level > 0.115 and number_project <= 2.5), THEN Class = Turnover

Rule 3: If (satisfaction_level <= 0.465 and satisfaction_level > 0.115 and number_project > 2.5), THEN Class = Non-Turnover

Rule 4: If (satisfaction_level > 0.465 and time_spend_company <= 4.5 and average_montly_hours <= 290.5), THEN Class = Non-Turnover

Rule 5: If (satisfaction_level > 0.465 and time_spend_company <= 4.5 and average_montly_hours > 290.5), THEN Class = Turnover

Rule 6: If (satisfaction_level > 0.465 and time_spend_company > 4.5 and last_evaluation <= 0.805), THEN Class = Non-Turnover

Rule 7: If (satisfaction_level > 0.465 and time_spend_company > 4.5 and last_evaluation > 0.805), THEN Class = Turnover.

6 Conclusion

This study proposed supervised ML models, which aimed to predict whether an employee would leave a company or not. The experiment was conducted with a combination of five predictive models (SVM, DT, NB, LR and the Adaboost classifier) using three different FS techniques (SelectKBest, RFE, and RF), while considering both train-validate-test and 10-fold cross-validation methods. Several important evaluation metrics were examined to analyse the performance of the supervised machine learning techniques. These metrics were accuracy, sensitivity, precision, specificity, F1-score, misclassification rate and AUC value.

The feature selection approaches were implemented within the HR dataset to identify the best predictors that lead to turnover. Finding the best predictors would also help an employer explore how to retain employees with high satisfaction and performance.

In the context of employee turnover prediction, sensitivity is one of the most critical metrics, as correctly identifying the potential staff that may leave the company is critical in the decision-making procedure. In this case, the decision maker would be able to provide a better solution and implement some form of retention planning as early as possible. Survival analysis was used to estimate patterns of time-to-the-event (i.e., the decision to leave), which was useful in measuring the length of time employees remained before finally leaving. This feature also allowed for the creation of a summary of survival data and made it possible to create comparisons across different situations. Within the context of this study and the dataset, satisfaction level, number of projects, last evaluation, time spent with company and average monthly hours were the most significant factors, as identified by the RF technique. This technique performed the best with the predictive models, followed by the SelectKBest and the RFE FS techniques.

The experimental results identified two models as most able to predict whether employee turnover: SVM using the RF algorithm and DT with SelectKBest method. It was found that when using ten-fold cross-validation, the SVM-RF algorithm performed best (accuracy = 0.97, precision = 0.94, specificity = 0.98, F1-score = 0.93, misclassification error = 0.3). While the DT considering SelectKBest performed better than other classifiers (sensitivity = 0.92 and AUC = 0.96).

On the other hand, when using the train-validate-test approach, the SVM-RF model provided very good indicators for predicting turnover. It performed best compared to other models in term of accuracy, precision, specificity, F1-score, misclassification rate and AUC value. The DT using SelectKBest method performed significantly better in sensitivity (i.e., the prediction of true turnover cases) with 0.93.

In future research, the best models identified in this study will be applied to various datasets (such as those containing the multi-class problem) in order to extend the performance evaluation in predicting employee turnover. Deep learning could be used to improve the results of the predictive models. Also, the genetic algorithm could be examined for feature selection in order to increase predictive model performance.

References

1. Sikaroudi, E., et al.: A data mining approach to employee turnover prediction (case study: Arak automotive parts manufacturing). J. Ind. Syst. Eng. **8**(4), 106–121 (2015)
2. Keramati, A., et al.: Improved churn prediction in telecommunication industry using data mining techniques. Appl. Soft Comput. **24**, 994–1012 (2014)
3. Fan, C.-Y., et al.: Using hybrid data mining and machine learning clustering analysis to predict the turnover rate for technology professionals. Expert Syst. Appl. **39**(10), 8844–8851 (2012)
4. Chien, C.-F., Chen, L.-F.: Data mining to improve personnel selection and enhance human capital: a case study in high-technology industry. Expert Syst. Appl. **34**(1), 280–290 (2008)
5. Saradhi, V.V., Palshikar, G.K.: Employee churn prediction. Expert Syst. Appl. **38**(3), 1999–2006 (2011)
6. Hung, S.-Y., Yen, D.C., Wang, H.-Y.: Applying data mining to telecom churn management. Expert Syst. Appl. **31**(3), 515–524 (2006)
7. Valle, M.A., Ruz, G.A.: Turnover prediction in a call center: behavioral evidence of loss aversion using random forest and Naïve Bayes algorithms. Appl. Artif. Intell. **29**(9), 923–942 (2015)
8. García, D.L., Nebot, À., Vellido, A.: Intelligent data analysis approaches to churn as a business problem: a survey. Knowl. Inf. Syst. **51**(3), 719–774 (2017)
9. Rombaut, E., Guerry, M.-A.: Predicting voluntary turnover through human resources database analysis. Manag. Res. Rev. **41**(1), 96–112 (2018)
10. Lima, E., Mues, C., Baesens, B.: Domain knowledge integration in data mining using decision tables: case studies in churn prediction. J. Oper. Res. Soc. **60**(8), 1096–1106 (2017)
11. De Caigny, A., Coussement, K., De Bock, K.W.: A new hybrid classification algorithm for customer churn prediction based on logistic regression and decision trees. Eur. J. Oper. Res. **269**(2), 760–772 (2018)
12. Vafeiadis, T., et al.: A comparison of machine learning techniques for customer churn prediction. Simul. Model. Pract. Theory **55**, 1–9 (2015)
13. Valle, M.A., Varas, S., Ruz, G.A.: Job performance prediction in a call center using a Naive Bayes classifier. Expert Syst. Appl. **39**(11), 9939–9945 (2012)
14. Shearer, C.: The CRISP-DM model: the new blueprint for data mining. J. Data Warehous. **5**(4), 13–22 (2000)

15. Kaggle. HR Analytics (2017). https://www.kaggle.com/colara/hr-analytics
16. Sainani, K.L.: Introduction to Survival Analysis. PM R **8**(6), 580–585 (2016)
17. Kartsonaki, C.: Survival analysis. Diagn. Histopathol. **22**(7), 263–270 (2016)
18. Amin, A., et al.: Comparing oversampling techniques to handle the class imbalance problem: a customer churn prediction case study. IEEE Access **4**, 7940–7957 (2016)
19. Jain, D., Singh, V.: Feature selection and classification systems for chronic disease prediction: a review. Egypt. Inform. J. **19**(3), 179–189 (2018)
20. Gao, X., Hou, J.: An improved SVM integrated GS-PCA fault diagnosis approach of Tennessee Eastman process. Neurocomputing **174**, 906–911 (2016)
21. Moosavi, M., Soltani, N.: Prediction of the specific volume of polymeric systems using the artificial neural network-group contribution method. Fluid Phase Equilib. **356**, 176–184 (2013)

Predicting Saudi Stock Market Index by Incorporating GDELT Using Multivariate Time Series Modelling

Rawan Alamro[1,2]([✉]), Andrew McCarren[2]([✉]), and Amal Al-Rasheed[1]([✉])

[1] Princess Nourah bint Abdulrahman University,
Riyadh, Kingdom of Saudi Arabia
`rawan.alamro3@mail.dcu.ie`, `aaalrasheed@pnu.edu.sa`
[2] Dublin City University, Dublin, Ireland
`andrew.mccarren@dcu.ie`

Abstract. Prediction of financial and economic markets is very challenging but valuable for economists, business owners, and traders. Forecasting stock market prices depends on many factors, such as other markets' performance, economic state of a country, and others. In behavioral finance, people's emotions and opinions influence their transactional decisions and therefore the financial markets. The focus of this research is to predict the Saudi Stock Market Index by utilizing its previous values and the impact of people's sentiments on their financial decisions. Human emotions and opinions are directly influenced by media and news, which we incorporated by utilizing the Global Data on Events, Location, and Tone (GDELT) dataset by Google. GDELT is a collection of news from all over the world from different types of media such as TV, broadcasts, radio, newspapers, and websites. We extracted two time series from GDELT, filtered for Saudi Arabian news. The two time series represent daily values of tone and social media attention. We studied the characteristics of the generated multivariate time series, then deployed and compared multiple multivariate models to predict the daily index of the Saudi stock market.

Keywords: Forecasting · Multivariate time series · Behavioral finance · Time series analysis

1 Introduction

People care a lot about the future: the future of their countries, families, finances, and relations. Predicting the future is considered a valuable skill nowadays. In the past, people dreamt of having this power. Ancient Greeks consulted the Oracle of Delphi, one of the most famous oracles of the Greek God Apollo. They consulted her knowing she was not infallible, and while they did not consider her revelations to be the objective truth, they still valued her visions. Interestingly, nowadays we take consultations from different experts and consultants with the

© Springer Nature Switzerland AG 2019
A. Alfaries et al. (Eds.): ICC 2019, CCIS 1097, pp. 317–328, 2019.
https://doi.org/10.1007/978-3-030-36365-9_26

same mentality of the ancient Greeks; we value their knowledge, but we do not believe in them blindly.

Experts use different types of metrics and data to predict a variety of measures. In the stock market, for example, economists use other markets to predict a single country's stock market movements. Other metrics used to predict stock markets are GDP, oil, financial freedom of a country, and many others. All previous predictors are based on reasoning and assume that people are logical creatures, which is not the case. People are emotional, and their emotions affect their decisions. Conventional economics assumes hard facts and rational decisions of people. This view has changed since the emergence of behavioural economics [1]. In behavioural economics, people's moods, emotions, and opinions have an impact on their transactional decisions and therefore on the financial markets. Nowadays, people are informed by different types of media such as news sites, news channels, forums, blogs, and even podcasts. Such vast amounts of information makes it very challenging to study the impact of news and information on financial markets. This leads us to the Global Data on Events, Location, and Tone (GDELT) dataset by Google. GDELT is a collection of news from all over the world from different types of media such as TV, broadcasts, radio, newspapers, and websites. Studying GDELT will provide a huge advantage to financial markets forecasters.

This research focuses on such effects on the Saudi Stock Market by studying the Tadawul All Share Index (TASI), which tracks the performance of all companies listed on the Saudi Stock Exchange. The research will use a time series analysis to predict the Saudi Stock Market Index by incorporating the GDELT dataset with the TASI.

2   Literature Review

The prediction of stock market trends is very important for the development of effective trading strategies [2]. Both statistical and machine-learning approaches are used to solve this type of problem and can provide traders with a reliable technique for predicting future prices [3,4]. In general, the prediction of the movement of stock prices is considered a difficult and important task for financial time series analysis. The accurate forecasting of stock prices is essential in assisting investors and traders to increase their stock returns. The natural noise and volatility in daily stock price fluctuation is the main reason for the high complexity in stock trends forecasting [5]. People opinions and emotions in media is showing promise for predicting financial markets. However, the true value of such data and which parameters can it predict is not agreed upon in the scientific society [1,6]. Modern financial theory is based on two main concepts: the efficient market hypothesis (EMH) and the capital asset pricing model (CAPM). Both concepts hold that investors can make rational responses to the market and that the stock market is unpredictable, ignoring the analysis of investors' actual decision-making behavior [1,6]. Since the development of behavioral finance, however, existing research shows that in the case of incomplete information, people's behavior, attitudes and preferences are not completely rational, that stock prices do not randomly fluctuate and, in some ways, the price is predictable. Not only will the news have an impact on the stock price, but so will the investors' mood [6]. Time series analysis and prediction are part of the wider field of data mining and analysis. A group of a large number of values within unified time interval is labelled as time series data. The time can be represented by year, month, week, day, etc. In time series analysis, the behavior and characteristics of a time series are studied and analyzed to predict future values and behavior, foreseeing the future data using the historical data in a timely structure [7,8].

2.1 Multivariate Time Series

Multivariate time series models are very valuable and popular in economics but much less so in other forecasting applications. Multivariate time series models, which are extensions to univariate ones, are given only a marginal position in standard textbooks on time series analysis. Outside economics, empirical examples are uncommon. In comparison, the multivariate perspective is fundamental in economics, where single factors are traditionally studied in the context of their relationships to other factors. Contrary to other fields of knowledge, economists may discard the use of univariate time series forecasting based on the interdependence theory, which appears to be an extravagant point of view [9].

Multivariate time series models are not necessarily better than univariate ones in forecasting, even in economics. While multivariate models are convenient in modeling fascinating interrelationships and achieving a better fit within a given sample, univariate methods are often found to outperform multivariate ones out of sample. And there are many possible reasons:

- There are more parameters for multivariate models than univariate ones. Each additional parameter is an unknown and has to be estimated. This estimate leads to an additional source of error due to variation in sampling.
- The number of potential multivariate model candidates exceeds their univariate counterpart. Therefore, model selection is more complex, takes longer time and more prone to errors, which affect prediction afterwards.
- Generalizing nonlinear algorithms to the multivariate models is difficult. In general, multivariate models need to be simple and to have basic structure compared to univariate models. This simplification is necessary to overcome the complication of multivariate models [9].

3 Methodology

This section discusses the methodologies used in this study to predict the Saudi Stock Market Index using a multivariate time series analysis. Integrating multivariate stochastic processes to be analyzed and modelled is a lengthy process that involves studying the time series characteristics and their integration and cointegration. We will use both statistical and machine learning approaches in the time series analysis to integrate GDELT dataset. Two time series from GDELT will be integrated to the model, which are Tone and Social Media Attention on Saudi Arabia. The Tone time series will represent a daily scale of the negativity and positivity of the news. While the Social Media Attention time series will represent how many news piece has been published daily concerning Saudi Arabia. The models chosen in this study are VAR, ARIMAX, multivariate GARCH, and LSTM, which have all proven successful in multivariate time series analyses and econometrics. Below is a generalized formula of the proposed models:

$$Y_t = aY_{(t-1)} + bZ_{(t-n)} + cX_{(t-m)} + e_t \tag{1}$$

where

Y_t = "stock market close price" at time t,
$Z_{(t-n)}$ = "Tone" at a previous lag n of time t,
$X_{(t-m)}$ = "Social Media Attention" at a previous lag m of time t,
e_t = error term at time t.

Figure 1 shows the methodology used in this study. Moreover, how the data is extracted from GDELT and Tadawul The Saudi Stock Exchange Company. We extracted both Tone and Social Media Attention time series from GDELT using Google's BigQuery language in Google Cloud Platform, and TASI time series from Tadawul's online portal. Finally, Fig. 1 represent the next phases of analysis, modeling and forecasting.

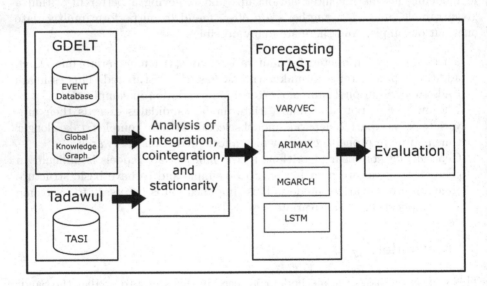

Fig. 1. Methodology graph.

3.1 Multivariate Time Series and Their Properties

Before explaining the methodology, we need to establish an understanding of multivariate time series and their special properties. Such understanding will give us a huge benefit in comprehending the data first and to examine any interrelationships. The following characteristics of multivariate time series are not all considered in the individual papers in the literature. Each research tries to cover one or two of them based on their choice of methodology. In this research, we try to cover all these characteristics to be able to apply it to the wide range of models used in the research.

Cross Correlation. One of the main objectives in multivariate time series analysis is to find relationships between the examined stochastic processes [12]. The study of cross correlation between time series help researchers to find any hidden relationships and connections. In the relationship between two time series X_t and Y_t, the series Y_t might be correlated to past lags of X_t. The Cross Correlation Function (CCF) is beneficial for detecting lags of X_t that might be usefull predictor of Y_t [10].

CCF is an important examining and assessment tool for modeling multivariate time series. The CCF generalizes the Autocorrelation Function (ACF) which is the autocorrelation function used on univariate time series to be used on the multivariate approach. Therefore, its main objective is to find linear dynamic correlations and interactions in time series data that have been produced from stationary processes [13]. Let X_t and Y_t represent a couple of stochastic processes that are stationary. Then the CCF is given as follows [13].

$$K_{XY}(T) = E[X_{t-T}Y_t] \tag{2}$$

Integration and Cointegration. In multivariate time series forecasting, cointegration is another important feature that need to be studied but usually neglected by beginners in statistics and econometrics. Cointegration examine non-stationary time series, which have variances, and means that differ over time. Therefore, cointegration allow researchers to identify the long-run relationships or equilibrium in systems.

Integration. In statistics and econometrics, the order of integration I(d) of a time series is a statistical summary that state the minimum number of differences needed to convert the time series to a stationary one.

Cointegration. Cointegration is a statistical characteristic of multivariate time series or a collection of time series variables, which identify the degree to which these variables are sensitive to the same average over time. Therefore, confirm whether the distance between them remains constant over time. In the contrary, correlation return if the variables move to the same or opposite direction, which makes them positively or negatively correlated.

Two stochastic processes (time series) X_t and Y_t are called cointegrated if the following two conditions are fulfilled:

1. X_t and Y_t are both integrated processes of order one, i.e. X_t $I(1)$ and Y_t $I(1)$.
2. There exists a constant $\beta \neq 0$ such that $Y_t - \beta X_t$ is a stationary process, i.e. $Y_t - \beta X_t$ $I(0)$.

The issue whether two integrated processes are cointegrated can be decided on the basis of a unit root test [3,13].

Endogenous Variables and Exogenous Variables. Endogenous and exogenous variables are widely used in econometrics and sometimes in statistics. Endogenous variables are similar to (but not the same as) dependent variables. Endogenous variables' values are influenced by other variables in the model. Meanwhile exogenous variable is not determined or influenced by any other variables in the model, although it could be affected by factors outside the model [3].

For example, a model trying to predict electricity consumption with the following available variables; electricity consumption, weather, financial situation of a country. The endogenous variables are electricity consumption, while the weather is considered an exogenous variable as it is not influenced by any other variable in the system. Financial situation is harder to classify as an exogenous variable, as we can argue that it could be influenced by weather and electricity consumption even in a subtle way. In this case, a variable can be considered partially exogenous and partially endogenous.

These characteristics of the variables are important in multivariate time series modeling, as some models are more appropriate to endogenous types such as VAR and some models are more appropriate to exogenous types such as ARI-MAX [3,10,15].

3.2 Vector Autoregressive and Vector Error Correction Models

In its basic form, a VAR consists of a set of K endogenous variables $y_t = (y_{1t}, \ldots, y_{kt}, \ldots, y_{Kt})$.

One important characteristic of a VAR(p)-process is its stability. This means that it generates stationary time series with time-invariant means, variances, and covariance structure, given sufficient starting values. One of the basic assumptions of VAR model is stationarity of all series, nonetheless differencing non-stationary time series individually considered a bad practice, as this might demolish important dynamic information. The critical issue is cointegration. In short, when there is cointegration, cointegrated models such as VEC (Vector Error Correction) should be used for forecasting. When there is no cointegration, series with an integrated appearance should be differenced [10,11].

The vector error correction (VEC) model is a special form of the VAR model which is used for variables that are stationary in their differences. VEC model is able to handle any cointegrating relationships between the variables and take it into consideration. VEC model is built with cointegration relations to restrict the long run effect of the endogenous variables to model their cointegrating relationship. The cointegration term is known in VEC as the error correction term as the deviation from long run equilibrium is corrected steadily through a series of short run amendments [10].

3.3 ARIMAX Model

Autoregressive Integrated Moving Average (ARIMA) models provide another approach to time series forecasting. ARIMA model is consider one of the widely used approaches in time series forecasting. ARIMA models aim to describe the autocorrelations in the data. ARIMA (p, d, q) is a combination of Autoregressive model AR(p) and a Moving Average model MA(q) for non-stationary time series where I(d) indicate the integration order.

Autoregressive Integrated Moving Average with Exogenous Variable (ARIMAX) model extend ARIMA models through the inclusion of exogenous variables X. ARIMA is also an extension to another model, which is the Autoregressive Moving Average (ARMA) model. ARIMA model is used in some scenarios where data are non-stationarity, a preliminary differencing step can be implemented once or more to remove the non-stationarity [15,16].

3.4 Multivariate GARCH Model

The autoregressive conditional heteroscedasticity model (ARCH) is a statistical model for stochastic process that explain the variance of the current error term. Various problems in finance have motivated the study of the volatility or variability, of a time series. ARMA models were used to model the conditional mean of a process when the conditional variance was constant. However, the assumption of a constant conditional variance will be violated. Models such as the autoregressive conditionally heteroscedastic or ARCH model, first introduced by Engle [17] were developed to model changes in volatility. These models were later extended to generalized ARCH or GARCH models by Bollerslev [16]. The ARCH model is used traditionally when the error variance follows an autoregressive (AR) model. Therefore, the generalized autoregressive conditional heteroscedasticity (GARCH) model will be used if an autoregressive moving average (ARMA) model is assumed for the error variance, GARCH is a statistical model usually used in analyzing financial time series data [17].

Heteroscedasticity explain the irregular pattern of variation of a variable, or an error term in a statistical model. Essentially, when heteroscedasticity is assumed, values do not follow a linear pattern. In the contrary, they tend to cluster. Therefore, the results and predictive value one can extract from the model will not be reliable hence the necessity for using ARCH/GARCH models [18].

Although modelling volatility of the prices and returns was the main objective, understanding the co-movements of financial metrics is greatly important in practical cases. therefore, it is substantial to extend the GARCH model to the multivariate case (MGARCH) [19].

3.5 LSTM Model

Long Short Term Memory networks (LSTM) are a special kind of Recurrent Neural Network with the ability to learn long term relationships. They were introduced by Hochreiter & Schmidhuber [20], and were polished and distributed by many people in preceding work. They work very well on a many types of problems, and are now extensively used. All recurrent neural networks have the form of a looping chain of neural network. In traditional RNNs, this looping unit will have a very simple structure, for example; an individual tanh layer [21]. LSTMs are designed explicitly to avoid the problem of long-term dependency. Their default behavior is to remember information for long periods of time. LSTM is used in the deep learning field, contrary to standard forward neural networks. LSTM has feedback functionality that enable it to be a general purpose model. LSTM special properties enable it to be successful in many applications such as speech recognition, video processing, time series, and medical predictions [20]. LSTM model is well suited to forecast, process, and analyze time series data, as the duration between important events can be unknown, because of the different lags [6,22].

A common LSTM unit is composed of a cell, an input gate, an output gate and a forget gate. cell remembers values over arbitrary time intervals and the three gates regulate the flow of information into and out of the cell [20].

4   Implementation

The dataset used in this study is GDELT developed by Google and TASI (Tadawul All Share Index), which is the Saudi stock market index. GDELT contains two main datasets; GDELT Event Database and GDELT Global Knowledge Graph (GKG). GDELT's entire quarter-billion-record database can be extracted using Google's BigQuery and Google Cloud Platform. The database is updated every 15 min and we can query, export, and analyze using SQL language [23].

Before forecasting, the data has been analyzed and pre-processed. The TASI data set represents the daily closing price of the Saudi market index. Media Attention represents the number of articles and new pieces across all media about Saudi Arabia, which is extracted from GDELT. Finally, Tone represents the tone of each of these news pieces from different media types, which is also extracted from GDELT. There was no missing values in the data. The Tone data has been smoothed to represent only one value per day; this aggregation has been completed using the mean Tone values for each day.

To analyze the time series, first we studied the cross correlation function to find any linear relationship between Tone, Media Attention, and TASI. The CCF shows that there is a strong negative relationship between TASI and SMA at lag 1 (as our data is daily, the lag is one day), and there is also a strong negative relationship between TASI and Tone at lag 1. These findings indicate that both Tone and Media Attention could have a predictive power over TASI [13,14] (Fig. 2).

Time Series Graph of GDELT and TASI

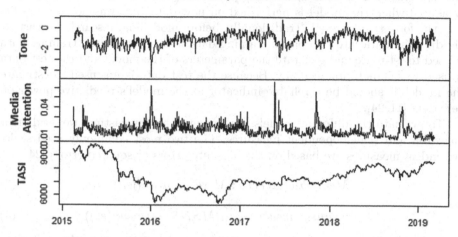

Fig. 2. Multivariate time series graph of GDELT and TASI.

Stationarity has been tested on all three time series using stationarity tests. Kwiatkowski-Phillips-Schmidt-Shin (KPSS), Augmented Dickey–Fuller (ADF), and Autocorrelation Function (ACF) stationarity tests have been conducted and showed that the TASI, Tone, and SMA are non-stationary and need to be differenced (first order) [10]. As all time series are non-stationary, we cannot model the data in the simplest form of VAR. In this case we also cannot difference the data before studying the cointegration of these time series, because if they are cointegrated some interrelation regressors might be lost in the process [10]. Johansen's test for cointegrating has been implemented and shows that there is cointegration between the series. Therefore we cannot use the simple form of VAR. The vector error correction (VEC) model has been used instead, which can handle the cointegration and non-stationarity.

After fitting the ARIMAX model, we studied the model residuals to ensure the good fit of the data. A residual analysis shows that the residuals have a constant mean, normally distributed, and goes gradually to zero in the ACF graph, which are all good indicators of a proper fit [15,16]. MGARCH was implemented using GO-MGARCH, which is one of the dynamic conditional correlation models (DCC) in GARCH modelling. Multivariate GO-GARCH is able to explain and model the fluctuating volatility that is mostly present in stock market data and financial data [17]. In LSTM modelling, we split the data to train and test sets. After that, the input variables were reshaped into 3D format as restricted by LSTM (samples, time, and features) [22].

5   Evaluation

It is essential to evaluate forecast accuracy using actual forecasts. Therefore, the quantity of the residuals is not a reliable indication of the likelihood of the forecast errors. The forecast's accuracy can only be considered and therefore measured when the model is performed on new data that was not used in fitting the forecasting model. Traditionally, before modelling, researchers start by dividing the data into two parts, training data and testing data. Training data is used to estimate and generate the parameters of the model and the test data is used to calculate its accuracy. Because the test data is not used to estimate the model, it should be a reliable indicator of the model's predictive power on new data [11,24].

To evaluate the different models implemented for forecasting, we used error measures and scale-dependent measures. The two most commonly used scale-dependent measures are based on the absolute errors or squared errors [24]:

$$Meanabsoluteerro : MAE = mean(|e_t|) \tag{3}$$

$$Rootmeansquarederror : RMSE = \sqrt{(mean(e_t^2))} \tag{4}$$

In forecasting time series, error measures are the most commonly used accuracy measures. A study forecasting crude oil prices based on internet concern used MAE, RMSE, and MAPE as error measures for the prediction [24]. Another study used MAE and RMSE to evaluate the prediction of crude oil prices based on deep learning modelling using text [4].

MAE is more popular than RMSE, as it is easier to implement and understand. The table below shows the results of each model. We can conclude that LSTM is the most accurate model, scoring 0.59 MAE, and that VAR and multivariate GARCH are the lowest performing models (Table 1).

Table 1. Forecasting results.

Model\error measure	RMSE	MAE
VAR\VEC	8080.49	8074.12
ARIMAX	325.06	284.75
Multivariate GARCH	8038.9	8032.5
LSTM	0.61	0.59

The LSTM loss function demonstrate that the training performance and the test performance were almost the same after the thirtieth iteration, which proves that the model is not overfitting.

The results shows that the VAR model performance is low compared to LSTM and ARIMAX, which can be explained by the endogenous/exogenous characteristics of the variables. The VAR model assumes all variables are endogenous. In our model, the TASI variable, which is the stock market index closing price, is endogenous, as it depends on the other two variables, Media Attention and Tone. Meanwhile, Media Attention and Tone can be partially endogenous and partially exogenous, as we are not certain. We can argue that the stock market index could affect Media Attention and Tone but not strongly, which makes them more exogenous, hence the success of ARIMAX compared to VAR [3].

A disadvantage of the multivariate GARCH model is that the number of parameters to be estimated in the equation increases rapidly, which consequently leads to a higher degree of errors, hence the high error measure of the multivariate GARCH in this research [19].

6 Conclusion

Predicting stock market movements is critical for the development of effective trading tactics. Both statistical and machine learning approaches are used to solve this problem and can provide traders a reliable technique for predicting future prices. Forecasting stock market prices is a challenging task, as stock markets depend on multiple factors that vary in type and extraction complexity. Financial markets can be influenced by economic factors and non-economic factors, which are harder to figure and to analyse. Human behaviours, emotions, and sentiments are an example of non-economic factors that are difficult to track and extract. In this study, we try to solve this issue by introducing GDELT as a global media dataset that has different useful features. We extracted two time series from GDELT, filtered for Saudi Arabian news. The two time series represent daily values of tone and social media attention. We studied the characteristics of the generated multivariate time series, then deployed and compared multiple multivariate models to predict the daily index of the Saudi stock market. The results show that the model with the highest performance is LSTM, with 0.59 MAE. This concludes that LSTM can give very accurate forecasts, as it has a very low MAE compared to the mean value of TASI, which is 7413.

References

1. Ogaki, M., Tanaka, S.C.: Behavioral Economics. Springer, Singapore (2017). https://doi.org/10.1007/978-981-10-6439-5
2. Elshendy, M., Fronzetti Colladon, A.: Big data analysis of economic news: hints to forecast macroeconomic indicators. Int. J. Eng. Bus. Manag. **9**, 1–12 (2017)
3. Mills, T.C.: Time Series Econometrics. Springer, Cham (2015). https://doi.org/10.1057/9781137525338
4. Li, X., Shang, W., Wang, S.: Text-based crude oil price forecasting: a deep learning approach. Int. J. Forecast. **35**, 1548–1560 (2018)
5. Ticknor, J.L.: A Bayesian regularized artificial neural network for stock market forecasting. Expert Syst. Appl. **40**(14), 5501–5506 (2013)
6. Zhang, G., Xu, L., Xue, Y.: Model and forecast stock market behavior integrating investor sentiment analysis and transaction data. Cluster Comput. **20**(1), 789–803 (2017)
7. Fakhrazari, A., Vakilzadian, H.: A survey on time series data mining. In: IEEE International Conference on Electro Information Technology, pp. 476–481 (2017)

8. Esling, P., Agon, C.: Time-series data mining. ACM Comput. Surv. **45**(1), 1–34 (2012)
9. Kunst, R.M., Franses, P.H.: The impact of seasonal constants on forecasting seasonally cointegrated time series. J. Forecast. **17**(2), 109–124 (1998)
10. Pfaff, B.: Analysis of Integrated and Cointegrated Time Series with R. Springer, New York (2008). https://doi.org/10.1007/978-0-387-75967-8
11. Shanmugam, R., Brockwell, P.J., Davis, R.A.: Introduction to time series and forecasting. Technometrics **39**(4), 426 (1997)
12. Kunst, R.: Multivariate forecasting methods. Building 28–39 (2000). https://homepage.univie.ac.at/robert.kunst/prognos4.pdf
13. Beran, J.: Mathematical Foundations of Time Series Analysis: A Concise Introduction. Springer, Cham (2018). https://doi.org/10.1007/978-3-319-74380-6
14. Hunter, J., Burke, S.P., Canepa, A.: Multivariate Modelling of Non-Stationary Economic Time Series. Palgrave Macmillan, London (2005)
15. Elshendy, M., Colladon, A.F., Battistoni, E., Gloor, P.A.: Using four different online media sources to forecast the crude oil price. J. Inf. Sci. **44**(3), 408–421 (2018)
16. De Gooijer, J.G., Hyndman, R.J.: 25 years of time series forecasting. Int. J. Forecast. **22**(3), 443–473 (2006)
17. Wenjing, S., Huang, Y.: Comparison of multivariate garch models with application to zero-coupon bond volatility. Thesis, pp. 1–55 (2010)
18. Kartsonakis Mademlis, D., Dritsakis, N.: Volatility between oil prices and stock returns of dow jones index: a bivariate GARCH (BEKK) approach. In: Tsounis, N., Vlachvei, A. (eds.) ICOAE 2018. SPBE, pp. 209–221. Springer, Cham (2018). https://doi.org/10.1007/978-3-030-02194-8_16
19. Bauwens, L., Laurent, S., Rombouts, J.V.K.: Multivariate GARCH models: a survey. J. Appl. Econom. **21**(1), 79–109 (2006)
20. Hochreiter, S., Schmidhuber, J.: Long short-term memory. Neural Comput. **9**, 1735–1780 (1997)
21. Greff, K., Srivastava, R.K., Koutnik, J., Steunebrink, B.R., Schmidhuber, J.: LSTM: a search space odyssey. IEEE Trans. Neural Netw. Learn. Syst. **28**(10), 2222–2232 (2017)
22. Fischer, T., Krauss, C.: Deep learning with long short-term memory networks for financial market predictions. Eur. J. Oper. Res. **270**(2), 654–669 (2018)
23. Leetaru, K., Schrodt, P.A.: GDELT: global data on events, location and tone. International Studies Association (2012)
24. Hyndman, R.J., Koehler, A.B.: Another look at measures of forecast accuracy. Int. J. Forecast. **22**(4), 679–688 (2006)

Author Index

Abbas, Safia I-43
Abd Latiff, Muhammad Shafie I-132
Abdelouhab, Fawzia Zohra II-201
Abdul Jalil, Masita I-99
Abel, Jürgen II-3
Abul Seoud, Rania Ahmed Abdel Azeem
    I-85
Abutile, Sarah II-126
Aguir, Khalifa II-286
Ahmad, Safaa II-241
AL Mansour, Hanan I-260
Alabdan, Rana II-144
Al-Akhras, Mousa II-241
Alalmaei, Shiyam II-265
Alamri, Rasha M. II-303
Alamro, Rawan I-317
Alanazi, Amal II-126
Alaskar, Lama I-301
Alawadh, Mohammed II-52
Alawadh, Monerah II-52
Alawairdhi, Mohammed II-241
Albrikan, Alanoud II-126
Aldossari, Amjad I-15
Alduailij, Mai I-301
Aleidi, Sumaya I-162
Alenazi, Azhar I-15
Alenazi, Tahani I-15
Algahtani, Ghada I-15
AlGarni, Abeer I-183, I-236
AlGuraibi, Norah II-228
Alhalawani, Sawsan I-148
AlHalawani, Sawsan I-170
Alhamdan, Ayah II-93
Alhamdan, Hanadi I-290
Alharbi, Lujain I-69
Alharthi, Haifa II-126
Alhenaki, Dana I-148
Aljamaan, Haneen II-228
Aljeaid, Dania I-69
Aljedaie, Alanoud M. I-57
Aljres, Rawan II-126
Aljulaud, Aseel II-228

Alkabkabi, Amal I-203
Alkhawaldeh, Abdullah A. K. I-119
Almuhajri, Mrouj I-275
Almuhana, Aljawharah M. I-57
Almutairi, Suad I-245
Alnabet, Nuha I-148
Alnanih, Reem II-40
Alrajebah, Nora I-162
Al-Rasheed, Amal I-211, I-317
Alrashidi, Bedour F. I-57
Alrobai, Amani I-224
Alrubaia, Reem II-126
Alrubaish, Fatimah A. II-303
Alrubei, Mariam II-228
Alsaiah, Anwar II-228
Alshaya, Sara I-211
Alsolai, Hadeel II-60
Alsuhaibani, Dalia I-162
Al-turaiki, Israa II-52
Altuwaijri, Sara II-93
Alzahrani, Hanaa II-40
Alzaid, Wafa I-15
Aoul, Nabil Tabet II-103
Atmani, Baghdad I-111, II-81, II-103,
    II-115, II-201

Bakali, Assia II-174
Bakara, Zuriana Abu II-30
Bashir, Mohammed Bakri I-132, II-71
Batouche, Mohamed II-161
Benamina, Mohamed I-111, II-81, II-115
Benbelkacem, Sofia I-111, II-81, II-115
Benfriha, Hichem II-103
Benhacine, Fatima Zohra II-81, II-201
Bezbradica, Marija I-245
Bouazza, Halima II-278, II-312
Boufama, Boubakeur II-161
Boughaci, Dalila I-3, I-119
Boughaci, Omar I-3
Brahimi, Samiha II-228
Broadbent, Matthew II-265
Broumi, Said II-174

Chelloug, Samia   II-265
Crane, Martin   I-301

Douah, Ali   II-103

Elamsy, Tarik   II-161
Elhussain, Mariam A.   II-303
ElMannai, Hela   I-183, I-236
Elsadig, Muna   II-252
Elsaid, Mayada   II-93
Elsaid, Shaimaa Ahmed   I-15, II-126
Elshakankiri, Maher   II-325

Hamdi, Monia   I-183, I-236
Hassan, M. M.   II-214
Humaid, Ghadah A.   II-303

Ismail, Suryani   I-99

Jilani, Musfira   I-224, I-290
John, Maya   I-193

Kenkar, Zubaydh   I-170
Khemliche, Belarbi   II-103
Kurdi, Heba   I-162

Lathamaheswari, Malayalan   II-174
Lundy, Michele   I-260

Maeeny, Samerah   I-15
Maher, Mohamed   II-214
Makram, Ibram   I-85
Mansoul, Abdelhak   I-111, II-115
Masmoudi, Mohamed   II-286
McCarren, Andrew   I-211, I-317
Mehdi, Ali   II-241
Menzli, Leila Jamel   II-252
Mohamad, Mumtazimah   I-99

Mohammad, Omer K. Jasim   I-43
Mohan, Amaliya Princy   II-325
Mohd, Fatihah   I-99
Mohemada, Rosmayati   II-30
Mostafa, Ayman Mohamed   II-185, II-214

Nagarajan, Deivanayagampillai   II-174
Nassar, Dua' A.   II-252
Nasser, Abanoub   I-85
Nebhen, Jamel   II-286
Noora, Noor Maizura Mohamad   I-99, II-30

Race, Nicholas   II-265
Rahajandraibe, Wenceslas   II-286
Rahim, Mohd Shafry Mohd   II-16
Roper, Marc   II-60
Roza, Rawand Abu   II-241

Said, Bachir   II-278, II-312
Salami, Fati Oiza   II-16
Shaheen, Sara M.   I-148
Shaiba, Hadil   I-193, I-245
Smarandache, Florentin   II-174
Suen, Ching   I-275
Suliman, Yusra Mohamed   II-71

Taileb, Mounira   I-203
Talea, Mohamed   II-174
Tallab, Shahad   II-52

Vidanagea, Kaneeka   II-30

Walke, Ashay   I-8

Yahya, Wan Fatin Fatihah   I-99
Yousif, Adil   I-132, II-71

Zohra, Laallam Fatima   II-278, II-312

Printed in the United States
by Bookmasters

Printed in the United States
By Bookmasters